The Acclaimed Chronological
Plan to Read the Bible in One Year

Through the Bible as it happened

The Acclaimed Chronological
Plan to Read the Bible in One Year

cover to cover

Through the Bible as it happened

In the year 2000 I pledge to read
through the Bible and dedicate time to prayer

Along with

Selwyn Hughes and **Trevor J Partridge**

 **CWR, Waverley Abbey House, Waverley Lane, Farnham, Surrey GU9 8EP**

UK (and countries not listed below)
CWR, PO Box 230, Farnham, Surrey GU9 8XG Tel: 01252 784710 Outside UK (44) 1252 784710
AUSTRALIA: CMC Australasia, PO Box 519, Belmont, Victoria 3216 Tel: (03) 5241 3288
CANADA: CMC Distribution Ltd., PO Box 7000, Niagara on the Lake, Ontario L0S 1J0
Tel: 1 800 325 1297
GHANA: Challenge Enterprises, PO Box 5723, Accra Tel: (21) 222437/223249
INDIA: Full Gospel Literature Stores, 254 Kilpauk Garden Road, Chennai 600010
Tel: (44) 644 3073
KENYA: Keswick Bookshop, PO Box 10422, Nairobi Tel: (02) 331692/226047
MALAYSIA: Salvation Book Centre (M) Sdn. Bhd., 23 Jalan SS2/64, Sea Park, 47300 Petaling Jaya, Selangor Tel: (03) 78766411/78766797   e-mail: salvat@tm.net.my
NEW ZEALAND: CMC New Zealand Ltd., Private Bag, 17910 Green Lane, Auckland
Tel: 09 5249393 Fax: 09 5222137
NIGERIA: FBFM, (Every Day with Jesus), Prince's Court, 37 Ahmed Onibudo Street, PO Box 70952, Victoria Island Tel: 01 2617721, 616832, 4700218
PHILIPPINES: Praise Incorporated, 145 Panay Avenue, Cor Sgt Esguerra St, Quezon City
Tel: 632 920 5291
REPUBLIC OF IRELAND: Scripture Union, 40 Talbot Street, Dublin 1 Tel: (01) 8363764
SINGAPORE: Campus Crusade Asia Ltd., 315 Outram Road, 06-08 Tan Boon Liat Building, Singapore 169074 Tel: (65) 222 3640
SOUTH AFRICA: Struik Christian Books (Pty Ltd), PO Box 193, Maitland 7405, Cape Town
Tel: (021) 551 5900
SRI LANKA: Christombu Investments, 27 Hospital Street, Colombo 1 Tel: (1) 433142/328909
TANZANIA: City Christian Bookshop, PO Box 33463, Dar es Salaam Tel: (51) 28915
UGANDA: New Day Ltd, PO Box 2021, Kampala Tel: (41) 255377
USA: CMC Distribution, PO Box 644, Lewiston, New York 14092-0644 Tel: 1 800 325 1297

Cover to Cover – Through the Bible as it happened

© CWR
The order of chronology in this book is based on the Chronological Bible edited by Edward Reese.
We are grateful to Robert Backhouse who supplied many of the background articles.
Concept Development, Editorial, Design and Production by CWR
Illustrations: Nick Spender of Advocate
Cover photograph: Roger Walker
Printed & Bound in Malaysia
ISBN 1 85345 136 3
First published in 1984 as a bi-monthly six-part work and reprinted 1985, 1986, 1990.
Revised, single volume edition first published © 1990. Reprinted 1992, 1993, 1994, 1995, 1996, 1997, 1998.
Previous editions published as *Through the Bible Every Day in One Year*
Published in this format 1999

All rights reserved. No part of this publication may be reproduced, stored in a retrieval system, or transmitted, in any form or by any means, electronic, mechanical, photocopying, recording or otherwise, without the prior permission in writing of CWR.

Unless otherwise identified, all Scripture quotations in this publication are taken from the Holy Bible, New International Version (NIV). Copyright © 1973, 1978, 1984, International Bible Society. Used by permission.

Introduction

For a number of years leading up to the new millennium I have felt an urge to recruit a million people to join me in reading through the whole of Scripture in this the year 2000. We live in difficult times. The world is oscillating between extreme optimism and despairing pessimism. We Christians need to have faith for the future and I know of no better way of reinforcing faith and equipping ourselves spiritually to face the challenges of a new millennium than to daily expose our hearts and minds to the Word that is alive (Hebrews 4:12).

There are many approaches to reading through the Bible in a year but the route I want to take you down is the chronological one, that is, following the events of Scripture as they happened. Though I have read through the Bible many times and followed different approaches (all have merit) I have found the chronological approach to be the most intriguing and fascinating.

I must warn you however that for some it's going to be a tough assignment. It requires self discipline and perhaps a re-ordering of priorities but I assure you the rewards are out of all proportion to the time spent. To come out at the end of the year with an overall view of how the events of Scripture fit together and to see something of how God has been working through history will buttress your faith and be a spiritual investment that you will never regret.

Here are a few tips to help you make it through the year. First, begin your reading with prayer. Ask God to speak to you through what you will read. God has not only spoken *in* Scripture; he speaks *through* it still.

Second, read not only with the view to gaining understanding but how to apply what you read to your own life. The Bible is full of principles and biographies. The principles tell us how to live and the biographies flesh out for us how those principles, when applied, lead to good and godly living. Let the truths of Scripture wrap themselves around you and pull you into the story.

Third, try and link up with a friend or a group who may be following this same Bible reading plan in the year 2000 so that you can discuss with each other the results of your reading. Experience has shown that sharing together in this way can be the difference between making it through the year or giving up. If no one in your church or fellowship is following this plan, invite someone to join you in it.

Fourth, if for any reason (such as sickness or unusual time pressures) you miss a day's or a few days' readings, don't be discouraged. Ask God to help you find the time to catch up. I have heard the most amazing testimonies in times past of how God has worked in people's lives to help them recapture the time they have lost. You have only to ask.

My prayer and wish for you as you begin this spiritually productive task of reading through the Bible is that through the written Word you might come to know in even greater measure than before the power and presence of the Living Word.

Selwyn Hughes

Selwyn Hughes

The Way In

God has spoken. In the Bible He has given us His thoughts in words we can understand. In Jesus He has given us His thoughts in flesh. That second Word, the Lord Jesus Christ, saw His entire life and direction predicted and guided by the Old Testament. The Scriptures, He said, were as vital as food and drink for our systems. They offer salvation, guidance and equipping "for every good work".

The comments and background material in this course will help you to understand and apply something from each day's reading in the Scriptures. But space is limited – God will also draw many other things to your attention to grasp and put into practice. To help you in your approach to these, there are some important guidelines to follow:

Trust it
The Bible was inspired or "God-breathed" (2 Tim. 3:16). He used the personalities of human writers but so guided their minds that their words were His words too. Treat them as Jesus did: as authoritative and entirely trustworthy. Jesus built His own life and ministry upon God's commands and promises, obeying them even to the cross (Luke 24:27, 45–47).

See the lasting principle
For most of us daily life is very different from the days of Israel's tent cities in the wilderness; far, too, from life in the Roman Empire. Where these differences exist, look to see the lasting principles below the instruction or event – what do they teach in general about God or about serving Him? Jesus' example and exhortation about foot washing, for instance, ought to lead us to other forms of service and care for one another relevant for our day (John 13:14).

Know the author
The Bible's human authors were "carried along" by the Holy Spirit to give us God's Word (2 Peter 1:21). So we need the Holy Spirit to be its interpreter. Knowing God personally as the Lord of our lives and Christ as our Saviour is the essential key to a proper understanding of the Bible.

See the background
Statements taken out of context can be misleading, to say the least – ask any public figure who is quoted in the press! Aim to understand the meaning and purpose of a passage as a whole. This will put into perspective the point of any verse or phrase within it.

See the whole picture

The Bible has one author and is a harmonious whole. This means we should interpret individual passages in the light of what we know generally from Scripture and from other sections on the same subject. Some of James' statements, for example, could imply that our works help to save us (James 2:20, 24). The entire force of Scripture contradicts this, however, and shows that this interpretation cannot be right (e.g. Eph. 2:8, 9; Rom. 3:23-24). Realising this, a careful rereading of James reveals that he is not answering the question about how we are saved; his message is that genuine faith in Christ must result in good works.

Value expert help

This year your aim is to read through the Bible – you won't have time to study all of it in detail. Even so, there may be particular passages you will want to dig deeper into, to apply in your own Christian living or to get to grips with difficult issues. Help in understanding harder passages can be found by using a good commentary by scholars who know the Bible and love its author. A further reading section is given below for your help.

Live it out

Always remember that your aim in reading the Scriptures is to draw closer to the Lord and live a life that brings praise to Him. Reading the whole sweep of Scripture is stimulating, but God's Word is to be obeyed! As you search God's Word, ask for His Spirit's empowering to put it into practice. Take it in and live it out!

Further Reading

Straightforward

The Lion Handbook for the Bible – Pat and David Alexander (Editors), Lion Publishing

30 Days to Understanding the Bible – Max Anders, Thomas Nelson Publishers

More detailed

New Bible Commentary – D. Carson (Editor), IVP

Matthew Henry's Commentary on the Whole Bible – Matthew Henry, Hendrickson Publishers

Individual commentaries in the **Bible Speaks Today** and **Tyndale Commentary Series**, IVP. Also, the **Focus on the Bible** series, Christian Focus, and the **Welwyn Commentary** series, Evangelical Press.

Time Chart

A specially prepared guide to help you chart your progress in reading 'Cover to Cover'.

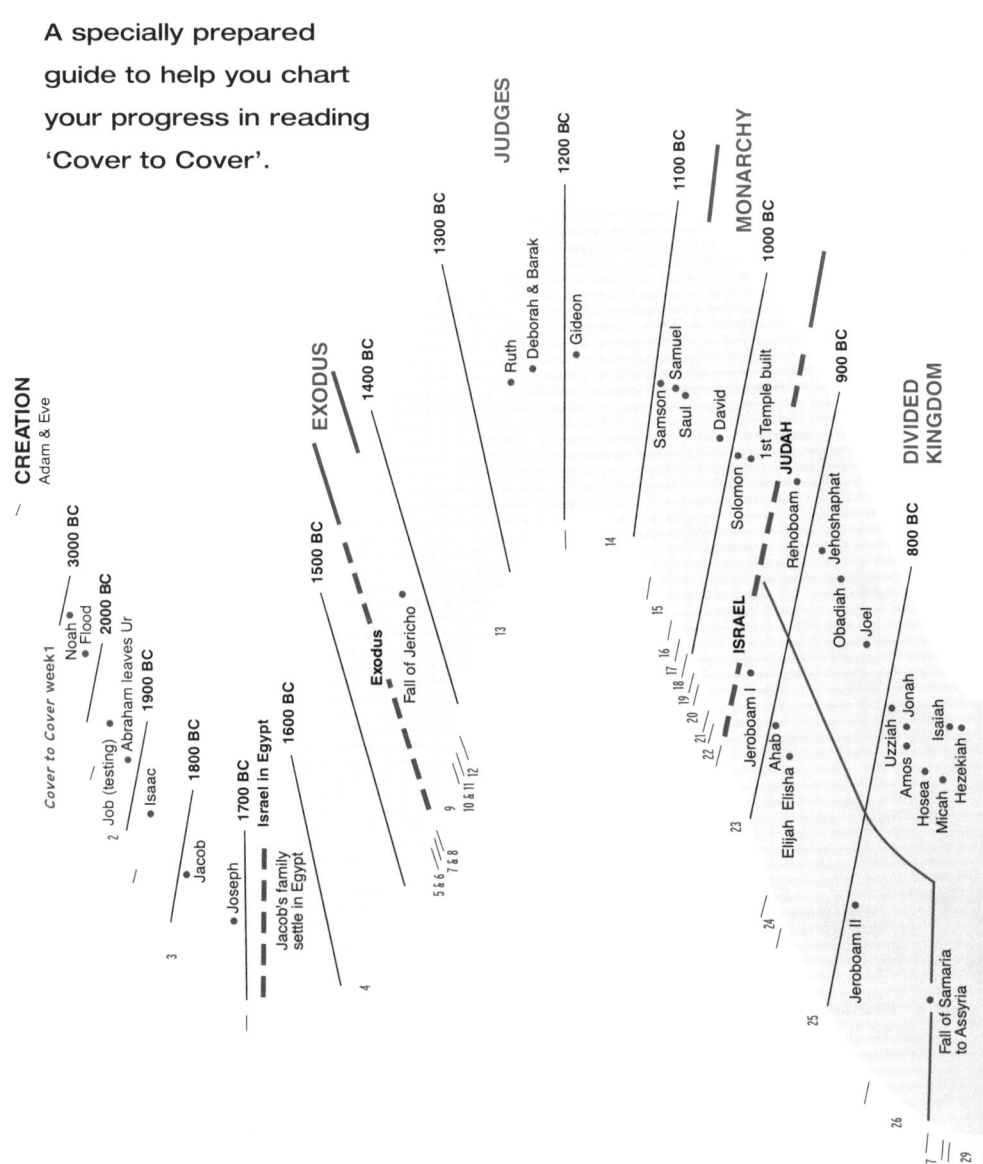

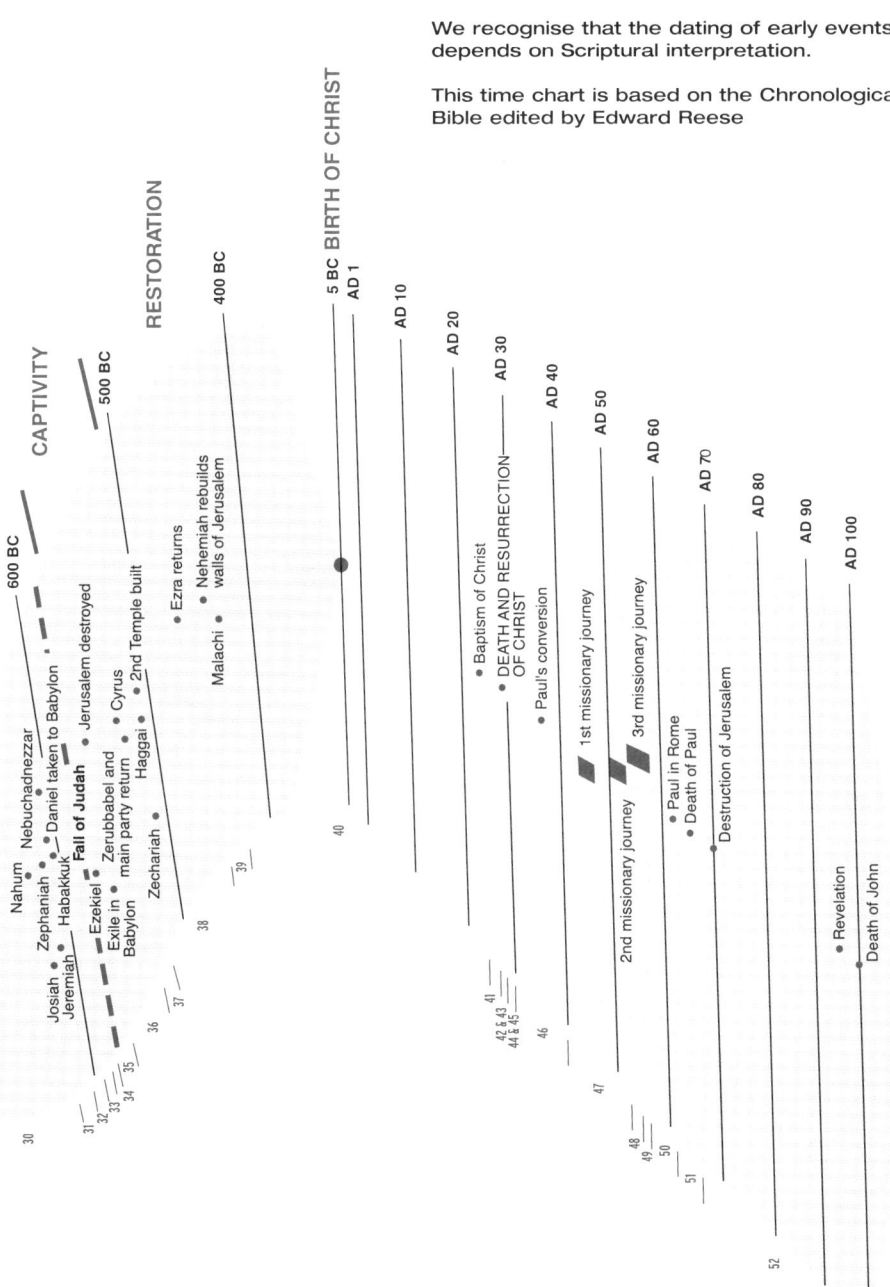

We recognise that the dating of early events depends on Scriptural interpretation.

This time chart is based on the Chronological Bible edited by Edward Reese

Getting Started

As you begin this year of discovering the Bible, you will naturally want to get the very best out of these studies. With that aim in mind, here are our suggestions:

1. Make sure that you have a good translation of the Bible.
2. Find a place and establish a specific time to follow these daily studies.
3. Pray before commencing to seek God's help and guidance as you study His Word.
4. Read the passages through to understand the general meaning.
5. Ponder upon the main truths the Holy Spirit is bringing to your attention.
6. Use the **Heart to Heart** page, at the end of each section, to jot down the main thoughts and how they apply to you. Four helpful words to remember are:
   Observation – what does it say?
   Interpretation – what does it mean?
   Application – how does it apply to me?
   Communication – how can I relate it to others?
7. If you miss a day, don't give up, remind yourself of the 4 d's of achievement – **desire, dedication, determination** and **discipline**.
8. After reading, spend a few moments in thanking God for what you have learned and asking Him for strength to put it into practice.

Follow the readings in the order given ticking each section as you complete it. This will enable you to keep track of your reading and avoid duplication.

The **Bird's Eye View** of each Bible book is intended to give a brief overview of that book. Other charts, maps and diagrams are included for additional background information in order to help your understanding of the Bible and Bible times and give insight into themes running through the whole of the Scriptures. The **Time Line** at the foot of the page is to give an indication of the date when events happened and to relate selected eras and landmarks in so-called secular history to the Bible. It is, of course, not an infallible guide; that is reserved for the Scriptures themselves.
A **Key reading** has been highlighted for you on each page of daily notes.

Visit the **Cover to Cover web site** where you will find news of the worldwide campaign, complementary articles written by Philip Greenslade, a contact point with other readers and many helps and encouragements.

http://**www.cover2cover.org**

In this section

The creation of the world
The consequences of sin
God's covenant with Abraham
The oppression in Egypt
Moses' liberation of God's people

Genesis
– The Beginning of Nations

THE WORD GENESIS means 'beginning' and within this book are recorded the origins of both sacred and secular history. Commencing this new year with the book of beginnings can be a new beginning in our lives of a deeper love for the Lord and His Word. The first 2,000 years of history are contained in the first eleven chapters and are characterised by four major and significant events.

Creation	**Origin of all things** Gen. 1–2 • In the beginning • Days of creation • Day of rest	
Corruption	**Sin of Adam** Gen. 3–5 • Satan's subtlety • Adam's sin • Strife and death	
Condemnation	**Flood of Noah** Gen. 6–9 • Conditions before flood • Salvation through flood • Tragedy following flood	
Confusion	**Tower of Babel** Gen. 10–11 • Arrogance of man • Judgment of God • Origin of nations	

The beginning of creation

DAY **1**

The pre-existent Christ
John 1:1–2

The creation declaration
Psalm 90:2

The origin of creation
Genesis 1:1

Satan cast out of heaven
Isaiah 14:12–17, Ezekiel 28:13–19

Judgment of creation
Genesis 1:2a

Creation for habitation
Isaiah 45:18

The Six Days of Creation

1st & 2nd Days
Genesis 1:2b–8

3rd Day
Genesis 2:5–6, 1:9–13

4th, 5th & 6th Days
Genesis 1:14–26, 2:7

Creation of Man in detail
Genesis 5:1, 1:27

Creation of the Woman
Genesis 2:18–25

Names given
Genesis 5:2, 3:20

Man's dominion over creation
Genesis 1:28–30

Creation completed
Genesis 1:31, 2:1 & John 1:3

Seventh day established
Genesis 2:2–3, Exodus 20:11

The Garden of Eden
Genesis 2:8–17

Genesis 1:27–28

²⁷So God created man in his own image,
 in the image of God he created him;
 male and female he created them.
²⁸God blessed them and said to them, "Be fruitful and increase in number; fill the earth and subdue it. Rule over the fish of the sea and the birds of the air and over every living creature that moves on the ground."

For Thought and **Contemplation**

If, as the Scripture teaches, man is the only being in creation who bears the "image" of God, then ask yourself today: How much of God's image is reflected in me?

"For by him all things were created: things in heaven and on earth, visible and invisible, whether thrones or powers or rulers or authorities; all things were created by him and for him. He is before all things, and in him all things hold together." (Col. 1:16–17)

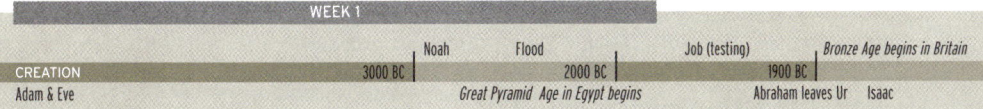

DAY 2 — The Fall & the beginning of civilisation

The temptation and fall
Genesis 3:1–7

God's judgment and curse
Genesis 3:8–19

Expulsion from Eden
Genesis 3:21–24

The story of Cain and Abel
Genesis 4:1–15

Seth and his descendants
1 Chronicles 1:1, Genesis 4:25–26, 5:3, 4:26, 5:6 & 9, 1 Chronicles 1:2, Genesis 5:12, 15 & 18

Cain and his descendants
Genesis 4:16–24

Adam's descendants continued
1 Chronicles 1:3, Genesis 5:21 & 25, 5:4–5, 5:22–24, 5:7–8, 5:28–29, 5:10–11, 5:13–14, 5:16–17, 5:19–20

Genesis 3:1–7

¹'Now the serpent was more crafty than any of the wild animals the Lord God had made. He said to the woman, "Did God really say, 'You must not eat from any tree in the garden'?" ²The woman said to the serpent, "We may eat fruit from the trees in the garden, ³but God did say, 'You must not eat fruit from the tree that is in the middle of the garden, and you must not touch it, or you will die.'" ⁴"You will not surely die," the serpent said to the woman. ⁵"For God knows that when you eat of it your eyes will be opened, and you will be like God, knowing good and evil." ⁶When the woman saw that the fruit of the tree was good for food and pleasing to the eye, and also desirable for gaining wisdom, she took some and ate it. She also gave some to her husband, who was with her, and he ate it. ⁷Then the eyes of both of them were opened, and they realised that they were naked; so they sewed fig leaves together and made coverings for themselves.

For Thought and **Contemplation**

Satan has a well worked-out strategy with which he tempts humanity. He appeals (1) to the lust of the flesh, (2) to the lust of the eyes and (3) to the pride of life. Are you able to discern this strategy at work in your life? And are you overcoming it?

"For since death came through a man, the resurrection of the dead comes also through a man." (1 Cor. 15:21)

a bird's eye view of **Genesis**

Place in the Bible	**Main Characters**	**Special Features**
First Old Testament book; first book of the Law.	Adam, Eve, Noah, Abraham, Jacob, Joseph.	The book of beginnings; the beginning of the world, of humankind, of sin, of God's chosen people.

The story of the Flood

DAY **3**

Genesis 7:1–9

¹The Lord then said to Noah, "Go into the ark, you and your whole family, because I have found you righteous in this generation. ²Take with you seven of every kind of clean animal, a male and its mate, and two of every kind of unclean animal, a male and its mate, ³and also seven of every kind of bird, male and female, to keep their various kinds alive throughout the earth. ⁴Seven days from now I will send rain on the earth for forty days and forty nights, and I will wipe from the face of the earth every living creature I have made." ⁵And Noah did all that the Lord commanded him.
⁶Noah was six hundred years old when the floodwaters came on the earth. ⁷And Noah and his sons and his wife and his sons' wives entered the ark to escape the waters of the flood. ⁸Pairs of clean and unclean animals, of birds and of all creatures that move along the ground, ⁹male and female, came to Noah and entered the ark, as God had commanded Noah.

Corrupt civilisation	Genesis 6:1–7, 11–12
Instructions for building the ark	Genesis 6:8, 13–21
Birth of Noah's sons	Genesis 5:32, 6:9–10, 1 Chronicles 1:4
Death of Lamech	Genesis 5:30–31
Death of Methuselah	Genesis 5:26–27
Entering the ark	Genesis 6:22, 7:1–9
The Flood: rain falls	Genesis 7:10–24
The Flood approx. 2319 BC	
The Flood: rain stops	Genesis 8:1–19
God's rainbow covenant	Genesis 8:20–22, 9:1–17

For Thought and **Contemplation**

God took Noah into the Flood – *and He also brought him out of it.* Similarly, He has not brought you to this point in your life to abandon you. Whatever the problems you face at this moment – *God will bring you through.*

"For in the days before the flood, people were eating and drinking, marrying and giving in marriage, up to the day Noah entered the ark; and they knew nothing about what would happen until the flood came and took them all away. That is how it will be at the coming of the Son of Man." (Matt. 24:38–39)

Jesus and the Book

Joseph is seen as a "type" of Jesus Christ because of the similarities between their lives. Both were bought for silver, both were innocent but condemned and both were raised up by God's power after terrible humiliation.

Teaching

God is the Creator of the world. Though man broke off his friendship with God by a deliberate act of disobedience, God still continually calls on man to live with Him in trust and obedience.

A Verse to Remember

"In the beginning God created the heavens and the earth" (Gen. 1:1).

DAY 4 — From the Flood to the Patriarchs

Noah's descendants
Genesis 9:18–19, 10:1–32,
1 Chronicles 1:5–27

Noah's vineyard and drunkenness
Genesis 9:20–21

Curse of Ham
Genesis 9:22–27

Death of Noah
Genesis 9:28–29

The Tower of Babel
Genesis 11:1–9

Shem to Abram
Genesis 11:10–26

Birth of Abram [Abraham] approx 1967 BC

Abram's family
Genesis 11:27–30

Genesis 11:1–9

¹Now the whole world had one language and a common speech ... ³They said to each other, "Come, let's make bricks and bake them thoroughly." They used brick instead of stone, and bitumen for mortar. ⁴Then they said, "Come, let us build ourselves a city, with a tower that reaches to the heavens, so that we may make a name for ourselves and not be scattered over the face of the whole earth." ⁵But the Lord came down to see the city and the tower that the men were building. ⁶The Lord said, "If as one people speaking the same language they have begun to do this, then nothing they plan to do will be impossible for them. ⁷Come, let us go down and confuse their language so they will not understand each other." ⁸So the Lord scattered them from there over all the earth, and they stopped building the city. ⁹That is why it was called Babel – because there the Lord confused the language of the whole world. From there the Lord scattered them over the face of the whole earth.

For Thought and **Contemplation**

Some regard the genealogies here as dull and uninteresting, but it is a lesson in how God pays attention to details. He is concerned not only about the general features of your life, but every detail of it. Remember that the next time you feel God doesn't care.

"... and Jacob the father of Joseph, the husband of Mary, of whom was born Jesus, who is called Christ." (Matt. 1:16)

WEEK 1

CREATION		Noah	Flood		Job (testing)	Bronze Age begins in Britain
Adam & Eve	3000 BC		2000 BC		1900 BC	
		Great Pyramid	Age in Egypt begins		Abraham leaves Ur	Isaac

Job's Four Comforters

Eliphaz
Chs. 4, 5, 15, 22

Zophar
Chs. 11, 20
You are deceitful 11:11

Bildad
Chs. 8, 18, 25
You don't know God 18:21

Elihu
Chs. 32–37
You rebel against God 34:37

Their speeches Their accusations

Their conclusion: "You are suffering because of your sin."

Job's conclusion: "I have heard many things like these; miserable comforters are you all!" 16:2

God's restoration: "After Job had prayed for his friends, the Lord made him prosperous again and gave him twice as much as he had before." 42:10

DAY 5 — Job's affliction

Early history of Job
Job 1:1–5

Birth of Job approx. 1967 BC

Satan discusses Job's character
Job 1:6–12

God gives him
permission to test Job
Job 1:13–2:10

Job complains to his three friends
Job 2:11–13, 3:1–26

The First Round of Speeches:

Eliphaz reproves Job
Job 4:1–11

The vision of Eliphaz
Job 4:12–21

The sin of sinners is their ruin
Job 5:1–7

God to be regarded with affection
Job 5:8–16

The happy result
of God's correction
Job 5:17–27

Job justifies his complaints
Job 6:1–7

He wishes for death
Job 6:8–13

Job reproves his friends
Job 6:14–30

Job 5:8–15

⁸"But if it were I, I would appeal to God;
 I would lay my cause before him.
⁹He performs wonders that cannot be fathomed,
 miracles that cannot be counted.
¹⁰He bestows rain on the earth;
 he sends water upon the countryside.
¹¹The lowly he sets on high,
 and those who mourn are lifted to safety.
¹²He thwarts the plans of the crafty,
 so that their hands achieve no success.
¹³He catches the wise in their craftiness,
 and the schemes of the wily are swept away.
¹⁴Darkness comes upon them in the daytime;
 at noon they grope as in the night.
¹⁵He saves the needy from the sword in their mouth;
 he saves them from the clutches of the powerful ..."

For Thought and **Contemplation**

Sometimes the greatest thing you can do for a person who is going through a difficult trial is to sit down with them, saying nothing, but show by your actions that you really care. This is usually far better than a round of speeches.

"When you pass through the waters, I will be with you; and when you pass through the rivers, they will not sweep over you. When you walk through the fire, you will not be burned; the flames will not set you ablaze. For I am the Lord, your God ..." (Isa. 43:2-3)

Place in the Bible	**Main Characters**	**Special Feature**
Eighteenth Old Testament book; first book of poetry and wisdom.	God, Satan, Job, Eliphaz, Bildad, Zophar, Elihu.	Discussion about undeserved suffering.

a bird's eye view of **Job**

Job's friends

DAY 6

Job's troubles
Job 7:1–6

Job expostulates
with God and begs release
Job 7:7–21

Bildad reproves Job
Job 8:1–7

Hypocrites will be destroyed
Job 8:8–19

Bildad applies God's
just dealing to Job
Job 8:20–22

Job acknowledges God's justice
Job 9:1–13

He is not able to
contend with God
Job 9:14–21

Job complains of
troubles and hardships
Job 9:22–35 & 10:1–7

Job pleads with God as his Maker
Job 10:8–13

He complains of God's severity
Job 10:14–22

Zophar reproves Job
Job 11:1–6

God's perfections
and almighty power
Job 11:7–12

Zophar assures Job
of blessings if he repents
Job 11:13–20

Job reproves his friends
Job 12:1–5

The wicked often prosper
Job 12:6–11

Job recognises the
wisdom and power of God
Job 12:12–25

Job 7:1–3

¹"Does not man have hard service on earth?
Are not his days like those of a hired man?
²Like a slave longing for the evening shadows,
or a hired man waiting eagerly for his wages,
³so I have been allotted months of futility,
and nights of misery have been assigned to me."

For Thought and **Contemplation**

It is not sinful or "unspiritual" to acknowledge one's confusion in the presence of sickness, distress or suffering. *Emotions that are not faced cause trouble.* You don't have to agree with them, but you do have to face them in God's strength.

"A man of many companions may come to ruin, but there is a friend who sticks closer than a brother." (Prov. 18:24)

Jesus and the Book

Bildad's question, "How can a man be righteous before God?" (Job 25:4) is answered in Jesus who gave Himself "to be sin for us, so that in him we might become the righteousness of God" (2 Cor. 5:21). Job looked to Jesus as his Redeemer (Job 19:25).

Teaching

No simple solution is given to the problem of suffering. The key comes in the last five chapters of the book, especially chapter 42. There Job sees God's greatness and that he is not to question but to trust and accept the Lord's perfect will.

A Verse to Remember

"I know that my Redeemer lives, and that in the end he will stand upon the earth" (Job 19:25).

DAY 7 — The story of Job continues

Job reproves his friends
Job 13:1–12

He professes his confidence in God and entreats to know his sins
Job 13:13–28

Job speaks of man's life and death
Job 14:1–15

By sin man is subject to corruption
Job 14:16–22

The Second Round of Speeches:

Eliphaz reproves Job
Job 15:1–16

The unease of wicked men
Job 15:17–35

Job reproves his friends
Job 16:1–5

He represents his case as deplorable and maintains his innocence
Job 16:6–22

Job appeals to God
Job 17:1–9

His hope is in death
Job 17:10–16

Bildad reproves Job
Job 18:1–4

Ruin awaits the wicked
Job 18:5–10

The ruin of the wicked
Job 18:11–21

Job 17:1–6

¹"My spirit is broken,
 my days are cut short,
 the grave awaits me.
²Surely mockers surround me;
 my eyes must dwell on their hostility.

³"Give me, O God, the pledge you demand.
 Who else will put up security for me?
⁴You have closed their minds to understanding;
 therefore you will not let them triumph.
⁵If a man denounces his friends for reward,
 the eyes of his children will fail.

⁶"God has made me a byword to everyone,
 a man in whose face people spit."

For Thought and **Contemplation**

Many in today's Church follow the pattern of Job's counsellors – giving advice before making sure they understand the problem. Never try to win a person to your point of view until you are sure you understand theirs.

"A man finds joy in giving an apt reply – and how good is a timely word!" (Prov. 15:23)

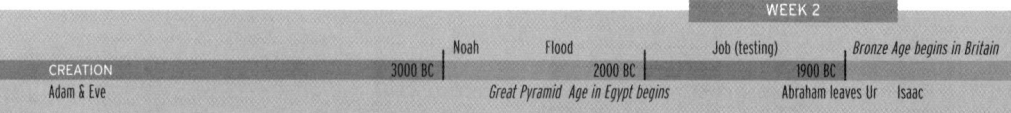

Job stands accused

DAY **8**

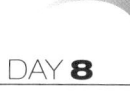

Job complains of unkind treatment
Job 19:1–7

God was the author of his afflictions
Job 19:8–22

Job's belief in the resurrection
Job 19:23–29

Zophar speaks of the short-lived joy of the wicked
Job 20:1–9

The ruin and the portion of the wicked
Job 20:10–29

Job entreats attention
Job 21:1–6

The prosperity of the wicked
Job 21:7–16

The dealings of God's providence
Job 21:17–26

The judgment of the wicked
Job 21:27–34

The Third Round of Speeches:

Eliphaz shows that man's goodness does not profit God
Job 22:1–4

Job accused of oppression
Job 22:5–14

The world before the flood
Job 22:15–20

Eliphaz exhorts Job to repentance
Job 22:21–30

Job complains that God has withdrawn
Job 23:1–7

He asserts his own integrity
Job 23:8–12

The divine terrors
Job 23:13–17

Job 22:21–22

21"Submit to God and be at peace with him;
in this way prosperity will come to you.
22Accept instruction from his mouth
and lay up his words in your heart.

For Thought and **Contemplation**

Life makes sense only when we learn to see it from God's point of view. This is what turned the tide for Job, and this is what will turn the tide for you. Is life unfair to you? Then look at it from God's perspective. Now what do you see?

"... keeping a clear conscience, so that those who speak maliciously against your good behaviour in Christ may be ashamed of their slander." (1 Pet. 3:16)

1800 BC | Jacob | 1700 BC | Joseph | ISRAEL IN EGYPT | 1600 BC | Jacob's family settle in Egypt | 1500 BC | EXODUS | 1400 BC | Fall of Jericho

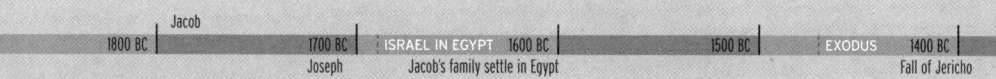

DAY 9 — Job defends himself

Wickedness often unpunished
Job 24:1–12

The wicked shun the light
Job 24:13–17

Judgments for the wicked
Job 24:18–25

Bildad shows that man cannot be justified before God
Job 25:1–6

Job reproves Bildad
Job 26:1–4

Job acknowledges the power of God
Job 26:5–14

Job protests his sincerity
Job 27:1–6

The hypocrite is without hope
Job 27:7–10

The miserable end of the wicked
Job 27:11–23

Concerning worldly wealth
Job 28:1–11

Wisdom is of inestimable value
Job 28:12–19

Wisdom is the gift of God
Job 28:20–28

Job's former comforts
Job 29:1–6

The honour paid to Job; his usefulness
Job 29:7–17

His prospect of prosperity
Job 29:18–25

Job's honour is turned into contempt
Job 30:1–14

Job a burden to himself
Job 30:15–31

Job 28:20–23

²⁰"Where then does wisdom come from?
 Where does understanding dwell?
²¹It is hidden from the eyes of every living thing,
 concealed even from the birds of the air.
²²Destruction and Death say,
 'Only a rumour of it has reached our ears.'
²³God understands the way to it
 and he alone knows where it dwells …"

For Thought and **Contemplation**

Why do bad things happen to good people? If you have often pondered that problem you are not alone. There is only one answer: God allows bad things to happen to His people only if He sees a way of turning the bad into a greater good.

"… And we know that in all things God works for the good of those who love him, who have been called according to his purpose." (Romans 8:28)

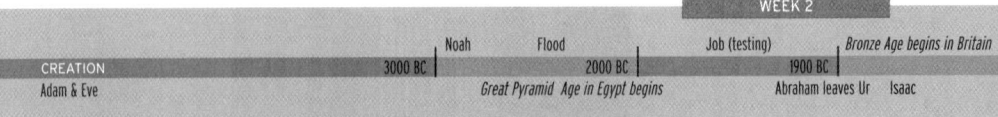

Elihu's perspective

DAY 10

Job 36:22–31

²²"God is exalted in his power.
  Who is a teacher like him?
²³Who has prescribed his ways for him,
  or said to him, 'You have done wrong'?
²⁴Remember to extol his work,
  which men have praised in song.
²⁵All mankind has seen it;
  men gaze on it from afar.
²⁶How great is God – beyond our understanding!
  The number of his years is past finding out.
²⁷He draws up the drops of water,
  which distil as rain to the streams;
²⁸the clouds pour down their moisture
  and abundant showers fall on mankind.
²⁹Who can understand how he spreads out the clouds,
  how he thunders from his pavilion?
³⁰See how he scatters his lightning about him,
  bathing the depths of the sea.
³¹This is the way he governs the nations ..."

Job declares his uprightness, integrity and mercy	Job 31:1–23
Job not guilty of covetousness, idolatry or hypocrisy	Job 31:24–40
Elihu is displeased at the dispute	Job 32:1–5
He reproves Job and his friends	Job 32:6–14
He speaks without partiality	Job 32:15–22
Elihu offers to reason with Job and entreats his attention	Job 33:1–33
Elihu accuses Job of charging God with injustice and reproves him	Job 34:1–37
Elihu speaks of man's conduct and reproves Job's impatience	Job 35:1–16
Elihu desires Job's attention and counsels him	Job 36:1–33

For Thought and **Contemplation**

The best time to learn the art of navigation is not when you are *in* a storm, but *prior* to it. How would you cope with a Job-sized problem? Have you a strategy for dealing with issues before they arise? If not perhaps now is the time to start working on it.

"Blessed are you when people insult you, persecute you and falsely say all kinds of evil against you because of me." (Matt. 5:11)

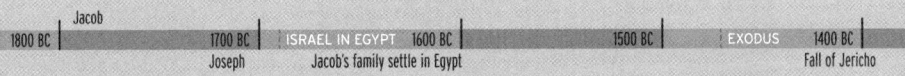

25

DAY 11 — God answers Job

Elihu observes the power of God
Job 37:1–13

Job required to explain
the works of nature
Job 37:14–20

God is great, and is to be feared
Job 37:21–24

Discourse with Jehovah:
God calls upon Job to answer
Job 38:1–3

God questions Job
Job 38:4–41

God inquires of Job concerning
several birds and animals
Job 39:1–30

Job humbles himself before God
Job 40:1–5

The Lord reasons with Job
Job 40:6–14

God's power shown
Job 40:15–24, 41:1–34

Discourse with Jehovah continued: Job humbly submits to God
Job 42:1–6

He intercedes for his friends
Job 42:7–10a

His renewed prosperity
Job 42:10b–17

Job 37:5–12

⁵"God's voice thunders in marvellous ways;
he does great things beyond our understanding.
⁶He says to the snow, 'Fall on the earth,'
and to the rain shower, 'Be a mighty downpour.'
⁷So that all men he has made may know his work,
he stops every man from his labour.
⁸The animals take cover;
they remain in their dens.
⁹The tempest comes out from its chamber,
the cold from the driving winds.
¹⁰The breath of God produces ice,
and the broad waters become frozen.
¹¹He loads the clouds with moisture;
he scatters his lightning through them.
¹²At his direction they swirl around over the face of the whole earth
to do whatever he commands them."

For Thought and **Contemplation**

God often deals with our problems and difficulties, not by removing them, but by giving us a greater vision of Himself. This may not remove the irritating circumstances, but it deepens our conviction that God knows what He is doing.

"'For my thoughts are not your thoughts, neither are your ways my ways,' declares the Lord." (Isa. 55:8)

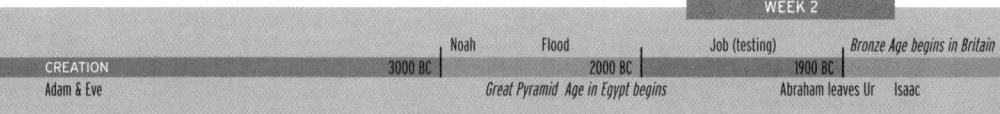

God calls Abram [Abraham]

DAY **12**

Genesis 12:4–9

⁴So Abram left, as the Lord had told him; and Lot went with him. Abram was seventy-five years old when he set out from Haran. ⁵He took his wife Sarai, his nephew Lot, all the possessions they had accumulated and the people they had acquired in Haran, and they set out for the land of Canaan, and they arrived there.

⁶Abram travelled through the land as far as the site of the great tree of Moreh at Shechem. At that time the Canaanites were in the land. ⁷The Lord appeared to Abram and said, "To your offspring I will give this land." So he built an altar there to the Lord, who had appeared to him.

⁸From there he went on toward the hills east of Bethel and pitched his tent, with Bethel on the west and Ai on the east. There he built an altar to the Lord and called on the name of the Lord. ⁹Then Abram set out and continued towards the Negev.

Abram travels from Ur to Haran	Genesis 12:1–3, 11:31
Death of Terah	Genesis 11:32
On to Canaan	Genesis 12:4–9
Trip to Egypt: journeys	Genesis 12:10
Lies about wife	Genesis 12:11–20
Abram leaves Egypt wealthy	Genesis 13:1–2
Arrives back in Bethel	Genesis 13:3–4
Abram and Lot separate	Genesis 13:5–13
Covenant renewed	Genesis 13:14–17
Abram goes to Hebron	Genesis 13:18

For Thought and **Contemplation**

The life of faith, though intriguing and exciting, is never without its periods of testing. Are you in such a period at this moment? Then take heart – God tests in order to entrust.

"By faith Abraham, when called to go to a place ... obeyed ..." (Heb. 11:8)

Important Places in Abraham's Life

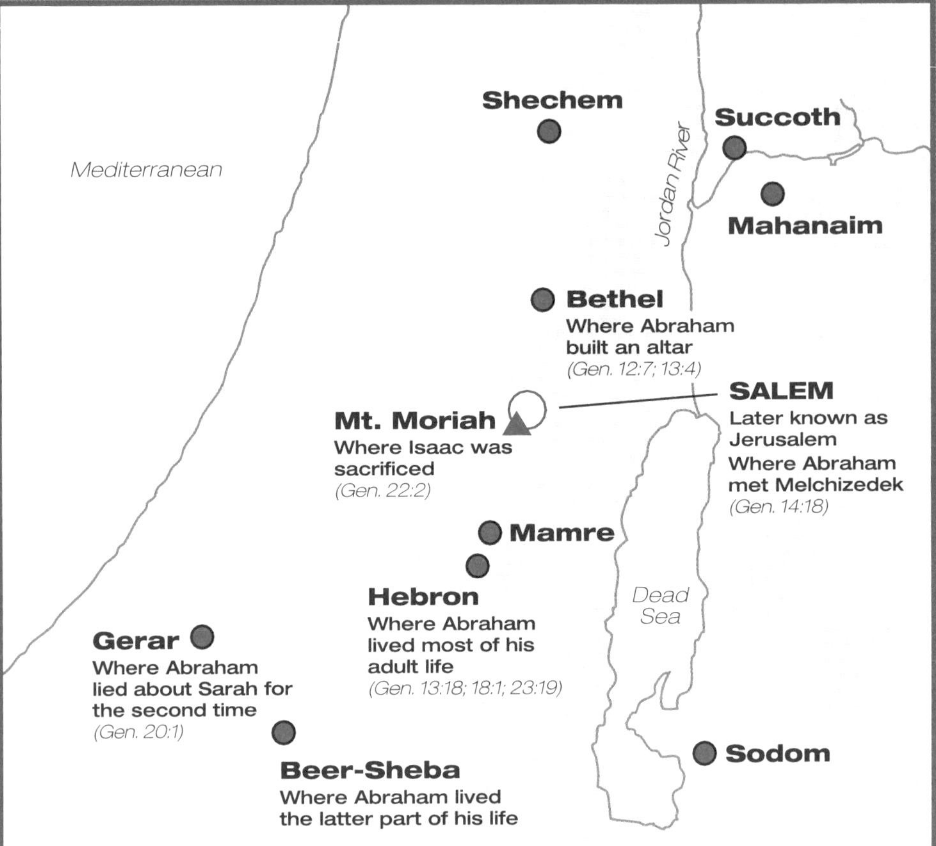

Shechem

Succoth

Mediterranean

Jordan River

Mahanaim

Bethel
Where Abraham built an altar
(Gen. 12:7; 13:4)

Mt. Moriah
Where Isaac was sacrificed
(Gen. 22:2)

SALEM
Later known as Jerusalem
Where Abraham met Melchizedek
(Gen. 14:18)

Mamre

Hebron
Where Abraham lived most of his adult life
(Gen. 13:18; 18:1; 23:19)

Dead Sea

Gerar
Where Abraham lied about Sarah for the second time
(Gen. 20:1)

Sodom

Beer-Sheba
Where Abraham lived the latter part of his life

God's Sevenfold Promise

- I will make you into a great nation
- I will make your name great
- I will bless those who bless you
- I will bless you
- You will be a blessing
- Whoever curses you I will curse
- All people on earth will be blessed through you

Acts 7:2, Genesis 12:1–4, Joshua 24:3

The Abrahamic covenant

DAY **13**

Kedorlaomer in power
Genesis 14:1–4

Lot taken captive
Genesis 14:5–13

Abram delivers Lot
Genesis 14:14–16

Abram with the king of Sodom
Genesis 14:17, 21–24

Melchizedek blesses Abram
Genesis 14:18–20

God's covenant with Abram
Genesis 15:1–21

Ishmael – Sarai
gives Hagar to Abram
Genesis 16:1–14

Birth of Ishmael
Genesis 16:15–16

Death of Arphaxad
Genesis 11:13

Abram becomes Abraham
Genesis 17:1–8

Circumcision a sign
Genesis 17:9–14

Son promised and
Sarai becomes Sarah
Genesis 17:15–19

Ishmael's destiny foretold
Genesis 17:20–27

Genesis 17:1–7

¹When Abram was ninety-nine years old, the Lord appeared to him and said, "I am God Almighty; walk before me and be blameless. ²I will confirm my covenant between me and you and will greatly increase your numbers." ³Abram fell face down, and God said to him, ⁴"As for me, this is my covenant with you: You will be the father of many nations. ⁵No longer will you be called Abram; your name will be Abraham, for I have made you a father of many nations. ⁶I will make you very fruitful; I will make nations of you, and kings will come from you. ⁷I will establish my covenant as an everlasting covenant between me and you and your descendants after you for the generations to come, to be your God and the God of your descendants after you.

For Thought and **Contemplation**

When God wants to turn a situation from despair to delight, all He has to do is breathe into it. The aspirate (the letter "h") is inserted in Abram's and Sarai's names, thus indicating that the breath of God was at work. He does the same with the word "impossible". He breathes into it and it becomes "*Him*-possible".

"For this reason Christ is the mediator of a new covenant, that those who are called may receive the promised eternal inheritance – now that he has died as a ransom to set them free from the sins committed under the first covenant." (Heb. 9:15)

DAY **14**

The birth of a nation

The Lord appears to Abraham
and Sarah is promised a son
Genesis 18:1–10

Sarah's unbelief reproved
Genesis 18:11–15

God reveals to Abraham the
impending destruction of Sodom
Genesis 18:16–22

Abraham's intercession
for Sodom
Genesis 18:23–33

Angels warn Lot
Genesis 19:1–22

The destruction of Sodom
and Gomorrah and Lot's wife
Genesis 19:23–28

Abraham's prayer for Lot
answered
Genesis 19:29

Abraham's later years:
lies to Abimelech
Genesis 20:1–18

Genesis 19:24–29

²⁴Then the Lord rained down burning sulphur on Sodom and Gomorrah – from the Lord out of the heavens. ²⁵Thus he overthrew those cities and the entire plain, including all those living in the cities – and also the vegetation in the land. ²⁶But Lot's wife looked back, and she became a pillar of salt.

²⁷Early the next morning Abraham got up and returned to the place where he had stood before the Lord. ²⁸He looked down towards Sodom and Gomorrah, towards all the land of the plain, and he saw dense smoke rising from the land, like smoke from a furnace. ²⁹So when God destroyed the cities of the plain, he remembered Abraham, and he brought Lot out of the catastrophe that overthrew the cities where Lot had lived.

For Thought and **Contemplation**

How do God's true servants react in times of emergency or great crisis? They react, as did Abraham, by turning to God in fervent, believing prayer. Life's best outlook is a prayerful uplook!

"This is the confidence we have in approaching God: that if we ask anything according to his will, he hears us. And if we know that he hears us – whatever we ask – we know that we have what we asked of him."
(1 Jn. 5:14–15)

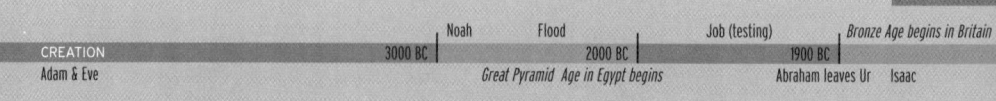

Incidents in Abraham's life — DAY **15**

Genesis 21:8–13

⁸The child grew and was weaned, and on the day Isaac was weaned Abraham held a great feast. ⁹But Sarah saw that the son whom Hagar the Egyptian had borne to Abraham was mocking, ¹⁰and she said to Abraham, "Get rid of that slave woman and her son, for that slave woman's son will never share in the inheritance with my son Isaac."

¹¹The matter distressed Abraham greatly because it concerned his son. ¹²But God said to him, "Do not be so distressed about the boy and your maidservant. Listen to whatever Sarah tells you, because it is through Isaac that your offspring will be reckoned. ¹³I will make the son of the maidservant into a nation also, because he is your offspring."

Lot's daughters give birth to sons
Genesis 19:30–38

Birth of Isaac
Genesis 21:1–7, 1 Chronicles 1:34

Conflict of Isaac and Ishmael
Genesis 21:8–13

Hagar and Ishmael cast out
Genesis 21:14–21

Death of Shelah
Genesis 11:15

Ishmael's children
Genesis 25:12–16, 1 Chronicles 1:29–31

Abimelech's covenant with Abraham
Genesis 21:22–34

Abraham's sacrifice of Isaac
Genesis 22:1–19

Abraham learns of Nahor's family
Genesis 22:20–24

Death of Sarah
Genesis 23:1–20

For Thought and **Contemplation**

Faith never quibbles at God's demands, even though those demands sometimes go against reason. But what is faith? No greater definition of faith has ever been given than that contained in the simple acrostic: **F**orsaking **A**ll **I** **T**rust **H**im

"Now faith is being sure of what we hope for and certain of what we do not see." (Heb. 11:1)

DAY 16 — The death of Abraham

Isaac marries Rebekah
Genesis 24:1–67, 25:20

Abraham's children by marriage to Keturah
Genesis 25:1–4, 1 Chronicles 1:32–33

Isaac heir of all things
Genesis 25:5–6

Death of Abraham
Genesis 25:7–10

Death of Shem
Genesis 11:11

Isaac blessed
Genesis 25:11

Ishmael and his descendants
Genesis 25:12–18, 1 Chronicles 1:28–29

Birth of Esau and Jacob
Genesis 25:19, 21–26

Death of Eber
Genesis 11:17

Genesis 25:21–26

²¹Isaac prayed to the Lord on behalf of his wife, because she was barren. The Lord answered his prayer, and his wife Rebekah became pregnant. ²²The babies jostled each other within her, and she said, "Why is this happening to me?" So she went to enquire of the Lord.
²³The Lord said to her,
"Two nations are in your womb,
  and two peoples from within you will be separated;
 one people will be stronger than the other,
  and the older will serve the younger."
²⁴When the time came for her to give birth, there were twin boys in her womb. ²⁵The first to come out was red, and his whole body was like a hairy garment; so they named him Esau. ²⁶After this, his brother came out, with his hand grasping Esau's heel; so he was named Jacob. Isaac was sixty years old when Rebekah gave birth to them.

For Thought and **Contemplation**

No matter how effective and important a man may be, his time and work on this earth are limited. How gratifying, therefore, to know that though God buries His workman, He always carries on His work.

"... Jesus answered, 'before Abraham was born, I am!'" (Jn. 8:58)

WEEK 3

| 1800 BC | Jacob | 1700 BC | ISRAEL IN EGYPT | 1600 BC | | 1500 BC | | EXODUS | 1400 BC |
| | | Joseph | Jacob's family settle in Egypt | | | | | | Fall of Jericho |

Important Places
in the lives of Jacob, Isaac and Joseph

Mediterranean

Haran — Where Jacob met and married Leah and Rachel (Gen. 29)

Mt. Gilead — Where Laban and Jacob built their boundary pillar of stones (Gen. 31)

Dothan — Where Joseph was sold into slavery by his brothers (Gen. 37:17)

Succoth — Where Jacob lived before re-entering Canaan (Gen. 33:17)

Jabbok River — Where Jacob wrestled with God (Gen. 32:22)

Shechem — Where two of Jacob's sons murdered some helpless pagan men (Gen. 34)

Mahanaim — Where Jacob saw the angelic host of God (Gen. 32:1–2)

Bethel — Where Jacob dreamed his ladder dream (Gen. 28:19)

Jordan River

Bethlehem — Where Rachel died giving birth to Benjamin (Gen. 35:19)

Dead Sea

Gerar — Where Isaac dug his well and lied about his wife (Gen. 26:6–12)

DAY **17**

Incidents in Isaac's life

Sale of birthright
Genesis 25:27–34

Esau marries two Canaanite women
Genesis 26:34–35

Famine and covenant renewal
Genesis 26:1–5

Isaac lies about Rebekah
Genesis 26:6–10

Isaac's success at Gerar
Genesis 26:11–16

Isaac the well-digger
Genesis 26:17–22

Isaac makes altar at Beersheba
Genesis 26:23–25

Isaac's truce with Abimelech
Genesis 26:26–33

Jacob obtains Esau's blessing
Genesis 27:1–46

Genesis 26:6–10

⁶So Isaac stayed in Gerar. ⁷When the men of that place asked him about his wife, he said, "She is my sister," because he was afraid to say, "She is my wife." He thought, "The men of this place might kill me on account of Rebekah, because she is beautiful."
⁸When Isaac had been there a long time, Abimelech king of the Philistines looked down from a window and saw Isaac caressing his wife Rebekah. ⁹So Abimelech summoned Isaac and said, "She is really your wife! Why did you say, 'She is my sister'?"
Isaac answered him, "Because I thought I might lose my life on account of her."
¹⁰Then Abimelech said, "What is this you have done to us? One of the men might well have slept with your wife, and you would have brought guilt upon us."

For Thought and **Contemplation**

When we lean upon our own reason rather than on God's clear commands, we run counter to the design of the universe. The theory that the end justifies the means may be part of man's order, but it is not part of the eternal scheme.

"Trust in the Lord with all your heart and lean not on your own understanding; in all your ways acknowledge him, and he will make your paths straight." (Prov. 3:5–6)

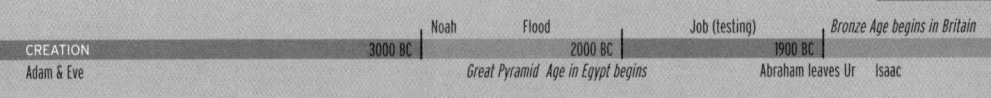

Jacob's history

DAY 18

Genesis 29:21-30

²¹Then Jacob said to Laban, "Give me my wife. My time is completed, and I want to lie with her." ²²So Laban brought together all the people of the place and gave a feast. ²³But when evening came, he took his daughter Leah and gave her to Jacob, and Jacob lay with her. ²⁴And Laban gave his servant girl Zilpah to his daughter as her maidservant.
²⁵When morning came, there was Leah! So Jacob said to Laban, "What is this you have done to me? I served you for Rachel, didn't I? Why have you deceived me?" ²⁶Laban replied, "It is not our custom here to give the younger daughter in marriage before the older one. ²⁷Finish this daughter's bridal week; then we will give you the younger one also, in return for another seven years of work." ²⁸And Jacob did so. He finished out the week with Leah, and then Laban gave him his daughter Rachel to be his wife ...³⁰Jacob lay with Rachel also, and he loved Rachel more than Leah. And he worked for Laban another seven years.

Jacob sent to Laban's house
Genesis 28:1-5

Dream at Bethel
Genesis 28:10-22

Arrives in Haran
Genesis 29:1-14

Works seven years to get Rachel
Genesis 29:15-20

Marriage to Leah then to Rachel
Genesis 29:21-30

Twelve children born while working for Laban
Genesis 29:31-30:24

Jacob's closing days with Laban
Genesis 30:25-43, 31:1-16

For Thought and **Contemplation**

Have you heard of the "Laban Principle"? It says that those who scheme to have their own way, as opposed to God's way, often have a head-on collision with someone who is their equal as a schemer.

"The heart is deceitful above all things and beyond cure. Who can understand it?" (Jer. 17:9)

DAY 19 — Esau's history

Esau marries Mahalath
Genesis 28:6–9

Esau's marriages and descendants
Genesis 36:1–30, 1 Chronicles 1:35–42

Kings of Edom: Bela, first king
Genesis 36:31–33, 1 Chronicles 1:43–44

Other kings
Genesis 36:34–39, 1 Chronicles 1:45–50

Chiefs of Edom
Genesis 36:40–43, 1 Chronicles 1:51–54

Jacob's departure from Laban
Genesis 31:17–32

Genesis 28:6–9

⁶Now Esau learned that Isaac had blessed Jacob and had sent him to Paddan Aram to take a wife from there, and that when he blessed him he commanded him, "Do not marry a Canaanite woman," ⁷and that Jacob had obeyed his father and mother and had gone to Paddan Aram. ⁸Esau then realised how displeasing the Canaanite women were to his father Isaac; ⁹so he went to Ishmael and married Mahalath, the sister of Nebaioth and daughter of Ishmael son of Abraham, in addition to the wives he already had.

For Thought and Contemplation

God often accomplishes His purposes with us despite our waywardness and stubbornness. But how much grief we would spare ourselves if we would learn to wait on God, and follow His bidding to the letter.

"If the Lord delights in a man's way, he makes his steps firm; though he stumble, he will not fall, for the Lord upholds him with his hand." (Psa. 37:23–24)

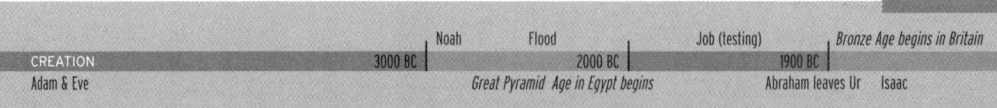

Jacob changes name — DAY **20**

Genesis 32:24–31

²⁴So Jacob was left alone, and a man wrestled with him till daybreak. ²⁵When the man saw that he could not overpower him, he touched the socket of Jacob's hip so that his hip was wrenched as he wrestled with the man. ²⁶Then the man said, "Let me go, for it is daybreak."

But Jacob replied, "I will not let you go unless you bless me."

²⁷The man asked him, "What is your name?"

"Jacob," he answered.

²⁸Then the man said, "Your name will no longer be Jacob, but Israel, because you have struggled with God and with men and have overcome."

²⁹Jacob said, "Please tell me your name."

But he replied, "Why do you ask my name?" Then he blessed him there.

³⁰So Jacob called the place Peniel, saying, "It is because I saw God face to face, and yet my life was spared."

³¹The sun rose above him as he passed Peniel, and he was limping because of his hip."

Jacob's departure from Laban continued
Genesis 31:33–55

Jacob's apprehension before his reunion with Esau
Genesis 32:1–23

Jacob wrestles with angel
Genesis 32:24–32

Jacob's name changed
Genesis 35:10

Jacob meets Esau
Genesis 33:1–16

Jacob's return to Shechem
Genesis 33:17–20

Dinah's defilement
Genesis 34:1–12

For Thought and **Contemplation**

Have you ever stopped everything and said this one thing to God – your name? What is your name? Ego? Fear? Resentment? Self-pity? A new name doesn't come until we say the old one. In other words, confession is catharsis.

"… I will also write on him my new name." (Rev. 3:12). "… rejoice that your names are written in heaven." (Lk. 10:20)

DAY 21 — The selling of Joseph

Jacob's sons take revenge
Genesis 34:13–31

Jacob's return to Bethel
Genesis 35:1–9, 11–15

Death of Rachel at Benjamin's birth
Genesis 35:16–19, 48:7, 35:20–22

Jacob's return to Hebron
Genesis 35:27, 37:1

Joseph's early days and dreams
Genesis 37:2–11

His brother's conspiracy
Genesis 37:12–35

Sold into Egypt
Genesis 37:36, 39:1

Judah's first three sons
Genesis 38:1–5, 1 Chronicles 2:3

Genesis 37:23–28

²³So when Joseph came to his brothers, they stripped him of his robe – the richly ornamented robe he was wearing – ²⁴and they took him and threw him into the cistern. Now the cistern was empty; there was no water in it.
²⁵As they sat down to eat their meal, they looked up and saw a caravan of Ishmaelites coming from Gilead. Their camels were loaded with spices, balm and myrrh, and they were on their way to take them down to Egypt.
²⁶Judah said to his brothers, "What will we gain if we kill our brother and cover up his blood? ²⁷Come, let's sell him to the Ishmaelites and not lay our hands on him; after all, he is our brother, our own flesh and blood." His brothers agreed.
²⁸So when the Midianite merchants came by, his brothers pulled Joseph up out of the cistern and sold him for twenty shekels of silver to the Ishmaelites, who took him to Egypt."

For Thought and **Contemplation**

Some use unpleasant situations and difficulties as an excuse for becoming bitter and hostile. But God intends that life's trials should make us better – not bitter. How are you reacting to what is happening in your life at the moment – with despair or delight?

"... If God is for us, who can be against us?" (Rom. 8.31)

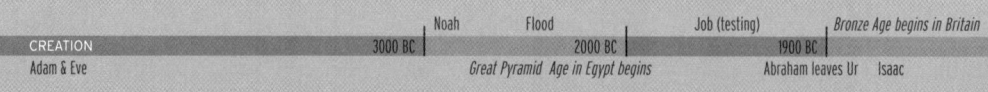

The ascent of Joseph

DAY 22

Genesis 41:38–44

³⁸So Pharaoh asked them, "Can we find anyone like this man, one in whom is the spirit of God?" ³⁹Then Pharaoh said to Joseph, "Since God has made all this known to you, there is no-one so discerning and wise as you. ⁴⁰You shall be in charge of my palace, and all my people are to submit to your orders. Only with respect to the throne will I be greater than you."

⁴¹So Pharaoh said to Joseph, "I hereby put you in charge of the whole land of Egypt." ⁴²Then Pharaoh took his signet ring from his finger and put it on Joseph's finger. He dressed him in robes of fine linen and put a gold chain around his neck. ⁴³He had him ride in a chariot as his second-in-command, and men shouted before him, "Make way!" Thus he put him in charge of the whole land of Egypt.

⁴⁴Then Pharaoh said to Joseph, "I am Pharaoh, but without your word no-one will lift hand or foot in all Egypt."

Joseph's early days in Egypt
Genesis 39:2–6

Joseph flees from committing adultery
Genesis 39:7–19

Joseph put in jail
Genesis 39:20–23

Sons of Levi
Exodus 6:16, Numbers 3:17, 1 Chronicles 6:1 & 16

Joseph interprets dream
Genesis 40:1–23

Death of Isaac
Genesis 35:28–29

Joseph interprets Pharaoh's dream
Genesis 41:1–37

Joseph made governor of Egypt
Genesis 41:38–44

For Thought and **Contemplation**

God has a marvellous and brilliant way of camouflaging opportunities to look like difficulties. Hundreds of Bible characters, including Joseph, discovered this. Have you?

"But God chose the foolish things of the world to shame the wise; God chose the weak things of the world to shame the strong." (1 Cor. 1:27)

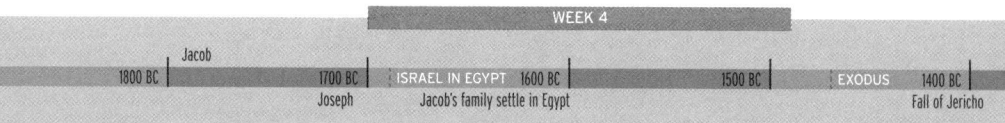

DAY 23 — Joseph's brothers travel to Egypt

Joseph marries Asenath
Genesis 41:45

The seven years of plenty
Genesis 41:46–49

Joseph's sons born
Genesis 41:50–52

Judah and Tamar
Genesis 38:6–26

Birth of Perez and Zerah
Genesis 38: 27–30, 1 Chronicles 2:4

The seven years of famine
Genesis 41:53–57

Joseph's brothers first journey to Egypt
Genesis 42:1–28

Their report to Jacob
Genesis 42:29–38

Jacob sends them to Egypt again
Genesis 43:1–14

Genesis 41:53–57

[53]The seven years of abundance in Egypt came to an end, [54]and the seven years of famine began, just as Joseph had said. There was famine in all the other lands, but in the whole land of Egypt there was food. [55]When all Egypt began to feel the famine, the people cried to Pharaoh for food. Then Pharaoh told all the Egyptians, "Go to Joseph and do what he tells you."
[56]When the famine had spread over the whole country, Joseph opened the storehouses and sold grain to the Egyptians, for the famine was severe throughout Egypt. [57]And all the countries came to Egypt to buy grain from Joseph, because the famine was severe in all the world.

For Thought and **Contemplation**

We must be careful not to interpret the days of obscurity and isolation as meaningless and unimportant. It is there that God prepares His servants for the spiritual challenges that lie ahead.

"... being confident of this, that he who began a good work in you will carry it on to completion until the day of Christ Jesus." (Phil. 1:6)

CREATION — Adam & Eve | 3000 BC — Noah / Great Pyramid Age in Egypt begins | 2000 BC — Flood | 1900 BC — Job (testing) / Abraham leaves Ur — Isaac | Bronze Age begins in Britain

Provision instead of famine

DAY 24

Genesis 46:1–7

¹So Israel set out with all that was his, and when he reached Beersheba, he offered sacrifices to the God of his father Isaac. ²And God spoke to Israel in a vision at night and said, "Jacob! Jacob!"

"Here I am," he replied.

³"I am God, the God of your father," he said. "Do not be afraid to go down to Egypt, for I will make you into a great nation there. ⁴I will go down to Egypt with you, and I will surely bring you back again. And Joseph's own hand will close your eyes."

⁵Then Jacob left Beersheba, and Israel's sons took their father Jacob and their children and their wives in the carts that Pharaoh had sent to transport him. ⁶They also took with them their livestock and the possessions they had acquired in Canaan, and Jacob and all his offspring went to Egypt. ⁷He took with him to Egypt his sons and grandsons and his daughters and granddaughters – all his offspring.

Joseph reunited with his brothers
Genesis 43:15–34, 44:1–34

Joseph makes himself known to his brothers
Genesis 45:1–15

Jacob hears good news
Genesis 45:16–28

Jacob goes to Egypt
Genesis 46:1–7

Summary of those who went to Egypt
Genesis 46:8–27, Exodus 1:1–5

Joseph's family settle in Egypt
Genesis 46:28–34, 47:1–12

His wise leadership continues
Genesis 47:13–26

Jacob's last days
Genesis 47:28–31

Jacob's blessing
Genesis 48:1–22

For Thought and **Contemplation**

Few people can be rejected, insulted, slandered and vilified without carrying a grudge and harbouring hatred in their hearts – but it's possible. Joseph did it. Jesus did it. And, in God's strength, so can you.

"For if you forgive men when they sin against you, your heavenly Father will also forgive you." (Matt 6:14)

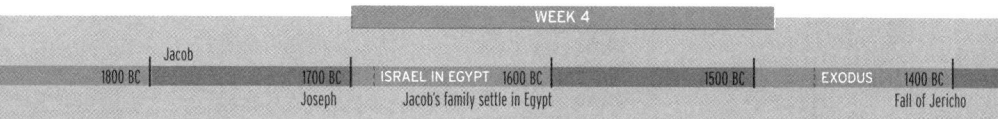

DAY 25 — A faithful Patriarch

Jacob speaks to his twelve sons
Genesis 49:1–32

Death of Jacob
Genesis 49:33

Burial of Jacob
Genesis 50:1–14

Joseph reassures his brothers
Genesis 50:15–21

Judah's descendants through Perez and Zerah
Ruth 4:18, 1 Chronicles 2:5–8

Joseph's latter days
Genesis 50:22–23

Joseph's last words
Genesis 50:24–25

Death of Joseph and his brothers
Genesis 50:26, Exodus 1:6

Genesis 50:14–20

¹⁴After burying his father, Joseph returned to Egypt, together with his brothers and all the others who had gone with him to bury his father.
¹⁵When Joseph's brothers saw that their father was dead, they said, "What if Joseph holds a grudge against us and pays us back for all the wrongs we did to him?" ¹⁶So they sent word to Joseph, saying, "Your father left these instructions before he died: ¹⁷'This is what you are to say to Joseph: I ask you to forgive your brothers the sins and the wrongs they committed in treating you so badly.' Now please forgive the sins of the servants of the God of your father." When their message came to him, Joseph wept.
¹⁸His brothers then came and threw themselves down before him. "We are your slaves," they said.
¹⁹But Joseph said to them, "Don't be afraid. Am I in the place of God? ²⁰You intended to harm me, but God intended it for good to accomplish what is now being done, the saving of many lives.

For Thought and **Contemplation**

God does not promise us a life free from difficulties or dangers. He does, however, promise us that, in all situations and problems, His wisdom will be at work to turn the dross into purest gold.

"These [trials] have come so that your faith – of greater worth than gold, which perishes even though refined by fire – may be proved genuine and may result in praise, glory and honour when Jesus Christ is revealed." (1 Pet. 1:7)

a bird's eye view of Exodus

Place in the Bible	Main Character	Special Features
Second Old Testament book; second book of the Law.	Moses	The account of the deliverance from Egypt, the Plagues, the Passover, the Exodus, and the giving of the Law.

The birth and commission of Moses — DAY **26**

Population of Israel grows
Genesis 47:27, Exodus 1:7

Egypt's bondage and oppression
Exodus 1:8–14

Moses' early days
Numbers 26:59, Exodus 6:20

Death of Israel's baby boys decreed
Exodus 1:15–22

Birth of Aaron
1 Chronicles 23:13

Birth of Moses
Exodus 2:1–9

Moses' childhood
Exodus 2:10

Aaron's family
Exodus 6:23, Numbers 26:60, 1 Chronicles 6:49

Moses slays Egyptian
Exodus 2:11–15

Moses flees to Midian
Exodus 2:16–20

Moses marries Zipporah
Exodus 2:21–22

Moses' sons
1 Chronicles 23:14–15

Birth of Phinehas
Exodus 6:25

God hears Israel's groanings
Exodus 2:23–25

Moses receives his commission
Exodus 3:1–22

Moses' objections
Exodus 4:1–13

Moses complies
Exodus 4:14–18

Exodus 2:11–14

¹¹One day ... Moses ... saw an Egyptian beating a Hebrew, one of his own people. ¹²Glancing this way and that and seeing no-one, he killed the Egyptian and hid him in the sand. ¹³The next day he went out and saw two Hebrews fighting. He asked the one in the wrong, "Why are you hitting your fellow Hebrew?"

¹⁴The man said, "Who made you ruler and judge over us? Are you thinking of killing me as you killed the Egyptian?" Then Moses was afraid and thought, "What I did must have become known."

For Thought and **Contemplation**

No one can do God's work effectively in this world until they have graduated from His "School of Patience". And patience, according to one definition, is "the ability to count down before blasting off".

"Therefore, since we are surrounded by such a great cloud of witnesses, let us throw off everything that hinders and the sin that so easily entangles, and let us run with perseverance the race marked out for us. Let us fix our eyes on Jesus, the author and per-fecter of our faith ..." (Heb.12:1–2)

Jesus and the Book

The New Testament shows in many ways that people and events in Exodus teach us about Christ: for example, Aaron the High Priest (Jesus Christ is "our great high priest", Heb. 4:14); the Passover (Jesus Christ is the Passover lamb, 1 Cor. 5:7).

Teaching

Exodus teaches that God is the God who in His love delivers His people from oppression. The day of the Exodus is the symbol and illustration of this truth.

A Verse to Remember

"Now if you obey me fully and keep my covenant, then out of all nations you will be my treasured possession" (Exod. 19:5).

DAY **27** — Moses becomes leader

Moses returns to Egypt
Exodus 4:19–28

Moses reports to the people
Exodus 4:29–31

Moses contends with Pharaoh
Exodus 5:1–3

Pharaoh increases burdens
Exodus 5:4–23

Final instructions to Moses
Exodus 6:1–13, 26–30, 7:1–6

First meeting with Pharaoh
Exodus 7:7

Rods turn to serpents
Exodus 7:8–13

The ten plagues

1. Rivers turned to blood
Exodus 7:14–25

2. Frogs
Exodus 8:1–15

Exodus 7:1–6

¹Then the Lord said to Moses, "See, I have made you like God to Pharaoh, and your brother Aaron will be your prophet. ²You are to say everything I command you, and your brother Aaron is to tell Pharaoh to let the Israelites go out of his country. ³But I will harden Pharaoh's heart, and though I multiply my miraculous signs and wonders in Egypt, ⁴he will not listen to you. Then I will lay my hand on Egypt and with mighty acts of judgment I will bring out my divisions, my people the Israelites. ⁵And the Egyptians will know that I am the Lord when I stretch out my hand against Egypt and bring the Israelites out of it."
⁶Moses and Aaron did just as the Lord commanded them.

For Thought and **Contemplation**

If we are to be successful in this life, then we must regard this as a central truth: there are no detours around God's will, and anything short of total obedience to God is disobedience.

"For he chose us in him before the creation of the world to be holy and blameless in his sight." (Eph. 1:4)

God continues the plagues

DAY 28

Exodus 10:21-27

²¹Then the Lord said to Moses, "Stretch out your hand towards the sky so that darkness will spread over Egypt – darkness that can be felt." ²²So Moses stretched out his hand towards the sky, and total darkness covered all Egypt for three days. ²³No-one could see anyone else or leave his place for three days. Yet all the Israelites had light in the places where they lived.

²⁴Then Pharaoh summoned Moses and said, "Go, worship the Lord. Even your women and children may go with you; only leave your flocks and herds behind."

²⁵But Moses said, "You must allow us to have sacrifices and burnt offerings to present to the Lord our God. ²⁶Our livestock too must go with us; not a hoof is to be left behind. We have to use some of them in worshipping the Lord our God, and until we get there we will not know what we are to use to worship the Lord."

²⁷But the Lord hardened Pharaoh's heart, and he was not willing to let them go.

3. Gnats
Exodus 8:16–19

4. Flies
Exodus 8:20–32

5. Death of livestock
Exodus 9:1–7

6. Boils
Exodus 9:8–12

7. Hail
Exodus 9:13–35

8. Locusts
Exodus 10:1–20

9. Darkness
Exodus 10:21–27

For Thought and **Contemplation**

The more we resist God's Word and the more we refuse to do the divine bidding, the harder and more stubborn our hearts become. The tragedy is that, when we insist on having our own way, God may let us have it.

"It is a dreadful thing to fall into the hands of the living God." (Heb. 10:31)

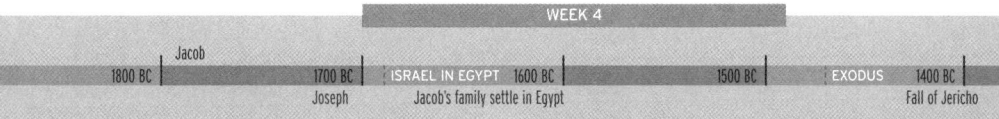

DAY 29

The Passover

10. Killing of firstborn: warning
Exodus 11:1–8

Pharaoh cancels negotiations
Exodus 10:28–29

Pharaoh's heart hardened
Exodus 11:9–10

Passover instructions
Exodus 12:1–12

Importance of the blood
Exodus 12:13–27

Israel's obedience
Exodus 12:28

Firstborn of Egypt killed
Exodus 12:29–30

Egyptians demand immediate departure
Exodus 12:31–36

Deliverance begins
Exodus 12:40–42, Numbers 33:1–4

The Exodus approx, 1462 BC

From Rameses to Succoth
Exodus 12:37, Numbers 33:5

At Succoth
Exodus 12:38–39, 43–51

Exodus 12:21–27

²¹Then Moses summoned all the elders of Israel and said to them, "Go at once and select the animals for your families and slaughter the Passover lamb. ²²Take a bunch of hyssop, dip it into the blood in the basin and put some of the blood on the top and on both sides of the door-frame. Not one of you shall go out of the door of his house until morning. ²³When the Lord goes through the land to strike down the Egyptians, he will see the blood on the top and sides of the door-frame and will pass over that doorway, and he will not permit the destroyer to enter your houses and strike you down.

²⁴"Obey these instructions as a lasting ordinance for you and your descendants. ²⁵When you enter the land that the Lord will give you as he promised, observe this ceremony. ²⁶And when your children ask you, 'What does this ceremony mean to you?' ²⁷then tell them, 'It is the Passover sacrifice to the Lord, who passed over the houses of the Israelites in Egypt and spared our homes when he struck down the Egyptians.'"

For Thought and **Contemplation**

The greatest celebration in the life of Israel is the Passover. They rejoice with great gladness as they remember their deliverance from Egypt. You have experienced a greater deliverance. Does it cause your heart to rejoice?

"... For Christ, our Passover lamb, has been sacrificed." (1 Cor. 5:7)

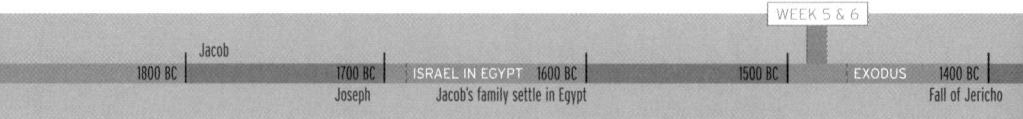

The Books of the Law

The first five books of the Old Testament, Genesis, Exodus, Leviticus, Numbers, Deuteronomy, are known as the **Pentateuch** (literally: the five-volumed book).

In the Old Testament the Pentateuch is referred to as:

- the Law (Ezra 10:3)
- the Book of the Law of Moses (Neh. 8:1)
- the Book of Moses (Neh. 13:1)
- the Law of the Lord (1 Chron. 16:40)
- the Law of God (Neh. 10:28)
- the Book of the Law of God (Neh. 8:18)
- the Book of the Law of the Lord (Neh. 9:3)
- the Law of Moses (Dan. 9:11)

In the New Testament the Pentateuch is referred to as:

- the Book of the Law (Gal. 3:10)
- the Book of Moses (Mark 12:26)
- the Law of the Lord (Luke 2:23–24)

The first five books of the Bible set down God's laws for humankind.

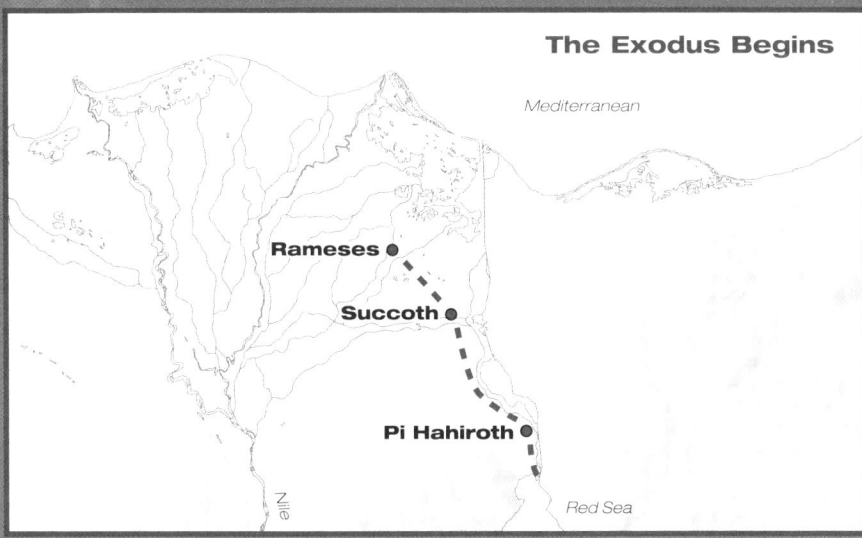

The Exodus Begins

DAY 30 — Crossing the Red Sea

Passover instructions
Exodus 13:1–19

From Succoth to Etham
Exodus 13:20, Numbers 33:6

Pillar of fire and cloud
Exodus 13:21–22

From Etham to Pi Hahiroth
Exodus 14:1–2, Numbers 33:7

Pharaoh pursues
Exodus 14:3–20

Crossing the Red Sea
Exodus 14:21–31

Song of victory
Exodus 15:1–21

Exodus 14:26–31

²⁶Then the Lord said to Moses, "Stretch out your hand over the sea so that the waters may flow back over the Egyptians and their chariots and horsemen." ²⁷Moses stretched out his hand over the sea, and at daybreak the sea went back to its place. The Egyptians were fleeing towards it, and the Lord swept them into the sea. ²⁸The water flowed back and covered the chariots and horsemen – the entire army of Pharaoh that had followed the Israelites into the sea. Not one of them survived. ²⁹But the Israelites went through the sea on dry ground, with a wall of water on their right and on their left. ³⁰That day the Lord saved Israel from the hands of the Egyptians, and Israel saw the Egyptians lying dead on the shore. ³¹And when the Israelites saw the great power the Lord displayed against the Egyptians, the people feared the Lord and put their trust in him and in Moses his servant.

For Thought and **Contemplation**

Has God placed you in a wilderness at this particular time? If so, then He has done it in order to teach you the important lesson of dependency. God will have you dependent on no one but Himself.

"He has delivered us from such a deadly peril, and he will deliver us. On him we have set our hope that he will continue to deliver us ..." (2 Cor. 1:10)

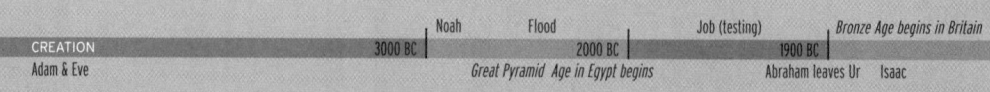

Into the Wilderness

DAY **31**

To the Desert of Shur
Exodus 15:22

From Shur to Marah
Numbers 33:8, Exodus 15:23–26

From Marah to Elim
Exodus 15:27, Numbers 33:9

From Elim to Desert of Sin
Exodus 16:1, Numbers 33:10–11

Murmuring about lack of food
Exodus 16:2–3

Manna promised
Exodus 16:4–12

Manna provided
Exodus 16:13–22, 31–36

Law of the Sabbath
Exodus 16:23–30

From wilderness of Sin to Rephidim
Exodus 17:1, Numbers 33:12–14

Murmuring about the lack of water
Exodus 17:2–4

Water from rock on Mount Horeb
Exodus 17:5–7

Conflict with Amalek
Exodus 17:8–16

Relatives visit Moses
Exodus 18:1–12

Jethro's wise counsel
Exodus 18:13–27

Sinai approx 1461 BC

From Rephidim to Sinai
Exodus 19:1–2, Numbers 33:15

Giving of the Law: Covenant reviewed and preliminary instructions
Exodus 19:3–8

Exodus 17:2–4

²So they quarrelled with Moses and said, "Give us water to drink."
  Moses replied, "Why do you quarrel with me? Why do you put the Lord to the test?"
³But the people were thirsty for water there, and they grumbled against Moses. They said, "Why did you bring us up out of Egypt to make us and our children and livestock die of thirst?"
⁴Then Moses cried out to the Lord, "What am I to do with these people? They are almost ready to stone me."

For Thought and **Contemplation**

Have you ever considered why it is that God allows us to go through bad days as well as good ones? Because we can learn things through adversity that we would never learn through prosperity.

"These things happened to them as examples and were written down as warnings for us ..." (1 Cor. 10:11)

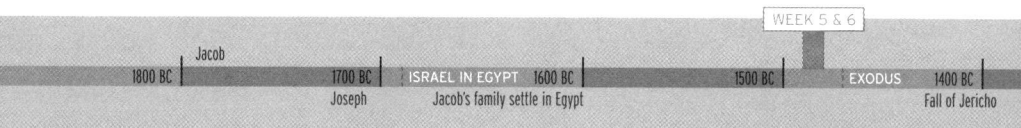

Heart to Heart

Section 1

Well done!! You are already one-twelfth of the way through the Bible. Don't be disheartened if it has been difficult or you have slipped a few days behind. Do what was suggested in the Introduction – ask the Lord to help you recover the time you have lost. A number of people at CWR are praying for you. The discipline of daily reading God's Word is building deep spiritual qualities within you.

2

In this section

God's laws for His people
The setting up of the Tabernacle
The ministry of the priests
Israel's years in the wilderness

DAY **32** — The Ten Commandments

Moses prepares Israel
to meet with God
Exodus 19:9–15

Moses holds Israel back
from the mount
Exodus 19:16–25

Ten Commandments given
Exodus 20:1–17

The people tremble
Exodus 20:18–21

Instructions for altar
Exodus 20:22–26

Various laws given:
Masters and servants
Exodus 21:1–11

Injuries to persons
Exodus 21:12–36

Exodus 20:1–10

¹And God spoke all these words: ²"I am the Lord your God, who brought you out of Egypt, out of the land of slavery. ³"You shall have no other gods before me. ⁴"You shall not make for yourself an idol in the form of anything in heaven above or on the earth beneath or in the waters below. ⁵You shall not bow down to them or worship them; for I, the Lord your God, am a jealous God, punishing the children for the sin of the fathers to the third and fourth generation of those who hate me, ⁶but showing love to a thousand [generations] of those who love me and keep my commandments. ⁷"You shall not misuse the name of the Lord your God, for the Lord will not hold anyone guiltless who misuses his name. ⁸"Remember the Sabbath day by keeping it holy. ⁹Six days you shall labour and do all your work, ¹⁰but the seventh day is a Sabbath to the Lord your God. ..."

For Thought and **Contemplation**

The Ten Commandments are God's moral guidelines for all people in all generations. If God wanted us to live in moral uncertainty, He would have given us Ten Suggestions, not Ten Commandments!

"This is the covenant I will make with them after that time, says the Lord. I will put my laws in their hearts, and I will write them on their minds." (Heb.10:16)

CREATION — Adam & Eve | 3000 BC | Noah | Flood — Great Pyramid Age in Egypt begins | 2000 BC | Job (testing) | 1900 BC — Abraham leaves Ur | Isaac | Bronze Age begins in Britain

God's covenant with Israel

DAY **33**

Exodus 23:20–26

²⁰"See, I am sending an angel ahead of you to guard you along the way and to bring you to the place I have prepared. ²¹Pay attention to him and listen to what he says. Do not rebel against him; he will not forgive your rebellion, since my Name is in him. ²²If you listen carefully to what he says and do all that I say, I will be an enemy to your enemies and will oppose those who oppose you. ²³My angel will go ahead of you and bring you into the land of the Amorites, Hittites, Perizzites, Canaanites, Hivites and Jebusites, and I will wipe them out. ²⁴Do not bow down before their gods or worship them or follow their practices. You must demolish them and break their sacred stones to pieces. ²⁵Worship the Lord your God, and his blessing will be on your food and water. I will take away sickness from among you, ²⁶and none will miscarry or be barren in your land. I will give you a full life span."

Rights of property
Exodus 22:1–15

Crimes against humanity
Exodus 22:16–31, 23:1–9

Land and the Sabbath
Exodus 23:10–13

Three national feasts
Exodus 23:14–19

God's covenant with Israel: future conquest
Exodus 23:20–33

Altar built
Exodus 24:3–8

Moses goes up Mount Sinai
Exodus 24:1–2, 9–17

Forty days of instruction begin
Exodus 24:18

Tabernacle items

Materials
Exodus 25:1–9

For Thought and **Contemplation**

Confucius said, "The faintest ink is better than the strongest memory." How easy it would be to forget God's principles if they were not written down. Aren't you thankful for the Bible?

"'... but the word of the Lord stands for ever'. And this is the word that was preached to you." (1 Pet. 1:25)

DAY 34 — The Tabernacle

Ark
Exodus 25:10–22

Table of shewbread
Exodus 25:23–30, Leviticus 24:5–9

Golden candlestick
Exodus 25:31–40

Curtains of linen
Exodus 26:1–6

Curtains of goats' hair
Exodus 26:7–13

Covering of rams' skins
Exodus 26:14

The construction of the framework
Exodus 26:15–29

According to the plan
Exodus 26:30

Inner veil
Exodus 26:31–35

Outer veil
Exodus 26:36–37

Brazen altar
Exodus 27:1–8

Court
Exodus 27:9–15

Exodus 25:17–22

¹⁷"Make an atonement cover of pure gold – two and a half cubits long and a cubit and a half wide. ¹⁸And make two cherubim out of hammered gold at the ends of the cover. ¹⁹Make one cherub on one end and the second cherub on the other; make the cherubim of one piece with the cover, at the two ends. ²⁰The cherubim are to have their wings spread upwards, overshadowing the cover with them. The cherubim are to face each other, looking towards the cover. ²¹Place the cover on top of the ark and put in the ark the Testimony, which I will give you. ²²There, above the cover between the two cherubim that are over the ark of the Testimony, I will meet with you and give you all my commands for the Israelites."

For Thought and **Contemplation**

God's greatest longing is not simply to visit His people, but to live with them. Divine visitation is wonderful, but how much more glorious is divine habitation. Blessed *Immanuel*.

"When Christ came as high priest of the good things that are already here, he went through the greater and more perfect tabernacle that is not man-made, that is to say, not a part of this creation." (Heb. 9:11)

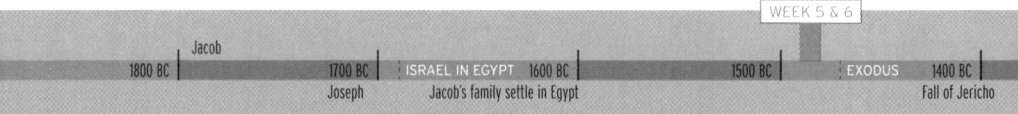

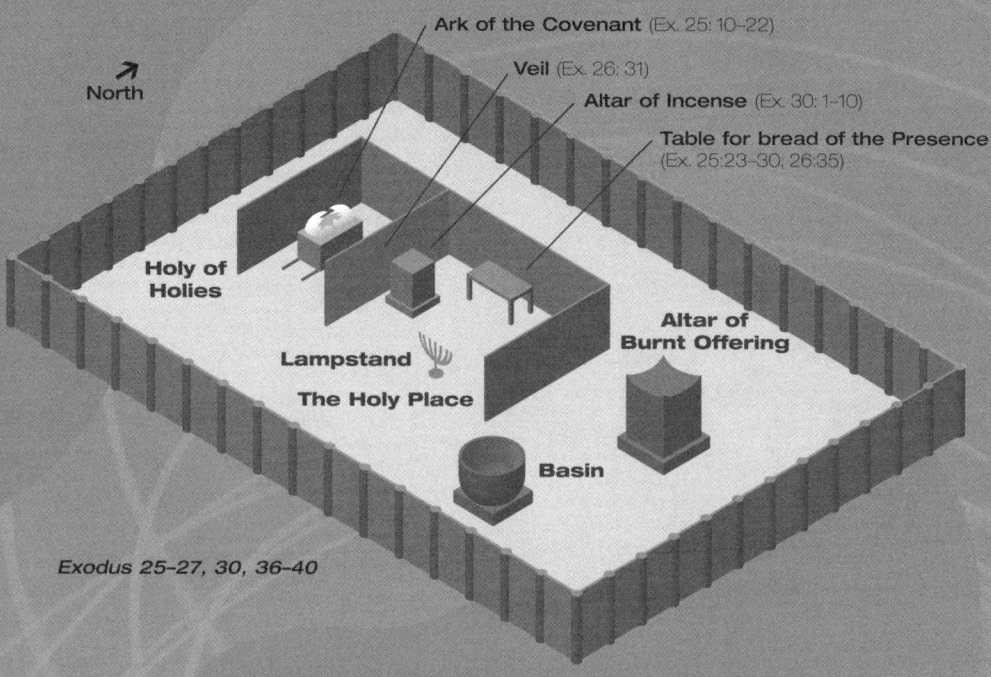

The Tabernacle
God dwells among his people

Exodus 25–27, 30, 36–40

Encampment position of the twelve tribes

DAY **35**

Tabernacle items

Hangings for gate of court
Exodus 27:16–19

Oil for the light
Exodus 27:20–21, Leviticus 24:1–4

Altar of incense
Exodus 30:1–10

Atonement money
Exodus 30:11–16

Bronze basin
Exodus 30:17–21

Incense and spices
Exodus 30:22–38

Workmen
Exodus 31:1–11

Priesthood items
Exodus 28:1

Garments of the priests
Exodus 28:2–30

Exodus 31:1–11

¹Then the Lord said to Moses, ²"See I have chosen Bezalel son of Uri, the son of Hur, of the tribe of Judah, ³and I have filled him with the Spirit of God, with skill, ability and knowledge in all kinds of crafts – ⁴to make artistic designs for work in gold, silver and bronze, ⁵to cut and set stones, to work in wood, and to engage in all kinds of craftsmanship. ⁶Moreover, I have appointed Oholiab son of Ahisamach, of the tribe of Dan, to help him. Also I have given skill to all the craftsmen to make everything I have commanded you: ⁷the Tent of Meeting, the ark of the Testimony with the atonement cover on it, and all the other furnishings of the tent – ⁸the table and its articles, the pure gold lampstand and all its accessories, the altar of incense, ⁹the altar of burnt offering and all its utensils, the basin with its stand – ¹⁰and also the woven garments, both the sacred garments for Aaron the priest and the garments for his sons when they serve as priests, ¹¹and the anointing oil and fragrant incense for the Holy Place …"

For Thought and **Contemplation**

If you are a believer, you are also a priest. You can come into God's presence and *linger* there – without dread or fear. What an exciting ministry! Are you using it?

"Now we know that if the earthly tent we live in is destroyed, we have a building from God, an eternal house in heaven, not built by human hands." (2 Cor 5:1)

The Priesthood

DAY **36**

Exodus 31:12-18

¹²Then the Lord said to Moses, ¹³"Say to the Israelites, 'You must observe my Sabbaths. This will be a sign between me and you for the generations to come, so that you may know that I am the Lord, who makes you holy.
¹⁴"'Observe the Sabbath, because it is holy to you. Anyone who desecrates it must be put to death; whoever does any work on that day must be cut off from his people. ¹⁵For six days work is to be done, but the seventh day is a Sabbath of rest, holy to the Lord. Whoever does any work on the Sabbath day must be put to death. ¹⁶The Israelites are to observe the Sabbath, celebrating it for the generations to come as a lasting covenant. ¹⁷It will be a sign between me and the Israelites for ever, for in six days the Lord made the heavens and the earth, and on the seventh day he abstained from work and rested.'"
¹⁸When the Lord finished speaking to Moses on Mount Sinai, he gave him the two tablets of the Testimony, the tablets of stone inscribed by the finger of God.

Garments of the priests continued
Exodus 28:31-43

Consecration of the priests
Exodus 29:1-25

Food for the priests
Exodus 29:26-37

Continual burnt offering
Exodus 29:38-46

Sabbath rest
Exodus 31:12-18

For Thought and **Contemplation**

If you were asked to write down the thought on which your mind most often focuses, what would it be? Money? Fame? Pleasure? Or God? If God doesn't have the central place in our thoughts, then whatever takes His place is an idol.

"For Christ did not enter a man-made sanctuary that was only a copy of the true one; he entered heaven itself, now to appear for us in God's presence." (Heb. 9:24)

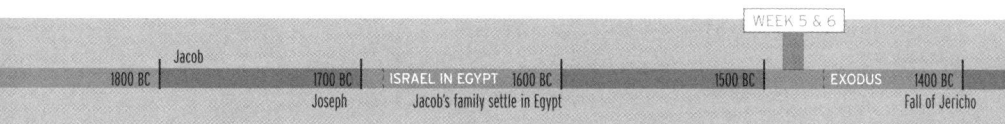

DAY 37 — Moses' anger and tablets broken

The golden calf
Exodus 32:1–6

Moses' anger
Exodus 32:7–29

Moses' plea and God's answer
Exodus 32:30–33:6

Temporary tabernacle erected
Exodus 33:7–11

Moses communes with God
Exodus 33:12–23

Instructions to hew stone
Exodus 34:1–3

Forty more days on mount: Tablets remade
Exodus 34:4

Directions renewed
Exodus 34:5–28

Law of the land given: Sabbatic year
Leviticus 25:1–7

Years of Jubilee
Leviticus 25:8–24

Exodus 34:5–10

⁵Then the Lord came down in the cloud and stood there with him and proclaimed his name, the Lord. ⁶And he passed in front of Moses, proclaiming, "The Lord, the Lord, the compassionate and gracious God, slow to anger, abounding in love and faithfulness, ⁷maintaining love to thousands, and forgiving wickedness, rebellion and sin. Yet he does not leave the guilty unpunished; he punishes the children and their children for the sin of the fathers to the third and fourth generation."

⁸Moses bowed to the ground at once and worshipped. ⁹"O Lord, if I have found favour in your eyes," he said, "then let the Lord go with us. Although this is a stiff-necked people, forgive our wickedness and our sin, and take us as your inheritance."

¹⁰Then the Lord said: "I am making a covenant with you. Before all your people I will do wonders never before done in any nation in all the world. The people you live among will see how awesome is the work that I, the Lord, will do for you."

For Thought and **Contemplation**

Whenever we fall into sin, the way out is not by indulging in excuses, but by an act of genuine repentance. When man covers his sin, he adds to it, but when God covers sin, He absolves it – eternally.

"If we confess our sins, he is faithful and just and will forgive us our sins and purify us from all unrighteousness." (1 Jn. 1:9)

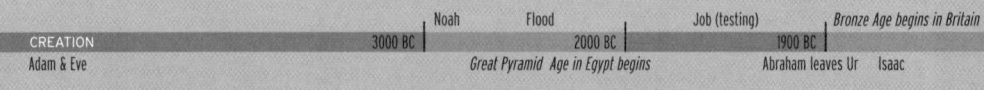

Further laws

DAY 38

Leviticus 26:1-8

¹"'Do not make idols or set up an image or a sacred stone for yourselves, and do not place a carved stone in your land to bow down before it. I am the Lord your God. ²"'Observe my Sabbaths and have reverence for my sanctuary. I am the Lord. ³"'If you follow my decrees and are careful to obey my commands, ⁴I will send you rain in its season, and the ground will yield its crops and the trees of the field their fruit. ⁵Your threshing will continue until grape harvest and the grape harvest will continue until planting, and you will eat all the food you want and live in safety in your land. ⁶"'I will grant peace in the land, and you will lie down and no-one will make you afraid. I will remove savage beasts from the land, and the sword will not pass through your country. ⁷You will pursue your enemies, and they will fall by the sword before you. ⁸Five of you will chase a hundred, and a hundred of you will chase ten thousand, and your enemies will fall by the sword before you.'"

Redemption of inheritance	Leviticus 25:25-34
Care of the poor	Leviticus 25:35-46
Redemption of the poor	Leviticus 25:47-55
Other laws given: conditions for blessing	Leviticus 26:1-13
Warnings of chastisement	Leviticus 26:14-31
Dispersion predicted	Leviticus 26:32-39
Covenant remains (conditional)	Leviticus 26:40-46
Dedicated persons and things (tax)	Leviticus 27:1-13

For Thought and **Contemplation**

God's warnings are clearly signposted everywhere in life – for those who have eyes to see. And no one can accuse God of enforcing any law that He has not clearly 'posted'.

"It is because of him that you are in Christ Jesus, who has become for us wisdom from God – that is, our righteousness, holiness and redemption." (1 Cor. 1:30)

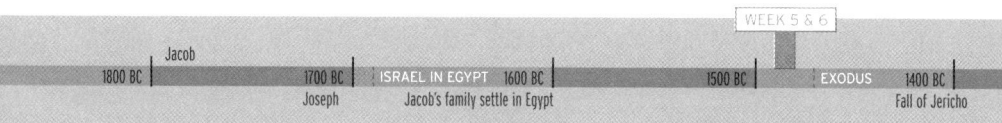

DAY 39 — Tabernacle contents

Dedicated persons and things (tax) continued
Leviticus 27:14–25

Three items that are the Lord's
Leviticus 27:26–34

Moses' face shines with God's glory
Exodus 34:29–35

Tabernacle built: materials given by people
Exodus 35:4–29, 36:1–7

Ark
Exodus 37:1–9

Table of shewbread
Exodus 37:10–16

Golden candlestick
Exodus 37:17–24

Curtains of linen
Exodus 36:8–13

Exodus 35:20–29
[20] Then the whole Israelite community withdrew from Moses' presence, [21] and everyone who was willing and whose heart moved him came and brought an offering to the Lord for the work on the Tent of Meeting, for all its service, and for the sacred garments. [22] All who were willing, men and women alike, came and brought gold jewellery of all kinds: brooches, earrings, rings and ornaments. They all presented their gold as a wave offering to the Lord. [23] Everyone who had blue, purple or scarlet yarn or fine linen, or goat hair, ram skins dyed red or hides of sea cows brought them. [24] Those presenting an offering of silver or bronze brought it as an offering to the Lord, and everyone who had acacia wood for any part of the work brought it. [25] Every skilled woman spun with her hands and brought what she had spun – blue, purple or scarlet yarn or fine linen. ... [29] All the Israelite men and women who were willing brought to the Lord freewill offerings for all the work the Lord through Moses had commanded them to do.

For Thought and **Contemplation**

It is a Scriptural principle to give according to one's income. Those whose giving is not according to their income, may find that God adjusts their income according to their giving.

"Give, and it will be given to you. A good measure, pressed down, shaken together and running over, will be poured into your lap. For with the measure you use, it will be measured to you." (Lk. 6:38)

The High Priest
and his garments

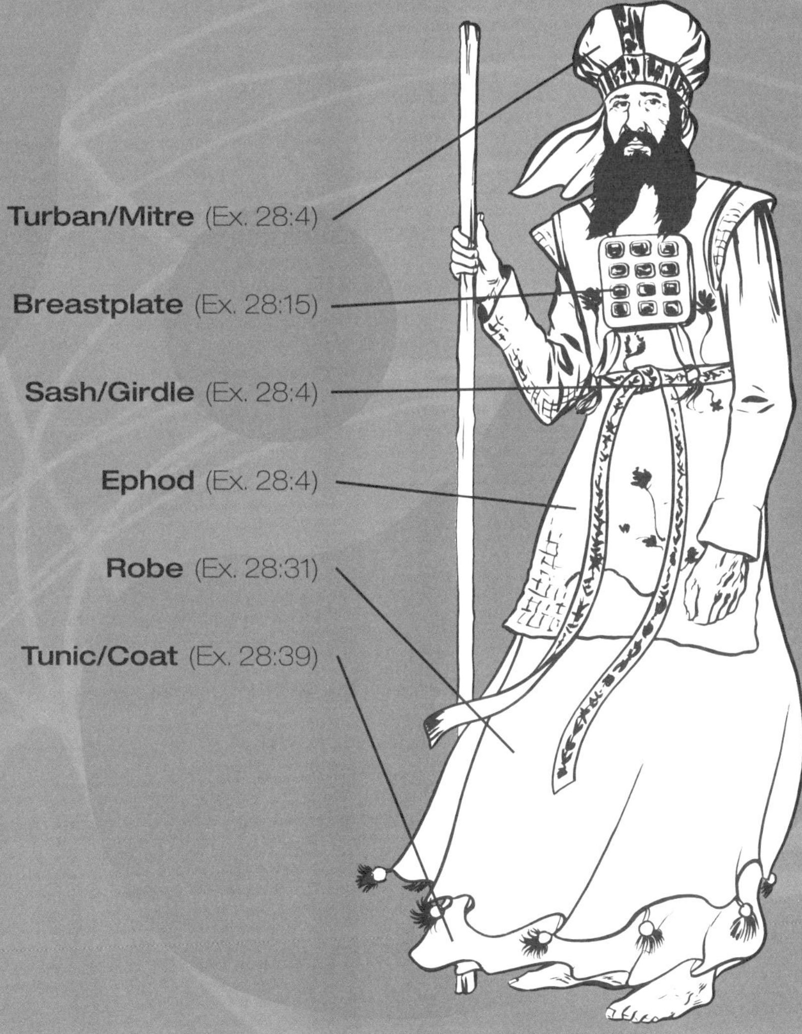

- **Turban/Mitre** (Ex. 28:4)
- **Breastplate** (Ex. 28:15)
- **Sash/Girdle** (Ex. 28:4)
- **Ephod** (Ex. 28:4)
- **Robe** (Ex. 28:31)
- **Tunic/Coat** (Ex. 28:39)

For Christians Jesus is our great high priest (Heb. 4:14).

DAY 40 — Tabernacle built

Tabernacle items continued: curtains of goats' hair
Exodus 36:14–18

Covering of rams' skins
Exodus 36:19

Boards and sockets
Exodus 36:20–30

Framework of the Tabernacle
Exodus 36:31–34

Inner veil
Exodus 36:35–36

Outer veil
Exodus 36:37–38

Altar of Burnt Offering
Exodus 38:1–7

Bronze basin
Exodus 38:8

Court
Exodus 38:9–17

Hangings for gate of court
Exodus 38:18–20

Altar of incense made
Exodus 37:25–28

Incense and spices
Exodus 37:29

Workmen
Exodus 35:30–35

Priesthood items: garments of the priests
Exodus 39:1–31

Exodus 35:30–35

³⁰Then Moses said to the Israelites, "See, the Lord has chosen Bezalel son of Uri, the son of Hur, of the tribe of Judah, ³¹and he has filled him with the Spirit of God, with skill, ability and knowledge in all kinds of crafts – ³²to make artistic designs for work in gold, silver and bronze, ³³to cut and set stones, to work in wood and to engage in all kinds of artistic craftsmanship. ³⁴And he has given both him and Oholiab son of Ahisamach, of the tribe of Dan, the ability to teach others. ³⁵He has filled them with skill to do all kinds of work as craftsmen, designers, embroiderers in blue, purple and scarlet yarn and fine linen, and weavers – all of them master craftsmen and designers. ..."

For Thought and Contemplation

Christ, our Great High Priest, when undertaking the work of our redemption, put on the garments of humility, girded Himself with resolution, took charge of God's spiritual Israel – the Church – and one day will present us perfect to the Father.

"Therefore, since we have a great high priest who has gone through the heavens, Jesus the Son of God, let us hold firmly to the faith we profess." (Heb. 4:14)

Levitical duties

DAY **41**

Numbers 3:5-13

⁵The Lord said to Moses, ⁶"Bring the tribe of Levi and present them to Aaron the priest to assist him. ⁷They are to perform duties for him and for the whole community at the Tent of Meeting by doing the work of the tabernacle. ⁸They are to take care of all the furnishings of the Tent of Meeting, fulfilling the obligations of the Israelites by doing the work of the tabernacle. ⁹Give the Levites to Aaron and his sons; they are the Israelites who are to be given wholly to him. ¹⁰Appoint Aaron and his sons to serve as priests; anyone else who approaches the sanctuary must be put to death."

¹¹The Lord also said to Moses, ¹²"I have taken the Levites from among the Israelites in place of the first male offspring of every Israelite woman. The Levites are mine, ¹³for all the firstborn are mine. When I struck down all the firstborn in Egypt, I set apart for myself every firstborn in Israel, whether man or animal. They are to be mine. I am the Lord."

Sabbath rest
Exodus 35:1-3

Summary of the building of tabernacle
Exodus 38:21-31, 39:32-43

Trumpets used to alert congregation
Numbers 10:1-10

Tabernacle made ready for service
Exodus 40:1-15

Instructions and duties prior to leaving wilderness of Sinai: to tribe of Levi
Numbers 3:5-13

To families of Levi
Numbers 3:14-16, 21-24

Responsibilities of Levi's sons
Numbers 3:25-39

For Thought and **Contemplation**

It took Israel a whole year before they learned the lessons of Sinai and were ready to move forward. How long does God have to keep us encamped at one spot because of our unco-operative and unsubmissive spirit?

"... To obey is better than sacrifice ..." (1 Sam. 15:22)

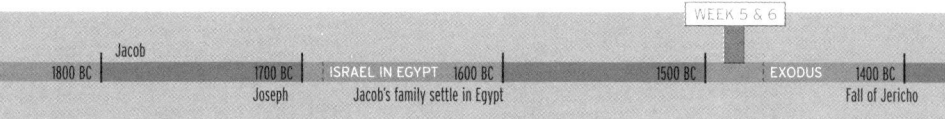

DAY 42

Duties apportioned

Firstborn redeemed
Numbers 3:40–51

Cleansing of the Levites
Numbers 8:5–26

Office of Eleazar
Numbers 4:16–20

Service of the Kohathites
Numbers 4:1–15

Service of the Gershonites
Numbers 4:21–28

Service of the Merarites
Numbers 4:29–33

Numbers 4:21-28

²¹The Lord said to Moses, ²²"Take a census also of the Gershonites by their families and clans. ²³Count all the men from thirty to fifty years of age who come to serve in the work at the Tent of Meeting.
²⁴"This is the service of the Gershonite clans as they work and carry burdens: ²⁵They are to carry the curtains of the tabernacle, the Tent of Meeting, its covering and the outer covering of hides of sea cows, the curtains for the entrance to the Tent of Meeting, ²⁶the curtains of the courtyard surrounding the tabernacle and altar, the curtain for the entrance, the ropes and all the equipment used in its service. The Gershonites are to do all that needs to be done with these things. ²⁷All their service, whether carrying or doing other work, is to be done under the direction of Aaron and his sons. You shall assign to them as their responsibility all they are to carry. ²⁸This is the service of the Gershonite clans at the Tent of Meeting. ..."

For Thought and **Contemplation**

An old cliche in Christian circles runs like this: We are saved to serve. It's true. And joy comes in exercising the gifts God has given us. An unhappy Christian is usually an indolent Christian.

"Therefore, I urge you, brothers, in view of God's mercy, to offer your bodies as living sacrifices, holy and pleasing to God – this is your spiritual act of worship." (Rom. 12:1)

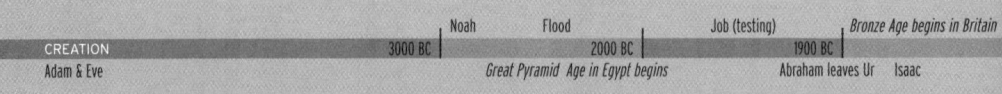

Tabernacle completed

DAY 43

Numbers 7:1-8

¹When Moses finished setting up the tabernacle, he anointed it and consecrated it and all its furnishings. He also anointed and consecrated the altar and all its utensils. ²Then the leaders of Israel, the heads of families who were the tribal leaders in charge of those who were counted, made offerings. ³They brought as their gifts before the Lord six covered carts and twelve oxen – an ox from each leader and a cart from every two. These they presented before the tabernacle.
⁴The Lord said to Moses, ⁵"Accept these from them, that they may be used in the work at the Tent of Meeting. Give them to the Levites as each man's work requires."
⁶So Moses took the carts and oxen and gave them to the Levites. ⁷He gave two carts and four oxen to the Gershonites, as their work required, ⁸and he gave four carts and eight oxen to the Merarites, as their work required. They were all under the direction of Ithamar son of Aaron, the priest.

Moses performs all as directed
Exodus 40:16–33

Aaron lights the lamps
Numbers 8:1–4

Cloud covers tabernacle
Exodus 40:34–35

Gifts and offerings brought at the dedication of the tabernacle and the altar
Numbers 7:1–88

For Thought and **Contemplation**

No matter how efficiently or effectively the hands of men contribute to God's work, the one thing that gives it meaning and purpose is the glory of God resting upon it. Without Him, the best we can produce is – nothing.

"The Word became flesh and made his dwelling among us. We have seen his glory, the glory of the One and Only, who came from the Father, full of grace and truth." (Jn. 1:14)

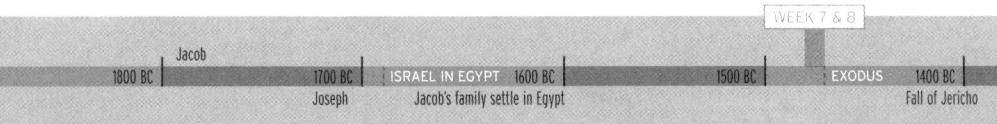

DAY **44**

Priestly ministry

Moses hears God's voice
Numbers 7:89

Aaron's sons' ministry described
Numbers 3:1–3, Leviticus 7:35–36

Consecration of Aaron
Leviticus 8:1–36

Ministry of priests begins
Leviticus 9:1–24

Unauthorised ("Strange" – AV) fire of Nadab and Abihu
Leviticus 10:1–7, Numbers 3:4

Leviticus 9:22–24

²²Then Aaron lifted his hands towards the people and blessed them. And having sacrificed the sin offering, the burnt offering and the fellowship offering, he stepped down. ²³Moses and Aaron then went into the Tent of Meeting. When they came out, they blessed the people; and the glory of the Lord appeared to all the people. ²⁴Fire came out from the presence of the Lord and consumed the burnt offering and the fat portions on the altar. And when all the people saw it, they shouted for joy and fell face down.

For Thought and **Contemplation**

Is the fire that burns on the altar of your heart strange fire or spiritual fire? *Strange* fire is fire that has its origin on earth. *Spiritual* fire is fire that comes down from heaven.

"To him who loves us and has freed us from our sins by his blood, and has made us to be a kingdom and priests to serve his God and Father – to him be glory and power for ever and ever! Amen." (Rev. 1:5–6)

a bird's eye view of **Leviticus**

Place in the Bible
Third Old Testament book; third book of the Law.

Special Features
Sacrifices, the day of atonement, detailed laws covering the whole of life.

Laws about sacrifice

DAY **45**

Leviticus 17:8–12

⁸"Say to them: 'Any Israelite or any alien living among them who offers a burnt offering or sacrifice ⁹and does not bring it to the entrance to the Tent of Meeting to sacrifice it to the Lord – that man must be cut off from his people.

¹⁰"'Any Israelite or any alien living among them who eats any blood – I will set my face against that person who eats blood and will cut him off from his people. ¹¹For the life of a creature is in the blood, and I have given it to you to make atonement for yourselves on the altar; it is the blood that makes atonement for one's life.

¹²Therefore I say to the Israelites, "None of you may eat blood, nor may an alien living among you eat blood.' "

Day of Atonement
Leviticus 16:1–34

Necessity of blood sacrifice
Leviticus 17:1–16

Offerings described: sacrifice system and priest's duties
Leviticus 7:37–38

The burnt offering from the herds
Leviticus 1:1–9

The burnt offering from the flocks, and from the fowls
Leviticus 1:10–17

Concerning the burnt offering
Leviticus 6:8–13

For Thought and **Contemplation**

How would you go about the task of atoning for your own sin? Would you offer the deeds of your home, your bank account, or some other material asset? Such things would be totally inadequate. God has paid your debt freely and fully in His Son. Think about it – and be glad!

"Not only is this so, but we also rejoice in God through our Lord Jesus Christ, through whom we have now received reconciliation." (Rom. 5:11)

Jesus and the Book

The details about sacrifices in Leviticus teach us about God's holiness and help us to understand Jesus' sacrifice. One way to appreciate this is to read the book of Hebrews as a commentary on the book of Leviticus.

Teaching

God's people are told how they can have access to God and how they are to live their lives in obedience to God: they are to be holy.

A Verse to Remember

"I am the Lord your God; consecrate yourselves and be holy, because I am holy." (Lev. 11:44)

DAY 46 — The offerings

The meal offering of flour
Leviticus 2:1–11

The offering of first fruits
Leviticus 2:12–16

Concerning the meal offering
Leviticus 6:14–23

The fellowship offering of the herd
Leviticus 3:1–5

The fellowship offering of the flock
Leviticus 3:6–17

Concerning the fellowship and wave offerings, and food prohibitions
Leviticus 7:11–36

The sin offering of ignorance for the priest
Leviticus 4:1–12

Leviticus 3:1–5

¹"'If someone's offering is a fellowship offering, and he offers an animal from the herd, whether male or female, he is to present before the Lord an animal without defect. ²He is to lay his hand on the head of his offering and slaughter it at the entrance to the Tent of Meeting. Then Aaron's sons the priests shall sprinkle the blood against the altar on all sides. ³From the fellowship offering he is to bring a sacrifice made to the Lord by fire: all the fat that covers the inner parts or is connected to them, ⁴both kidneys with the fat around them near the loins, and the covering of the liver, which he will remove with the kidneys. ⁵Then Aaron's sons are to burn it on the altar on top of the burnt offering that is on the burning wood, as an offering made by fire, an aroma pleasing to the Lord.'"

For Thought and **Contemplation**

Israel were commanded to present many sacrifices, but the only sacrifice God asks of His Church is a "sacrifice of praise" (Heb. 13:15). And it is a sacrifice He requires continually. How consistently does this flame burn on the altar of your heart?

"... so Christ was sacrificed once to take away the sins of many people; and he will appear a second time, not to bear sin, but to bring salvation to those who are waiting for him." (Heb. 9:28)

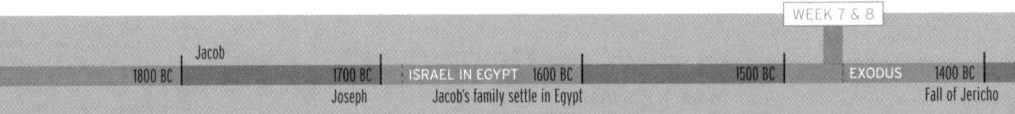

Fellowship with God:
The five main Levitical offerings

Offering	Reference	Purpose

Burnt offering — Lev. 1 — Dedication
Bullocks, lambs, goats, doves, pigeons – were wholly consumed on the altar. It was offered every day, each morning and night.

Cereal offering — Lev. 2 — Thanksgiving
Fine flour, unleavened bread, cakes, wafers, grain – always with salt. A handful was burned on the altar; the rest was for the priests, who ate it in a holy place – always followed the morning and evening burnt offerings.

Peace offering — Lev. 3 — Fellowship
Oxen, sheep, goats. This was a shared sacrifice. The fat was burned: the rest was eaten by priests, and by the sacrificer and his friends. A meal and drink offering always accompanied this sacrifice.

Sin offering — Lev. 4 — Cleansing
Bullocks, goats, lambs. The whole animal was burned outside the camp. A sin offering was made for the whole congregation on all the feast days, especially on the Day of Atonement.

Trespass offering — Lev. 5 — Reconciliation
Always a lamb, with one exception (Lev. 14:12). The ritual was the same as in the sin offering except that the blood was poured and not sprinkled over the surface of the altar. Where wrong had been done to another, restitution was made, including an additional 20% of its value.

DAY 47 — Atonement for sin

The sin offering for the whole congregation
Leviticus 4:13–21

The sin offering for a ruler and for any of the people
Leviticus 4:22–35

Concerning the sin offering
Leviticus 6:24–30

Concerning various sins
Leviticus 5:1–13

Concerning sins against the Lord
Leviticus 5:14–19

Concerning sins against our neighbour
Leviticus 6:1–7

Concerning the guilt offering
Leviticus 7:1–10

Instructions to Aaron and his sons about offerings
Leviticus 10:8–20

Leviticus 5:1–5

¹ "'If a person sins because he does not speak up when he hears a public charge to testify regarding something he has seen or learned about, he will be held responsible.

² "'Or if a person touches anything ceremonially unclean – whether the carcasses of unclean wild animals or of unclean livestock or of unclean creatures that move along the ground – even though he is unaware of it, he has become unclean and is guilty.

³ "'Or if he touches human uncleanness – anything that would make him unclean – even though he is unaware of it, when he learns of it he will be guilty.

⁴ "'Or if a person thoughtlessly takes an oath to do anything, whether good or evil – in any matter one might carelessly swear about – even though he is unaware of it, in any case when he learns of it he will be guilty.

⁵ "'When anyone is guilty in any of these ways, he must confess in what way he has sinned ...'"

For Thought and **Contemplation**

Someone has said that the first step towards thanking is thinking. Think, therefore, of how marvellously God has dealt with your sin in Christ, and let your thinking turn into thanking.

"For Christ died for sins once for all, the righteous for the unrighteous, to bring you to God. He was put to death in the body but made alive by the Spirit." (1 Pet. 3:18)

Laws for the people

DAY **48**

Leviticus 11:41–47

⁴¹"'Every creature that moves about on the ground is detestable; it is not to be eaten. ⁴²You are not to eat any creature that moves about on the ground, whether it moves on its belly or walks on all fours or on many feet; it is detestable. ⁴³Do not defile yourselves by any of these creatures. Do not make yourselves unclean by means of them or be made unclean by them. ⁴⁴I am the Lord your God; consecrate yourselves and be holy, because I am holy. Do not make yourselves unclean by any creature that moves about on the ground. ⁴⁵I am the Lord who brought you up out of Egypt to be your God; therefore be holy, because I am holy.

⁴⁶"'These are the regulations concerning animals, birds, every living thing that moves in the water and every creature that moves about on the ground. ⁴⁷You must distinguish between the unclean and the clean, between living creatures that may be eaten and those that may not be eaten.'"

Food: clean and unclean animals
Leviticus 11:1–47

Ceremonial purification: cleansing after childbirth
Leviticus 12:1–8

Directions to the priest to judge concerning leprosy
Leviticus 13:1–17

Further directions
Leviticus 13:18–44

For Thought and **Contemplation**

God has a personal concern for the holiness and well-being of His people. And why? Because the holier we are, the more clearly others see Him in us. How clearly do others see God in you?

"... through Christ Jesus the law of the Spirit of life set me free from the law of sin and death." (Rom. 8:2)

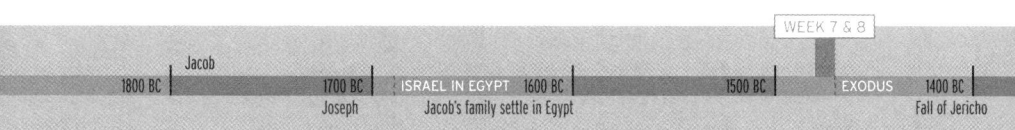

DAY 49 — The problem of leprosy

The treatment of lepers
Leviticus 13:45–46

Concerning the leprosy in garments
Leviticus 13:47–59

Rules to be observed after cleansing of leprosy: declaring the leper to be clean
Leviticus 14:1–9

The sacrifices to be offered by him
Leviticus 14:10–32

Leprosy in a house
Leviticus 14:33–53

Summary of the law concerning leprosy
Leviticus 14:54–57

Laws concerning ceremonial uncleanness
Leviticus 15:1–33

Leviticus 14:1–8

¹The Lord said to Moses, ²"These are the regulations for the diseased person at the time of his ceremonial cleansing, when he is brought to the priest: ³The priest is to go outside the camp and examine him. If the person has been healed of his infectious skin disease, ⁴the priest shall order that two live clean birds and some cedar wood, scarlet yarn and hyssop be brought for the one to be cleansed. ⁵Then the priest shall order that one of the birds be killed over fresh water in a clay pot. ⁶He is then to take the live bird and dip it, together with the cedar wood, the scarlet yarn and the hyssop, into the blood of the bird that was killed over the fresh water. ⁷Seven times he shall sprinkle the one to be cleansed of the infectious disease and pronounce him clean. Then he is to release the live bird in the open fields.
⁸"The person to be cleansed must wash his clothes, shave off all his hair and bathe with water; then he will be ceremonially clean. ... "

For Thought and **Contemplation**

No wonder preachers refer to leprosy as an illustration of sin, for it is one of the most disfiguring and debilitating of all diseases. How wonderful a leper must have felt when healed. How much more wonderful to be cleansed from sin!

"Jesus reached out his hand and touched the man ... Immediately he was cured of his leprosy." (Matt. 8:3)

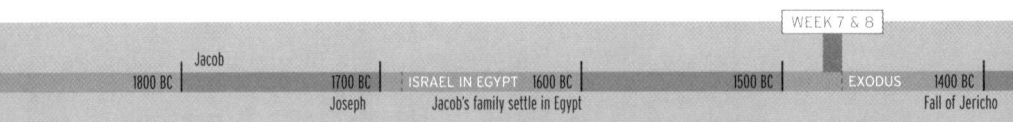

Feasts of the Lord

Passover and Unleavened Bread — Leviticus 23 vv. 5-8
Purpose
Beginning of the religious year, commemorating the Exodus and the establishment of Israel as a nation by God's redeeming power.

NT Spiritual significance
Calvary and Christ's death

Pentecost — vv. 15-22
Purpose
Commemorating the firstfruits of harvest and later the giving of the Law. Observed 50 days after the Passover (also see Ex. 23:16; 34:22; Num. 28:26; Deut. 16:9–10).

NT Spiritual significance
The coming of the Holy Spirit

Trumpets — vv. 23-25
Purpose
Beginning of the civil year, corresponding to our New Year's Day.

NT Spiritual significance
The coming again of the Lord Jesus

Atonement — vv. 26-32
Purpose
A day of remembrance when the High Priest made confession of all the sins of the past year and made atonement in the Most Holy Place.

NT Spiritual significance
Redemption and righteousness in Christ

Tabernacles — vv. 33-43
Purpose
Commemorating life in the wilderness; thanksgiving for harvest; the last feast of the religious year.

NT Spiritual significance
The rule and reign of Christ

The purpose of these feasts was a spiritual one – for God to meet with His people.

DAY 50 — The Feasts of Israel

Regulations concerning marriage
Leviticus 18:1–30

Idolatry and child sacrifice forbidden
Leviticus 20:1–6 & 27

The Feasts of the Lord: the Sabbath
Leviticus 23:1–3

The Passover; the Feast of Unleavened Bread; the Offering of Firstfruits
Leviticus 23:4–14

The Feast of Weeks/Pentecost
Leviticus 23:15–22

The Feast of Trumpets
Leviticus 23:23–25

The Day of Atonement
Leviticus 23:26–32

The Feast of Tabernacles
Leviticus 23:33–44

Leviticus 23:33–38

³³The Lord said to Moses, ³⁴"Say to the Israelites: 'On the fifteenth day of the seventh month the Lord's Feast of Tabernacles begins, and it lasts for seven days. ³⁵The first day is a sacred assembly; do no regular work. ³⁶For seven days present offerings made to the Lord by fire, and on the eighth day hold a sacred assembly and present an offering made to the Lord by fire. It is the closing assembly; do no regular work.

³⁷("'These are the Lord's appointed feasts, which you are to proclaim as sacred assemblies for bringing offerings made to the Lord by fire – the burnt offerings and grain offerings, sacrifices and drink offerings required for each day. ³⁸These offerings are in addition to those for the Lord's Sabbaths and in addition to your gifts and whatever you have vowed and all the freewill offerings you give to the Lord.)' "

For Thought and **Contemplation**

The Christian life is characterised by both fasting and feasting, by curtailment and celebration. Those who do not take this into account have a very lopsided Christian experience.

"I know what it is to be in need, and I know what it is to have plenty. I have learned the secret of being content in any and every situation, whether well fed or hungry, whether living in plenty or in want." (Phil. 4:12)

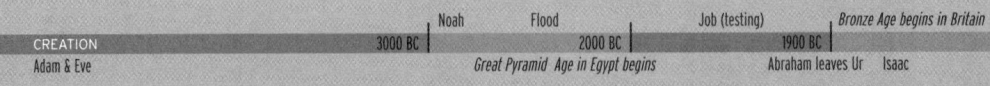

A time of sanctification

DAY **51**

Leviticus 19:1-8

¹The Lord said to Moses, ²"Speak to the entire assembly of Israel and say to them: 'Be holy because I, the Lord your God, am holy.
³"'Each of you must respect his mother and father, and you must observe my Sabbaths. I am the Lord your God.
⁴"'Do not turn to idols or make gods of cast metal for yourselves. I am the Lord your God.
⁵"'When you sacrifice a fellowship offering to the Lord, sacrifice it in such a way that it will be accepted on your behalf. ⁶It shall be eaten on the day you sacrifice it or on the next day; anything left over until the third day must be burned up. ⁷If any of it is eaten on the third day, it is impure and will not be accepted. ⁸Whoever eats it will be held responsible because he has desecrated what is holy to the Lord; that person must be cut off from his people.'"

Conduct of God's people
Leviticus 19:1-8

Laws concerning neighbours, the land, and foreigners
Leviticus 19:9-37

Punishments for disobedience
Leviticus 20:7-26

Instructions for priests
Leviticus 21:1-9

Concerning the High Priest
Leviticus 21:10-15

Physical requirements for priests
Leviticus 21:16-24

Priests and the holy things
Leviticus 22:1-16

For Thought and **Contemplation**

Before God's people can take possession of God's fulness (Canaan), there must, of necessity, be a time of preparation, training and testing. God always prepares His children before He entrusts them with greater possessions and responsibility.

"... But you were washed, you were sanctified, you were justified in the name of the Lord Jesus Christ and by the Spirit of our God." (1 Cor. 6:11)

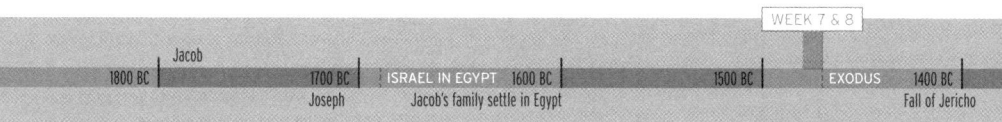

DAY **52**

The second Passover

Requirements for animals
to be sacrificed
Leviticus 22:17–33

Death penalties: blasphemy
Leviticus 24:10–16 & 23

Murder
Leviticus 24:17–22

Camp laws explained
Numbers 5:1–10

Law of jealous husband
Numbers 5:11–31

Vow of Nazarites
Numbers 6:1–21

The priestly blessing
Numbers 6:22–27

God reminds Israel to keep
Passover
Numbers 9:1–4

Passover held in Sinai
Numbers 9:5–14

Numbers 9:1–5

¹The Lord spoke to Moses in the Desert of Sinai in the first month of the second year after they came out of Egypt. He said, ²"Have the Israelites celebrate the Passover at the appointed time. ³Celebrate it at the appointed time, at twilight on the fourteenth day of this month, in accordance with all its rules and regulations."
⁴So Moses told the Israelites to celebrate the Passover, ⁵and they did so in the Desert of Sinai at twilight on the fourteenth day of the first month. The Israelites did everything just as the Lord commanded Moses.

For Thought and **Contemplation**

How grateful we ought to be that, in Jesus Christ, God has provided a lamb – not merely for the sins of an individual, not merely for the sins of a family, not even for the sins of a nation. Jesus Christ is the Lamb of God who takes away the sins of the *world*.

"... 'This is my body, which is for you; do this in remembrance of me.' In the same way, after supper he took the cup, saying, 'This cup is the new covenant in my blood; do this, whenever you drink it, in remembrance of me.'" (1 Cor. 11:24–25)

a bird's eye view of
Numbers

Place in the Bible

Fourth Old Testament book; fourth book of the Law.

Main Characters

Moses, the Levites, Miriam, Aaron, Caleb, Balaam.

Special Features

Two censuses, the spies in the Promised Land, wandering in the wilderness, Balaam's talking donkey.

Getting ready to move

DAY **53**

Deuteronomy 1:6–14

⁶The Lord our God said to us at Horeb, "You have stayed long enough at this mountain. ⁷Break camp and advance into the hill country of the Amorites; go to all the neighbouring peoples in the Arabah, in the mountains, in the western foothills, in the Negev and along the coast, to the land of the Canaanites and to Lebanon, as far as the great river, the Euphrates. ⁸See, I have given you this land. Go in and take possession of the land that the Lord swore he would give to your fathers – to Abraham, Isaac and Jacob – and to their descendants after them."

⁹At that time I said to you, "You are too heavy a burden for me to carry alone. ¹⁰The Lord your God has increased your numbers so that today you are as many as the stars in the sky. ¹¹May the Lord, the God of your fathers, increase you a thousand times and bless you as he has promised! ¹²But how can I bear your problems and your burdens and your disputes all by myself? ¹³Choose some wise, understanding and respected men from each of your tribes, and I will set them over you."

Preparations for leaving Sinai: numbering of the people
Numbers 1:1–54

General arrangement of the camp
Numbers 2:1–2, 17, 32–34

Eastern division
Numbers 2:3–9

Southern division
Numbers 2:10–16

Western division
Numbers 2:18–24

Northern division
Numbers 2:25–31

Journey to resume
Numbers 33:1–6

Moses reminds the people
Deuteronomy 1:6–18

From Sinai to Kadesh-Barnea: journey starts
Numbers 10:11 & 13

For Thought and **Contemplation**

A relationship with God always begins with the knowledge of the law and humiliation for sin. After that comes the long march toward Canaan and all the fulness of His blessings.

"The wind blows wherever it pleases. You hear its sound, but you cannot tell where it comes from or where it is going. So it is with everyone born of the Spirit." (Jn. 3:8)

Jesus and the Book

In chapter 3 of John's Gospel Jesus speaks of Moses' raising of the bronze snake (Num. 21:4–9) as a picture of His own lifting up "that all who believe in Him may receive eternal life".

Teaching

In chapter 14 the people rebel against God, so for 40 years they are to wander in the wilderness. They learn from this that they can only make progress as they trust and obey God. (v.34)

A Verse to Remember

"... my servant Caleb has a different spirit and follows me wholeheartedly ..." (Num. 14:24).

DAY 54

Journeyings continue

Order of the divisions
Numbers 10:14–28

Cloud leads them
Exodus 40:36–38, Numbers 9:15–23

In Paran wilderness
Numbers 10:12, 29–32

Fire at Taberah
Numbers 10:33–36, 11:1–3

Arrival at Kibroth
Numbers 33:16

Murmuring about manna
Numbers 11:4–9

Moses complains
Numbers 11:10–15

Seventy elders chosen
Numbers 11:16–25

Prophecy in the camp
Numbers 11:26–30

Plague of quails
Numbers 11:31–34

From Kibroth to Hazeroth
Numbers 11:35, 33:17

Miriam's leprosy
Numbers 12:1–15

Numbers 11:10–15

¹⁰Moses heard the people of every family wailing, each at the entrance to his tent. The Lord became exceedingly angry, and Moses was troubled. ¹¹He asked the Lord, "Why have you brought this trouble on your servant? What have I done to displease you that you put the burden of all these people on me? ¹²Did I conceive all these people? Did I give them birth? Why do you tell me to carry them in my arms, as a nurse carries an infant, to the land you promised on oath to their forefathers? ¹³Where can I get meat for all these people? They keep wailing to me, 'Give us meat to eat!' ¹⁴I cannot carry all these people by myself; the burden is too heavy for me. ¹⁵If this is how you are going to treat me, put me to death right now – if I have found favour in your eyes – and do not let me face my own ruin."

For Thought and **Contemplation**

Today's pressing problems sometimes create within us a hankering for times past – "the good old days". If we forget God's promise of *future* blessing, we will suffer from a lack of perspective.

"... But one thing I do: Forgetting what is behind and straining towards what is ahead, I press on towards the goal to win the prize for which God has called me heavenwards in Christ Jesus." (Phil. 3:13–14)

a bird's eye view of **Deuteronomy**

Place in the Bible	**Main Characters**	**Special Features**
Fifth Old Testament book; fifth book of the Law.	Moses, Joshua	The title of the book of Deuteronomy comes from the Greek, meaning "Second Law", since it expands on the laws God had already given at Sinai. Deuteronomy gives God's laws for His people as they prepare to live in Canaan.

Turning back from Canaan

DAY **55**

Numbers 13:25–33

²⁵At the end of forty days they returned from exploring the land. ... ²⁷They gave Moses this account: "We went into the land to which you sent us, and it does flow with milk and honey! Here is its fruit. ²⁸But the people who live there are powerful, and the cities are fortified and very large. We even saw descendants of Anak there. ²⁹The Amalekites live in the Negev; the Hittites, Jebusites and Amorites live in the hill country; and the Canaanites live near the sea and along the Jordan." ³⁰Then Caleb silenced the people before Moses and said, "We should go up and take possession of the land, for we can certainly do it." ³¹But the men who had gone up with him said, "We can't attack those people; they are stronger than we are." ³²And they spread among the Israelites a bad report about the land they had explored. They said, "The land we explored devours those living in it. All the people we saw there are of great size. ³³We saw the Nephilim there (the descendants of Anak come from the Nephilim). ..."

From Hazeroth to Kadesh-Barnea
Numbers 33:18–36, 12:16, Deuteronomy 1:19–20

From Kadesh-Barnea to Jordan crossing: spies sent out to Canaan
Numbers 13:1–24, Deuteronomy 1:21–24

Spies return
Numbers 13:25–33, Deuteronomy 1:25–33

Unbelief of Israel
Numbers 14:1–24

Generation cursed to die in wilderness
Numbers 14:25–30

For Thought and **Contemplation**

How often have we stepped right up to the edge of God's fulness, only to draw back because of unbelief? Are you there right now? Press on, despite the giants. God will give you all the ground you place your feet upon.

"So we see that they were not able to enter, because of their unbelief. Therefore, since the promise of entering his rest still stands, let us be careful that none of you be found to have fallen short of it." (Heb. 3:19–4:1)

Jesus and the Book
The writer to the Hebrews picks up the covenant theme and states that, "... Jesus the mediator of a new covenant" (Heb. 12:24). Jesus Himself quoted from Deuteronomy each time the devil tempted Him in the wilderness.

Teaching
Deuteronomy consists mainly of three sermons of Moses to the Israelites emphasising how God has saved the people He loves. On the verge of Canaan Moses reminds them of God's great power and faithfulness. Blessing or disaster depends on their response.

A Verse to Remember
"Love the Lord your God with all your heart and with all your soul and with all your strength" (Deut. 6:5)

DAY 56 — Wilderness wanderings

Generation cursed continued
Numbers 14:31-38,
Deuteronomy 1:34-40

Defeat at Hormah
Numbers 14:39-45,
Deuteronomy 1:41-44

Repentance too late
Deuteronomy 1:45-46

Earliest Psalm
Psalm 90:1-17

Instructions: offerings
Numbers 15:1-31

Separation
Numbers 15:37-41

Man stoned for working on Sabbath
Numbers 15:32-36

The rebellion of Korah, Dathan and Abiram
Numbers 16:1-2

Numbers 14:31-38

³¹'As for your children that you said would be taken as plunder, I will bring them in to enjoy the land you have rejected. ³²But you – your bodies will fall in this desert. ³³Your children will be shepherds here for forty years, suffering for your unfaithfulness, until the last of your bodies lies in the desert. ³⁴For forty years – one year for each of the forty days you explored the land – you will suffer for your sins and know what it is like to have me against you.' ³⁵I, the Lord, have spoken, and I will surely do these things to this whole wicked community, which has banded together against me. They will meet their end in this desert; here they will die."

³⁶So the men Moses had sent to explore the land, who returned and made the whole community grumble against him by spreading a bad report about it – ³⁷these men responsible for spreading the bad report about the land were struck down and died of a plague before the Lord. ³⁸Of the men who went to explore the land, only Joshua son of Nun and Caleb son of Jephunneh survived.

For Thought and Contemplation

God often allows His people a second chance when they fail to enter into a blessing, but only after they have undergone some painful discipline. Make up your mind to say "yes" to God, no matter what fears arise within you.

"So, as the Holy Spirit says: 'Today, if you hear his voice, do not harden your hearts as you did in the rebellion, during the time of testing in the desert ...'" (Heb. 3:7-8)

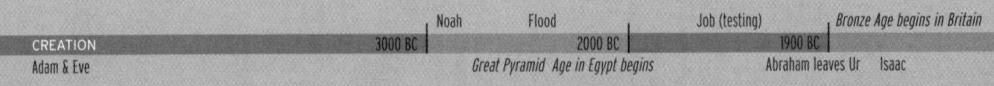

The people murmur

DAY **57**

Numbers 16:41-48

⁴¹The next day the whole Israelite community grumbled against Moses and Aaron. "You have killed the Lord's people," they said.
⁴²But when the assembly gathered in opposition to Moses and Aaron and turned towards the Tent of Meeting, suddenly the cloud covered it and the glory of the Lord appeared. ⁴³Then Moses and Aaron went to the front of the Tent of Meeting, ⁴⁴and the Lord said to Moses, ⁴⁵"Get away from this assembly so that I can put an end to them at once." And they fell face down.
⁴⁶Then Moses said to Aaron, "Take your censer and put incense in it, along with fire from the altar, and hurry to the assembly to make atonement for them. Wrath has come out from the Lord; the plague has started." ⁴⁷So Aaron did as Moses said, and ran into the midst of the assembly. The plague had already started among the people, but Aaron offered the incense and made atonement for them. ⁴⁸He stood between the living and the dead, and the plague stopped.

The rebellion of Korah, Dathan and Abiram continued: Korah contends for the priesthood
Numbers 16:3-11

The disobedience of Dathan and Abiram
Numbers 16:12-15

The glory of the Lord appears and the intercession of Moses and Aaron
Numbers 16:16-22

The ground swallows up Dathan and Abiram
Numbers 16:23-34

The company of Korah consumed
Numbers 16:35-40

The people murmur and a plague is sent
Numbers 16:41-50

The budding of Aaron's rod
Numbers 17:1-13

Levite responsibilities
Numbers 18:1-24

For Thought and **Contemplation**

How easy it is when things go wrong in our lives to lash out at others and say, "It's all your fault." This is the oldest defence in history. Adam and Eve used it in the Garden of Eden. Is it also a favourite defence of yours?

"With the tongue we praise our Lord and Father, and with it we curse men, who have been made in God's likeness. Out of the same mouth come praise and cursing. My brothers, this should not be." (Jas. 3:9-10)

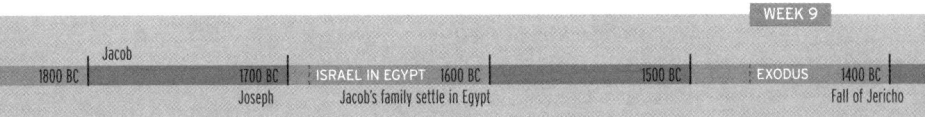

DAY 58 — Water from the Rock

Levite responsibilities
Numbers 18:25–32

Red heifer ordinance: instructions about dead
Numbers 19:1–22

Death of Miriam
Numbers 20:1

Water from Meribah
Numbers 20:2–13

Birth of Moses' grandchildren
1 Chronicles 23:16–17

Permission to pass through Edom denied
Numbers 20:14–21

To Mount Hor
Numbers 20:22, 33:37

Death of Aaron
Numbers 20:23–28, 33:38–39, Deuteronomy 10:6–7

Mourning for Aaron
Numbers 20:29

Victory at Hormah
Numbers 33:40, 21:1–3

Numbers 20:7–13

⁷The Lord said to Moses, ⁸"Take the staff, and you and your brother Aaron gather the assembly together. Speak to that rock before their eyes and it will pour out its water. You will bring water out of the rock for the community so that they and their livestock can drink."
⁹So Moses took the staff from the Lord's presence, just as he commanded him. ¹⁰He and Aaron gathered the assembly together in front of the rock and Moses said to them, "Listen, you rebels, must we bring you water out of this rock?" ¹¹Then Moses raised his arm and struck the rock twice with his staff. Water gushed out, and the community and their livestock drank.
¹²But the Lord said to Moses and Aaron, "Because you did not trust in me enough to honour me as holy in the sight of the Israelites, you will not bring this community into the land I give them."
¹³These were the waters of Meribah, where the Israelites quarrelled with the Lord and where he showed himself holy among them.

For Thought and **Contemplation**

Our vulnerability does not always lie in our weaknesses: it can also lie in our strengths. Moses, the meekest man on the face of the earth, sinned through losing his temper. We are strong only in Christ.

"'In your anger do not sin': Do not let the sun go down while you are still angry, and do not give the devil a foothold." (Eph. 4:26–27)

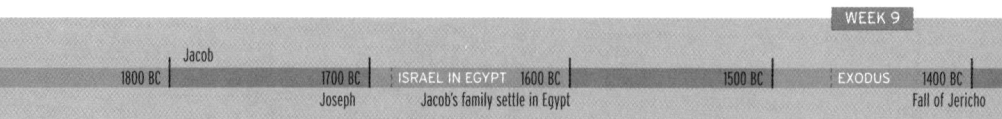

Wilderness Wanderings

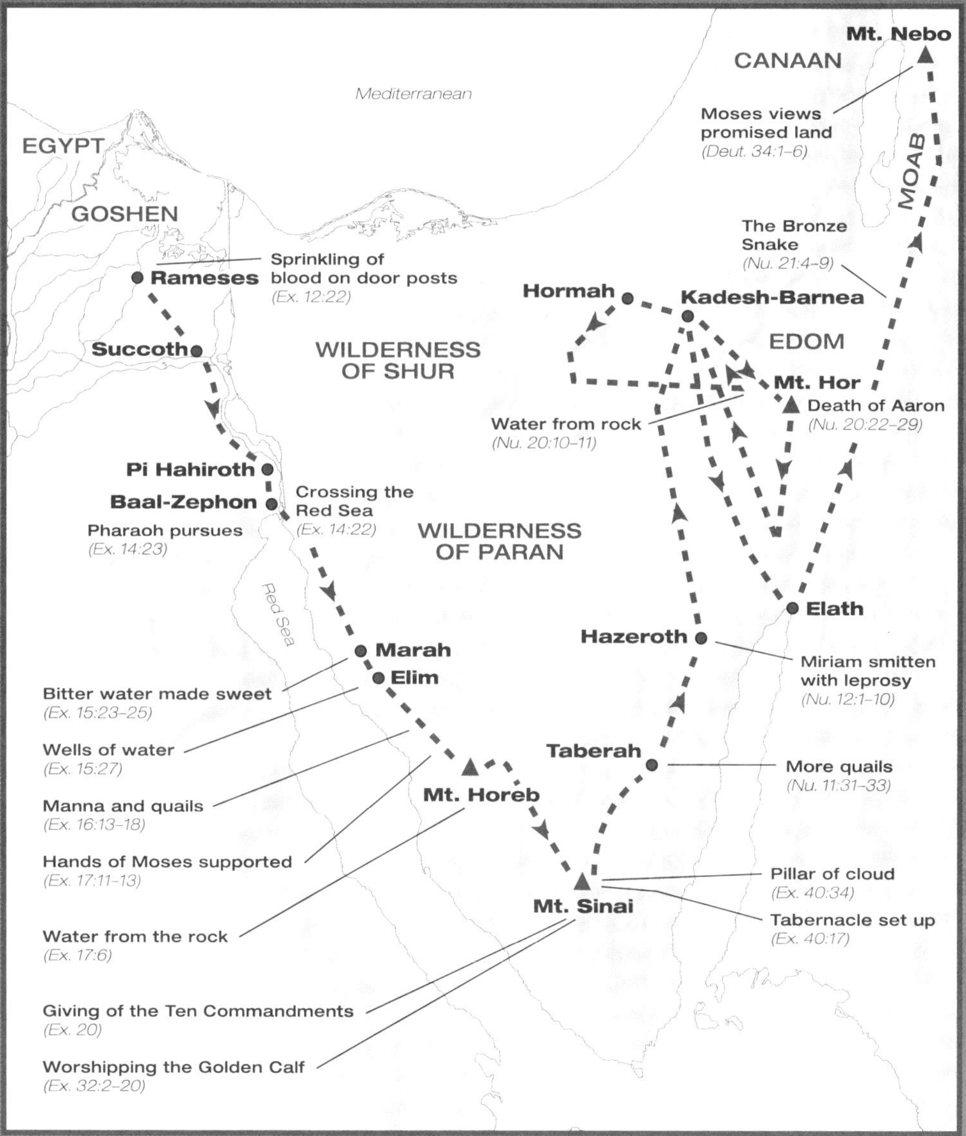

DAY 59 — Healing for sickness

From Mount Hor around Edom
Deuteronomy 2:1–12,
Numbers 21:4, 33:41–42

The bronze snake
Numbers 21:5–9

To Oboth and Iye Abarim
Numbers 21:10–11, 33:43–44

Northward through Moab
Numbers 21:12–20,
Deuteronomy 2:13–18,
Numbers 33:45

**Victory over Amorites:
in Gilead (over Sihon)**
Numbers 33:46–47, 21:21–32,
Deuteronomy 2:19–37

In Bashan (over Og)
Deuteronomy 3:1–11, Numbers 21:33–35

Numbers 21:4–9

⁴They travelled from Mount Hor along the route to the Red Sea, to go round Edom. But the people grew impatient on the way; ⁵they spoke against God and against Moses, and said, "Why have you brought us up out of Egypt to die in the desert? There is no bread! There is no water! And we detest this miserable food!"
⁶Then the Lord sent venomous snakes among them; they bit the people and many Israelites died. ⁷The people came to Moses and said, "We sinned when we spoke against the Lord and against you. Pray that the Lord will take the snakes away from us." So Moses prayed for the people.
⁸The Lord said to Moses, "Make a snake and put it up on a pole; anyone who is bitten can look at it and live." ⁹So Moses made a bronze snake and put it up on a pole. Then when anyone was bitten by a snake and looked at the bronze snake, he lived.

For Thought and **Contemplation**

A history of failure does not mean that victory is not possible. When we align ourselves with God, no matter the defeats of the past, victory is not only possible, but assured.

"Just as Moses lifted up the snake in the desert, so the Son of Man must be lifted up, that everyone who believes in him may have eternal life." (Jn. 3:14–15)

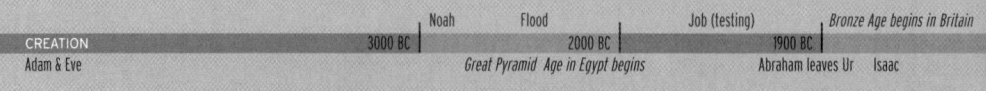

Balak meets Balaam

DAY **60**

Numbers 22:20–25

²⁰That night God came to Balaam and said, "Since these men have come to summon you, go with them, but do only what I tell you." ²¹Balaam got up in the morning, saddled his donkey and went with the princes of Moab. ²²But God was very angry when he went, and the angel of the Lord stood in the road to oppose him. Balaam was riding on his donkey, and his two servants were with him. ²³When the donkey saw the angel of the Lord standing in the road with a drawn sword in his hand, she turned off the road into a field. Balaam beat her to get her back on the road. ²⁴Then the angel of the Lord stood in a narrow path between two vineyards, with walls on both sides. ²⁵When the donkey saw the angel of the Lord, she pressed close to the wall, crushing Balaam's foot against it. So he beat her again.

The Israelites camp in Moab
Numbers 22:1, 33:48–49

Balak sends for Balaam
Numbers 22:2–14

Balaam goes to Balak
Numbers 22:15–21

Balaam's ass talks
Numbers 22:22–35

Balaam and Balak meet
Numbers 22:36–41

Balak's sacrifice and Balaam's blessing
Numbers 23:1–10

Balak's disappointment
Numbers 23:11–15

Balaam again blesses Israel
Numbers 23:16–24

Balak's third sacrifice
Numbers 23:25–30

Balaam predicts Israel's happiness
Numbers 24:1–9

Balak dismisses Balaam
Numbers 24:10–14

For Thought and **Contemplation**

Failure to obey God's commands leads inevitably to spiritual insensitivity. This is illustrated by Balaam's inability to see the angel barring his way. Even the ass seemed to have more spiritual sensitivity than Balaam!

"Trust in the Lord with all your heart and lean not on your own understanding; in all your ways acknowledge him, and he will make your paths straight." (Prov. 3:5–6)

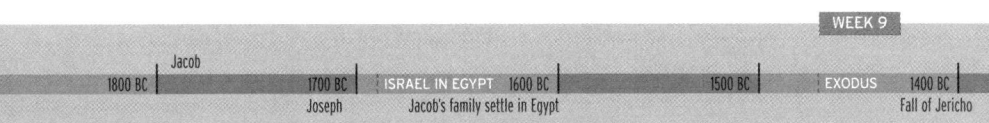

Heart to Heart

Section 2

Just like the Israelites you too are on a journey. Their journey was 40 years through a wilderness – yours is just one year through God's Word. They were led by Moses and the pillar of fire – you are led by Jesus and the Holy Spirit. Don't be discouraged but be like Joshua and Caleb who overcame every temptation to give up and remained faithful to complete the task God had given them.

Visit the web site: **www.cover2cover.org**

3

In this section

Moses' farewell addresses
The conquest of Canaan
The division of the land
God's appointment of the judges
The story of Ruth

DAY **61** — Second numbering of Israel

Balaam's prophecies
Numbers 24:15–25

The Israelites enticed
Numbers 25:1–5

Phinehas puts Zimri and Cozbi to death
Numbers 25:6–15

The Midianites to be punished
Numbers 25:16–18

Second numbering of Israel
Numbers 26:1–51

Division of the land
Numbers 26:52–56

Number of Levites
Numbers 26:57–58, 62

None remaining of first numbering
Numbers 26:63–65

The inheritance law
Numbers 27:1–11

Numbers 25:6–13

⁶Then an Israelite man brought to his family a Midianite woman right before the eyes of Moses and the whole assembly of Israel while they were weeping at the entrance to the Tent of Meeting. ⁷When Phinehas son of Eleazar, the son of Aaron, the priest, saw this, he left the assembly, took a spear in his hand ⁸and followed the Israelite into the tent. He drove the spear through both of them – through the Israelite and into the woman's body. Then the plague against the Israelites was stopped; ⁹but those who died in the plague numbered 24,000. ¹⁰The Lord said to Moses, ¹¹"Phinehas son of Eleazar, the son of Aaron, the priest, has turned my anger away from the Israelites; for he was as zealous as I am for my honour among them, so that in my zeal I did not put an end to them. ¹²Therefore tell him I am making my covenant of peace with him. ¹³He and his descendants will have a covenant of a lasting priesthood, because he was zealous for the honour of his God and made atonement for the Israelites."

For Thought and **Contemplation**

How sad that between the first census and this second census a whole generation – with the exceptions of Caleb and Joshua – had died in the wilderness. Disobedience makes havoc of God's purposes.

"... you will cross the Jordan here to go in and take possession of the land the Lord your God is giving you for your own." (Josh. 1:11) "Not one of you will enter the land I swore with uplifted hand to make your home, except Caleb son of Jephunneh and Joshua son of Nun." (Num. 14:30)

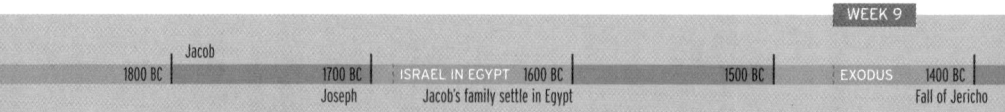

Wilderness Wanderings

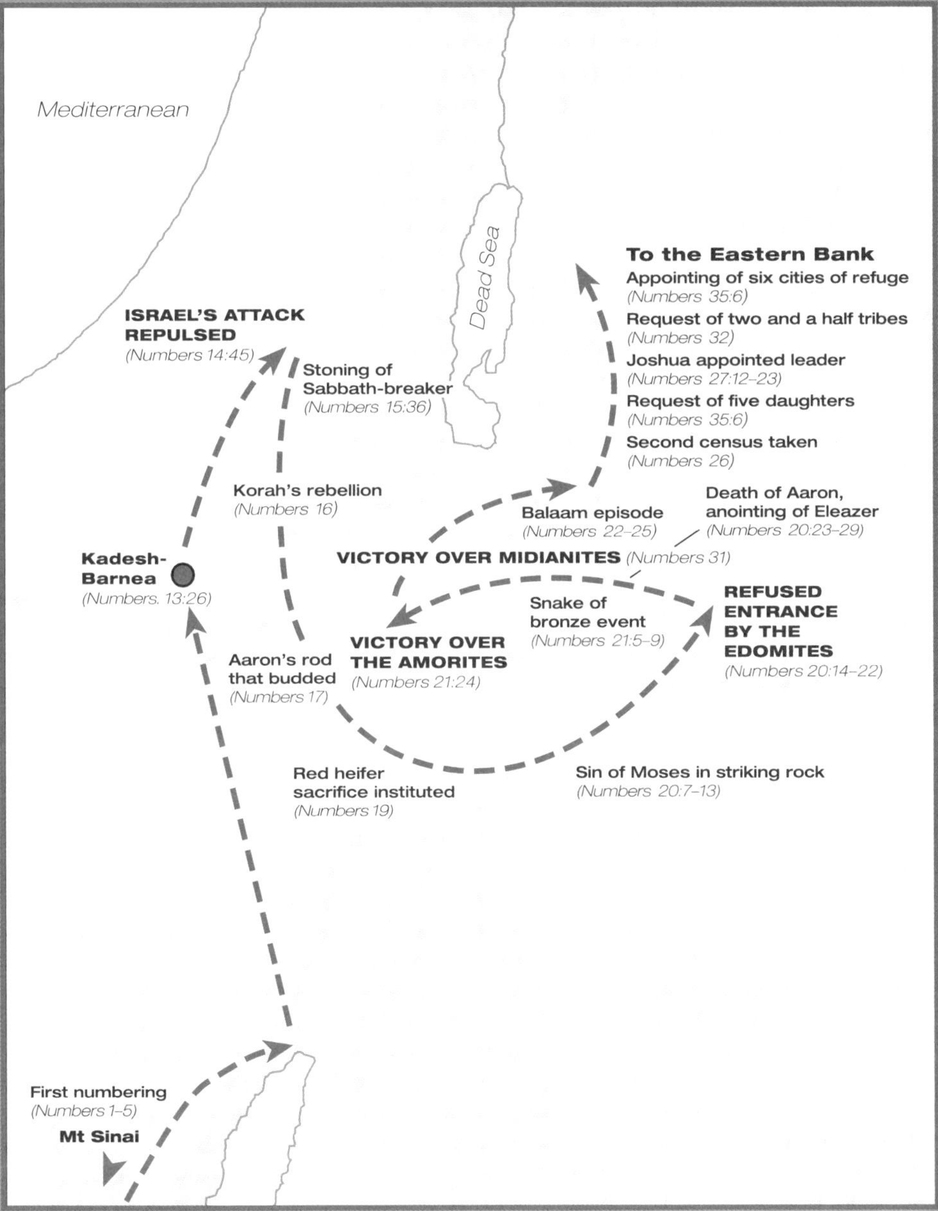

DAY 62 — Sacrifices and offerings

The daily sacrifice
Numbers 28:1-8

Sabbath and new moon offerings
Numbers 28:9-15

Passover and Firstfruits offerings
Numbers 28:16-31

Feast of Trumpets and Day of Atonement offering
Numbers 29:1-11

Offerings at the Feast of Tabernacles
Numbers 29:12-40

Laws about vows
Numbers 30:1-2

When vows might be released
Numbers 30:3-16

Numbers 28:1-8

¹'The Lord said to Moses, ²"Give this command to the Israelites and say to them: 'See that you present to me at the appointed time the food for my offerings made by fire, as an aroma pleasing to me.' ³Say to them: 'This is the offering made by fire that you are to present to the Lord: two lambs a year old without defect, as a regular burnt offering each day. ⁴Prepare one lamb in the morning and the other at twilight, ⁵together with a grain offering of a tenth of an ephah of fine flour mixed with a quarter of a hin of oil from pressed olives. ⁶This is the regular burnt offering instituted at Mount Sinai as a pleasing aroma, an offering made to the Lord by fire. ⁷The accompanying drink offering is to be a quarter of a hin of fermented drink with each lamb. Pour out the drink offering to the Lord at the sanctuary. ⁸Prepare the second lamb at twilight, along with the same kind of grain offering and drink offering that you prepare in the morning. This is an offering made by fire, an aroma pleasing to the Lord.

For Thought and **Contemplation**

Of the many varied sacrifices and offerings in ancient Israel, one offering was a daily occurrence – *the sin offering*. How beautifully this illustrates the fact that our 'burnt offerings' are of no interest to God until we have first showed an interest in the great Sin-offering which He Himself made for us on Calvary.

"For Christ died for sins once for all, the righteous for the unrighteous, to bring you to God. He was put to death in the body but made alive by the Spirit." (1 Pet. 3:18)

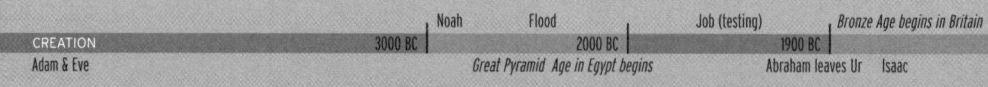

The Reubenites and Gadites — DAY **63**

Numbers 32:6-13

⁶Moses said to the Gadites and Reubenites, "Shall your countrymen go to war while you sit here? ⁷Why do you discourage the Israelites from going over into the land the Lord has given them? ⁸This is what your fathers did when I sent them from Kadesh Barnea to look over the land. ⁹After they went up to the Valley of Eshcol and viewed the land, they discouraged the Israelites from entering the land the Lord had given them. ¹⁰The Lord's anger was aroused that day and he swore this oath: ¹¹'Because they have not followed me wholeheartedly, not one of the men twenty years old or more who came up out of Egypt will see the land I promised on oath to Abraham, Isaac and Jacob – ¹²not one except Caleb son of Jephunneh the Kenizzite and Joshua son of Nun, for they followed the Lord wholeheartedly.' ¹³The Lord's anger burned against Israel and he made them wander in the desert for forty years, until the whole generation of those who had done evil in his sight was gone.

War with Midian	Numbers 31:1-7
Balaam and kings of Midian slain	Numbers 31:8-12
Those slain who caused sin	Numbers 31:13-18
Purification of Israelites	Numbers 31:19-24
Division of the spoil	Numbers 31:25-47
Offerings to the Lord	Numbers 31:48-54
Tribes of Reuben and Gad request an inheritance	Numbers 32:1-5
Moses reproves Reubenites and Gadites	Numbers 32:6-15
Their views explained	Numbers 32:16-27
They settle to the east of the Jordan	Numbers 32:28-42

For Thought and **Contemplation**

What a tragedy that some of God's people, within sight of the *Land of Promise*, should prefer to settle for something less than God's best. How is it with you? Are you content to remain this side of Jordan? Are you settling for less than God's best?

"Anyone, then, who knows the good he ought to do and doesn't do it, sins." (Jas 4:17)

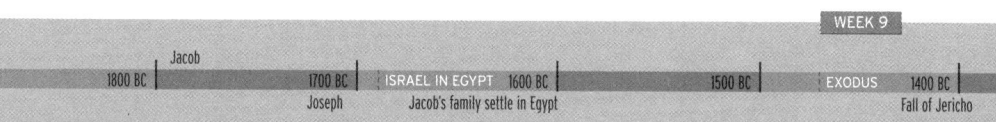

DAY 64 — Preparing to enter Canaan

Inheritance of the tribes
Deuteronomy 3:12–17,
Joshua 13:8–13, 15–32

Recap of victories
Joshua 12:1–6

Command for conquest
Numbers 33:50–56,
Deuteronomy 3:18–29

Boundaries given
Numbers 34:1–15

Men chosen to divide the land
Numbers 34:16–29

Cities promised to Levites
Numbers 35:1–8

Numbers 33:50-56

⁵⁰On the plains of Moab by the Jordan across from Jericho the Lord said to Moses, ⁵¹"Speak to the Israelites and say to them: 'When you cross the Jordan into Canaan, ⁵²drive out all the inhabitants of the land before you. Destroy all their carved images and their cast idols, and demolish all their high places. ⁵³Take possession of the land and settle in it, for I have given you the land to possess. ⁵⁴Distribute the land by lot, according to your clans. To a larger group give a larger inheritance, and to a smaller group a smaller one. Whatever falls to them by lot will be theirs. Distribute it according to your ancestral tribes.

⁵⁵"'But if you do not drive out the inhabitants of the land, those you allow to remain will become barbs in your eyes and thorns in your sides. They will give you trouble in the land where you will live. ⁵⁶And then I will do to you what I plan to do to them.'"

For Thought and **Contemplation**

In dividing the land *before* they entered it, the Israelites demonstrated their faith in God's great promise. Has God made you a personal promise? Then remember that faith is acting as if you are already in possession of it.

"For no matter how many promises God has made, they are 'Yes' in Christ. And so through him the 'Amen' is spoken by us to the glory of God."
(2 Cor. 1:20)

Review of Jewish law and history

DAY **65**

Deuteronomy 4:9–14

⁹Only be careful, and watch yourselves closely so that you do not forget the things your eyes have seen or let them slip from your heart as long as you live. Teach them to your children and to their children after them. ¹⁰Remember the day you stood before the Lord your God at Horeb, when he said to me, "Assemble the people before me to hear my words so that they may learn to revere me as long as they live in the land and may teach them to their children." ¹¹You came near and stood at the foot of the mountain while it blazed with fire to the very heavens, with black clouds and deep darkness. ¹²Then the Lord spoke to you out of the fire. You heard the sound of words but saw no form; there was only a voice. ¹³He declared to you his covenant, the Ten Commandments, which he commanded you to follow and then wrote them on two stone tablets. ¹⁴And the Lord directed me at that time to teach you the decrees and laws you are to follow in the land that you are crossing the Jordan to possess.

The laws about murder
Numbers 35:9–34

Cities of refuge appointed
Deuteronomy 4:41–49

Law settled regarding murder
Deuteronomy 19:1–13

Inheritance law reviewed
Numbers 36:1–12

Review of Jewish law and history:
Moses' words to Israel
Deuteronomy 1:1–5

Moses' exhortation to obedience
Deuteronomy 4:1–24

For Thought and **Contemplation**

Have you ever wondered why some enjoy the blessing of God more than others? One great key is *obedience*. That key opened up the whole of Canaan to the Israelites. It will open up your own personal "Canaan" too – but only as you use it.

"Don't you know that when you offer yourselves to someone to obey him as slaves, you are slaves to the one whom you obey – whether you are slaves to sin, which leads to death, or to obedience, which leads to righteousness?" (Rom. 6:16)

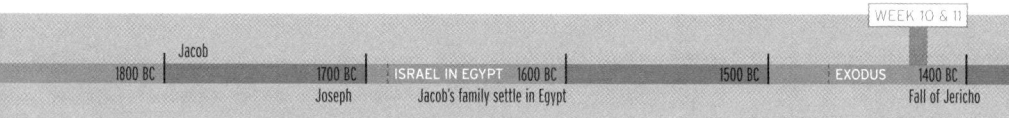

DAY 66 — Restating of the Ten Commandments

God's warning and promise of mercy
Deuteronomy 4:25–40

The covenant in Horeb
Deuteronomy 5:1–5

The Ten Commandments repeated
Deuteronomy 5:6–22

The people's request
Deuteronomy 5:23–33

An incentive to obedience
Deuteronomy 6:1–3

An exhortation to obedience
Deuteronomy 6:4–5

Obedience taught
Deuteronomy 6:6–19

Instruction of children
Deuteronomy 6:20–25

Caution against association with idolaters
Deuteronomy 7:1–11

Deuteronomy 6:3–9
³Hear, O Israel, and be careful to obey so that it may go well with you and that you may increase greatly in a land flowing with milk and honey, just as the Lord, the God of your fathers, promised you. ⁴Hear, O Israel: The Lord our God, the Lord is one. ⁵Love the Lord your God with all your heart and with all your soul and with all your strength. ⁶These commandments that I give you today are to be upon your hearts. ⁷Impress them on your children. Talk about them when you sit at home and when you walk along the road, when you lie down and when you get up. ⁸Tie them as symbols on your hands and bind them on your foreheads. ⁹Write them on the door-frames of your houses and on your gates.

For Thought and **Contemplation**

In restating the Ten Commandments, Moses underlined the command: "Thou shalt have no other gods before me." Why this emphasis? Moses knew the ever-present danger of substituting *something* for the all-important Someone.

"For although they knew God, they neither glorified him as God nor gave thanks to him, but their thinking became futile and their foolish hearts were darkened. ... They exchanged the truth of God for a lie, and worshipped and served created things rather than the Creator ..." (Rom. 1:21, 25)

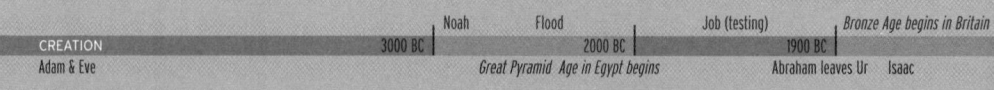

Exhortations and cautions

DAY **67**

Deuteronomy 8:1-7

¹Be careful to follow every command I am giving you today, so that you may live and increase and may enter and possess the land that the Lord promised on oath to your forefathers. ²Remember how the Lord your God led you all the way in the desert these forty years, to humble you and to test you in order to know what was in your heart, whether or not you would keep his commands. ³He humbled you, causing you to hunger and then feeding you with manna, which neither you nor your fathers had known, to teach you that man does not live on bread alone but on every word that comes from the mouth of the Lord. ⁴Your clothes did not wear out and your feet did not swell during these forty years. ⁵Know then in your heart that as a man disciplines his son, so the Lord your God disciplines you.

⁶Observe the commands of the Lord your God, walking in his ways and revering him. ⁷For the Lord your God is bringing you into a good land – a land with streams and pools of water, with springs flowing in the valleys and hills ...

Rewards for obedience
Deuteronomy 7:12-26
Exhortations and cautions
Deuteronomy 8:1-9
Exhortations and cautions further enforced
Deuteronomy 8:10-20
Success not due to worthiness
Deuteronomy 9:1-6
Moses reminds the Israelites of God's mercies
Deuteronomy 9:7-29
Moses tells the Israelites how he made new stone tablets
Deuteronomy 10:1-11
Moses' exhortation to obedience
Deuteronomy 10:12-22

For Thought and **Contemplation**

Moses' reminder that success is due, not to human worthiness, but Divine mercy, is something that relates equally to His Church of today. Hold it as an axiom and repeat it as often as you can: *I am what I am because He is what He is!*

"Because of the Lord's great love we are not consumed, for his compassions never fail. They are new every morning; great is your faithfulness."
(Lam. 3:22-23)

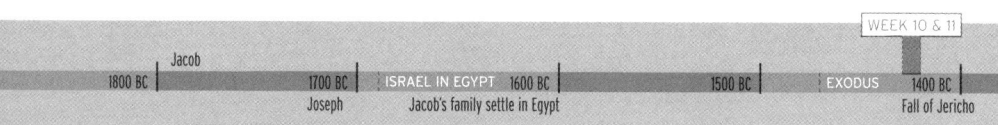

DAY 68 — Further exhortations and instructions

Results of obedience and disobedience
Deuteronomy 11:1–7

Promises and warnings
Deuteronomy 11:8–17

Study of God's Word imperative
Deuteronomy 11:18–25

Choice between blessing or curse
Deuteronomy 11:26–32

Monuments of idolatry to be destroyed
Deuteronomy 12:1–4

The place of God's service
Deuteronomy 12:5–32

Punishment of the wicked
Deuteronomy 13:1–11

Idolatrous cities to be destroyed
Deuteronomy 13:12–18

Deuteronomy 11:26–32

²⁶See, I am setting before you today a blessing and a curse – ²⁷the blessing if you obey the commands of the Lord your God that I am giving you today; ²⁸the curse if you disobey the commands of the Lord your God and turn from the way that I command you today by following other gods, which you have not known. ²⁹When the Lord your God has brought you into the land you are entering to possess, you are to proclaim on Mount Gerizim the blessings, and on Mount Ebal the curses. ³⁰As you know, these mountains are across the Jordan, west of the road, towards the setting sun, near the great trees of Moreh, in the territory of those Canaanites living in the Arabah in the vicinity of Gilgal. ³¹You are about to cross the Jordan to enter and take possession of the land the Lord your God is giving you. When you have taken it over and are living there, ³²be sure that you obey all the decrees and laws I am setting before you today.

For Thought and **Contemplation**

In all our duties as Christians the reading and study of God's Word is one of the highest priorities, for the more we love God, the more we will love the Bible, and the more we love the Bible, the more we will love God. Don't give up. The benefits of reading through the Bible and meditation are worth more than the cost in the time and effort involved.

"Do your best to present yourself to God as one approved, a workman who does not need to be ashamed and who correctly handles the word of truth." (2 Tim. 2:15)

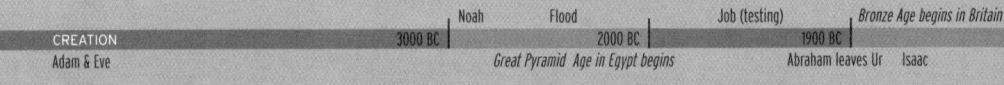

Laws and directives

DAY **69**

Deuteronomy 14:22-27

²²Be sure to set aside a tenth of all that your fields produce each year. ²³Eat the tithe of your grain, new wine and oil, and the firstborn of your herds and flocks in the presence of the Lord your God at the place he will choose as a dwelling for his Name, so that you may learn to revere the Lord your God always. ²⁴But if that place is too distant and you have been blessed by the Lord your God and cannot carry your tithe (because the place where the Lord will choose to put his Name is so far away), ²⁵then exchange your tithe for silver, and take the silver with you and go to the place the Lord your God will choose. ²⁶Use the silver to buy whatever you like: cattle, sheep, wine or other fermented drink, or anything you wish. Then you and your household shall eat there in the presence of the Lord your God and rejoice. ²⁷And do not neglect the Levites living in your towns, for they have no allotment or inheritance of their own.

Israelites to be a distinguished people
Deuteronomy 14:1–21

Regarding tithes
Deuteronomy 14:22–29

The seventh year of release
Deuteronomy 15:1–11

The release of servants
Deuteronomy 15:12–18

Regarding the firstlings of cattle
Deuteronomy 15:19–23

The yearly feasts
Deuteronomy 16:1–17

Appointment of judges, and other directives
Deuteronomy 16:18–22

Sacrifices to be perfect
Deuteronomy 17:1

Penalty for idolatry
Deuteronomy 17:2–7

For Thought and **Contemplation**

God's purpose for Israel was that they might be His *distinguished* people – a nation *in* the world, yet *different* from it. This is equally His purpose for you and me – today. But how sad that our similarities to the world are sometimes more clearly seen than our differences.

"But you are a chosen people, a royal priesthood, a holy nation, a people belonging to God, that you may declare the praises of him who called you out of darkness into his wonderful light." (1 Pet. 2:9)

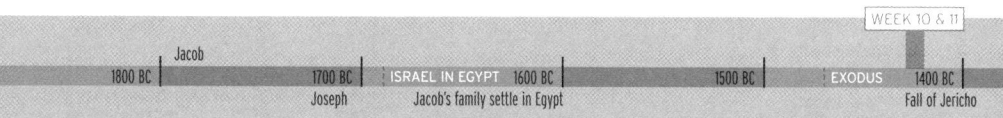

DAY 70 — National laws

Settling of controversies
Deuteronomy 17:8-13

The choice of a king
Deuteronomy 17:14-20

Provision for the Levites
Deuteronomy 18:1-8

Abominations to be avoided
Deuteronomy 18:9-14

Christ the great Prophet
Deuteronomy 18:15-22

Landmarks not to be removed
Deuteronomy 19:14

The punishment of the false witnesses
Deuteronomy 19:15-21

Proclamation regarding war
Deuteronomy 20:1-9

Instructions about captured cities
Deuteronomy 20:10-20

Various instructions
Deuteronomy 21:1-14

Deuteronomy 17:8-13

⁸If cases come before your courts that are too difficult for you to judge – whether bloodshed, lawsuits or assaults – take them to the place the Lord your God will choose. ⁹Go to the priests, who are Levites, and to the judge who is in office at that time. Enquire of them and they will give you the verdict. ¹⁰You must act according to the decisions they give you at the place the Lord will choose. Be careful to do everything they direct you to do. ¹¹Act according to the law they teach you and the decisions they give you. Do not turn aside from what they tell you, to the right or to the left. ¹²The man who shows contempt for the judge or for the priest who stands ministering there to the Lord your God must be put to death. You must purge the evil from Israel. ¹³All the people will hear and be afraid, and will not be contemptuous again.

For Thought and Contemplation

The rules and regulations of God may seem at times to be onerous and unnecessary. But God's laws are designed to help us – not hurt us. It is better to build a fence at the top of a cliff than a hospital at the bottom.

"For in my inner being I delight in God's law." (Rom. 7:22)

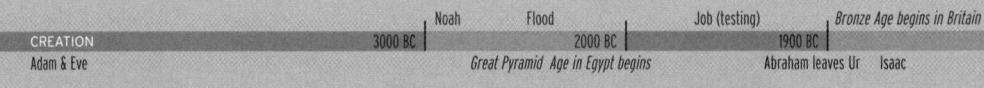

Further regulations for Israel

DAY **71**

Deuteronomy 21:15-17

¹⁵If a man has two wives, and he loves one but not the other, and both bear him sons but the firstborn is the son of the wife he does not love, ¹⁶when he wills his property to his sons, he must not give the rights of the firstborn to the son of the wife he loves in preference to his actual firstborn, the son of the wife he does not love. ¹⁷He must acknowledge the son of his unloved wife as the firstborn by giving him a double share of all he has. That son is the first sign of his father's strength. The right of the firstborn belongs to him.

The firstborn
Deuteronomy 21:15-17

A stubborn son
Deuteronomy 21:18-21

Rule about hanging
Deuteronomy 21:22-23

Extent of punishment
Deuteronomy 25:1-3

Regarding the ox
Deuteronomy 25:4

Marriage of a brother's wife
Deuteronomy 25:5-12

Regarding unjust weights
Deuteronomy 25:13-16

War against Amalek
Deuteronomy 25:17-19

Various laws
Deuteronomy 22:1-30

Regulations of the congregation
Deuteronomy 23:1-25

For Thought and **Contemplation**

The wisdom which Moses shows by anticipating problems that might arise in Canaan, and then giving clear answers for them, is the kind of wisdom that is characteristic of a true leader. Has God given you a leadership role in your home, the church or the community? Then pray for wisdom. Remember – it's yours for the asking.

"If any of you lacks wisdom, he should ask God, who gives generously to all without finding fault, and it will be given to him." (Jas. 1:5)

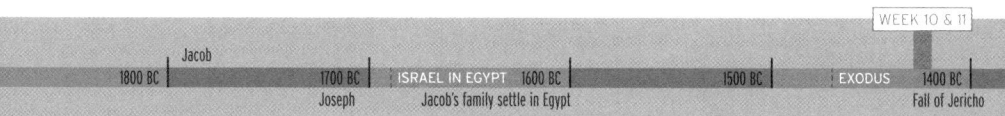

DAY **72**

Personal laws

Divorce and other laws
Deuteronomy 24:1–22

Firstfruits offering
Deuteronomy 26:1–11

Obedience and prayer
Deuteronomy 26:12–19

Law to be written on stones
Deuteronomy 27:1–10

The curses to be pronounced
Deuteronomy 27:11–26

Prophecy concerning Israel's future
Deuteronomy 28:1–14

Deuteronomy 27:1–7

¹Moses and the elders of Israel commanded the people: "Keep all these commands that I give you today. ²When you have crossed the Jordan into the land the Lord your God is giving you, set up some large stones and coat them with plaster. ³Write on them all the words of this law when you have crossed over to enter the land the Lord your God is giving you, a land flowing with milk and honey, just as the Lord, the God of your fathers, promised you. ⁴And when you have crossed the Jordan, set up these stones on Mount Ebal, as I command you today, and coat them with plaster. ⁵Build there an altar to the Lord your God, an altar of stones. Do not use any iron tool upon them. ⁶Build the altar of the Lord your God with stones from the field and offer burnt offerings on it to the Lord your God. ⁷Sacrifice fellowship offerings there, eating them and rejoicing in the presence of the Lord your God.

For Thought and **Contemplation**

As free agents, we may choose for ourselves which path to take, but in the divine scheme of things it always works out like this: obedience brings results; disobedience brings consequences. We are free to choose, but we are not free to choose the consequences of our choosing. Today, therefore – choose life!

"... See, I am setting before you today a blessing and a curse – the blessing if you obey the commands of the Lord your God ... the curse if you disobey the commands of the Lord your God ..." (Deut. 11:26–28)

Moses
– God's messenger

God's Faithfulness
Deuteronomy 2:7; 4:33–38; 7:6–9 ; 8:3, 4; 9:4–6;
29:5, 6; 32:9–14

God's Character 6:4, 5; 7:9; 32:39

God's Love 7:13

God's Glory 4:39; 10:17, 18

God's Grace 7:6–9; 9:4–6

God's Will 10:12–16

God's Coming Messiah 18:15–19

God's Word 4:1, 2, 7, 9; 11:18–21; 30:11–14

"The Lord would speak to Moses face to face, as a man speaks with his friend."
(Ex. 33:11)

DAY 73 — Prophecy concerning Israel's future

Curses for disobedience
Deuteronomy 28:15–44

Result of disobedience
Deuteronomy 28:45–68

Moses calls God's mercies to remembrance
Deuteronomy 29:1–9

Divine wrath
Deuteronomy 29:10–21

The result of idolatry
Deuteronomy 29:22–28

Secret things belong to God
Deuteronomy 29:29

Deuteronomy 29:2–9

²Moses summoned all the Israelites and said to them:
Your eyes have seen all that the Lord did in Egypt to Pharaoh, to all his officials and to all his land. ³With your own eyes you saw those great trials, those miraculous signs and great wonders. ⁴But to this day the Lord has not given you a mind that understands or eyes that see or ears that hear. ⁵During the forty years that I led you through the desert, your clothes did not wear out, nor did the sandals on your feet. ⁶You ate no bread and drank no wine or other fermented drink. I did this so that you might know that I am the Lord your God.
⁷When you reached this place, Sihon king of Heshbon and Og king of Bashan came out to fight against us, but we defeated them. ⁸We took their land and gave it as an inheritance to the Reubenites, the Gadites and the half-tribe of Manasseh.
⁹Carefully follow the terms of this covenant, so that you may prosper in everything you do.

For Thought and **Contemplation**

Never be afraid of the Almighty's chastisement. God's disciplines are designed not to demean and deter, but develop us. Parents who are afraid to put their foot down usually have children who step on their toes!

" '... the Lord disciplines those he loves, and he punishes everyone he accepts as a son.' Endure hardship as discipline; God is treating you as sons. For what son is not disciplined by his father?" (Heb. 12:6–7)

Moses' final words and song

DAY 74

Deuteronomy 31:1–6

¹Then Moses went out and spoke these words to all Israel: ²"I am now a hundred and twenty years old and I am no longer able to lead you. The Lord has said to me, 'You shall not cross the Jordan.' ³The Lord your God himself will cross over ahead of you. He will destroy these nations before you, and you will take possession of their land. Joshua also will cross over ahead of you, as the Lord said. ⁴And the Lord will do to them what he did to Sihon and Og, the kings of the Amorites, whom he destroyed along with their land. ⁵The Lord will deliver them to you, and you must do to them all that I have commanded you. ⁶Be strong and courageous. Do not be afraid or terrified because of them, for the Lord your God goes with you; he will never leave you nor forsake you."

Mercies promised to repentant
Deuteronomy 30:1–10

Life and death set before them
Deuteronomy 30:11–20, Numbers 36:13

Joshua replaces Moses
Numbers 27:15–23

Final words of Moses to people
Deuteronomy 31:1–6

Final words of Moses to Joshua
Deuteronomy 31:7–8, 23

Final words of Moses to priests
Deuteronomy 31:9–13

Final words of Moses to Levites
Deuteronomy 31:24–29

Israelites' apostasy foretold
Deuteronomy 31:14–22, 30, 32:1–18

For Thought and **Contemplation**

The last words of any great man are usually of great importance and have special significance. It was so with Moses, and it was so with Jesus. Remember the last words of Jesus? They have cosmic significance! "Go into all the world and preach the good news to all creation" (Mark 16:15).

"Write on a scroll what you see and send it to the seven churches ... I am the Living One; I was dead, and behold I am alive for ever and ever! And I hold the keys of death and Hades."
(Rev. 1:11, 18)

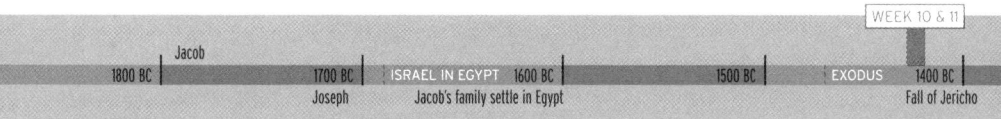

DAY 75 — Moses' death

Judgments for sins
Deuteronomy 32:19–25

God's deliverance
Deuteronomy 32:26–43

Moses' exhortation
Deuteronomy 32:44–47

Moses goes to Mount Nebo
Numbers 27:12–14,
Deuteronomy 32:48–52

Final words to the tribes
Deuteronomy 33:1–29

Death of Moses
Deuteronomy 34:1–7

Deuteronomy 34:1–7

¹Then Moses climbed Mount Nebo from the plains of Moab to the top of Pisgah, across from Jericho. There the Lord showed him the whole land – from Gilead to Dan, ²all of Naphtali, the territory of Ephraim and Manasseh, all the land of Judah as far as the western sea, ³the Negev and the whole region from the Valley of Jericho, the City of Palms, as far as Zoar. ⁴Then the Lord said to him, "This is the land I promised on oath to Abraham, Isaac and Jacob when I said, 'I will give it to your descendants.' I have let you see it with your eyes, but you will not cross over into it."

⁵And Moses the servant of the Lord died there in Moab, as the Lord had said. ⁶He buried him in Moab, in the valley opposite Beth Peor, but to this day no-one knows where his grave is. ⁷Moses was a hundred and twenty years old when he died, yet his eyes were not weak nor his strength gone.

For Thought and **Contemplation**

It is always a sad moment when a great leader, particularly a spiritual leader, goes to his reward in heaven. But we must never fail to hold fast to the truth that though death comes to everyone, God continues His work.

"... the time has come for my departure. I have fought the good fight, I have finished the race, I have kept the faith. Now there is in store for me the crown of righteousness, which the Lord ... will award to me ... and not only to me, but also to all who have longed for his appearing." (2 Tim. 4:6–8)

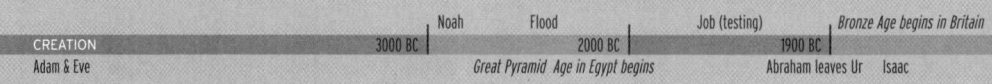

A summary of Israel's history

DAY 76

Psalm 106:1-8

¹Praise the Lord.
Give thanks to the Lord, for he is good; his love endures for ever.
²Who can proclaim the mighty acts of the Lord
or fully declare his praise?
³Blessed are they who maintain justice,
who constantly do what is right.
⁴Remember me, O Lord, when you show favour to your people,
come to my aid when you save them,
⁵that I may enjoy the prosperity of your chosen ones,
that I may share in the joy of your nation
and join your inheritance in giving praise.
⁶We have sinned, even as our fathers did;
we have done wrong and acted wickedly.
⁷When our fathers were in Egypt, they gave no thought to your miracles;
they did not remember your many kindnesses,
and they rebelled by the sea, the Red Sea.
⁸Yet he saved them for his name's sake, to make his mighty power known.

Thirty days of mourning for Moses
Deuteronomy 34:8, 10-12

Joshua, the new leader
Deuteronomy 34:9

Psalms summing up previous history of Israel
Psalm 78:12-66, 105:16-45, 106:1-33, 135:1-20

For Thought and **Contemplation**

When God called Joshua to lead the nation, He did not ask him to be another Moses. Leading Israel *out* was a task for a Moses, leading Israel *in* was a task for a Joshua. Joshua could not be Moses, nor Moses Joshua. You, too, have a place in God's eternal scheme of things, but you can only fit into it as you are yourself.

"Just as each of us has one body with many members, and these members do not all have the same function, so in Christ we who are many form one body, and each member belongs to all the others. We have different gifts, according to the grace given us ..." (Rom. 12:4-6)

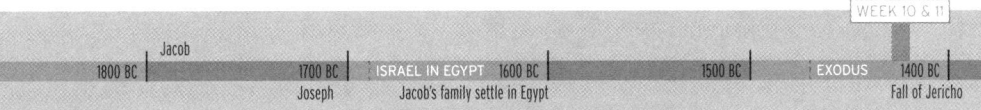

DAY **77**  The crossing into Canaan

God appoints Joshua
Joshua 1:1–4

God promises His assistance
Joshua 1:5–9

Joshua and the
Israelites go to Jordan
Joshua 3:1

Rahab protects the spies
Joshua 2:1–21

The return of the spies
Joshua 2:22–24

Joshua instructs the people
Joshua 1:10–18

The ark's importance
Joshua 3:2–13

Crossing the Jordan
Joshua 3:14–17

The memorial stones
Joshua 4:1–18

Joshua 4:1–7

¹When the whole nation had finished crossing the Jordan, the Lord said to Joshua, ²"Choose twelve men from among the people, one from each tribe, ³and tell them to take up twelve stones from the middle of the Jordan from right where the priests stood and to carry them over with you and put them down at the place where you stay tonight."

⁴So Joshua called together the twelve men he had appointed from the Israelites, one from each tribe, ⁵and said to them, "Go over before the ark of the Lord your God into the middle of the Jordan. Each of you is to take up a stone on his shoulder, according to the number of the tribes of the Israelites, ⁶to serve as a sign among you. In the future, when your children ask you, 'What do these stones mean?' ⁷tell them that the flow of the Jordan was cut off before the ark of the covenant of the Lord. When it crossed the Jordan, the waters of the Jordan were cut off. These stones are to be a memorial to the people of Israel for ever."

For Thought and **Contemplation**

When our focus is on what God has for us in the future, it is so easy to forget the past. But reminding ourselves of God's past victories buttresses our faith in His continuing goodness in the future. What "memorial stones" can you raise in your mind today?

"... I have written ... to stimulate you to wholesome thinking. I want you to recall the words spoken in the past by the holy prophets and the command given by our Lord and Saviour through your apostles." (2 Pet. 3:1–2)

a bird's eye view of **Joshua**

Place in the Bible	**Main Character**	**Special Features**
Sixth Old Testament book; first book of history.	Joshua	The conquest of the Promised Land dominates this book. Much of it reads like an exciting epic with spies being sent into Canaan, the Israelites crossing the Jordan and then the conquest and settlement of the Promised Land under Joshua's leadership.

The battle of Jericho

DAY **78**

Joshua 6:2–5

²Then the Lord said to Joshua, "See, I have delivered Jericho into your hands, along with its king and its fighting men. ³March around the city once with all the armed men. Do this for six days. ⁴Make seven priests carry trumpets of rams' horns in front of the ark. On the seventh day, march around the city seven times, with the priests blowing the trumpets. ⁵When you hear them sound a long blast on the trumpets, make all the people give a loud shout; then the wall of the city will collapse and the people will go up, every man straight in."

An exhortation to fear God
Psalm 114:1–8

Camp at Gilgal
Joshua 4:19–24, 5:1

Circumcision renewed
Joshua 5:2–9

Change of food
Joshua 5:10–12

Jericho shut up
Joshua 6:1

The Captain of the Lord's host
Joshua 5:13–15

The siege of Jericho
Joshua 6:2–5

The city is compassed
Joshua 6:6–16

Jericho is taken
Joshua 6:17–20

Rahab and her family are saved
Joshua 6:21–27

Defeat at Ai
Joshua 7:1–5

Joshua's humiliation and prayer
Joshua 7:6–9

God instructs Joshua
Joshua 7:10–15

For Thought and **Contemplation**

Victory at Jericho – but defeat at Ai. Why? A simple reason – *sinful disobedience*. When the sin is purged, then victory is given. Is there something in your heart that is holding up the victories you ought to be experiencing? Then root it out – today.

"A little yeast works through the whole batch of dough." (Gal. 5:9) "Catch for us the foxes, the little foxes that ruin the vineyards …" (Song of Songs 2:15)

Jesus and the Book

Many examples of salvation are given in this book. Joshua, who leads the Israelites to take possession of Canaan, is a "type" of Jesus Christ who is "bringing many sons to glory"! (Heb. 2:10).

Teaching

The main message of this book is that God always keeps His promises. The land that He had promised to Moses is now possessed by the Israelites. In this, God's will, His goodness and His great power are all demonstrated.

A Verse to Remember

"Not one of all the Lord's good promises to the house of Israel failed; every one was fulfilled" (Josh. 21:45)

DAY 79 — The victory at Ai

Achan is detected and destroyed
Joshua 7:16–26

God encourages Joshua
Joshua 8:1–2

The capture of Ai
Joshua 8:3–22

The destruction of Ai
Joshua 8:23–29

Altar built at Mount Ebal
Joshua 8:30–35

The kings against Israel
Joshua 9:1–2

The Gibeonites apply for peace
Joshua 9:3–13

They are soon detected
Joshua 9:14–21

They are to be bondmen
Joshua 9:22–27

Joshua 8:23–29

²³But they took the king of Ai alive and brought him to Joshua. ²⁴When Israel had finished killing all the men of Ai in the fields and in the desert where they had chased them, and when every one of them had been put to the sword, all the Israelites returned to Ai and killed those who were in it. ²⁵Twelve thousand men and women fell that day – all the people of Ai. ²⁶For Joshua did not draw back the hand that held out his javelin until he had destroyed all who lived in Ai. ²⁷But Israel did carry off for themselves the livestock and plunder of this city, as the Lord had instructed Joshua. ²⁸So Joshua burned Ai and made it a permanent heap of ruins, a desolate place to this day. ²⁹He hung the king of Ai on a tree and left him there until evening. At sunset, Joshua ordered them to take his body from the tree and throw it down at the entrance of the city gate. And they raised a large pile of rocks over it, which remains to this day.

For Thought and **Contemplation**

What a perilous path we walk when we rely upon our own wisdom and neglect to include God in our decisions (Josh. 9:14–15). Are you facing a major decision today? Then don't make a move until you have prayed and invited God's involvement in your decision-making.

"Guide me in your truth and teach me, for you are God my Saviour, and my hope is in you all day long." (Psa. 25:5)

Continued victory in Canaan

DAY 80

Joshua 10:28-33

²⁸That day Joshua took Makkedah. He put the city and its king to the sword and totally destroyed everyone in it. He left no survivors. And he did to the king of Makkedah as he had done to the king of Jericho.
²⁹Then Joshua and all Israel with him moved on from Makkedah to Libnah and attacked it. ³⁰The Lord also gave that city and its king into Israel's hand. The city and everyone in it Joshua put to the sword. He left no survivors there. And he did to its king as he had done to the king of Jericho.
³¹Then Joshua and all Israel with him moved on from Libnah to Lachish; he took up positions against it and attacked it. ³²The Lord handed Lachish over to Israel, and Joshua took it on the second day. The city and everyone in it he put to the sword, just as he had done to Libnah. ³³Meanwhile, Horam king of Gezer had come up to help Lachish, but Joshua defeated him and his army – until no survivors were left.

The angel of the Lord rebukes the people
Judges 2:1-5

Five kings attack Gibeon
Joshua 10:1-6

Joshua aids Gibeon
Joshua 10:7-15

The kings' armies are defeated
Joshua 10:16-27

Other victories
Joshua 10:28-43

The kings at Merom
Joshua 11:1-9

Hazor is burned
Joshua 11:10-14

The country is subdued
Joshua 11:15-23

For Thought and **Contemplation**

Need a miracle in your life today? Then ponder again the story of the sun and moon standing still. This miracle of "daylight saving time" has stretched the credulity of millions. But is anything too hard for the Lord? Well – is there anything?

"Ah, Sovereign Lord, you have made the heavens and the earth by your great power and outstretched arm. Nothing is too hard for you."
(Jer. 32:17)

DAY 81 — Caleb and Joshua

Kings defeated by Joshua
Joshua 12:7–24

The land not yet conquered
Joshua 13:1–6

The division of Canaan
Joshua 13:7, 14:1–5

Caleb obtains Hebron and his daughter receives a blessing
Joshua 14:6–15, 15:13–19, Judges 1:20, 10–16, 1 Chronicles 6:56

Judah's portion
Joshua 15:1–12

Israel's first sabbatical year 1415 BC

The cities of Judah
Joshua 15:20–47

Joshua 15:13–19

¹³In accordance with the Lord's command to him, Joshua gave to Caleb son of Jephunneh a portion in Judah – Kiriath Arba, that is, Hebron. (Arba was the forefather of Anak.) ¹⁴From Hebron Caleb drove out the three Anakites – Sheshai, Ahiman and Talmai – descendants of Anak. ¹⁵From there he marched against the people living in Debir (formerly called Kiriath Sepher). ¹⁶And Caleb said, "I will give my daughter Acsah in marriage to the man who attacks and captures Kiriath Sepher." ¹⁷Othniel son of Kenaz, Caleb's brother, took it; so Caleb gave his daughter Acsah to him in marriage.

¹⁸One day when she came to Othniel, she urged him to ask her father for a field. When she got off her donkey, Caleb asked her, "What can I do for you?"
¹⁹She replied, "Do me a special favour. Since you have given me land in the Negev, give me also springs of water." So Caleb gave her the upper and lower springs.

For Thought and **Contemplation**

After forty years of strife in the wilderness and months of bitter warfare, the Israelites finally take control of Canaan. And guess what? They could have occupied the Promised Land far sooner had they been obedient. Got the point?

"Do not let this Book of the Law depart from your mouth; meditate on it day and night, so that you may be careful to do everything written in it. Then you will be prosperous and successful." (Josh. 1:8)

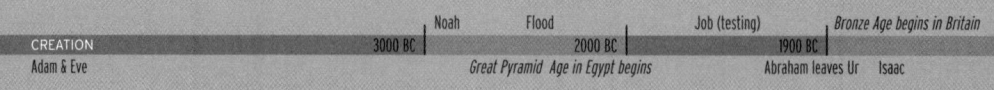

Division of the land

DAY 82

Joshua 17:1–4

¹This was the allotment for the tribe of Manasseh as Joseph's firstborn, that is, for Makir, Manasseh's firstborn. Makir was the ancestor of the Gileadites, who had received Gilead and Bashan because the Makirites were great soldiers. ²So this allotment was for the rest of the people of Manasseh – the clans of Abiezer, Helek, Asriel, Shechem, Hepher and Shemida. These are the other male descendants of Manasseh son of Joseph by their clans.

³Now Zelophehad son of Hepher, the son of Gilead, the son of Makir, the son of Manasseh, had no sons but only daughters, whose names were Mahlah, Noah, Hoglah, Milcah and Tirzah. ⁴They went to Eleazar the priest, Joshua son of Nun, and the leaders and said, "The Lord commanded Moses to give us an inheritance among our brothers." So Joshua gave them an inheritance along with the brothers of their father, according to the Lord's command.

The cities of Judah	Joshua 15:48–63, Judges 1:21
The portion of Joseph's sons	Joshua 16:1–10
Manasseh's portion	Joshua 17:1–6
The boundaries of Manasseh	Joshua 17:7–13
Joseph desires a larger portion	Joshua 17:14–18
The tabernacle set up	Joshua 18:1
The remainder of the land divided	Joshua 18:2–10
The lot of Benjamin	Joshua 18:11–28
The lot of Simeon	Joshua 19:1–9, 1 Chronicles 4:28–33

For Thought and **Contemplation**

Many people "yawn" their way through this part of the Bible. But as "all Scripture is profitable" (2 Tim. 3:16), there are nuggets of gold in every page. Here's one – the word "inheritance". It occurs many times. You, too, have an inheritance in God. Do you know what it is? Have you entered into it?

"I pray also that the eyes of your heart may be enlightened in order that you may know the hope to which he has called you, the riches of his glorious inheritance in the saints." (Eph. 1:18)

The Twelve Tribes

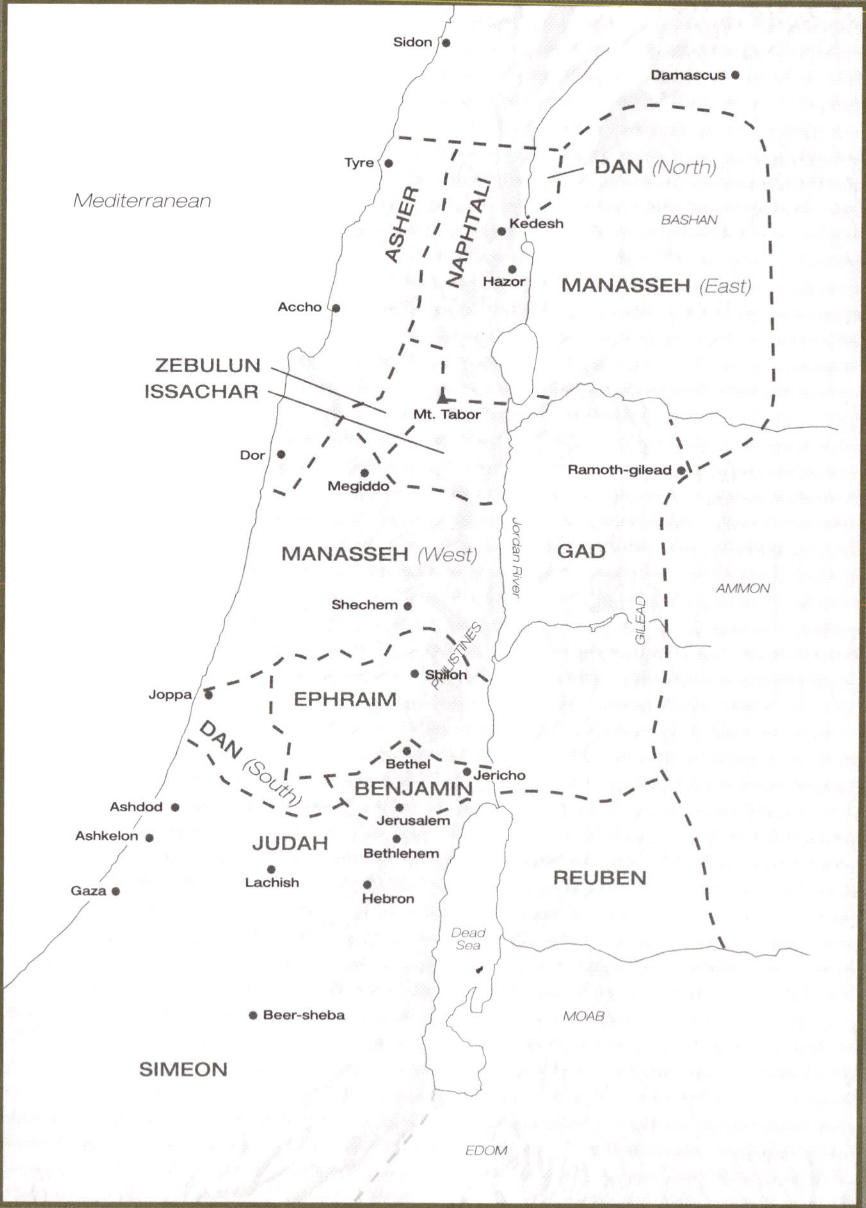

The cities of refuge

DAY **83**

Joshua 20:1-6

¹Then the Lord said to Joshua: ²"Tell the Israelites to designate the cities of refuge, as I instructed you through Moses, ³so that anyone who kills a person accidentally and unintentionally may flee there and find protection from the avenger of blood.
⁴"When he flees to one of these cities, he is to stand in the entrance of the city gate and state his case before the elders of that city. Then they are to admit him into their city and give him a place to live with them. ⁵If the avenger of blood pursues him, they must not surrender the one accused, because he killed his neighbour unintentionally and without malice aforethought. ⁶He is to stay in that city until he has stood trial before the assembly and until the death of the high priest who is serving at that time. Then he may go back to his own home in the town from which he fled."

The lot of Zebulun	Joshua 19:10-16
The lot of Issachar	Joshua 19:17-23
The lot of Asher	Joshua 19:24-31
The lot of Naphtali	Joshua 19:32-39
The lot of Dan	Joshua 19:40-48
Joshua's portion	Joshua 19:49-51
The cities of refuge	Joshua 20:1-9
No inheritance for the Levites	Joshua 13:14, 33
Cities allotted to the Levites out of the other Israelites' inheritance	Joshua 21:1-42, 1 Chronicles 6:54-81

For Thought and **Contemplation**

The cities of refuge were so appointed that a person who committed unintentional murder could reach them within a day. They were easily accessible, well signposted, and their gates were open day and night. How beautifully illustrative of our Lord Jesus Christ – our eternal City of Refuge – to whom we run, when in trouble, and find perfect peace and rest. Hallelujah!

"God is our refuge and strength, an ever-present help in trouble." (Psa. 46:1)

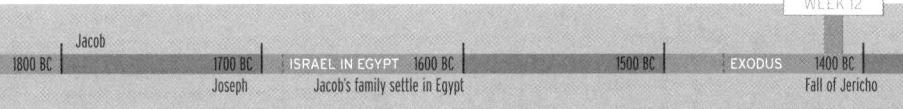

DAY **84**   Misunderstandings arise

The Lord's promise fulfilled
Joshua 21:43–45

Reuben and Gad sent to their homes
Joshua 22:1–9

Altar of testimony built which offends the Israelites
Joshua 22:10–20

The Reubenites' answer
Joshua 22:21–29

The Israelites are satisfied
Joshua 22:30–34

Joshua 22:30–34

³⁰When Phinehas the priest and the leaders of the community – the heads of the clans of the Israelites – heard what Reuben, Gad and Manasseh had to say, they were pleased. ³¹And Phinehas son of Eleazar, the priest, said to Reuben, Gad and Manasseh, "Today we know that the Lord is with us, because you have not acted unfaithfully towards the Lord in this matter. Now you have rescued the Israelites from the Lord's hand."

³²Then Phinehas son of Eleazar, the priest, and the leaders returned to Canaan from their meeting with the Reubenites and Gadites in Gilead and reported to the Israelites. ³³They were glad to hear the report and praised God. And they talked no more about going to war against them to devastate the country where the Reubenites and the Gadites lived.

³⁴And the Reubenites and the Gadites gave the altar this name: A Witness Between Us that the Lord is God.

For Thought and **Contemplation**

Misunderstandings and disagreements between God's people over spiritual matters are often the most difficult to resolve. This is when we must heed the Scripture's advice, and *endeavour* (strive earnestly) to maintain "the unity of the Spirit through the bond of peace" (Eph. 4:3).

"The Peter came to Jesus and asked, 'Lord, how many times shall I forgive my brother when he sins against me? Up to seven times?' Jesus answered, 'I tell you, not seven times, but seventy-seven times.' " (Matt. 18:21–22)

a bird's eye view of **Judges**

Place in the Bible	**Main Characters**	**Special Features**
Seventh Old Testament book; second book of history.	Gideon, Samson.	The special feature of this book is what has become known as the "sin-cycle". Six times the prospering Israelites forget God, are oppressed, then repent and are delivered by Him before they neglect Him and start the cycle all over again!

The death of Joshua

DAY **85**

Joshua 23:1–6

¹After a long time had passed and the Lord had given Israel rest from all their enemies around them, Joshua, by then old and well advanced in years, ²summoned all Israel – their elders, leaders, judges and officials – and said to them: "I am old and well advanced in years. ³You yourselves have seen everything the Lord your God has done to all these nations for your sake; it was the Lord your God who fought for you. ⁴Remember how I have allotted as an inheritance for your tribes all the land of the nations that remain – the nations I conquered – between the Jordan and the Great Sea in the west. ⁵The Lord your God himself will drive them out of your way. He will push them out before you, and you will take possession of their land, as the Lord your God promised you.

⁶"Be very strong; be careful to obey all that is written in the Book of the Law of Moses, without turning aside to the right or to the left."

Joshua's final exhortation	Joshua 23:1–10
Joshua warns the people	Joshua 23:11–16
God's benefits to their fathers	Joshua 24:1–14
Joshua renews the covenant	Joshua 24:15–28, Judges 2:6–7
Death of Joshua	Joshua 24:29–31, Judges 2:8–9
Joseph's bones buried	Joshua 24:32
Battles of the tribes of Judah and Simeon	Judges 1:1–9, 17–19
Tribe of Joseph attacks Bethel	Judges 1:22–26
Establishment of the Judges	Judges 2:16–19
First apostasy and servitude (Mesopotamia)	Judges 3:5–8
Othniel, the first Judge, delivers Israel	Judges 3:9–10

For Thought and **Contemplation**

Israel had lost Moses, and now they lose Joshua. But the nation continued to serve the Lord because of the spiritual impact of its elders. Spiritual leadership begets spiritual leadership.

"Be strong and courageous, because you will lead these people to inherit the land I swore to their forefathers to give them." (Josh. 1:6) "Israel served the Lord throughout the lifetime of Joshua and of the elders who outlived him and who had experienced everything the Lord had done for Israel." (Josh. 24:31)

Jesus and the Book

Jesus came as a despised carpenter from Nazareth to save the humble, weak and oppressed, and often in Judges it is the lowly and insignificant whom God uses. Gideon asked: "How can I save Israel? My clan is the weakest in Manasseh …" (6:15).

Teaching

Judges is a sobering illustration of what disastrous consequences occur when God is rejected by a nation.

A Verse to Remember

"But when they cried out to the Lord, he raised up for them a deliverer …" (Judg. 3:9)

DAY 86 — Micah's idolatry

Some Canaanites remain
Judges 1:27–36

Israel's backsliding
Judges 2:10–15, 20

Some nations left
Judges 2:21–23, 3:1–4, 11

Second apostasy and servitude (Moab)
Judges 3:12–14

Death of Eleazar
Joshua 24:33

Second Judge, Ehud, delivers Israel
Judges 3:15–30

Micah and his mother
Judges 17:1–6

Micah hires a Levite to be his priest
Judges 17:7–13

The Danites seek to enlarge their inheritance
Judges 18:1–15

Judges 17:1–6

¹Now a man named Micah from the hill country of Ephraim ²said to his mother, "The eleven hundred shekels of silver that were taken from you and about which I heard you utter a curse – I have that silver with me; I took it."
 Then his mother said, "The Lord bless you, my son!"
 ³When he returned the eleven hundred shekels of silver to his mother, she said, "I solemnly consecrate my silver to the Lord for my son to make a carved image and a cast idol. I will give it back to you."
 ⁴So he returned the silver to his mother, and she took two hundred shekels of silver and gave them to a silversmith, who made them into the image and the idol. And they were put in Micah's house.
 ⁵Now this man Micah had a shrine, and he made an ephod and some idols and installed one of his sons as his priest. ⁶In those days Israel had no king; everyone did as he saw fit.

For Thought and **Contemplation**

Micah thought it a sign of God's favour to him and his images that a Levite should knock on his door. His mistake was that he interpreted Scripture in the light of circumstances rather than circumstances in the light of Scripture.

"But when he, the Spirit of truth, comes, he will guide you into all truth. He will not speak on his own; he will speak only what he hears, and he will tell you what is yet to come." (Jn. 16:13)

a bird's eye view of **Ruth**

Place in the Bible	**Main Characters**	**Special Features**
Eighth Old Testament book; third book of history.	Naomi, Ruth, Boaz	The book shows how a Gentile, Ruth, becomes an ancestor of Jesus Christ (she was King David's great-grandmother).

Civil war in Israel

DAY 87

Judges 20:18–25

¹⁸The Israelites went up to Bethel and inquired of God. They said, "Who of us shall go first to fight against the Benjamites?"

The Lord replied, "Judah shall go first."

¹⁹The next morning the Israelites got up and pitched camp near Gibeah. ²⁰The men of Israel went out to fight the Benjamites and took up battle positions against them at Gibeah. ²¹The Benjamites came out of Gibeah and cut down twenty-two thousand Israelites on the battlefield that day. ²²But the men of Israel encouraged one another and again took up their positions where they had stationed themselves the first day. ²³The Israelites went up and wept before the Lord until evening, and they enquired of the Lord. They said, "Shall we go up again to battle against the Benjamites, our brothers?"

The Lord answered, "Go up against them."

²⁴Then the Israelites drew near to Benjamin the second day. ²⁵This time, when the Benjamites came out from Gibeah to oppose them, they cut down another eighteen thousand Israelites …

The Danites rob Micah and invade Laish	Judges 18:16–31
A Levite and his concubine	Judges 19:1–13
The wickedness of the men of Gibeah	Judges 19:14–30
Israel prepares for civil war	Judges 20:1–17
War against the Benjamites and their defeat	Judges 20:18–36a

For Thought and **Contemplation**

Why do God's people one moment climb to great heights of spiritual attainment, then the next descend into the depths of degradation and despair? There is only one answer – the waywardness of the human heart. Keep that in mind when next you stand on a peak of spiritual attainment.

"The heart is deceitful above all things and beyond cure. Who can understand it?" (Jer. 17:9)

Jesus and the Book
The book of Ruth mentions the word "kinsman-redeemer" (see 3:9) thirteen times. Boaz, Ruth's "kinsman-redeemer" prefigures our Redeemer, Jesus.

Teaching
The book is a wonderful portrayal of God's care for an insignificant widow.

A Verse to Remember
"'Your people will be my people and your God my God.'" (Ruth 1:16)

DAY **88** — Ruth and Naomi

How the Israelites won
Judges 20:36b–48

Mourning for the tribe of Benjamin
Judges 21:1–25

Third judge, Shamgar
Judges 3:31

Third apostasy and servitude (Canaan)
Judges 4:1–3

The death of Elimelech and his sons
Ruth 1:1–5

Naomi returns home
Ruth 1:6–13

Ruth goes with Naomi
Ruth 1:14–18

Ruth and Naomi arrive at Bethlehem
Ruth 1:19–22

Ruth 1:14–19

¹⁴At this they wept again. Then Orpah kissed her mother-in-law good-bye, but Ruth clung to her. ¹⁵"Look," said Naomi, "your sister-in-law is going back to her people and her gods. Go back with her." ¹⁶But Ruth replied, "Don't urge me to leave you or to turn back from you. Where you go I will go, and where you stay I will stay. Your people will be my people and your God my God. ¹⁷Where you die I will die, and there I will be buried. May the Lord deal with me, be it ever so severely, if anything but death separates you and me." ¹⁸When Naomi realised that Ruth was determined to go with her, she stopped urging her.

¹⁹So the two women went on until they came to Bethlehem. When they arrived in Bethlehem, the whole town was stirred because of them, and the women exclaimed, "Can this be Naomi?"

For Thought and **Contemplation**

The decisions of Ruth and Orpah present a picture of what is involved in true conversion. Orpah draws back to end her days in heathen idolatry. Ruth moves on to have her name inscribed in the divine record. How sad that some can travel with God's people, yet fail to make that "leap of faith" and entrust all to the Saviour.

"... Agrippa said to Paul, 'Do you think that in such a short time you can persuade me to be a Christian?' Paul replied, 'Short time or long – I pray God that not only you but all who are listening to me today may become what I am ...'" (Acts 26:28–29)

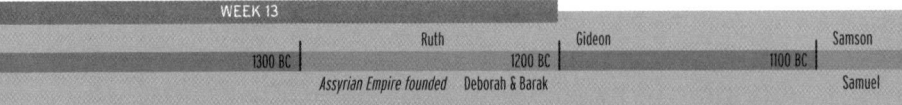

Ruth and Boaz

DAY **89**

Ruth 4:9-12

⁹Then Boaz announced to the elders and all the people, "Today you are witnesses that I have bought from Naomi all the property of Elimelech, Kilion and Mahlon. ¹⁰I have also acquired Ruth the Moabitess, Mahlon's widow, as my wife, in order to maintain the name of the dead with his property, so that his name will not disappear from among his family or from the town records. Today you are witnesses!"

¹¹Then the elders and all those at the gate said, "We are witnesses. May the Lord make the woman who is coming into your home like Rachel and Leah, who together built up the house of Israel. May you have standing in Ephrathah and be famous in Bethlehem. ¹²Through the offspring the Lord gives you by this young woman, may your family be like that of Perez, whom Tamar bore to Judah."

Ruth gleans in Boaz' fields	Ruth 2:1-3
Boaz' kindness to Ruth	Ruth 2:4-16
Ruth returns to Naomi	Ruth 2:17-23
Naomi's instructions	Ruth 3:1-5
Boaz acknowledges the duty of a kinsman	Ruth 3:6-13
Ruth's return to Naomi	Ruth 3:14-18
The kinsman refuses to redeem Ruth's inheritance	Ruth 4:1-8
Boaz marries Ruth	Ruth 4:9-12
Birth of Obed	Ruth 4:13-17
Deborah and Barak, the fourth and fifth judges	Judges 4:4-9
Sisera defeated	Judges 4:10-16

For Thought and **Contemplation**

In the controlled life nothing happens by chance. Ruth's meeting with Boaz was not an accident, it was providentially arranged. Aren't you glad that your life is guided, not by luck, but by the *Lord* – not by the stars, but by the *Saviour*?

"If the Lord delights in a man's way, he makes his steps firm." (Psa. 37:23)

Saul		Solomon	Rehoboam		Jehoshaphat	Obadiah	Joel		Uzziah Jonah Amos Hosea Micah Isaiah Hezekiah
	1000 BC			900 BC		JUDAH		800 BC	700 BC
	David	1st Temple built	Jeroboam I		Ahab Elijah Elisha			Jeroboam II	Fall of Samaria to Assyria
					ISRAEL				
					Homer's epics written				Rome founded

DAY 90

Israel – a world power

Sisera put to death
Judges 4:17–24

Praise and glory ascribed to God
Judges 5:1–5

The deliverance of Israel
Judges 5:6–11

**Israel is the world power
(1200–750 BC)**

Some commended,
others censured
Judges 5:12–23

Sisera's mother disappointed
Judges 5:24–31

Fourth apostasy and
servitude (Midian)
Judges 6:1–6

Israel rebuked
Judges 6:7–10

Sixth Judge, Gideon,
set to deliver Israel
Judges 6:11–24

Gideon destroys Baal's altar
Judges 6:25–35

Gideon's fleece
Judges 6:36–40

Judges 5:1–5

¹On that day Deborah and Barak son of Abinoam sang this song:
²"When the princes in Israel take the lead,
 when the people willingly offer themselves –
 praise the Lord!

³"Hear this, you kings! Listen, you rulers!
 I will sing to the Lord, I will sing;
 I will make music to the
Lord, the God of Israel.
⁴"O Lord, when you went out from Seir,
 when you marched from the land of Edom,
 the earth shook, the heavens poured,
 the clouds poured down water.
⁵The mountains quaked before the Lord, the One of Sinai,
 before the Lord, the God of Israel."

For Thought and **Contemplation**

Israel's rise as a world power came about only through God's blessing and the people's obedience. As long as they remained faithful, their power was certain. When they became disobedient, their power diminished. This is not only the story of nations, it is the story of individuals too.

"My eyes will be on the faithful in the land, that they may dwell with me; he whose walk is blameless will minister to me." (Psa. 101:6)

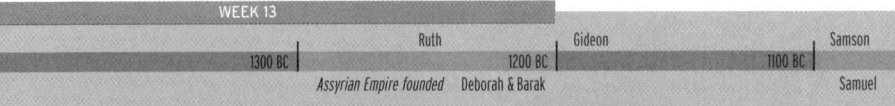

The story of Gideon

DAY 91

Judges 7:9-14

⁹During that night the Lord said to Gideon, "Get up, go down against the camp, because I am going to give it into your hands. ¹⁰If you are afraid to attack, go down to the camp with your servant Purah ¹¹and listen to what they are saying. Afterwards, you will be encouraged to attack the camp." So he and Purah his servant went down to the outposts of the camp. ¹²The Midianites, the Amalekites and all the other eastern peoples had settled in the valley, thick as locusts. Their camels could no more be counted than the sand on the seashore. ¹³Gideon arrived just as a man was telling a friend his dream. "I had a dream," he was saying. "A round loaf of barley bread came tumbling into the Midianite camp. It struck the tent with such force that the tent overturned and collapsed." ¹⁴His friend responded, "This can be nothing other than the sword of Gideon son of Joash, the Israelite. God has given the Midianites and the whole camp into his hands."

Gideon's army reduced
Judges 7:1-8

Gideon encouraged
Judges 7:9-15

The defeat of the Midianites
Judges 7:16-22

The Ephraimites take Oreb and Zeeb
Judges 7:23-25

Gideon pacifies the Ephraimites
Judges 8:1-3

Succoth and Penuel are punished
Judges 8:4-17

Gideon avenges his brethren
Judges 8:18-21

Gideon gives occasion for idolatry
Judges 8:22-30

Birth of Abimelech
Judges 8:31

Gideon's death
Judges 8:32-35

Abimelech made king
Judges 9:1-6

For Thought and **Contemplation**

Just as God gave Gideon a strategy to overcome the Midianites, so He is able to provide you with a divine plan to resolve your most pressing problems. Who and what are the "Midianites" in your life? Pinpoint a problem right now, and ask God to give you His strategy for dealing with it.

"What, then, shall we say in response to this? If God is for us, who can be against us?" (Rom. 8:31)

Saul		Solomon		Rehoboam		Jehoshaphat	Obadiah	Joel		Uzziah	Jonah	Amos	Hosea	Micah	Isaiah	Hezekiah
1000 BC				900 BC		JUDAH			800 BC						700 BC	
David		1st Temple built		Jeroboam 1		Ahab	Elijah	Elisha		Jeroboam II			Fall of Samaria to Assyria			
						ISRAEL										
						Homer's epics written							Rome founded			

Heart to Heart

Section 3

Congratulations. You have now completed a quarter of the whole Bible. The hard work is behind you. There is now a daily discipline of Bible reading in your life. Just like an athlete or body builder, this daily exercise is beginning to form spiritual muscles of power that will build faith for you to overcome obstacles to experiencing more of the peace and joy of God's kingdom.

In this section

Samson's exploits
Israel's demand for a king
Saul's pursuit of David
David's many victories

DAY 92 — The story of Abimelech

Jotham rebukes the Shechemites
Judges 9:7–21

The Shechemites conspiracy
Judges 9:22–29

Abimelech destroys Shechem
Judges 9:30–49

Abimelech slain
Judges 9:50–57

Seventh Judge,
Tola, defends Israel
Judges 10:1–2

Eighth Judge, Jair
10:3–5 **(Ninth Judge, Eli)**

Samson's conception
Judges 13:2–7

The angel appears to Manoah
Judges 13:8–14

Manoah's sacrifice
Judges 13:15–23

Judges 9:50–57

⁵⁰Next Abimelech went to Thebez and besieged it and captured it. ⁵¹Inside the city, however, was a strong tower, to which all the men and women – all the people of the city – fled. They locked themselves in and climbed up on the tower roof. ⁵²Abimelech went to the tower and stormed it. But as he approached the entrance to the tower to set it on fire, ⁵³a woman dropped an upper millstone on his head and cracked his skull.
⁵⁴Hurriedly he called to his armour-bearer, "Draw your sword and kill me, so that they can't say, 'A woman killed him.'" So his servant ran him through, and he died. ⁵⁵When the Israelites saw that Abimelech was dead, they went home.
⁵⁶Thus God repaid the wickedness that Abimelech had done to his father by murdering his seventy brothers. ⁵⁷God also made the men of Shechem pay for all their wickedness. The curse of Jotham son of Jerub-Baal came on them.

For Thought and **Contemplation**

"The measure of a man," said a great philosopher, "is what he does with power." Gideon's son, Abimelech, misused it, and ended his life in failure and defeat. How do you use the power God has given you? Carefully – or carelessly?

"For God did not give us a spirit of timidity, but a spirit of power, of love and of self-discipline." (2 Tim. 1:7)

a bird's eye view of 1 Samuel

Place in the Bible	Main Characters	Special Features
Ninth Old Testament book; fourth book of history.	Hannah, Eli, Samuel, Saul, David, Goliath, Jonathan.	The special feature of 1 Samuel is kingship. We see the people's rejection of God's Kingship and their desire to have a king like the other nations. It also records Saul's failure, and David's friendship with Jonathan.

The story of Samson

Judges 14:1–7

¹Samson went down to Timnah and saw there a young Philistine woman. ²When he returned, he said to his father and mother, "I have seen a Philistine woman in Timnah; now get her for me as my wife."

³His father and mother replied, "Isn't there an acceptable woman among your relatives or among all our people? Must you go to the uncircumcised Philistines to get a wife?"

But Samson said to his father, "Get her for me. She's the right one for me." ⁴(His parents did not know that this was from the Lord, who was seeking an occasion to confront the Philistines; for at that time they were ruling over Israel.) ⁵Samson went down to Timnah together with his father and mother. As they approached the vineyards of Timnah, suddenly a young lion came roaring towards him. ⁶The Spirit of the Lord came upon him in power so that he tore the lion apart with his bare hands as he might have torn a young goat. But he told neither his father nor his mother what he had done. ⁷Then he went down and talked with the woman, and he liked her.

Samson's birth	Judges 13:24–25
Jephthah's youth	Judges 11:1–3
Elkanah and his family	1 Samuel 1:1–8
Hannah's prayer	1 Samuel 1:9–18
Samuel's birth	1 Samuel 1:19–23
Samuel's dedication	1 Samuel 1:24–28
Hannah's song	1 Samuel 2:1–10
The oppression of Israel	Judges 10:6–9
Israel's repentance	Judges 10:10–18
The Philistines in the west	Judges 13:1, Psalm 106:34–46
Samson desires a Philistine wife	Judges 14:1–4
Samson kills a lion	Judges 14:5–9
Samson's riddle	Judges 14:10–14

For Thought and **Contemplation**

One important fact spells out Samson's downfall – he was careless in the day of his power. Those who are careless about their God-given duties and responsibilities end up like Samson – disappointed, disillusioned and powerless.

"Now it is required that those who have been given a trust must prove faithful." (1 Cor. 4:2)

Jesus and the Book
Hannah's prayer in 1 Samuel 2 is remarkably similar to Mary's in Luke 1. Jesus is the great prophet and king who, by His obedience to God, has the power to deliver His people.

Teaching
Through the historical ups and downs of the lives of Samuel, Saul, and David, 1 Samuel teaches that rejection of God spells disaster, while faith in God brings His blessing.

A Verse to Remember
"To obey is better than sacrifice ..." (1 Sam. 15:22)

The Judges of Israel

Othniel	*v. Nomads*	Judges 3:7–11
Ehud	*v. Moabites*	Judges 3:12–30
Shamgar	*v. Philistines*	Judges 3:31
Deborah	*v. Canaanites*	Judges 4–5
Gideon	*v. Midianites*	Judges 6:11–8:33
Tola	*of Issachar*	Judges 10:1–2
Jair	*of Gilead*	Judges 10:3–5
Jephthah	*v. Ammonites*	Judges 10:6 to 12:7
Ibzan	*of Bethlehem*	Judges 12:8–10
Elon	*of Zebulun*	Judges 12:11–12
Abdon	*of Ephraim*	Judges 12:13–15
Samson	*v. Philistines*	Judges 13–16

God calls Samuel

DAY 94

1 Samuel 3:7–11

⁷Now Samuel did not yet know the Lord: The word of the Lord had not yet been revealed to him. ⁸The Lord called Samuel a third time, and Samuel got up and went to Eli and said, "Here I am; you called me."
Then Eli realised that the Lord was calling the boy. ⁹So Eli told Samuel, "Go and lie down, and if he calls you, say, 'Speak, Lord, for your servant is listening.'" So Samuel went and lay down in his place.
¹⁰The Lord came and stood there, calling as at the other times, "Samuel! Samuel!"
Then Samuel said, "Speak, for your servant is listening."
¹¹And the Lord said to Samuel: "See, I am about to do something in Israel that will make the ears of everyone who hears of it tingle.

Samson's riddle continued	Judges 14:15–20
Samson denied his wife	Judges 15:1–2
Eli's wicked sons	1 Samuel 2:12–17
Samuel's childhood	1 Samuel 2:11, 18–21, 26
Warning to Eli	1 Samuel 2:22–25, 27–36
Birth of Saul	1 Samuel 9:1, 14:51
God calls Samuel	1 Samuel 3:1–10
God tells Samuel of the destruction of Eli's house	1 Samuel 3:11–18
Samuel established as a prophet	1 Samuel 3:19–21
Jephthah and the Gileadites	Judges 11:4–11
He attempts to make peace	Judges 11:12–28

For Thought and **Contemplation**

Who can tell the far-reaching effects of prayer? Hannah prayed, and from her prayer came Samuel, the first great prophet and the last Judge in Israel. Pray on – your *persistent* praying can produce results you never dreamed possible.

"This is the confidence we have in approaching God: that if we ask anything according to his will, he hears us. And if we know that he hears us – whatever we ask – we know that we have what we asked of him."
(1 Jn. 5:14–15)

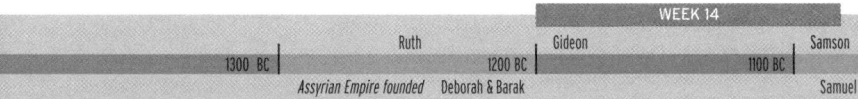

DAY 95 — The ark taken

Jephthah's vow
Judges 11:29–40

The Ephraimites quarrel with Jephthah
Judges 12:1–6

Tenth Judge, Jephthah, dies
Judges 12:7

Eleventh Judge, Samson
Judges 15:20

The ark is taken
1 Samuel 4:1–11

Eli's death and Ichabod's birth
1 Samuel 4:12–22

Dagon is broken
1 Samuel 5:1–5

The Philistines afflicted
1 Samuel 5:6–12, 6:1

Ark restored
1 Samuel 6:2–12

1 Samuel 5:1–5

¹After the Philistines had captured the ark of God, they took it from Ebenezer to Ashdod. ²Then they carried the ark into Dagon's temple and set it beside Dagon. ³When the people of Ashdod rose early the next day, there was Dagon, fallen on his face on the ground before the ark of the Lord! They took Dagon and put him back in his place. ⁴But the following morning when they rose, there was Dagon, fallen on his face on the ground before the ark of the Lord! His head and hands had been broken off and were lying on the threshold; only his body remained. ⁵That is why to this day neither the priests of Dagon nor any others who enter Dagon's temple at Ashdod step on the threshold.

For Thought and **Contemplation**

Why did Israel lose the battle even though the ark was with them? Perhaps they came to rely more on the ark than on God. When faith in God wavers, faith in inanimate objects increased. And when that happens, victory is no longer assured.

"By faith we understand that the universe was formed at God's command, so that what is seen was not made out of what was visible." (Heb. 11:3)

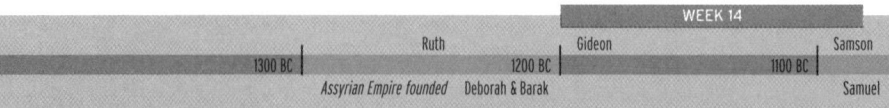

Samson and Delilah

DAY 96

Judges 16:25–30
... they called Samson out of the prison, and he performed for them. When they stood him among the pillars, ²⁶Samson said to the servant who held his hand, "Put me where I can feel the pillars that support the temple, so that I may lean against them." ²⁷Now the temple was crowded with men and women; all the rulers of the Philistines were there, and on the roof were about three thousand men and women watching Samson perform. ²⁸Then Samson prayed to the Lord, "O Sovereign Lord, remember me. O God, please strengthen me just once more, and let me with one blow get revenge on the Philistines for my two eyes." ²⁹Then Samson reached towards the two central pillars on which the temple stood. Bracing himself against them, his right hand on the one and his left hand on the other, ³⁰Samson said, "Let me die with the Philistines!" Then he pushed with all his might, and down came the temple on the rulers and all the people in it. Thus he killed many more when he died than while he lived.

Ark at Beth Shemesh
1 Samuel 6:13–18

The people destroyed
1 Samuel 6:19–21

The ark taken to Kiriath Jearim
1 Samuel 7:1–2

Twelfth Judge, Ibzan
Judges 12:8–10

Samson and the Philistines
Judges 15:3–19

Samson's escape
Judges 16:1–3

Saul's marriage and family
1 Samuel 14:49, 50

Thirteenth Judge, Elon
Judges 12:11–12

Samson and Delilah
Judges 16:4–22

Samson's death
Judges 16:23–31

Revival at Mizpeh
1 Samuel 7:3–8

For Thought and **Contemplation**

How reassuring is the truth that God is the God of the "second chance" – Samson's hair began to grow again! Have you failed in something God gave you to do? Then be encouraged – tell Him you are sorry, ask His forgiveness, and He will give you another chance.

"I will repay you for the years the locusts have eaten – the great locust and the young locust ... my great army that I sent among you. You will have plenty to eat, until you are full, and you will praise the name of the Lord your God, who has worked wonders for you; never again will my people be shamed." (Joel 2:25–26)

DAY 97 — The story of Saul

The Philistines defeated
1 Samuel 7:9–14

Samuel's leadership
1 Samuel 7:15–17

Fourteenth Judge, Abdon
Judges 12:13–15

The corrupt government of Samuel's sons
1 Samuel 8:1–3

Israel desires a king
1 Samuel 8:4–9

The manner of a king
1 Samuel 8:10–22

Saul directed to Samuel
1 Samuel 9:2–10

Samuel told about Saul
1 Samuel 9:11–17

Samuel's treatment of Saul
1 Samuel 9:18–27

Reign of Saul 1065–1025 BC

Samuel anoints Saul
1 Samuel 10:1–16

Saul chosen to be king
1 Samuel 10:17–27

1 Samuel 9:17–22

¹⁷When Samuel caught sight of Saul, the Lord said to him, "This is the man I spoke to you about; he will govern my people." ¹⁸Saul approached Samuel in the gateway and asked, "Would you please tell me where the seer's house is?"
¹⁹"I am the seer," Samuel replied. "Go up ahead of me to the high place, for today you are to eat with me, and in the morning I will let you go and will tell you all that is in your heart. ²⁰As for the donkeys you lost three days ago, do not worry about them; they have been found. And to whom is all the desire of Israel turned, if not to you and all your father's family?"
²¹Saul answered, "But am I not a Benjamite, from the smallest tribe of Israel, and is not my clan the least of all the clans of the tribe of Benjamin? Why do you say such a thing to me?"
²²Then Samuel brought Saul and his servant into the hall and seated them at the head of those who were invited – about thirty in number.

For Thought and **Contemplation**

Israel's desire for a king was really a cover-up. Deep down inside, they resented the rule of God over them. They were like the boy who said, "My father told me to sit down, but I was still standing up on the inside." Remind you of anyone?

"If you love me, you will obey what I command." (Jn. 14:15)

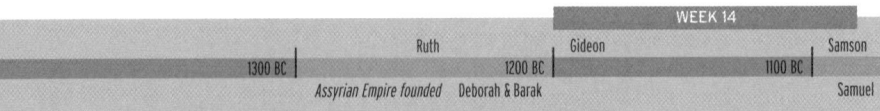

War with the Philistines

DAY **98**

1 Samuel 13:1–7

¹Saul was [thirty] years old when he became king, and he reigned over Israel [forty-] two years. ²Saul chose three thousand men from Israel; two thousand were with him at Michmash and in the hill country of Bethel, and a thousand were with Jonathan at Gibeah in Benjamin. The rest of the men he sent back to their homes. ³Jonathan attacked the Philistine outpost at Geba, and the Philistines heard about it. Then Saul had the trumpet blown throughout the land and said, "Let the Hebrews hear!" ⁴So all Israel heard the news: "Saul has attacked the Philistine outpost, and now Israel has become an offence to the Philistines." And the people were summoned to join Saul at Gilgal. ⁵The Philistines assembled to fight Israel, with three thousand chariots, six thousand charioteers, and soldiers as numerous as the sand on the seashore. They went up and camped at Michmash, east of Beth Aven. ⁶When the men of Israel saw that their situation was critical and that their army was hard pressed, they hid in caves ...

Jabesh Gilead delivered	1 Samuel 11:1–11
Saul confirmed as king	1 Samuel 11:12–15
Saul defeats Hagrites	1 Chronicles 5:10, 18–22
Samuel declares his integrity	1 Samuel 12:1–5
Samuel reproves the people	1 Samuel 12:6–15
Thunder sent in harvest time	1 Samuel 12:16–18
Samuel's love for the people	1 Samuel 12:19–25
The Philistines' invasion	1 Samuel 13:1–7, 16–22
Saul sacrifices and is reproved	1 Samuel 13:8–15

For Thought and **Contemplation**

God never acts out of character. Despite the rebellion of His people, He promises not to forsake them "for the sake of his great name" (1 Sam. 12:22). And for that same reason, God will not forsake you. Remember that the next time you feel discouraged.

"... because God has said, 'Never will I leave you; never will I forsake you.'" (Heb. 13:5)

DAY 99 — The decline of Saul

Jonathan's victory
1 Samuel 13:23–14:23

The people forbidden to eat
1 Samuel 14:24–35

Jonathan – the offender
1 Samuel 14:36–46

Continual war with the Philistines
1 Samuel 14:47–48, 52

Saul sent to destroy Amalek
1 Samuel 15:1–9

Saul commends himself
1 Samuel 15:10–21

Samuel's reply
1 Samuel 15:22–23

Saul's imperfect humiliation
1 Samuel 15:24–31

Agag put to death, Samuel and Saul part
1 Samuel 15:32–35

1 Samuel 15:22–27

²²But Samuel replied:
 "Does the Lord delight in burnt offerings and sacrifices
  as much as in obeying the voice of the Lord?
 To obey is better than sacrifice,
  and to heed is better than the fat of rams.
²³For rebellion is like the sin of divination,
  and arrogance like the evil of idolatry.
 Because you have rejected the word of the Lord,
  he has rejected you as king."
²⁴Then Saul said to Samuel, "I have sinned. I violated the Lord's command and your instructions. I was afraid of the people and so I gave in to them. ²⁵Now I beg you, forgive my sin and come back with me, so that I may worship the Lord."
²⁶But Samuel said to him, "I will not go back with you. You have rejected the word of the Lord, and the Lord has rejected you as king over Israel!"
²⁷As Samuel turned to leave, Saul caught hold of the hem of his robe, and it tore.

For Thought and **Contemplation**

Failure to carry out God's instructions, however contradictory to reason they may appear to be, always results in great spiritual loss. Make it a life principle to do whatever God asks, even though you may not feel like it. God says, "To obey is better than sacrifice." It is.

"'For my thoughts are not your thoughts, neither are your ways my ways,' declares the Lord. 'As the heavens are higher than the earth, so are my ways higher than your ways and my thoughts than your thoughts.'" (Isa. 55:8–9)

The rise of David

DAY **100**

1 Samuel 16:7,10–13

⁷But the Lord said to Samuel, "Do not consider his appearance or his height, for I have rejected him. The Lord does not look at the things man looks at. Man looks at the outward appearance, but the Lord looks at the heart."
... ¹⁰Jesse made seven of his sons pass before Samuel, but Samuel said to him, "The Lord has not chosen these." ¹¹So he asked Jesse, "Are these all the sons you have?"
"There is still the youngest," Jesse answered, "but he is tending the sheep."
Samuel said, "Send for him; we will not sit down until he arrives."
¹²So he sent and had him brought in. He was ruddy, with a fine appearance and handsome features.
Then the Lord said, "Rise and anoint him; he is the one."
¹³So Samuel took the horn of oil and anointed him in the presence of his brothers, and from that day on the Spirit of the Lord came upon David in power. Samuel then went to Ramah.

Samuel sent to Bethlehem	1 Samuel 16:1–11
Samuel anoints David	1 Samuel 16:12–13
The glory of God's creation	Psalm 19:1–14, 8:1–9
David calms Saul	1 Samuel 16:14–23
Goliath's challenge	1 Samuel 17:1–11
David comes to the camp	1 Samuel 17:12–30

For Thought and **Contemplation**

Anger can be righteous as well as unrighteous. David's anger at Goliath's taunting of the Israelites was righteous because it arose from grief at what was happening to others, not from a grudge because of what was happening to him. Discerning the difference is vital.

"'In your anger do not sin': Do not let the sun go down while you are still angry." (Eph. 4:26)

DAY 101 — David's popularity increases

David and Goliath
1 Samuel 17:31–58

Jonathan's friendship
1 Samuel 18:1–4

David's confidence in God's grace and care
Psalm 23:1–6

David is praised
1 Samuel 18:5–9

Saul tries to kill David
1 Samuel 18:10–13

David prays for protection
Psalm 5:1–12

David's wisdom
1 Samuel 18:14–19

David marries Michal
1 Samuel 18:20–30

David's prayer for help
Psalm 12:1–8

1 Samuel 18:5–9

⁵Whatever Saul sent him to do, David did it so successfully that Saul gave him a high rank in the army. This pleased all the people, and Saul's officers as well. ⁶When the men were returning home after David had killed the Philistine, the women came out from all the towns of Israel to meet King Saul with singing and dancing, with joyful songs and with tambourines and lutes. ⁷As they danced, they sang:

"Saul has slain his thousands,
 and David his tens of thousands."

⁸Saul was very angry; this refrain galled him. "They have credited David with tens of thousands," he thought, "but me with only thousands. What more can he get but the kingdom?" ⁹And from that time on Saul kept a jealous eye on David.

For Thought and **Contemplation**

David dressing up in Saul's armour was not the way to victory over Goliath. His defeat required special insight and sanctified cunning. When facing your "Goliath" today, keep in mind that it is "'Not by might nor by power, but by my Spirit,' says the Lord Almighty" (Zech. 4:6).

"If any of you lacks wisdom, he should ask God, who gives generously to all without finding fault, and it will be given to him." (Jas. 1:5)

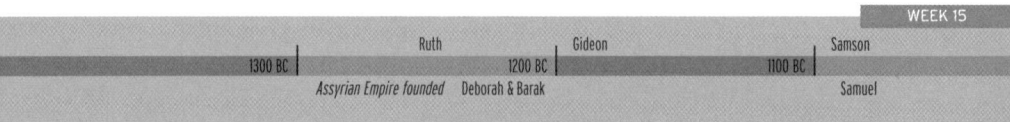

King Saul
His Rise and Fall

The Rise of Saul

1. Israel demands a king. (1 Sam. 8)
   Israel wanted to be like other nations.
2. Saul is chosen (1 Sam. 9)
   God instructs Samuel to look Saul out.
3. Samuel anoints him. (1 Sam. 10)
   God's Spirit comes on him and he prophesies.
4. His leadership is confirmed. (1 Sam. 11)
   Saul raises an army and delivers the city.

The Fall of Saul

1. He desecrates the priesthood. (1 Sam. 13)
   He offers a burnt offering. Samuel reproves him.
2. He spares Amalek.
   God had commanded the Amalekites to be destroyed.
   Samuel reproves him.
3. He is oppressed by an evil spirit. (1 Sam. 16)
   He attempts to kill and destroy David. David escapes, then confronts him.
4. He commands the killing of the priests of God. (1 Sam. 22)
   He was jealous of David and thought they were his supporters.
5. He visits the witch of Endor. (1 Sam. 28)
   Saul is full of fear and commits suicide with his armour-bearer. (1 Sam. 31)

"Now the Spirit of the Lord had departed from Saul ..."
(1 Sam. 16:14)

DAY 102 — David turns to his God

Jonathan warns David
1 Samuel 19:1–3

David's confidence in the Lord
Psalm 11:1–7

Saul's behaviour towards David
1 Samuel 19:4–11

Michal helps David
1 Samuel 19:12–17

David's prayer for safety
Psalm 59:1–17

David flees to Samuel
1 Samuel 19:18–24

David's prayer for justice
Psalm 7:1–17

David's prayer for guidance and protection
Psalm 25:1–22

David consults Jonathan
1 Samuel 20:1–11

Psalm 11:1–7

¹In the Lord I take refuge.
 How then can you say to me:
 "Flee like a bird to your mountain.
²For look, the wicked bend their bows;
 they set their arrows against the strings
 to shoot from the shadows
 at the upright in heart.
³When the foundations are being destroyed,
 what can the righteous do?"
⁴The Lord is in his holy temple;
 the Lord is on his heavenly throne.
 He observes the sons of men;
 his eyes examine them.
⁵The Lord examines the righteous,
 but the wicked and those who love violence
 his soul hates.
⁶On the wicked he will rain
 fiery coals and burning sulphur;
 a scorching wind will be their lot.
⁷For the Lord is righteous,
 he loves justice;
 upright men will see his face.

For Thought and **Contemplation**

Where do you turn for confidence when you are up against the wall? To art? To literature? To music? To alcohol? David turned to the Lord, and reminded himself that God was on the throne (Psa. 11:4). In the midst of life's insecurities, He is the greatest security.

"God is our refuge and strength, an ever-present help in trouble." (Psa. 46:1)

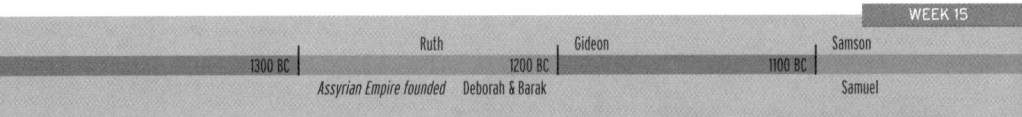

David in difficulties

DAY **103**

Psalm 56:1–8

¹Be merciful to me, O God, for men hotly pursue me;
all day long they press their attack.
²My slanderers pursue me all day long;
many are attacking me in their pride.
³When I am afraid,
I will trust in you.
⁴In God, whose word I praise,
in God I trust; I will not be afraid.
What can mortal man do to me?
⁵All day long they twist my words;
they are always plotting to harm me.
⁶They conspire, they lurk,
they watch my steps,
eager to take my life.
⁷On no account let them escape;
in your anger, O God, bring down the nations.
⁸Record my lament;
list my tears on your scroll –
are they not in your record? ...

Jonathan's covenant with David
1 Samuel 20:12–23

Saul seeks to kill Jonathan
1 Samuel 20:24–34

Jonathan and David part
1 Samuel 20:35–42

David's prayer
Psalm 26:1–12

David flees to Ahimelech
1 Samuel 21:1–9

David's praise of God's goodness
Psalm 34:1–22

David's prayer of trust in God
Psalm 56:1–13

For Thought and **Contemplation**

While fleeing from Saul, David finds time to compose two magnificent psalms. This is what is meant by turning a setback into a springboard. Can you turn life's trials and setbacks into a song? Try it today.

"About midnight Paul and Silas were praying and singing hymns to God, and the other prisoners were listening to them." (Acts 16:25)

DAY 104 — David's victory

David at cave of Adullam 1 Samuel 22:1	Psalm 64:1–7 ¹Hear me, O God, as I voice my complaint;
David's prayer for help Psalm 142:1–7	protect my life from the threat of the enemy.
Many come to David 1 Samuel 22:2, 1 Chronicles 12:16–18	²Hide me from the conspiracy of the wicked,
David's evening prayer Psalm 141:1–10	from that noisy crowd of evildoers.
David flees to Moab 1 Samuel 22:3–5	³They sharpen their tongues like swords
David's prayer for protection Psalm 64:1–10	and aim their words like deadly arrows.
Doeg slays the priests 1 Samuel 22:6–20	⁴They shoot from ambush at the innocent man;
David's prayer for help Psalm 35:1–28	they shoot at him suddenly, without fear.
David saves the people of Keilah 1 Samuel 23:1–5	⁵They encourage each other in evil plans,
David offers Abiathar protection 1 Samuel 22:21–23	they talk about hiding their snares;

David at cave of Adullam — 1 Samuel 22:1
David's prayer for help — Psalm 142:1–7
Many come to David — 1 Samuel 22:2, 1 Chronicles 12:16–18
David's evening prayer — Psalm 141:1–10
David flees to Moab — 1 Samuel 22:3–5
David's prayer for protection — Psalm 64:1–10
Doeg slays the priests — 1 Samuel 22:6–20
David's prayer for help — Psalm 35:1–28
David saves the people of Keilah — 1 Samuel 23:1–5
David offers Abiathar protection — 1 Samuel 22:21–23

Psalm 64:1–7

¹Hear me, O God, as I voice my complaint;
 protect my life from the threat of the enemy.
²Hide me from the conspiracy of the wicked,
 from that noisy crowd of evildoers.
³They sharpen their tongues like swords
 and aim their words like deadly arrows.
⁴They shoot from ambush at the innocent man;
 they shoot at him suddenly, without fear.
⁵They encourage each other in evil plans,
 they talk about hiding their snares;
 they say, "Who will see them?"
⁶They plot injustice and say,
 "We have devised a perfect plan!"
 Surely the mind and heart of man are cunning.
⁷But God will shoot them with arrows;
 suddenly they will be struck down ...

For Thought and **Contemplation**

Imagine taking a band of men who were "in distress or in debt or discontented" and turning them into a formidable army! What a picture it presents of One greater than David – Jesus – who takes utterly unworthy men and women and turns them into a mighty army – the Church of the Living God!

"These ... follow the Lamb wherever he goes. They were purchased from among men and offered as firstfruits to God and the Lamb." (Rev. 14:4)

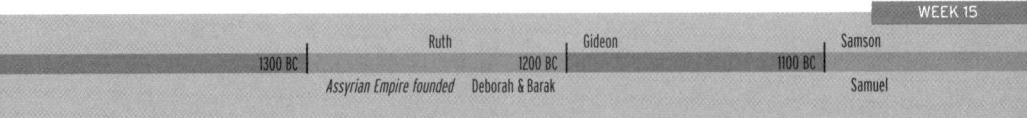

Saul in pursuit of David

DAY **105**

Psalm 52:1–8

¹Why do you boast of evil, you mighty man?
 Why do you boast all day long,
 you who are a disgrace in the eyes of God?
²Your tongue plots destruction;
 it is like a sharpened razor,
 you who practise deceit.
³You love evil rather than good,
 falsehood rather than speaking the truth. *Selah*
⁴You love every harmful word,
 O you deceitful tongue!
⁵Surely God will bring you down to everlasting ruin:
 He will snatch you up and tear you from your tent;
 he will uproot you from the land of the living. *Selah*
⁶The righteous will see and fear;
 they will laugh at him, saying,
⁷"Here now is the man
 who did not make God his stronghold
 but trusted in his great wealth
 and grew strong by destroying others!"
⁸But I am like an olive tree
 flourishing in the house of God;
 I trust in God's unfailing love
 for ever and ever ...

David speaks of God's judgment and grace
Psalm 52:1–9

David's complaint
Psalm 109:1–31

David's prayer for protection
Psalm 140:1–13

God warns David
1 Samuel 23:6–13

David's prayer of trust in God
Psalm 31:1–24

David still sought by Saul
1 Samuel 23:14–15

David's prayer for help
Psalm 13:1–6

Jonathan comforts David
1 Samuel 23:16–18

David betrayed by the Ziphites
1 Samuel 23:19–23

David escapes
1 Samuel 23:24–28

David's prayer for protection
Psalm 54:1–7

For Thought and **Contemplation**

Do you feel at this moment that Satan seems to be pursuing you to an unusual degree? Then do as David did, and focus your thoughts upon God. This is why God recorded David's words in His book, the Bible. He wanted you to focus your thoughts on Him. And when you do, you will find the same comfort that David did.

" ... when the enemy comes in like a flood, the Spirit of the Lord will put him to flight." (Isa. 59:19 NIV footnote)

DAY 106 — David spares Saul's life

David goes to En Gedi
1 Samuel 23:29

David's prayer
Psalm 17:1–15

David spares Saul's life
1 Samuel 24:1–7

David shows his innocence
1 Samuel 24:8–15

Saul acknowledges his fault
1 Samuel 24:16–22

David's confidence in God
Psalm 57:1–11, 108:1–13

Death of Samuel
1 Samuel 25:1

David's request
1 Samuel 25:2–11

David's intention to destroy Nabal
1 Samuel 25:12–17

Abigail pacifies David and Nabal dies
1 Samuel 25:18–38

1 Samuel 24:1–7

¹After Saul returned from pursuing the Philistines, he was told, "David is in the Desert of En Gedi." ²So Saul took three thousand chosen men from all Israel and set out to look for David and his men near the Crags of the Wild Goats. ³He came to the sheep pens along the way; a cave was there, and Saul went in to relieve himself. David and his men were far back in the cave. ⁴The men said, "This is the day the Lord spoke of when he said to you, 'I will give your enemy into your hands for you to deal with as you wish.'" Then David crept up unnoticed and cut off a corner of Saul's robe. ⁵Afterwards, David was conscience-stricken for having cut off a corner of his robe. ⁶He said to his men, "The Lord forbid that I should do such a thing to my master, the Lord's anointed, or lift my hand against him; for he is the anointed of the Lord." ⁷With these words David rebuked his men and did not allow them to attack Saul. And Saul left the cave and went his way.

For Thought and **Contemplation**

One of the great principles of spiritual success is to honour leadership, even when that leadership seems to be working against you or shows signs of failure. David knew that Saul's authority was given him by God. He respected that – and moved on to success.

"Obey your leaders and submit to their authority. They keep watch over you as men who must give an account. Obey them so that their work will be a joy, not a burden, for that would be of no advantage to you." (Heb. 13:17)

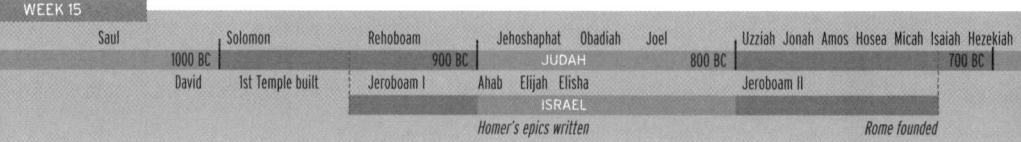

From Shepherd
to King

DAVID, THE SHEPHERD and son of a Bethlehem farmer, was a man of many parts and endowed with outstanding abilities. He was an accomplished musician, the poet who gave us so many of the Psalms, a shrewd statesman and a fearless general. He was responsible for uniting the divided tribes of Israel and is remembered as Israel's greatest king. 1 Samuel 13:14 reveals the key to David's passionate devotion to his Lord. David, it says, was a man "after God's own heart."

DAY 107 — David builds a great army

David marries Abigail
1 Samuel 25:39–44

David again spares Saul's life
1 Samuel 26:1–12

David confronts Saul
1 Samuel 26:13–25

David retires to Gath
1 Samuel 27:1–7

David deceives Achish
1 Samuel 27:8–12

David's friends
1 Chronicles 12:1–7

The Philistines gather for battle; Achish's confidence in David
1 Samuel 28:1–2

David prevented from fighting
1 Samuel 29:1–11

Men who joined David
1 Chronicles 12:19–22

1 Samuel 27:1–7

¹But David thought to himself, "One of these days I shall be destroyed by the hand of Saul. The best thing I can do is to escape to the land of the Philistines. Then Saul will give up searching for me anywhere in Israel, and I will slip out of his hand." ²So David and the six hundred men with him left and went over to Achish son of Maoch king of Gath. ³David and his men settled in Gath with Achish. Each man had his family with him, and David had his two wives: Ahinoam of Jezreel and Abigail of Carmel, the widow of Nabal. ⁴When Saul was told that David had fled to Gath, he no longer searched for him.
⁵Then David said to Achish, "If I have found favour in your eyes, let a place be assigned to me in one of the country towns, that I may live there. Why should your servant live in the royal city with you?"
⁶So on that day Achish gave him Ziklag, and it has belonged to the kings of Judah ever since. ⁷David lived in Philistine territory for a year and four months.

For Thought and **Contemplation**

Building anything for God requires dedication, determination and persistence. There are sure to be times of doubt and difficulty. David had his time of doubt, but he acknowledged it, resisted it, and moved ahead in the direction God told him to go. And so must you.

"We are hard pressed on every side, but not crushed; perplexed, but not in despair; persecuted, but not abandoned; struck down, but not destroyed." (2 Cor. 4:8–9)

a bird's eye view of **1 Chronicles**

Place in the Bible	Main Character	Special Feature
Thirteenth Old Testament book; eighth book of history.	David	Family histories (genealogies)

The deaths of Saul and Jonathan

DAY **108**

1 Chronicles 10:1–8

¹Now the Philistines fought against Israel; the Israelites fled before them, and many fell slain on Mount Gilboa. ²The Philistines pressed hard after Saul and his sons, and they killed his sons Jonathan, Abinadab and Malki-Shua. ³The fighting grew fierce around Saul, and when the archers overtook him, they wounded him.

⁴Saul said to his armour-bearer, "Draw your sword and run me through, or these uncircumcised fellows will come and abuse me."

But his armour-bearer was terrified and would not do it; so Saul took his own sword and fell on it. ⁵When the armour-bearer saw that Saul was dead, he too fell on his sword and died. ⁶So Saul and his three sons died, and all his house died together.

⁷When all the Israelites in the valley saw that the army had fled and that Saul and his sons had died, they abandoned their towns and fled. And the Philistines came and occupied them.

⁸The next day, when the Philistines came to strip the dead, they found Saul and his sons fallen on Mount Gilboa ...

Ziklag spoiled
1 Samuel 30:1–6

David pursues the Amalekites
1 Samuel 30:7–15

He recovers everything
1 Samuel 30:16–20

David's distribution of the spoil
1 Samuel 30:21–31

Battle positions
1 Samuel 28:4

Saul consults the witch of Endor
1 Samuel 28:3, 5–19

Saul's terror
1 Samuel 28:20–25

Saul's defeat and death
1 Samuel 31:1–13, 1 Chronicles 10:1–14

For Thought and **Contemplation**

In God's sovereignty the destruction of David's home – which outwardly seemed a calamity – was but the preparation for his next phase of service – kingship. The words "calamity" and "sovereignty" are incompatible.

"And we know that in all things God works for the good of those who love him, who have been called according to his purpose." (Rom. 8:28)

Jesus and the Book

This book teaches that God's people should worship and obey Him. Jesus said that "God is spirit, and his worshippers must worship in spirit and in truth" (Jn. 4:24), and, "if anyone loves me, he will obey my teaching" (Jn. 14:23).

Teaching

1 Chronicles, which covers the same period as 2 Samuel, recounts Israel's story to the end of David's reign. The Chronicler, however, writing for exiles returned from Babylon, concentrates on telling the religious history of the nation, starting with its origins.

A Verse to Remember

"'Be strong and courageous, and do the work. Do not be afraid or discouraged, for the Lord God, my God, is with you.'" (1 Chron. 28:20).

DAY 109 — David becomes King

Mephibosheth's lameness
2 Samuel 4:4

David hears of Saul's death
2 Samuel 1:1–16

David's lamentation
2 Samuel 1:17–27

Saul's descendants
1 Chronicles 8:29–40, 9:35–44

David becomes king
2 Samuel 5:4, 1 Kings 2:11,
1 Chronicles 29:27

Reign of David 1025–985 BC

David anointed King of Judah
2 Samuel 2:1–7

Ish-Bosheth made King of Israel
2 Samuel 2:8–11

Civil war in Israel
2 Samuel 2:12–32, 2 Samuel 3:1

Children born in Hebron
2 Samuel 3:2–5, 1 Chronicles 3:1–4

2 Samuel 2:1–7

¹In the course of time, David enquired of the Lord. "Shall I go up to one of the towns of Judah?" he asked.
The Lord said, "Go up."
David asked, "Where shall I go?"
"To Hebron," the Lord answered. ²So David went up there with his two wives, Ahinoam of Jezreel and Abigail, the widow of Nabal of Carmel. ³David also took the men who were with him, each with his family, and they settled in Hebron and its towns. ⁴Then the men of Judah came to Hebron and there they anointed David king over the house of Judah.
When David was told that it was the men of Jabesh Gilead who had buried Saul, ⁵he sent messengers to the men of Jabesh Gilead to say to them, "The Lord bless you for showing this kindness to Saul your master by burying him. ⁶May the Lord now show you kindness and faithfulness, and I too will show you the same favour because you have done this. ⁷Now then, be strong and brave, for Saul your master is dead, and the house of Judah has anointed me king over them."

For Thought and **Contemplation**

David's lament over Jonathan's death – "Your love for me was wonderful" – is one of the most beautiful passages in the Bible. When you consider the death of Christ, and what it meant for you, do not those selfsame words describe your feelings also?

"This is love: not that we loved God, but that he loved us and sent his Son as an atoning sacrifice for our sins." (1 Jn 4:10)

---

a bird's eye view of **2 Samuel**

Place in the Bible	**Main Characters**	**Special Features**
Tenth Old Testament book; fifth book of history.	Saul, David, Bathsheba, Nathan, Absalom.	The establishment of Jerusalem and the reign of David, Israel's greatest king.

Israel united

DAY 110

1 Chronicles 11:1–3

¹All Israel came together to David at Hebron and said, "We are your own flesh and blood. ²In the past, even while Saul was king, you were the one who led Israel on their military campaigns. And the Lord your God said to you, 'You will shepherd my people Israel, and you will become their ruler.'" ³When all the elders of Israel had come to King David at Hebron, he made a compact with them at Hebron before the Lord, and they anointed David king over Israel, as the Lord had promised through Samuel.

Michal and Abner return to David
2 Samuel 3:6–21

Joab murders Abner
2 Samuel 3:22–29

Murder of Ish-Bosheth
2 Samuel 4:1–3, 5–12

David made king over Israel
2 Samuel 5:1–3, 1 Chronicles 11:1–3

List of David's warriors
1 Chronicles 12:23–40

Israel united under David
1 Chronicles 29:26

For Thought and **Contemplation**

What explains David's great success? One thing above all else – early in his life he made a commitment to the God of the covenant. And the God of the covenant made a commitment to him. Without this understanding, no life can be secure.

"This is my blood of the covenant, which is poured out for many for the forgiveness of sins." (Matt. 26:28)

Jesus and the Book

The Lord promised David that his lineage and throne would stand for ever (2 Sam. 7:16). This was fulfilled in Jesus Christ, who is called the "Son of David" (Matt. 21:9), and who will be given "the throne of his father David" (Luke 1:32).

Teaching

Despite his grievous sins, King David was a man who loved God. In public he showed his joy in God. In private he prayed frequently and confessed that God's grace made him what he was. "The Lord is my rock, my fortress and my deliverer" (2 Sam. 22:2).

A Verse to Remember

"... I will raise up your offspring to succeed you ... and I will establish his kingdom. He is the one who will build a house for my Name, and I will establish the throne of his kingdom for ever" (2 Sam. 7:12–13).

DAY 111 — David: King of Israel and Judah

Length of David's reign
2 Samuel 5:5

Punishment of the wicked
Psalm 58:1–11

God the great King
Psalm 93:1–5

A song of praise
Psalm 95:1–11

Jerusalem becomes the capital city
2 Samuel 5:6–10, 1 Chronicles 11:4–9

A prayer of thanksgiving
Psalm 118:1–29

House built for David
2 Samuel 5:11–12, 1 Chronicles 14:1–2

David's promise
Psalm 101:1–8

Children born in Jerusalem
2 Samuel 5:13–16,
1 Chronicles 3:5–9, 14:3–7

Wars against the Philistines
2 Samuel 5:17, 1 Chronicles 14:8

The Gadites join David
1 Chronicles 12:8–15

The Philistines gather
2 Samuel 5:18, 1 Chronicles 14:9

David brought water from Bethlehem
2 Samuel 23:13–17,
1 Chronicles 11:15–19

Psalm 93:1–5

¹The Lord reigns, he is robed in majesty;
 the Lord is robed in majesty
 and is armed with strength.
The world is firmly established;
 it cannot be moved.
²Your throne was established long ago;
 you are from all eternity.
³The seas have lifted up, O Lord,
 the seas have lifted up their voice;
 the seas have lifted up their pounding waves.
⁴Mightier than the thunder of the great waters,
 mightier than the breakers of the sea—
 the Lord on high is mighty.
⁵Your statutes stand firm;
 holiness adorns your house
 for endless days, O Lord.

For Thought and **Contemplation**

David's act of sacrifice in pouring out the water that came from the well of Bethlehem shows the depth of his sincerity and dedication. How does his action compare with your own willingness for self-sacrifice? Moderately? Closely? Or remotely?

"Therefore, I urge you, brothers, in view of God's mercy, to offer your bodies as living sacrifices, holy and pleasing to God – which is your spiritual act of worship." (Rom. 12:1)

Israel's victory

DAY **112**

2 Samuel 6:1–5

¹David again brought together out of Israel chosen men, thirty thousand in all. ²He and all his men set out from Baalah of Judah to bring up from there the ark of God, which is called by the Name, the name of the Lord Almighty, who is enthroned between the cherubim that are on the ark. ³They set the ark of God on a new cart and brought it from the house of Abinadab, which was on the hill. Uzzah and Ahio, sons of Abinadab, were guiding the new cart ⁴with the ark of God on it, and Ahio was walking in front of it. ⁵David and the whole house of Israel were celebrating with all their might before the Lord, with songs and with harps, lyres, tambourines, sistrums and cymbals.

Victory at Baal Perazim
2 Samuel 5:19–21, 1 Chronicles 14:10–12

The second conflict
2 Samuel 5:22–25, 1 Chronicles 14:13–17

Decision to bring ark back
1 Chronicles 13:1–4

God's complete knowledge and care
Psalm 139:1–24

Journey of ark from Kiriath Jearim
2 Samuel 6:1–5, 1 Chronicles 13:5–8

God and His people
Psalm 78:1–11, 67–72

Ark brought to the house of Obed-Edom
2 Samuel 6:6–11, 1 Chronicles 13:9–14

David's song of triumph
Psalm 68:1–18

For Thought and **Contemplation**

For God's blessing to flow, He must have the central place. The ark, which was the symbol of God's presence, had to be brought to Jerusalem – the city of God. Where does God dwell in your life? Is He marginal? Or central?

"Being confident of this, that he who began a good work in you will carry it on to completion until the day of Christ Jesus." (Phil. 1:6)

DAY 113 — The ark restored

David's song of triumph
Psalm 68:19–35

Preparation for the ark
1 Chronicles 15:1–14

The temple praised
Psalm 132:1–18

Musicians chosen
1 Chronicles 15:15–24

Ark brought to Jerusalem
2 Samuel 6:12–15, 1 Chronicles 15:25–28

God the supreme Ruler
Psalm 97:1–12

Ark set in its place
2 Samuel 6:16, 17, 1 Chronicles 15:29, 16:1, 2 Chronicles 1:4

What God requires
Psalm 15:1–5

The great King
Psalm 24:1–10

David blesses the people
2 Samuel 6:18–19, 1 Chronicles 16:2–3

2 Samuel 6:12–17

¹²Now King David was told, "The Lord has blessed the household of Obed-Edom and everything he has, because of the ark of God." So David went down and brought up the ark of God from the house of Obed-Edom to the City of David with rejoicing. ¹³When those who were carrying the ark of the Lord had taken six steps, he sacrificed a bull and a fattened calf. ¹⁴David, wearing a linen ephod, danced before the Lord with all his might, ¹⁵while he and the entire house of Israel brought up the ark of the Lord with shouts and the sound of trumpets.

¹⁶As the ark of the Lord was entering the City of David, Michal daughter of Saul watched from a window. And when she saw King David leaping and dancing before the Lord, she despised him in her heart.

¹⁷They brought the ark of the Lord and set it in its place inside the tent that David had pitched for it, and David sacrificed burnt offerings and fellowship offerings before the Lord.

For Thought and **Contemplation**

When the ark of God's presence is given its rightful place, the inevitable result is jubilation and rejoicing. If your heart is not singing today, perhaps this is the reason – God does not have His rightful place in your life.

"Let them give thanks to the Lord for his unfailing love and his wonderful deeds for men. Let them sacrifice thank-offerings and tell of his works with songs of joy." (Psa. 107:21–22)

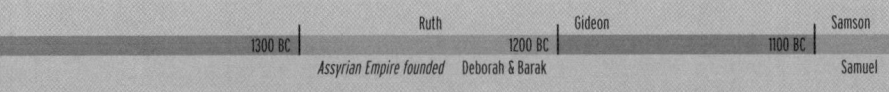

Psalms of praise

DAY **114**

Psalm 98:1-7

¹Sing to the Lord a new song,
 for he has done marvellous things;
 his right hand and his holy arm
 have worked salvation for him.
²The Lord has made his salvation known
 and revealed his righteousness to the nations.
³He has remembered his love
 and his faithfulness to the house of Israel;
 all the ends of the earth have seen
 the salvation of our God.
⁴Shout for joy to the Lord, all the earth,
 burst into jubilant song with music;
⁵make music to the Lord with the harp,
 with the harp and the sound of singing,
⁶with trumpets and the blast of the ram's horn –
 shout for joy before the Lord, the King.
⁷Let the sea resound, and everything in it,
 the world, and all who live in it ...

Hymn of praise prepared	1 Chronicles 16:4-7
Hymn of praise sung	1 Chronicles 16:8-22
God and His people	Psalm 105:1-15, 1 Chronicles 16:23-36, Psalm 96:1-13, Psalm 98:1-9, Psalm 106:47-48
Daily sacrifices instituted	1 Chronicles 16:37-43
Michal despises David	2 Samuel 6:20-23
David's care for the ark	2 Samuel 7:1-3, 1 Chronicles 17:1-2
God's covenant with David	2 Samuel 7:4-17

For Thought and **Contemplation**

When God has His rightful place in the hearts of not just some, but all of His people, then the Church becomes like the temple in David's day – a habitation of continuous delight and endless praise. Why is it not so?

"The Lord is my strength and my song; he has become my salvation. Shouts of joy and victory resound in the tents of the righteous: 'The Lord's right hand has done mighty things!'" (Psa. 118:14-15)

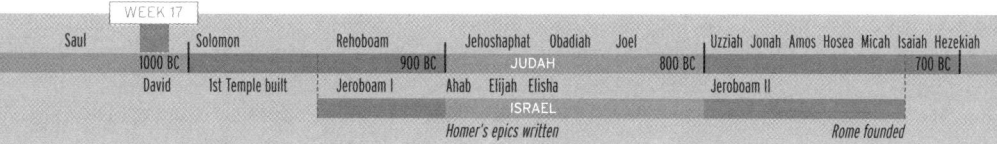

DAY 115 — Israel increases her territory

God's covenant with David
1 Chronicles 17:3–15

David's prayer and thanksgiving
2 Samuel 7:18–29, 1 Chronicles 17:16–27

God's chosen King
Psalm 2:1–12, 110:1–7

David's prayer of confidence
Psalm 16:1–11

Territorial gains over the Philistines, Moab, the King of Zobah and Syria
2 Samuel 8:1–8, 1 Chronicles 18:1–8

David's thanksgiving
Psalm 9:1–20

2 Samuel 8:1–6

¹In the course of time, David defeated the Philistines and subdued them, and he took Metheg Ammah from the control of the Philistines. ²David also defeated the Moabites. He made them lie down on the ground and measured them off with a length of cord. Every two lengths of them were put to death, and the third length was allowed to live. So the Moabites became subject to David and brought tribute. ³Moreover, David fought Hadadezer son of Rehob, king of Zobah, when he went to restore his control along the Euphrates River. ⁴David captured a thousand of his chariots, seven thousand charioteers and twenty thousand foot soldiers. He hamstrung all but a hundred of the chariot horses. ⁵When the Arameans of Damascus came to help Hadadezer king of Zobah, David struck down twenty-two thousand of them. ⁶He put garrisons in the Aramean kingdom of Damascus, and the Arameans became subject to him and brought tribute. The Lord gave David victory wherever he went.

For Thought and **Contemplation**

Despite all that Israel had gained, God led them to embark upon gaining even more territory. How is it with you in your Christian life? Is God leading you on to even greater gains? Then don't hold back. S-t-r-e-t-c-h yourself. God is with you.

"Enlarge the place of your tent, stretch your tent curtains wide, do not hold back; lengthen your cords, strengthen your stakes." (Isa. 54:2)

David's military victories

DAY 116

2 Samuel 23:8–12

⁸These are the names of David's mighty men:
Josheb-Basshebeth, a Tahkemonite, was chief of the Three; he raised his spear against eight hundred men, whom he killed in one encounter.
⁹Next to him was Eleazar son of Dodai the Ahohite. As one of the three mighty men, he was with David when they taunted the Philistines gathered [at Pas Dammim] for battle. Then the men of Israel retreated, ¹⁰but he stood his ground and struck down the Philistines till his hand grew tired and froze to the sword. The Lord brought about a great victory that day. The troops returned to Eleazar, but only to strip the dead.
¹¹Next to him was Shammah son of Agee the Hararite. When the Philistines banded together at a place where there was a field full of lentils, Israel's troops fled from them. ¹²But Shammah took his stand in the middle of the field. He defended it and struck the Philistines down, and the Lord brought about a great victory.

Joram congratulates David
2 Samuel 8:9–10, 1 Chronicles 18:9–10

David's prayer for deliverance
Psalm 60:1–12, 108:6–13

Edom subdued
2 Samuel 8:13–14, 1 Chronicles 18:12–13

Hadad flees to Egypt
1 Kings 11:15–20

Spoils dedicated
2 Samuel 8:12, 1 Chronicles 18:11

David's mighty men
2 Samuel 23:8–12, 18–39,
1 Chronicles 11:10–14, 20–47

David's government and officers
2 Samuel 8:15–18, 1 Chronicles 18:14-17

For Thought and **Contemplation**

The list of David's victories is staggering. But had he gone to battle without God, it would not be his victories we would be reading about, but his defeats. When God sends, He fends – wards off all fatal harm on the way.

"But thanks be to God! He gives us the victory through our Lord Jesus Christ." **(1 Cor. 15:57)**

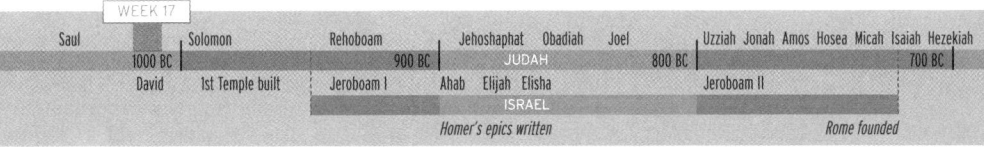

DAY 117 — David's songs of thanksgiving

David's psalm of thanksgiving
2 Samuel 22:1–51

David's song of victory
Psalm 18:1–50

He thanks God for victory
Psalm 144:1–15

2 Samuel 22:44–51

⁴⁴"You have delivered me from the attacks of my people;
 you have preserved me as the head of nations.
 People I did not know are subject to me,
⁴⁵and foreigners come cringing to me;
 as soon as they hear me, they obey me.
⁴⁶They all lose heart;
 they come trembling
from their strongholds.
⁴⁷The Lord lives! Praise be to my Rock!
 Exalted be God, the Rock, my Saviour!
⁴⁸He is the God who avenges me,
 who puts the nations under me,
⁴⁹who sets me free from my enemies.
 You exalted me above my foes;
 from violent men you rescued me.
⁵⁰Therefore I will praise you, O Lord, among the nations;
 I will sing praises to your name.
⁵¹He gives his king great victories;
 he shows unfailing kindness to his anointed,
 to David and his descendants for ever."

For Thought and **Contemplation**

One of the things God delights in is His people's praise. Has God given you a victory in the last few days or weeks? Then do as David did, and compose your own psalm of praise. You'll be surprised at the result.

"I will extol the Lord at all times;
his praise will always be on my lips."
(Psa. 34:1)

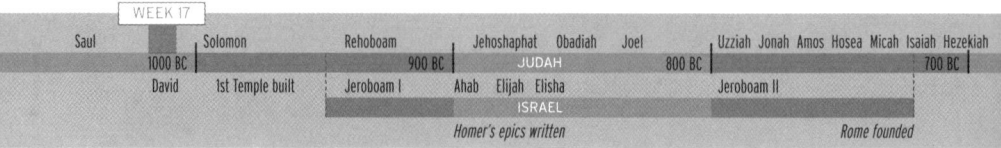

Names of God

Elohim – used 2,570 times, refers to God's power and might (Gen. 1:1; Psa. 19:1).

El – four compounds of this name:

- **Elyon**, the strongest strong One (Gen. 14:17–20; Isa. 14:13, 14)
- **Roi**, the strong One who sees (Gen. 16:13)
- **Shaddai**, the breasted One (used 48 times in the Old Testament; see Gen. 17:1; Psa. 91:1)
- **Olam**, the everlasting God (Isa. 40:28)

Adonai – Master, Lord. God owns all His creation (Mal. 1:6)

Jehovah – the most common name. Occurs 6,823 times. The Self-existent One, the God of the covenant (Gen. 2:4). There are nine compound names of this name:

- **Jireh** – the Lord will provide (Gen. 22:13, 14)
- **Nissi** – the Lord, my banner (Ex. 17:15)
- **Shalom** – the Lord is Peace (Judg. 6:24)
- **Sabbaoth** – the Lord of Hosts (1 Sam. 1:3; Isa. 6:1–3)
- **Maccaddeshoem** – the Lord thy Sanctifier (Ex. 31:13)
- **Rohi** (Raah) – the Lord my Shepherd (Psa. 23:1)
- **Tsidkenu** – the Lord our Righteousness (Jer. 23:6)
- **Shammah** – the Lord who is present (Ezek. 48:35)
- **Rapha** – the Lord our Healer (Ex. 15:26)

DAY 118

David and Bathsheba

David and Mephibosheth
2 Samuel 9:1–13

Decisive victories over Ammonite-Syrian forces
2 Samuel 10:1–14, 1 Chronicles 19:1–15

David defeats Syrian forces
2 Samuel 10:15–19, 1 Chronicles 19:16–19

David's prayer for victory
Psalm 20:1–9

David's sin
1 Kings 15:5

David's adultery
2 Samuel 11:1–5

His attempt at concealment
2 Samuel 11:6–13

Uriah murdered
2 Samuel 11:14–27

2 Samuel 11:1–5

¹**In the spring, at the time when kings go off to war, David sent Joab out with the king's men and the whole Israelite army. They destroyed the Ammonites and besieged Rabbah. But David remained in Jerusalem.**
²**One evening David got up from his bed and walked around on the roof of the palace. From the roof he saw a woman bathing. The woman was very beautiful,** ³**and David sent someone to find out about her. The man said, "Isn't this Bathsheba, the daughter of Eliam and the wife of Uriah the Hittite?"** ⁴**Then David sent messengers to get her. She came to him, and he slept with her. (She had purified herself from her uncleanness.) Then she went back home.** ⁵**The woman conceived and sent word to David, saying, "I am pregnant."**

For Thought and **Contemplation**

How sad that David – "the man after God's own heart" – could fall into the sins of adultery and murder. Somewhere inside David's heart, spiritual erosion had set in. Is there any spiritual erosion taking place in your life? Check now – before it is too late!

"If we confess our sins, he is faithful and just and will forgive us our sins and purify us from all unrighteousness." (1 Jn. 1:9)

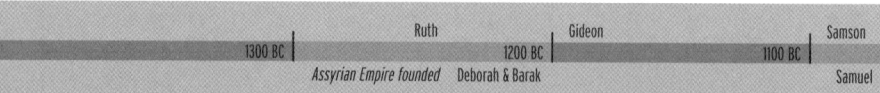

The birth of Solomon

DAY **119**

Psalm 103:13–20
¹³As a father has compassion on his children,
  so the Lord has compassion on those who fear him;
¹⁴for he knows how we are formed,
  he remembers that we are dust.
¹⁵As for man, his days are like grass,
  he flourishes like a flower of the field;
¹⁶the wind blows over it and it is gone,
  and its place remembers it no more.
¹⁷But from everlasting to everlasting the Lord's love is with those who fear him,
  and his righteousness with their children's children –
¹⁸with those who keep his covenant
  and remember to obey his precepts.
¹⁹The Lord has established his throne in heaven,
  and his kingdom rules over all.
²⁰Praise the Lord, you his angels,
  you mighty ones who do his bidding,
  who obey his word …

Nathan's parable and David's confession	2 Samuel 12:1–15
His prayer for forgiveness	Psalm 51:1–19, 32:1–11, 38:1–22
God's love and mercy	Psalm 103:1–22
David's intercession	2 Samuel 12:16
His prayer for help	Psalm 6:1–10
David's child dies	2 Samuel 12:17–23
Solomon's birth	2 Samuel 12:24–25

For Thought and **Contemplation**

The greatest deception in life is self-deception. David had deceived himself to such an extent that it took Nathan's barbed parable to bring him out into the open. "To thine own self be true, and it must follow as the night the day, thou canst not then be false to any man." (*Hamlet,* Shakespeare)

"Surely you desire truth in the inner parts; you teach me wisdom in the inmost place." (Psa. 51:6)

DAY **120**

David's family troubles

David and Joab capture Rabbath
2 Samuel 12:26–31, 1 Chronicles 20:1–3

Praise for victory
Psalm 21:1–13

Amnon rapes his sister Tamar
2 Samuel 13:1–20

Absalom murders Amnon
2 Samuel 13:21–29

Absalom flees to Geshur
2 Samuel 13:30–39

Absalom persuaded to return
2 Samuel 14:1–33

2 Samuel 14: 28–33

[28]Absalom lived two years in Jerusalem without seeing the king's face. [29]Then Absalom sent for Joab in order to send him to the king, but Joab refused to come to him. So he sent a second time, but he refused to come. [30]Then he said to his servants, "Look, Joab's field is next to mine, and he has barley there. Go and set it on fire." So Absalom's servants set the field on fire.

[31]Then Joab did go to Absalom's house and he said to him, "Why have your servants set my field on fire?"

[32]Absalom said to Joab, "Look, I sent word to you and said, 'Come here so that I can send you to the king to ask, "Why have I come from Geshur? It would be better for me if I were still there!" ' Now then, I want to see the king's face, and if I am guilty of anything, let him put me to death."

[33]So Joab went to the king and told him this. Then the king summoned Absalom, and he came in and bowed down with his face to the ground before the king. And the king kissed Absalom.

For Thought and **Contemplation**

"Most problems in children," said one famous family counsellor, "are the reflection of what lies in the hearts of the parents." Did David's weaknesses work themselves out in his own offspring? We can only speculate – but it's a thought worth pondering.

"Train a child in the way he should go, and when he is old he will not turn from it." (Prov. 22:6)

Absalom's rebellion

DAY **121**

2 Samuel 15:7–12

⁷At the end of four years, Absalom said to the king, "Let me go to Hebron and fulfil a vow I made to the Lord. ⁸While your servant was living at Geshur in Aram, I made this vow: 'If the Lord takes me back to Jerusalem, I will worship the Lord in Hebron.'"
⁹The king said to him, "Go in peace." So he went to Hebron.
¹⁰Then Absalom sent secret messengers throughout the tribes of Israel to say, "As soon as you hear the sound of the trumpets, then say, 'Absalom is king in Hebron.'" ¹¹Two hundred men from Jerusalem had accompanied Absalom. They had been invited as guests and went quite innocently, knowing nothing about the matter. ¹²While Absalom was offering sacrifices, he also sent for Ahithophel the Gilonite, David's counsellor, to come from Giloh, his home town. And so the conspiracy gained strength, and Absalom's following kept on increasing.

Absalom's ambition
2 Samuel 15:1–6

David's trust in God
Psalm 62:1–12

Absalom's conspiracy
2 Samuel 15:7–12

David's prayer
Psalm 41:1–13

David leaves Jerusalem
2 Samuel 15:13–16

His confidence in
God's protection
Psalm 63:1–11

Ittai's loyalty
2 Samuel 15:17–23

David sends ark back
2 Samuel 15:24–28

His prayer for protection
Psalm 61:1–8

David on the Mount of Olives
2 Samuel 15:29–30

David's prayer for help
Psalm 3:1–8

His cry of anguish
Psalm 22:1–18

For Thought and **Contemplation**

David's response to the conspiracy against him was not to wallow in self-pity, but to draw from it the lessons that would make him a better servant of the Lord. When we see God's hand in all events, then we shall see all events in God's hand.

"This is what the Lord says – your Redeemer, the Holy One of Israel: 'I am the Lord your God, who teaches you what is best for you, who directs you in the way you should go.'" (Isa. 48:17)

Heart to Heart

Section 4

David and his soldiers were trained in the knowledge of warfare so they could overcome God's enemies and see His rule extended throughout the land. You are being trained in the knowledge of God's Word to overcome doubt and opposition and see God working in and through you to extend Christ's kingdom. As a soldier of Christ remain faithful to your commitment to read through the Bible - the best is yet to come!

Visit the web site: **www.cover2cover.org**

In this section

Absalom's rebellion against David
The initial preparations for the Temple
David's praise and prayers
The dedication of Solomon's Temple
The wealth and wisdom of Solomon

DAY **122** — Absalom's advisors

David's prayer and praise
Psalm 22:19-31

Man's wickedness
Psalm 14:1-7, 53:1-6

David and Hushai
2 Samuel 15:31-37

David and Ziba
2 Samuel 16:1-4

Shimei curses David
2 Samuel 16:5-14

David cries to God
Psalm 39:1-13

Absalom enters Jerusalem
2 Samuel 16:15-23

Ahithophel and Hushai advise Absalom
2 Samuel 17:1-14

David escapes
2 Samuel 17:15-24

2 Samuel 15:31-37

³¹Now David had been told, "Ahithophel is among the conspirators with Absalom." So David prayed, "O Lord, turn Ahithophel's counsel into foolishness."
³²When David arrived at the summit, where people used to worship God, Hushai the Arkite was there to meet him, his robe torn and dust on his head. ³³David said to him, "If you go with me, you will be a burden to me. ³⁴But if you return to the city and say to Absalom, 'I will be your servant, O king; I was your father's servant in the past, but now I will be your servant,' then you can help me by frustrating Ahithophel's advice. ³⁵Won't the priests Zadok and Abiathar be there with you? Tell them anything you hear in the king's palace. ³⁶Their two sons, Ahimaaz son of Zadok and Jonathan son of Abiathar, are there with them. Send them to me with anything you hear."
³⁷So David's friend Hushai arrived at Jerusalem as Absalom was entering the city.

For Thought and **Contemplation**

How do you feel when you are ridiculed or abused? David did not allow Shimei's cursing to provoke him to anger, but viewed it as a "divine reproof". How much easier it is to stand up to life when we can make all things serve.

"Blessed are you when people insult you, persecute you and falsely say all kinds of evil against you because of me. Rejoice and be glad, because great is your reward in heaven …" (Matt. 5:11-12)

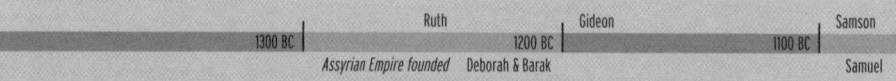

Absalom pursues David

DAY **123**

Psalm 4:1–8

¹Answer me when I call to you,
  O my righteous God.
 Give me relief from my distress;
  be merciful to me and hear my prayer.
²How long, O men, will you turn my glory into shame?
 How long will you love delusions and seek false gods?   *Selah*
³Know that the Lord has set apart the godly for himself;
 the Lord will hear when I call to him.
⁴In your anger do not sin;
 when you are on your beds,
  search your hearts and be silent.
                              Selah
⁵Offer right sacrifices
 and trust in the Lord.
⁶Many are asking, "Who can show us any good?"
 Let the light of your face shine upon us, O Lord.
⁷You have filled my heart with greater joy
 than when their grain and new wine abound.
⁸I will lie down and sleep in peace,
 for you alone, O Lord,
 make me dwell in safety.

David's prayer for help	Psalm 4:1–8
Absalom pursues David	2 Samuel 17:25–26
David is provided for	2 Samuel 17:27–29
The prayer of an exiled man	Psalm 42:1–11, 43:1–5
David's prayer after his betrayal	Psalm 55:1–23
An old man's prayer	Psalm 71:1–24
David's prayer for help	Psalm 28:1–9, 143:1–12
His praises to God	Psalm 40:1–12

For Thought and **Contemplation**

Someone has said that there are two ways of handling life's problems: we can either let them drive us to despair – or drive us to prayer. David learned how to turn his irritations into intercessions. Have you?

"... My grace is sufficient for you, for my power is made perfect in weakness."
(2 Cor. 12:8–9)

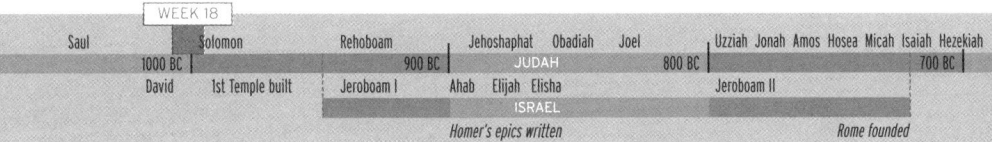

DAY **124**

The Battle of Mount Ephraim

David's prayer for help
Psalm 40:13–17, 70:1–5

His prayer of praise
Psalm 27:1–14

His cry for help
Psalm 69:1–36

A prayer for help
Psalm 120:1–7

The Lord our protector
Psalm 121:1–8

Absalom is slain
2 Samuel 18:1–18

2 Samuel 18:9–14

⁹Now Absalom happened to meet David's men. He was riding his mule, and as the mule went under the thick branches of a large oak, Absalom's head got caught in the tree. He was left hanging in mid-air, while the mule he was riding kept on going. ¹⁰When one of the men saw this, he told Joab, "I have just seen Absalom hanging in an oak tree." ¹¹Joab said to the man who had told him this, "What! You saw him? Why didn't you strike him to the ground right there? Then I would have had to give you ten shekels of silver and a warrior's belt." ¹²But the man replied, "Even if a thousand shekels were weighed out into my hands, I would not lift my hand against the king's son. In our hearing the king commanded you and Abishai and Ittai, 'Protect the young man Absalom for my sake.' ¹³And if I had put my life in jeopardy – and nothing is hidden from the king – you would have kept your distance from me." ¹⁴Joab said, "I'm not going to wait like this for you." So he took three javelins in his hand and plunged them into Absalom's heart ...

For Thought and **Contemplation**

How ironic that Absalom's glory – a head of hair, from which seven pounds in weight was trimmed annually – proved to be the cause of his death. Be careful about your *strengths* – they may turn out to be your greatest weaknesses.

"That is why, for Christ's sake, I delight in weaknesses, in insults, in hardships, in persecutions, in difficulties. For when I am weak, then I am strong."
(2 Cor. 12:10)

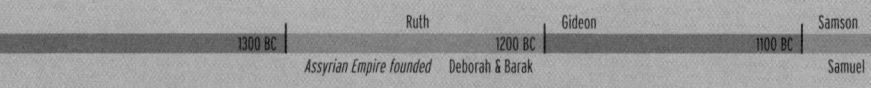

David restored to the throne

DAY **125**

2 Samuel 19:11–15

[11]"King David sent this message to Zadok and Abiathar, the priests: "Ask the elders of Judah, 'Why should you be the last to bring the king back to his palace, since what is being said throughout Israel has reached the king at his quarters? [12]You are my brothers, my own flesh and blood. So why should you be the last to bring back the king?' [13]And say to Amasa, 'Are you not my own flesh and blood? May God deal with me, be it ever so severely, if from now on you are not the commander of my army in place of Joab.'"
[14]He won over the hearts of all the men of Judah as though they were one man. They sent word to the king, "Return, you and all your men." [15]Then the king returned and went as far as the Jordan ...

David learns of Absalom's death
2 Samuel 18:19–33

Prayer for justice
Psalm 10:1–18

Joab reproaches David
2 Samuel 19:1–8

David's praise of Jerusalem
Psalm 122:1–9

David returns to Jerusalem
2 Samuel 19:9–15

He pardons Shimei
2 Samuel 19:16–23

A song of praise
Psalm 92:1–15

David and Mephibosheth
2 Samuel 19:24–30

For Thought and **Contemplation**

"The true measure of a person," said someone, "is seen not only in their readiness to ask forgiveness of those against whom they have sinned, but in their willingness to forgive those who have sinned against them." By that standard, David was great. How about you?

"'And when you stand praying, if you hold anything against anyone, forgive him, so that your Father in heaven may forgive you your sins.'" (Mk. 11:25)

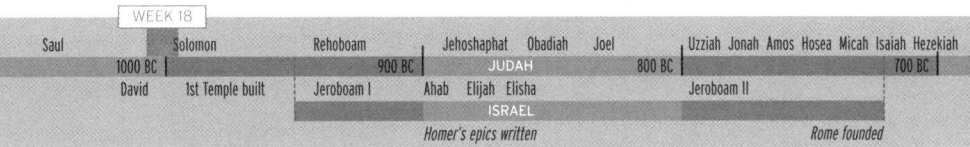

DAY 126 — Israel and Judah quarrel

David and Barzillai
2 Samuel 19:31–40

Israel quarrels with Judah
2 Samuel 19:41–43

Sheba's rebellion
2 Samuel 20:1–3

Joab kills Amasa
2 Samuel 20:4–12

Sheba seeks refuge but is killed
2 Samuel 20:13–22

David's officers
2 Samuel 20:23–26

The Gibeonites avenged
2 Samuel 21:1–9

Rizpah's care
2 Samuel 21:10–14

David honours God's majesty
Psalm 29:1–11

His thanksgiving
Psalm 65:1–13

2 Samuel 19:41–43

⁴¹"Soon all the men of Israel were coming to the king and saying to him, "Why did our brothers, the men of Judah, steal the king away and bring him and his household across the Jordan, together with all his men?"

⁴²All the men of Judah answered the men of Israel, "We did this because the king is closely related to us. Why are you angry about it? Have we eaten any of the king's provisions? Have we taken anything for ourselves?"

⁴³Then the men of Israel answered the men of Judah, "We have ten shares in the king; and besides, we have a greater claim on David than you have. So why do you treat us with contempt? Were we not the first to speak of bringing back our king?"

But the men of Judah responded even more harshly than the men of Israel.

For Thought and **Contemplation**

The quarrel between the men of Israel and the men of Judah (whose words were "fiercer than the words of the men of Israel" 2 Sam. 19:43, AV) might have been avoided if they had acted according to the key truth in today's verse. Try it the next time you find yourself on the verge of a quarrel.

"A gentle answer turns away wrath, but a harsh word stirs up anger." (Prov. 15:1)

a bird's eye view of 1 Kings

Place in the Bible	Main Characters	Special Features
Eleventh Old Testament book; sixth book of history.	David, Solomon, Elijah, Ahab.	1 Kings is the story of two nations: Judah and Israel. The building of Solomon's temple is followed by the division of David's kingdom into two. Elijah dramatically confronts the prophets of Baal who play a major role in the country's spiritual life.

David numbers the people

DAY 127

1 Chronicles 21:1–7

¹Satan rose up against Israel and incited David to take a census of Israel. ²So David said to Joab and the commanders of the troops, "Go and count the Israelites from Beersheba to Dan. Then report back to me so that I may know how many there are."

³But Joab replied, "May the Lord multiply his troops a hundred times over. My lord the king, are they not all my lord's subjects? Why does my lord want to do this? Why should he bring guilt on Israel?"

⁴The king's word, however, overruled Joab; so Joab left and went throughout Israel and then came back to Jerusalem. ⁵Joab reported the number of the fighting men to David: In all Israel there were one million one hundred thousand men who could handle a sword, including four hundred and seventy thousand in Judah.

⁶But Joab did not include Levi and Benjamin in the numbering, because the king's command was repulsive to him. ⁷This command was also evil in the sight of God; so he punished Israel.

Battles with the Philistines
2 Samuel 21:15–22, 1 Chronicles 20:4–8

David speaks of man's wickedness and God's goodness
Psalm 36:1–12

David numbers the people
2 Samuel 24:1–9, 1 Chronicles 21:1–6

Numbering hindered
1 Chronicles 27:23–24

David's choice
2 Samuel 24:10–14, 1 Chronicles 21:7–13

The pestilence
2 Samuel 24:15–17, 1 Chronicles 21:14–17

David's sacrifice
2 Samuel 24:18–25, 1 Chronicles 21:18–30

For Thought and Contemplation

In the light of David's sacrificial giving, examine your own attitude to this important matter. Some give like a sponge – only when they are squeezed. Others give like Moses' rock – only when they are hit. But others give like a flower opening up to the sun – they *delight* to give. The latter was David's method. What's yours?

"Each man should give what he has decided in his heart to give, not reluctantly or under compulsion, for God loves a cheerful giver." (2 Cor. 9:7)

Jesus and the Book

The Queen of Sheba mentions Solomon's wisdom (1 Kings 10:8). Solomon is taken to be a "type" of Christ who "has become for us wisdom from God" (1 Cor. 1:30).

Teaching

After the division of the kingdom (chapters 12 to 14), the book traces the history of the kings of Judah, who ruled from Jerusalem, and the kings of Israel, who ruled from Samaria. It teaches that failure to obey God led to their destruction.

A Verse to Remember

"God gave Solomon wisdom and very great insight, and a breadth of understanding as measureless as the sand on the seashore" (1 Kings 4:29).

DAY 128 — Solomon is made king

David's thanksgiving
Psalm 30:1–12

A song of praise
Psalm 33:1–22

David's humble trust
Psalm 131:1–3

David's old age
1 Kings 1:1–4

Adonijah's plot
1 Kings 1:5–9

David makes Solomon king
1 Kings 1:10–37

Solomon is anointed
1 Kings 1:38–40

The supreme ruler
Psalm 47:1–9

Adonijah's submission
1 Kings 1:41–53

1 Kings 1:32–37

³²King David said, "Call in Zadok the priest, Nathan the prophet and Benaiah son of Jehoiada." When they came before the king, ³³he said to them: "Take your lord's servants with you and set Solomon my son on my own mule and take him down to Gihon. ³⁴There shall Zadok the priest and Nathan the prophet anoint him king over Israel. Blow the trumpet and shout, 'Long live King Solomon!' ³⁵Then you are to go up with him, and he is to come and sit on my throne and reign in my place. I have appointed him ruler over Israel and Judah." ³⁶Benaiah son of Jehoiada answered the king, "Amen! May the Lord, the God of my lord the king, so declare it. ³⁷As the Lord was with my lord the king, so may he be with Solomon to make his throne even greater than the throne of my lord King David!"

For Thought and **Contemplation**

The knowledge that David's son, Solomon, had come to the throne of Israel caused the heart of every true Israelite to rejoice. But here is a reason for greater joy: Jesus – "the son of David" – has ascended a throne from which He will never be deposed. Hallelujah! Our God reigns!

"... the appearing of our Lord Jesus Christ, which God will bring about in his own time – God, the blessed and only Ruler, the King of kings and Lord of lords ..." (1 Tim. 6:14–15)

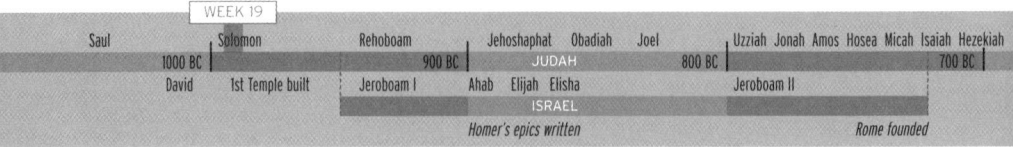

Samuel
– The circuit-riding preacher

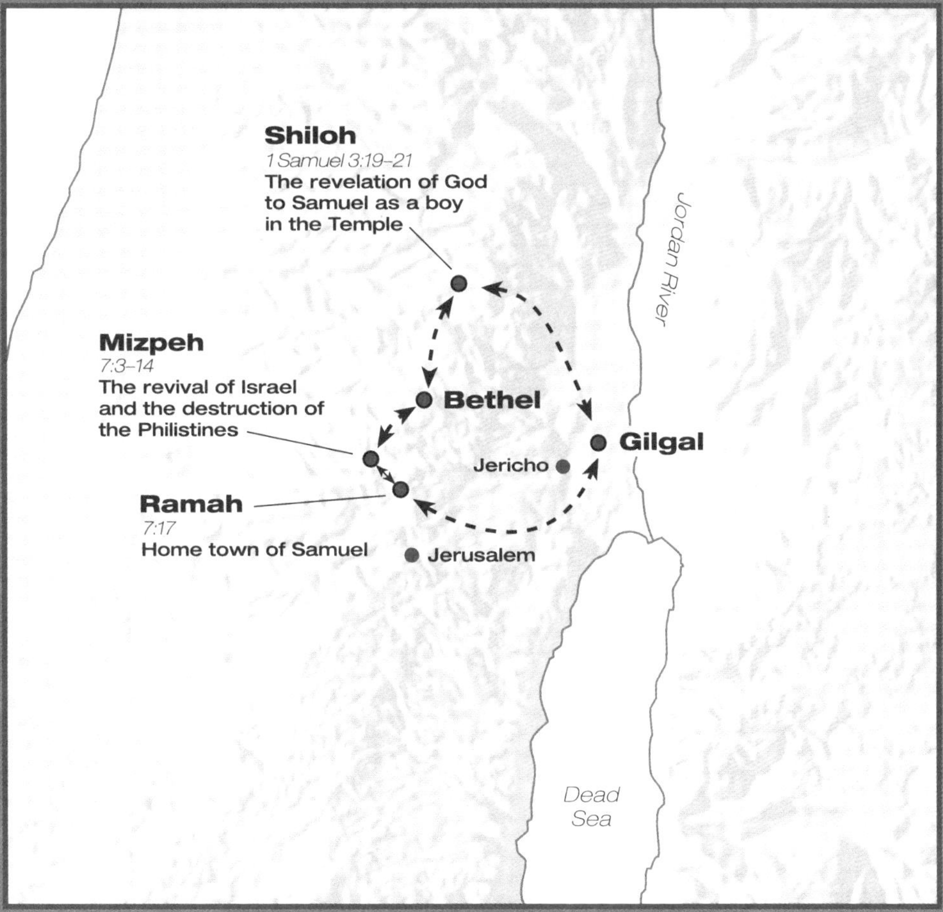

Shiloh
1 Samuel 3:19–21
The revelation of God to Samuel as a boy in the Temple

Mizpeh
7:3–14
The revival of Israel and the destruction of the Philistines

Ramah
7:17
Home town of Samuel

Bethel

Gilgal

Jericho

Jerusalem

Jordan River

Dead Sea

DAY 129 — David's preparations for the Temple

David's preparations
1 Chronicles 22:1–5

His instructions to Solomon
1 Chronicles 22:6–16

His commands to the princes
1 Chronicles 22:17–19

The Levites and their duties
1 Chronicles 23:2–6, 24–32, 24:20–31

Divisions of priests
1 Chronicles 24:1–19

Singers and musicians
1 Chronicles 25:1–31

1 Chronicles 22:1–5

¹Then David said, "The house of the Lord God is to be here, and also the altar of burnt offering for Israel."

²So David gave orders to assemble the aliens living in Israel, and from among them he appointed stone-cutters to prepare dressed stone for building the house of God. ³He provided a large amount of iron to make nails for the doors of the gateways and for the fittings, and more bronze than could be weighed. ⁴He also provided more cedar logs than could be counted, for the Sidonians and Tyrians had brought large numbers of them to David.

⁵David said, "My son Solomon is young and inexperienced, and the house to be built for the Lord should be of great magnificence and fame and splendour in the sight of all the nations. Therefore I will make preparations for it." So David made extensive preparations before his death.

For Thought and **Contemplation**

In Christ's Church, as in Solomon's Temple, everyone has a place and a purpose. Have you discovered your place in the Body of Christ?* If not, you may end up trying to do someone else's job instead of your own. And that's frustrating!

*For more guidance on this subject, see the chart 'Discovering Your Basic Gift', available from CWR.

"… in Christ we who are many form one body, and each member belongs to all the others. We have different gifts, according to the grace given us …" (Rom. 12:5–6)

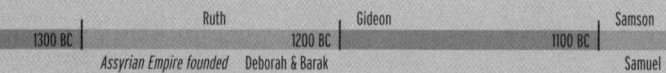

Temple duties

DAY **130**

Psalm 145:1–8

¹'I will exalt you, my God the King;
   I will praise your name for ever and ever.
²Every day I will praise you
   and extol your name for ever and ever.
³Great is the Lord and most worthy of praise;
   his greatness no-one can fathom.
⁴One generation will commend your works to another;
   they will tell of your mighty acts.
⁵They will speak of the glorious splendour of your majesty,
   and I will meditate on your wonderful works.
⁶They will tell of the power of your awesome works,
   and I will proclaim your great deeds.
⁷They will celebrate your abundant goodness
   and joyfully sing of your righteousness.
⁸The Lord is gracious and compassionate,
   slow to anger and rich in love ...

The temple guards
1 Chronicles 26:1–19

The temple treasurers
1 Chronicles 26:20–28

Administrative duties
1 Chronicles 26:29–32

David's military force
1 Chronicles 27:1–15

Chiefs of the 12 tribes
1 Chronicles 27:16–22

David's overseers and officers
1 Chronicles 27:25–34

David assembles and addresses the people
1 Chronicles 28:1–10

Solomon is made king
1 Chronicles 23:1

David's hymn of praise
Psalm 145:1–8

For Thought and **Contemplation**

David wisely provided not only for worship, but also for war. The spiritual life involves not only benedictions, but battles. Alert Christians learn to worship with their armour on!

"Finally, be strong in the Lord and in his mighty power. Put on the full armour of God so that you can take your stand against the devil's schemes."
(Eph. 6:10–11)

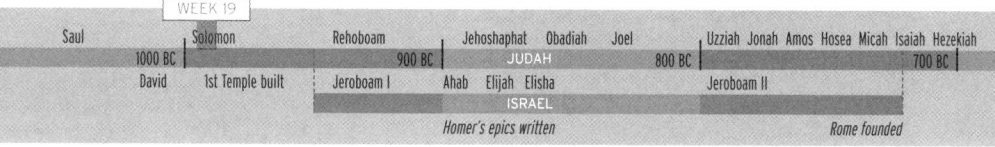

DAY 131 — David's instructions

David's hymn of praise
Psalm 145:9–21

David's directions concerning the temple
1 Chronicles 28:11–21

In praise of the Creator
Psalm 104:1–35

David speaks of God's protection
Psalm 124:1–8

His praises brotherly love
Psalm 133:1–3

His prayer for help
Psalm 86:1–17

His instructions regarding giving
1 Chronicles 29:1–9

His thanksgiving
1 Chronicles 29:10–13

1 Chronicles 29:1–5

¹Then King David said to the whole assembly: "My son Solomon, the one whom God has chosen, is young and inexperienced. The task is great, because this palatial structure is not for man but for the Lord God. ²With all my resources I have provided for the temple of my God – gold for the gold work, silver for the silver, bronze for the bronze, iron for the iron and wood for the wood, as well as onyx for the settings, turquoise, stones of various colours, and all kinds of fine stone and marble – all of these in large quantities. ³Besides, in my devotion to the temple of my God I now give my personal treasures of gold and silver for the temple of my God, over and above everything I have provided for this holy temple: ⁴three thousand talents of gold (gold of Ophir) and seven thousand talents of refined silver, for the overlaying of the walls of the buildings, ⁵for the gold work and the silver work, and for all the work to be done by the craftsmen. Now, who is willing to consecrate himself today to the Lord?"

For Thought and **Contemplation**

David had only to contemplate the glories of creation and his heart would swell in endless praise. Ever tried to compose a psalm? Try it today. Meditate on God's love and goodness as it relates to your life, and then compose your own personal paean of praise.

"Speak to one another with psalms, hymns and spiritual songs. Sing and make music in your heart to the Lord, always giving thanks to God the Father for everything, in the name of our Lord Jesus Christ." (Eph. 5:19–20)

a bird's eye view of 2 Chronicles

Place in the Bible	Main Characters	Special Features
Fourteenth Old Testament book; ninth book of history	Solomon, Queen of Sheba.	The reigns of twenty-one kings and one queen are recounted. 2 Chronicles starts with Solomon – especially emphasising the building and finishing of the temple, and ends with Cyrus' decree permitting the exiled Jews of Babylon to return home.

David's final words

DAY **132**

2 Samuel 23:1–5

¹These are the last words of David:
"The oracle of David son of Jesse,
  the oracle of the man exalted by the Most High,
  the man anointed by the God of Jacob,
  Israel's singer of songs:
²The Spirit of the Lord spoke through me;
  his word was on my tongue.
³The God of Israel spoke,
  the Rock of Israel said to me:
'When one rules over men in righteousness,
  when he rules in the fear of God,
⁴he is like the light of morning at sunrise
  on a cloudless morning,
  like the brightness after rain
  that brings the grass from the earth.'
⁵Is not my house right with God?
  Has he not made with me an everlasting covenant,
  arranged and secured in every part?
  Will he not bring to fruition my salvation
  and grant me my every desire? ..."

David's prayer	1 Chronicles 29:14–19
His prayer for the king	Psalm 72:1–20
Solomon enthroned	1 Chronicles 29:20–22
David's last words	2 Samuel 23:1–7, 1 Kings 2:1–9
His death	1 Kings 2:10, 1 Chronicles 29:28–30
Unclassified psalms of David	Psalm 37:1–40, 138:1–8

For Thought and **Contemplation**

A great man's final words are usually carefully noted and recorded for posterity. This is how it was with Moses, David, Elijah – and with many others. You have read David's last words – now read the last words of Jesus. Are they saying something to you – today?

"... you will receive power when the Holy Spirit comes on you; and you will be my witnesses in Jerusalem, and in all Judea and Samaria, and to the ends of the earth." (Acts 1:8)

Jesus and the Book

In chapter 9 the Queen of Sheba visited Solomon and was overwhelmed by his wisdom and wealth. In Matthew 12:42, speaking of Himself, Jesus says, "... now one greater than Solomon is here."

Teaching

The book's theme is the consequences of keeping or breaking God's covenant. God rewards those who faithfully keep His laws. The book outlines many attributes of God: He is great (2:6), good (5:13), just (12:6), and faithful (21:7).

A Verse to Remember

"'... if my people, who are called by my name, will humble themselves and pray and seek my face and turn from their wicked ways, then will I hear from heaven and will forgive their sin and will heal their land.'" (2 Chron. 7:14)

DAY 133 — King Solomon

Solomon's reign begins
1 Kings 2:12, 1 Chronicles 29:23–25, 2 Chronicles 1:1

Adonijah put to death
1 Kings 2:13–25

Abiathar banished
1 Kings 2:26–27

Reign of Solomon 985–945 BC

Joab put to death
1 Kings 2:28–34

Solomon's instructions to Shimei
1 Kings 2:35–38

Solomon and Pharaoh's daughter
1 Kings 3:1

A royal wedding song
Psalm 45:1–17

Solomon's love of God
1 Kings 3:2–3

His sacrifice
1 Kings 3:4, 2 Chronicles 1:2–3, 5–6

His prayer for wisdom
1 Kings 3:5–15, 2 Chronicles 1:7–12

His return to Jerusalem
2 Chronicles 1:13

2 Chronicles 1:7–12

⁷That night God appeared to Solomon and said to him, "Ask for whatever you want me to give you."
⁸Solomon answered God, "You have shown great kindness to David my father and have made me king in his place. ⁹Now, Lord God, let your promise to my father David be confirmed, for you have made me king over a people who are as numerous as the dust of the earth. ¹⁰Give me wisdom and knowledge, that I may lead this people, for who is able to govern this great people of yours?"
¹¹God said to Solomon, "Since this is your heart's desire and you have not asked for wealth, riches or honour, nor for the death of your enemies, and since you have not asked for a long life but for wisdom and knowledge to govern my people over whom I have made you king, ¹²therefore wisdom and knowledge will be given you. And I will also give you wealth, riches and honour, such as no king who was before you ever had and none after you will have."

For Thought and Contemplation

Great though Solomon became in wisdom, riches and honour, the most significant thing that was ever said about him was that "he loved the Lord" (1 Kings 3:3, AV). Would those words be true of you if they were written on your epitaph?

"Keep yourselves in God's love as you wait for the mercy of our Lord Jesus Christ to bring you to eternal life." (Jude v. 21)

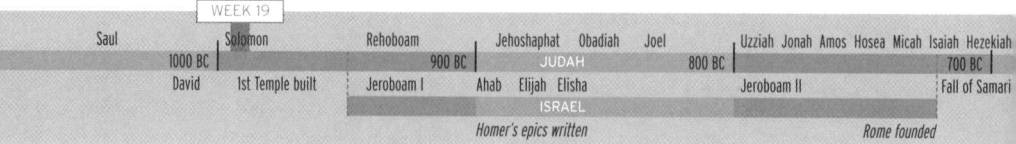

Solomon

SOLOMON'S PRAYER for wisdom assured his place in Israel's history, for God generously answered that request. Wisdom in the Old Testament has a very practical emphasis – the skilful application of knowledge to daily life. The ancient Near East in Solomon's day, and before, was full of wise men and seekers of wisdom. Egyptian and Mesopotamian sages have left us their writings, but Solomon surpassed them all. One is always amazed how Solomon the wise man, the Temple builder, the king of God's choosing, could also become Solomon the despot and backslider. Wisdom, wealth, and wives were a potent combination that Solomon could not handle.

Solomon's reign has sometimes been called the Augustan age of the Jewish nation. But Solomon was not only its Augustus – he was also, according to tradition, its Aristotle. With the accession of Solomon, a new world of thought was opened to the Israelites. We find the first beginnings of that wider view which ended, at last, when Judaism was eclipsed by the coming of Christ, "in whom are hidden all the treasures of wisdom and knowledge." (Col. 2:3).

DAY 134 — Preparations for building the Temple

Solomon's judgment
1 Kings 3:16–28

Hadad's response to David's death
1 Kings 11:21–22

Solomon's court
1 Kings 4:1–19

His daily provision
1 Kings 4:22–23, 27–28

His agreement with Hiram
1 Kings 5:1–12, 7:13–14

His treaty with Hiram
2 Chronicles 2:1, 3–16

His workmen
1 Kings 5:13–18, 2 Chronicles 2:2, 17–18

1 Kings 5:13–18

¹³King Solomon conscripted labourers from all Israel – thirty thousand men. ¹⁴He sent them off to Lebanon in shifts of ten thousand a month, so that they spent one month in Lebanon and two months at home. Adoniram was in charge of the forced labour. ¹⁵Solomon had seventy thousand carriers and eighty thousand stonecutters in the hills, ¹⁶as well as thirty-three hundred foremen who supervised the project and directed the workmen. ¹⁷At the king's command they removed from the quarry large blocks of quality stone to provide a foundation of dressed stone for the temple. ¹⁸The craftsmen of Solomon and Hiram and the men of Gebal cut and prepared the timber and stone for the building of the temple.

For Thought and **Contemplation**

Building a temple for the worship of God was a colossal task. It involved careful planning, skilful negotiation and great faith. But Solomon discovered, as will you, that God's work done in God's way will receive God's support.

"May the God of peace ... equip you with everything good for doing his will, and may he work in us what is pleasing to him, through Jesus Christ, to whom be glory for ever and ever ..."
(Heb. 13:20–21)

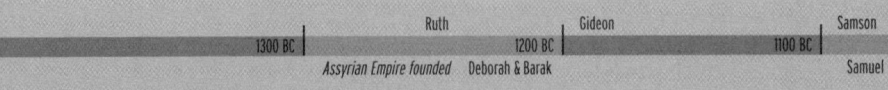

The Temple is built

DAY **135**

1 Kings 6:1–6

¹In the four hundred and eightieth year after the Israelites had come out of Egypt, in the fourth year of Solomon's reign over Israel, in the month of Ziv, the second month, he began to build the temple of the Lord. ²The temple that King Solomon built for the Lord was sixty cubits long, twenty wide and thirty high. ³The portico at the front of the main hall of the temple extended the width of the temple, that is twenty cubits, and projected ten cubits from the front of the temple. ⁴He made narrow clerestory windows in the temple. ⁵Against the walls of the main hall and inner sanctuary he built a structure around the building, in which there were side rooms. ⁶The lowest floor was five cubits wide, the middle floor six cubits and the third floor seven. He made offset ledges around the outside of the temple so that nothing would be inserted into the temple walls.

Shimei's execution
1 Kings 2:39–46

A mother's advice
Proverbs 31:1–9

God's ideal woman
Proverbs 31:10–31

The construction of the Temple
1 Kings 6:1–10, 14–37, 2 Chronicles 3:1–14

For Thought and **Contemplation**

Solomon's temple was constructed not only with infinite care, but with the minimum of noise: "no hammer, chisel or any other iron tool was heard" (1 Kings 6:7). Clamour and frenzy hinder rather than foster spiritual growth. God's kingdom develops, not with great noise and the fanfare of trumpets, but quietly, effortlessly and silently.

"... 'In repentance and rest is your salvation, in quietness and trust is your strength ...'" (Isa. 30:15)

DAY 136 — The Temple furnishings

The reward of obedience
Psalm 128:1–6, 1 Kings 6:38

Solomon's buildings
1 Kings 7:1–12

Temple furnishings
1 Kings 7:15–50, 2 Chronicles 4:1–22

1 Kings 7:15–22

¹⁵He cast two bronze pillars, each eighteen cubits high and twelve cubits round, by line. ¹⁶He also made two capitals of cast bronze to set on the tops of the pillars; each capital was five cubits high. ¹⁷A network of interwoven chains festooned the capitals on top of the pillars, seven for each capital. ¹⁸He made pomegranates in two rows encircling each network to decorate the capitals on top of the pillars. He did the same for each capital. ¹⁹The capitals on top of the pillars in the portico were in the shape of lilies, four cubits high. ²⁰On the capitals of both pillars, above the bowl-shaped part next to the network, were the two hundred pomegranates in rows all around. ²¹He erected the pillars at the portico of the temple. The pillar to the south he named Jakin and the one to the north Boaz. ²²The capitals on top were in the shape of lilies. And so the work on the pillars was completed.

For Thought and **Contemplation**

The priests who ministered in Solomon's temple were required to cleanse themselves frequently as they ministered before the Lord. As God's "royal priesthood", we, too, must take advantage of the full means provided for our cleansing, the blood of Christ and the water of the Word.

"... Christ loved the church and gave himself up for her to make her holy, cleansing her by the washing with water through the word ..." (Eph. 5:25–26)

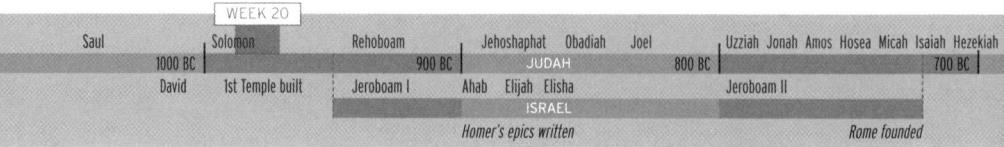

Solomon's Temple

A PERMANENT RESTING PLACE for the Ark of the Covenant. Similar to the tabernacle, but the Holy Place and the Holy of Holies were doubled in size. Known in the ancient world for its breathtaking beauty and craftsmanship. It stood for four hundred years until destroyed by the Babylonians.

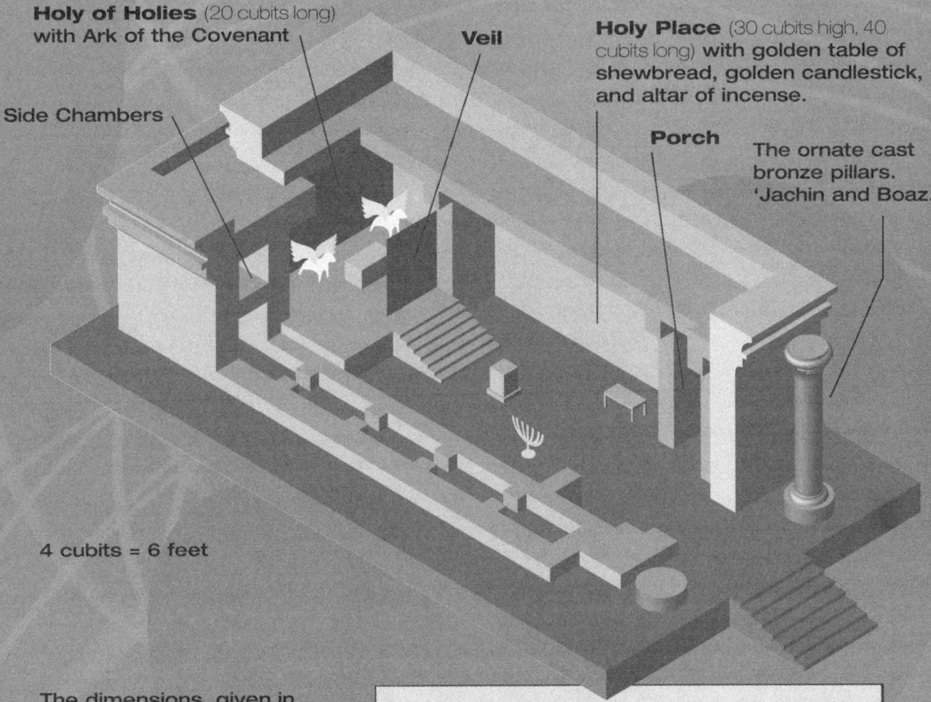

Holy of Holies (20 cubits long) with Ark of the Covenant

Veil

Holy Place (30 cubits high, 40 cubits long) with golden table of shewbread, golden candlestick, and altar of incense.

Side Chambers

Porch

The ornate cast bronze pillars. 'Jachin and Boaz.'

4 cubits = 6 feet

The dimensions, given in Scripture, are usually understood to refer to the inner measurements of the rooms.

The Temple

Altar

Laver

"The temple that King Solomon built for the Lord was sixty cubits long, twenty wide and thirty high." (1 Kings 6:2)

David wanted to build a permanent house where the people could worship God. He made very full plans for the building of a Temple, but, because many people had been killed in the battles he had fought against Israel's enemies, God did not allow him to go ahead. Instead, Solomon, his son, was given the job.

DAY 137 — The dedication of the Temple

Final completion
1 Kings 7:51, 2 Chronicles 5:1

The dedication of the Temple
1 Kings 8:1–11, 2 Chronicles 5:2–14

Dedication of Temple 972 BC

A prayer of thanks
Psalm 118:1–4, 29

The one true God
Psalm 115:1–18

A call to praise God
Psalm 134:1–3, 135:21

A hymn of thanksgiving
Psalm 136:1–26

Solomon's address
1 Kings 8:12–21. 2 Chronicles 6:1–11

1 Kings 8:3–9

³When all the elders of Israel had arrived, the priests took up the ark, ⁴and they brought up the ark of the Lord and the Tent of Meeting and all the sacred furnishings in it. The priests and Levites carried them up, ⁵and King Solomon and the entire assembly of Israel that had gathered about him were before the ark, sacrificing so many sheep and cattle that they could not be recorded or counted.
⁶The priests then brought the ark of the Lord's covenant to its place in the inner sanctuary of the temple, the Most Holy Place, and put it beneath the wings of the cherubim. ⁷The cherubim spread their wings over the place of the ark and overshadowed the ark and its carrying poles. ⁸These poles were so long that their ends could be seen from the Holy Place in front of the inner sanctuary, but not from outside the Holy Place; and they are still there today. ⁹There was nothing in the ark except the two stone tablets that Moses had placed in it at Horeb, where the Lord made a covenant with the Israelites after they came out of Egypt.

For Thought and Contemplation

God required not only that the temple be built for Him but also *dedicated* to Him. Dedication goes further than hoping God will accept what we offer – it gathers up those hopes in a distinct and definite commitment. Don't just hope God will use you – dedicate your talents to Him – now.

"…. I urge you, brothers, in view of God's mercy, to offer your bodies as living sacrifices, holy and pleasing to God – this is your spiritual act of worship." (Rom. 12:1)

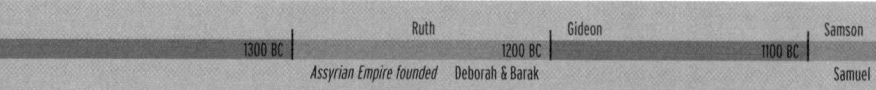

Solomon's prayer

DAY **138**

1 Kings 8:22–26

²²Then Solomon stood before the altar of the Lord in front of the whole assembly of Israel, spread out his hands towards heaven ²³and said:

"O Lord, God of Israel, there is no God like you in heaven above or on earth below – you who keep your covenant of love with your servants who continue wholeheartedly in your way. ²⁴You have kept your promise to your servant David my father; with your mouth you have promised and with your hand you have fulfilled it – as it is today.

²⁵"Now Lord, God of Israel, keep for your servant David my father the promises you made to him when you said, 'You shall never fail to have a man to sit before me on the throne of Israel, if only your sons are careful in all they do to walk before me as you have done.' ²⁶And now, O God of Israel, let your word that you promised your servant David my father come true."

Solomon reminds God of His promises
1 Kings 8:22–26, 2 Chronicles 6:12–17

He pleads for forgiveness
1 Kings 8:27–30, 2 Chronicles 6:18–21

He prays for God's justice
1 Kings 8:31–32, 2 Chronicles 6:22–23

He prays for mercy
1 Kings 8:33–40, 2 Chronicles 6:24–31

He asks God to answer the foreigner's prayer
1 Kings 8:41–43, 2 Chronicles 6:32–33

Prayer for victory
1 Kings 8:44–45, 2 Chronicles 6:34–35

Prayer for Israelites
1 Kings 8:46–53, 2 Chronicles 6:36–39

His final petitions
2 Chronicles 6:40–42

Solomon's blessing and exhortation
1 Kings 8:54–61

For Thought and **Contemplation**

The prayers of God's servants in the Old Testament, Solomon's included, contain a common characteristic – spiritual boldness. This boldness stemmed from their knowledge that God was under an obligation to fulfil his promises (see 1 Kings 8:25). Follow this principle, and it could add a whole new dimension to your prayer life.

"Let us then approach the throne of grace with confidence, so that we may receive mercy and find grace to help us in our time of need." (Heb. 4:16)

DAY 139 — Building programme completed

The glory of the Lord
2 Chronicles 7:1–3

Solomon's peace-offerings
1 Kings 8:62–66, 2 Chronicles 7:4–10

God, the supreme King
Psalm 99:1–9

A hymn of praise
Psalm 100:1–5

Building programme finished
1 Kings 9:1, 2 Chronicles 7:11

God warns Solomon
1 Kings 9:2–9, 2 Chronicles 7:12–22

Solomon and Hiram
1 Kings 9:10–14, 2 Chronicles 8:1–2

Hamath Zobah conquered
2 Chronicles 8:3

Solomon's wife's house
1 Kings 9:24, 2 Chronicles 8:11

Love's beginning
Song of Solomon 1:1–17

Psalm 100:1–5

'Shout for joy to the Lord, all the earth.
²Worship the Lord with gladness;
    come before him with joyful songs.
³Know that the Lord is God.
    It is he who made us, and we are his;
    we are his people, the sheep of his pasture.

⁴Enter his gates with thanksgiving
    and his courts with praise;
    give thanks to him and praise his name.
⁵For the Lord is good and his love endures for ever;
    his faithfulness continues through all generations.

For Thought and **Contemplation**

Another evidence of Solomon's wisdom was the fact that he had his priorities in the right order – he build a house for God before he built one for himself. When we put God *first*, then prosperity and blessing follow. Whose interests come first in your life? Yours – or God's?

"'... seek first his kingdom and his righteousness, and all these things will be given to you as well.'" (Matt. 6:33)

a bird's eye view of Song of Songs

Place in the Bible	**Main Characters**	**Special Features**
Twenty-second Old Testament book; fifth book of poetry and wisdom.	Solomon, Shulammite girl.	A series of love poems.

Bride and bridegroom — DAY 140

Song of Songs 3:1–5

¹All night long on my bed
I looked for the one my heart loves;
I looked for him but did not find him.
²I will get up now and go about the city,
through its streets and squares;
I will search for the one my heart loves.
So I looked for him but did not find him.
³The watchmen found me
as they made their rounds in the city.
"Have you seen the one my heart loves?"
⁴Scarcely had I passed them
when I found the one my heart loves.
I held him and would not let him go
till I had brought him to my mother's house,
to the room of the one who conceived me.
⁵Daughters of Jerusalem, I charge you
by the gazelles and by the does of the field:
Do not arouse or awaken love
until it so desires.

Love's beginning
Song of Songs 2:1–7

Love's absence
Song of Songs 2:8–17, 3:1–5

Love's restoration
Song of Songs 3:6–11, 4:1–16, 5:1

Love delayed
Song of Songs 5:2–16, 6:1–3

Love's fulfilment
Song of Songs 6:4–13, 7:1–13, 8:1–4

Love's triumph
Song of Songs 8:5–14

For Thought and Contemplation

A popular modern conception of "love" is "never having to say you are sorry". This implies that where true love exists, asking forgiveness is unnecessary. But is it? Solomon's bride did not think so. Love means *wanting* to say you are sorry – and saying it.

"Be kind and compassionate to one another, forgiving each other, just as in Christ God forgave you." (Eph. 4:32)

Jesus and the Book
The most famous verse in the Bible states how much God loves everyone: "For God so loved the world that he gave his one and only Son, that whoever believes in him shall not perish but have eternal life" (John 3:16).

Teaching
The beauty and value of love between a woman and a man are joyously depicted. The Song is also a picture of Christ's love for the Church. God's love for His people and their love in return is often compared in Scripture to the love of husband and wife.

A Verse to Remember
"Many waters cannot quench love; rivers cannot wash it away" (Song of Songs 8:7).

DAY 141 — Solomon and the Queen of Sheba

Levy of forced labour
1 Kings 9:20–23 & 15, 2 Chronicles 8:7–10

Building the cities
1 Kings 9:16–19, 2 Chronicles 8:4–6

Burnt offerings
1 Kings 9:25, 2 Chronicles 8:12–16

Solomon's prosperity
1 Kings 9:26–28, 10:22,
2 Chronicles 8:17–18, 9:21

The Queen of Sheba
1 Kings 10:1–13, 2 Chronicles 9:1–12

Solomon's wealth
1 Kings 10:14–21, 27, 23–25,
2 Chronicles 1:15, 9:13–19

1 Kings 10:1–7

¹When the queen of Sheba heard about the fame of Solomon and his relation to the name of the Lord, she came to test him with hard questions. ²Arriving at Jerusalem with a very great caravan – with camels carrying spices, large quantities of gold, and precious stones – she came to Solomon and talked with him about all that she had on her mind. ³Solomon answered all her questions; nothing was too hard for the king to explain to her. ⁴When the queen of Sheba saw all the wisdom of Solomon and the palace he had built, ⁵the food on his table, the seating of his officials, the attending servants in their robes, his cupbearers, and the burnt offerings he made at the temple of the Lord, she was overwhelmed.

⁶She said to the king, "The report I heard in my own country about your achievements and your wisdom is true. ⁷But I did not believe these things until I came and saw with my own eyes. Indeed, not even half was told me; in wisdom and wealth you have far exceeded the report I heard ...

For Thought and **Contemplation**

When the Queen of Sheba saw the magnitude of Solomon's wealth and wisdom, her conclusion was that "not even half was told me". Those who come to know God through His Son Jesus Christ arrive at a similar conclusion. Jesus is such a wonder that the combined reports of all the teachers and preachers who have ever lived cannot do Him justice.

"... 'No eye has seen, no ear has heard, no mind has conceived what God has prepared for those who love him' – but God has revealed it to us by his Spirit." (1 Cor. 2:9–10)

a bird's eye view of **Proverbs**

Place in the Bible
Twentieth Old Testament book; third book of poetry and wisdom.

Special Features
A collection of about nine hundred short, memorable, pithy sayings, concluding with the famous acrostic poem on the ideal wife in chapter 31.

Solomon's wealth and wisdom

DAY **142**

1 Kings 4:29–33

²⁹God gave Solomon wisdom and very great insight, and a breadth of understanding as measureless as the sand on the seashore. ³⁰Solomon's wisdom was greater than the wisdom of all the men of the East, and greater than all the wisdom of Egypt. ³¹He was wiser than any other man, including Ethan the Ezrahite – wiser than Heman, Calcol and Darda, the sons of Mahol. And his fame spread to all the surrounding nations. ³²He spoke three thousand proverbs and his songs numbered a thousand and five. ³³He described plant life, from the cedar of Lebanon to the hyssop that grows out of walls. He also taught about animals and birds, reptiles and fish. ³⁴Men of all nations came to listen to Solomon's wisdom, sent by all the kings of the world, who had heard of his wisdom.

Solomon's wealth
2 Chronicles 9:20, 27, 22–24,
1 Kings 4:26, 10:26, 28–29,
2 Chronicles 1:14, 16–17, 9:25, 28

His kingdom
1 Kings 4:21, 24, 20, 25,
2 Chronicles 9:26

His visitors
1 Kings 4:34

His wisdom
1 Kings 4:29–33

A cry for help
Psalm 88:1–18

A hymn in time of national trouble
Psalm 89:1–52

Value of proverbs
Proverbs 1:1–6

Advice to young men
Proverbs 1:7–19

For Thought and **Contemplation**

If, today, God told you that you could have whatever you wanted – what would you choose? Wealth? Fame? Happiness? Solomon, when faced with that question, chose the greatest of all qualities – *wisdom*. And God was so pleased with his request that He added riches and honour also.

"If any of you lacks wisdom, he should ask God, who gives generously to all without finding fault, and it will be given to him." (Jas. 1:5)

Jesus and the Book

Wisdom is personified in chapter 8 and from the New Testament we also know that wisdom became incarnate in Christ "in whom are hidden all the treasures of wisdom and knowledge" (Col. 2:3).

Teaching

Proverbs chapter 1:2–7 explains the purpose of these proverbs. They can provide the reader with wisdom, discipline and understanding. The fear of the Lord is the starting point for anybody who seeks to become wise.

A Verse to Remember

"The fear of the Lord is the beginning of wisdom, and knowledge of the Holy One is understanding" (Prov. 9:10)

DAY 143 — The wisdom of moral restraint

Virtue of wisdom
Proverbs 1:20–33

Rewards of wisdom
Proverbs 2:1–22

Trusting God's wisdom
Proverbs 3:1–35

Benefits of wisdom
Proverbs 4:1–27

Warning against adultery
Proverbs 5:1–23

Caution about putting up security
Proverbs 6:1–5

Warning against laziness
Proverbs 6:6–11

Things God hates
Proverbs 6:12–19

Proverbs 2:1–10

¹My son, if you accept my words
  and store up my commands within you,
²turning your ear to wisdom
  and applying your heart to understanding,
³and if you call out for insight
  and cry aloud for understanding,
⁴and if you look for it as for silver
  and search for it as for hidden treasure,
⁵then you will understand the fear of the Lord
  and find the knowledge of God.
⁶For the Lord gives wisdom,
  and from his mouth come knowledge and understanding.
⁷He holds victory in store for the upright,
  he is a shield to those whose walk is blameless,
⁸for he guards the course of the just
  and protects the way of his faithful ones.
⁹Then you will understand what is right and just
  and fair – every good path.
¹⁰For wisdom will enter your heart,
  and knowledge will be pleasant to your soul.

For Thought and **Contemplation**

Have you ever reflected on what wisdom really is? "Wisdom," said a great man, "is more than knowledge: knowledge is just knowing things, but wisdom is the ability to put knowledge to its best effect." Ask God once again to help you "wise up".

"... the wisdom that comes from heaven is first of all pure; then peace-loving, considerate, submissive, full of mercy and good fruit, impartial and sincere." (Jas 3:17)

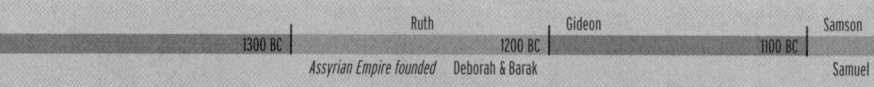

The importance of wisdom

DAY 144

Proverbs 8:1–9

¹Does not wisdom call out?
  Does not understanding raise her voice?
²On the heights along the way,
  where the paths meet, she takes her stand;
³beside the gates leading into the city,
  at the entrances, she cries aloud:
⁴"To you, O men, I call out;
  I raise my voice to all mankind.
⁵You who are simple, gain prudence;
  you who are foolish, gain understanding.
⁶Listen, for I have worthy things to say;
  I open my lips to speak what is right.
⁷My mouth speaks what is true,
  for my lips detest wickedness.
⁸All the words of my mouth are just;
  none of them is crooked or perverse.
⁹To the discerning all of them are right;
  they are faultless to those who have knowledge.

Further warning against adultery
Proverbs 6:20–35

The importance of learning wisdom
Proverbs 7:1–5

The immoral woman
Proverbs 7:6–27

The nature and riches of wisdom
Proverbs 8:1–21

Wisdom (Christ) at the creation
Proverbs 8:22–31

Listen to wisdom (Christ)
Proverbs 8:32–36

Wisdom and foolishness
Proverbs 9:1–18

Solomon's proverbs
Proverbs 10:1

The benefits of righteousness
Proverbs 10:2–32, 11:1–6

For Thought and **Contemplation**

One of the greatest definitions of wisdom, and one based on the Scriptures is this: wisdom is "seeing life from God's point of view" (Col. 1:9, J.B. Phillips). The proverbs you are now reading are part of God's plan to make you wise, or, in other words, to help you see life "from God's point of view".

"... in whom [Christ] are hidden all the treasures of wisdom and knowledge."
Colossians 2:3

DAY 145 — The benefits of righteousness

The benefits of righteousness
(continued)
Proverbs 11:7–11

The foolishness of
quarrelling and wrongdoing
Proverbs 11:12–31

The wicked and the righteous
Proverbs 12:1–11

The wise and the foolish
Proverbs 12:12–28

Watch your words
Proverbs 13:1–6

The rich and the poor
Proverbs 13:7–25

Contrast between wise
and foolish
Proverbs 14:1–35

Wisdom, the better way
Proverbs 15:1–19

Proverbs 15:1–8

¹A gentle answer turns away wrath,
but a harsh word stirs up anger.
²The tongue of the wise commends knowledge,
but the mouth of the fool gushes folly.
³The eyes of the Lord are everywhere,
keeping watch on the wicked and the good.
⁴The tongue that brings healing is a tree of life,
but a deceitful tongue crushes the spirit.
⁵A fool spurns his father's discipline,
but whoever heeds correction shows prudence.
⁶The house of the righteous contains great treasure,
but the income of the wicked brings them trouble.
⁷The lips of the wise spread knowledge;
not so the hearts of fools.
⁸The Lord detests the sacrifice of the wicked,
but the prayer of the upright pleases him.

For Thought and **Contemplation**

Words are more powerful than we realise. When God "spoke", He created a world – a glorious cosmos. And when you speak, you, too, create a world – a world of harmony, or a world of disharmony. Ask yourself now: what kind of world will I create by my words today?

"May the words of my mouth and the meditation of my heart be pleasing in your sight, O Lord, my Rock and my Redeemer." (Psa. 19:14)

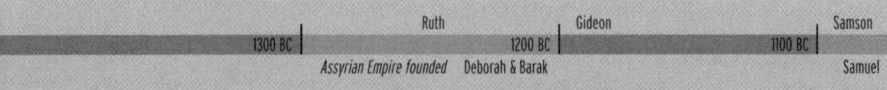

Good conduct

DAY **146**

Proverbs 16:6-14

⁶Through love and faithfulness sin is atoned for;
  through the fear of the Lord a man avoids evil.
⁷When a man's ways are pleasing to the Lord,
  he makes even his enemies live at peace with him.
⁸Better a little with righteousness than much gain with injustice.
⁹In his heart a man plans his course,
  but the Lord determines his steps.
¹⁰The lips of a king speak as an oracle,
  and his mouth should not betray justice.
¹¹Honest scales and balances are from the Lord;
  all the weights in the bag are of his making.
¹²Kings detest wrongdoing,
  for a throne is established through righteousness.
¹³Kings take pleasure in honest lips;
  they value a man who speaks the truth.
¹⁴A king's wrath is a messenger of death,
  but a wise man will appease it.

Wisdom, the better way	Proverbs 15:20-33
Warning against pride	Proverbs 16:1-5
The better way of life	Proverbs 16:6-26
Warning against violence	Proverbs 16:27-33
Good conduct	Proverbs 17:1-28, 18:1-5
A fool's words	Proverbs 18:6-9
Warnings against pride	Proverbs 18:10-14
The way of knowledge and justice	Proverbs 18:15-18
The power of the tongue	Proverbs 18:19-24
Personal conduct	Proverbs 19:1-29

For Thought and **Contemplation**

Question: why do so many Christians land up in trouble? Answer: one major reason is pride (see Proverbs 18:12). It was this that made a devil out of an angel and emptied heaven of many of its inhabitants (see Isa. 14:12-14 & Jude 6). Watch out that it doesn't topple you.

"Pride goes before destruction,
a haughty spirit before a fall."
(Prov. 16:18)

"'Blessed are the poor in spirit,
for theirs is the kingdom of heaven.'"
(Matt. 5:3)

DAY 147 — Wise sayings

Honourable conduct
Proverbs 20:1–3

Wise counsel
Proverbs 20:4–21

The way of the Lord
Proverbs 20:22–30

The importance of justice
Proverbs 21:1–31

The importance of prudence
Proverbs 22:1–5

Wise teaching
Proverbs 22:6–16

The sayings of wise men
Proverbs 22:17–29, 23:1–14

The blessing of a wise son
Proverbs 23:15–25

Warnings against vice
Proverbs 23:26–35

The way of wisdom
Proverbs 24:1–14

Proverbs 22:6–12

⁶Train a child in the way he should go,
 and when he is old he will not turn from it.
⁷The rich rule over the poor,
 and the borrower is servant to the lender.
⁸He who sows wickedness reaps trouble,
 and the rod of his fury will be destroyed.
⁹A generous man will himself be blessed,
 for he shares his food with the poor.
¹⁰Drive out the mocker, and out goes strife;
 quarrels and insults are ended.
¹¹He who loves a pure heart and whose speech is gracious
 will have the king for his friend.
¹²The eyes of the Lord keep watch over knowledge,
 but he frustrates the words of the unfaithful.

For Thought and **Contemplation**

Are you aware of what God wants to happen to you as you read these proverbs? If not, take a look at Proverbs 22:17–21. He wants you (1) to absorb their truth into your personality, so that (2) your trust in Him might be deepened, and (3) that His truth might be passed on, through you, to others. Are you letting that happen?

"A man finds joy in giving an apt reply – and how good is a timely word! (Prov. 15:23)

More proverbs

DAY 148

Proverbs 24:15–22

¹⁵Do not lie in wait like an outlaw against a righteous man's house,
  do not raid his dwelling-place;
¹⁶for though a righteous man falls seven times, he rises again,
  but the wicked are brought down by calamity.
¹⁷Do not gloat when your enemy falls;
  when he stumbles, do not let your heart rejoice,
¹⁸or the Lord will see and disapprove
  and turn his wrath away from him.
¹⁹Do not fret because of evil men
  or be envious of the wicked,
²⁰for the evil man has no future hope,
  and the lamp of the wicked will be snuffed out.
²¹Fear the Lord and the king, my son,
  and do not join with the rebellious,
²²for those two will send sudden destruction upon them,
  and who knows what calamities they can bring?

More wise sayings
Proverbs 24:15–34

Solomon's later proverbs
Proverbs 25:1

Wise conduct
Proverbs 25:2–28

Other sins
Proverbs 26:1–28

Other maxims
Proverbs 27:1–27

Contrast between good and evil
Proverbs 28:1–18

The way to lasting wealth
Proverbs 28:19–28

For Thought and **Contemplation**

Ever been hurt by a friend who told you the truth about yourself? Well, according to Proverbs 27:5–6, that's what friends are for! If you don't *have* a friend such as proverbs describes, then *be* such a friend – perhaps today.

"It is better to heed a wise man's rebuke than to listen to the song of fools." (Eccl. 7:5)

DAY 149 — Solomon's backsliding

More wise advice
Proverbs 29:1–27

The words of Agur
Proverbs 30:1–6

The way of moderation
Proverbs 30:7–9

More proverbs
Proverbs 30:10–33

Solomon's backsliding
1 Kings 11:1–13

His adversaries: Hadad
1 Kings 11:14

Rezon
1 Kings 11:23–25

Jeroboam
1 Kings 11:26–40

Unhappy condition of backsliders
Ecclesiastes 1:1–11

1 Kings 11:1–6

¹King Solomon, however, loved many foreign women besides Pharaoh's daughter – Moabites, Ammonites, Edomites, Sidonians and Hittites. ²They were from nations about which the Lord had told the Israelites, "You must not intermarry with them, because they will surely turn your hearts after their gods." Nevertheless, Solomon held fast to them in love. ³He had seven hundred wives of royal birth and three hundred concubines, and his wives led him astray. ⁴As Solomon grew old, his wives turned his heart after other gods, and his heart was not fully devoted to the Lord his God, as the heart of David his father had been. ⁵He followed Ashtoreth the goddess of the Sidonians, and Molech the detestable god of the Ammonites. ⁶So Solomon did evil in the eyes of the Lord; he did not follow the Lord completely, as David his father had done.

For Thought and **Contemplation**

Wisdom and greatness, although admirable and highly desirable qualities, are insufficient in themselves to guarantee spiritual progress and stability. We must walk in daily dependence upon God – or else, like Solomon, we will fall and fail.

"Trust in the Lord with all your heart and lean not on your own understanding; in all your ways acknowledge him, and he will make your paths straight." (Prov. 3:5–6)

a bird's eye view of **Ecclesiastes**

Place in the Bible
Twenty-first Old Testament book; fourth book of poetry and wisdom.

The contradictions of life

DAY **150**

Ecclesiastes 1:12–18

¹²I, the Teacher, was king over Israel in Jerusalem. ¹³I devoted myself to study and to explore by wisdom all that is done under heaven. What a heavy burden God has laid on men! ¹⁴I have seen all the things that are done under the sun; all of them are meaningless, a chasing after the wind.
¹⁵What is twisted cannot be straightened;
  what is lacking cannot be counted.
¹⁶I thought to myself, "Look, I have grown and increased in wisdom more than anyone who has ruled over Jerusalem before me; I have experienced much of wisdom and knowledge." ¹⁷Then I applied myself to the understanding of wisdom, and also of madness and folly, but I learned that this, too, is a chasing after the wind.
¹⁸For with much wisdom comes much sorrow;
  the more knowledge, the more grief.

Wisdom is vain
Ecclesiastes 1:12–18

Emptiness of pleasure
Ecclesiastes 2:1–3

Vanity of material wealth
Ecclesiastes 2:4–11

Result of wisdom and folly
Ecclesiastes 2:12–26

A time for everything
Ecclesiastes 3:1–8

Weariness of life
Ecclesiastes 3:9–22

The foolishness of trusting in riches
Psalm 49:1–20

Oppressions and inequalities of life
Ecclesiastes 4:1–16

Warning against rash promises
Ecclesiastes 5:1–7

For Thought and **Contemplation**

One question Christians frequently ask is this: how can we make sense out of the apparently meaningless events of life? There is only one way. We must endeavour to see life "from God's point of view". You can't make sense out of life, but you can make sense out of God.

"Oh, the depth of the riches of the wisdom and knowledge of God! How unsearchable his judgments, and his paths beyond tracing out! ... For from him and through him and to him are all things. To him be the glory for ever! Amen." (Rom 11:33 & 36)

Jesus and the Book

In contrast to the emptiness of a life which has no relation to God, Jesus offers his followers a life that is to be lived with God, "I have come that they may have life, and have it to the full" (John 10:10).

Teaching

The message of Ecclesiastes exposes the meaninglessness of life when it is lived without God.

A Verse to Remember

"Now all has been heard; here is the conclusion of the matter: Fear God and keep his commandments, for this is the whole duty of man" (Eccles. 12:13).

DAY 151 — Thoughts about Life

Riches and poverty
Ecclesiastes 5:8–20

Man's inevitable end
Ecclesiastes 6:1–12

Incurable evil of man
Ecclesiastes 7:1–29

Mystery of divine providence
Ecclesiastes 8:1–17

World's wrong values
Ecclesiastes 9:1–18

Ecclesiastes 8:14–17

¹⁴There is something else meaningless that occurs on earth: righteous men who get what the wicked deserve, and wicked men who get what the righteous deserve. This too, I say, is meaningless. ¹⁵So I commend the enjoyment of life, because nothing is better for a man under the sun than to eat and drink and be glad. Then joy will accompany him in his work all the days of the life God has given him under the sun. ¹⁶When I applied my mind to know wisdom and to observe man's labour on earth – his eyes not seeing sleep day or night – ¹⁷then I saw all that God has done. No-one can comprehend what goes on under the sun. Despite all his efforts to search it out, man cannot discover its meaning. Even if a wise man claims he knows, he cannot really comprehend it.

For Thought and **Contemplation**

Faith alone can hold the heart steady in a world where it seems the righteous suffer and the wicked prosper. When we can leave it to the Lord to clear up the difficulties in His own good time, then we are free to absorb the grace that enables us to turn the difficulties into doors of opportunity.

"O righteous God, who searches minds and hearts, bring to an end the violence of the wicked and make the righteous secure. My shield is God Most High, who saves the upright in heart." (Psa. 7:9–10)

Solomon's death

DAY **152**

Ecclesiastes 12:1–5

¹Remember your Creator
 in the days of your youth,
 before the days of trouble come
 and the years approach when you will say,
 "I find no pleasure in them" –
²before the sun and the light
 and the moon and the stars grow dark,
 and the clouds return after the rain;
³when the keepers of the house tremble,
 and the strong men stoop,
 when the grinders cease because they are few,
 and those looking through the windows grow dim;
⁴when the doors to the street are closed
 and the sound of grinding fades;
 when men rise up at the sound of birds,
 but all their songs grow faint;
⁵when men are afraid of heights
 and of dangers in the streets;
 when the almond tree blossoms
 and the grasshopper drags himself along
 and desire no longer is stirred.
 Then man goes to his eternal home …

Anarchy of the world
Ecclesiastes 10:1–20

Wise advice
Ecclesiastes 11:1–6

Advice to young people
Ecclesiastes 11:7–12:8

An optimistic conclusion
Ecclesiastes 12:9–14

Solomon's death
1 Kings 11:41–43, 2 Chronicles 9:29–31

His descendants
1 Chronicles 3:10–24

The 12 tribes
Genesis 35:23–26, 1 Chronicles 2:1–2

Judah and his lineage
1 Chronicles 4:1–14, 16–23

Hezron to David
Ruth 4:19–22

Hezron to David's nephews
1 Chronicles 2:9–17

For Thought and **Contemplation**

If wealth and honour alone could satisfy the soul, then Solomon would have known complete fulfilment. His disappointment can be summed up in the words, "All is vanity and vexation of spirit." True joy is found not "under the sun", but above the sun – in God's eternal presence.

"You have made known to me the path of life; you will fill me with joy in your presence, with eternal pleasures at your right hand." (Psa. 16:11)

Heart to Heart

Section 5

The Word of God was placed in the temple of God so the priests of God could encourage and teach the people of God in the presence of God. The New Testament shows that we are now priests of God in the new living temple of God and God is placing His Word in you so that you can encourage and reach others to experience His presence. What a Book! What a Message! What an Author!

6

In this section

The division of the kingdom
The reigns of good and evil kings
Elijah's championing of God's cause
The miracles Elisha performed
Prophecies of judgment and eventual restoration

DAY 153 — Genealogies

Hezron to Elishama
1 Chronicles 2:21–41

Caleb, son of Hezron
1 Chronicles 2:18–20

Descendants of Caleb
1 Chronicles 2:42–55

Caleb, son of Jephunneh
1 Chronicles 4:15

Descendants of Gershon
Exodus 6:17, Numbers 3:18,
1 Chronicles 6:17, 20–21, 23:7–11

Descendants of Kohath
Exodus 6:18, Numbers 3:19,
1 Chronicles 6:2, 18, 23:12,
Exodus 6:21–22, 24,
1 Chronicles 6:22–28, 23:18–20

Aaron's descendants
1 Chronicles 6:3–15, 50–53, Ezra 7:1–5

Descendants of Merari
Exodus 6:19, Numbers 3:20,
1 Chronicles 6:19, 29–30, 23:21–23

Ancestors of songmasters
1 Chronicles 6:31–48

1 Chronicles 2:42–50a

⁴²The sons of Caleb the brother of Jerahmeel:
   Mesha his firstborn, who was the father of Ziph, and his son Mareshah, who was the father of Hebron. ⁴³The sons of Hebron:
   Korah, Tappuah, Rekem and Shema. ⁴⁴Shema was the father of Raham, and Raham the father of Jorkeam. Rekem was the father of Shammai. ⁴⁵The son of Shammai was Maon, and Maon was the father of Beth Zur.
⁴⁶Caleb's concubine Ephah was the mother of Haran, Moza and Gazez. Haran was the father of Gazez.
⁴⁷The sons of Jahdai:
   Regem, Jotham, Geshan, Pelet, Ephah and Shaaph.
⁴⁸Caleb's concubine Maacah was the mother of Sheber and Tirhanah. ⁴⁹She also gave birth to Shaaph the father of Madmannah and to Sheva the father of Macbenah and Gibea. Caleb's daughter was Acsah. ⁵⁰These were the descendants of Caleb.

For Thought and **Contemplation**

Genealogies may seem boring and irrelevant to some, but they are the evidence of God's interest in individuals. People are not just a part of history – they are a part of God's purposes for history. Remember this – you are in the world not simply as part of a family tree, you are here for a purpose.

"Before I formed you in the womb I knew you, before you were born I set you apart ..." (Jer. 1:5)

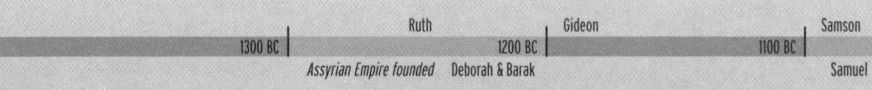

The tribes

DAY 154

1 Chronicles 5:11–17

¹¹The Gadites lived next to them in Bashan, as far as Salecah: ¹²Joel was the chief, Shapham the second, then Janai and Shaphat, in Bashan.
¹³Their relatives, by families, were: Michael, Meshullam, Sheba, Jorai, Jacan, Zia and Eber – seven in all. ¹⁴These were the sons of Abihail son of Huri, the son of Jaroah, the son of Gilead, the son of Michael, the son of Jeshishai, the son of Jahdo, the son of Buz.
¹⁵Ahi son of Abdiel, the son of Guni, was head of their family.
¹⁶The Gadites lived in Gilead, in Bashan and its outlying villages, and on all the pasturelands of Sharon as far as they extended.
¹⁷All these were entered in the genealogical records during the reigns of Jotham king of Judah and Jeroboam king of Israel.

Tribe of Reuben
Exodus 6:14, 1 Chronicles 5:1–9

Tribe of Gad
1 Chronicles 5:11–17

Tribe of Manasseh (east)
1 Chronicles 5:23–24

Tribe of Manasseh (west)
1 Chronicles 7:14–19

Tribe of Simeon
Exodus 6:15,
1 Chronicles 4:24–27, 34–38

Tribe of Issachar
1 Chronicles 7:1–5

Tribe of Naphtali
1 Chronicles 7:13

Tribe of Ephraim
1 Chronicles 7:20–29

Tribe of Asher
1 Chronicles 7:30–40

Tribe of Benjamin
1 Chronicles 7:6–12, 8:1–28

Summary
1 Chronicles 9:1

For Thought and **Contemplation**

Have you ever wondered why the family of Israel should be split up into various tribes? One reason is that we need to identify with a small group before we can take our place in a large group. The more easily you relate to your church locally, the more easily you will relate to the Church universally.

"For where two or three come together in my name, there am I with them."
(Matt. 18:20)

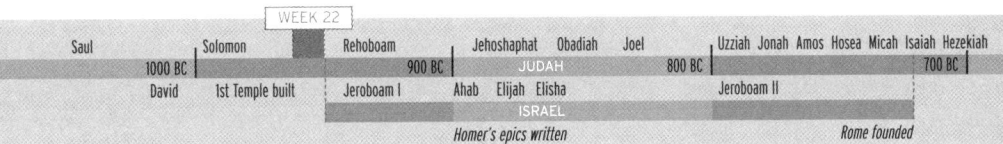

DAY 155 — The divided kingdom 945–721 BC

Revolt of the tribes
2 Chronicles 10:1–19

Wrong advice causes revolt
1 Kings 12:1–19

Jeroboam
1 Kings 12:20

Rehoboam
1 Kings 14:21, 2 Chronicles 12:13

People led into idolatry
1 Kings 12:25–33, 2 Chronicles 11:15

Warning to Rehoboam
1 Kings 12:21–24, 2 Chronicles 11:1–4

Prophecy concerning the altar at Bethel
1 Kings 13:1–10

2 Chronicles 11:1–4

¹When Rehoboam arrived in Jerusalem, he mustered the house of Judah and Benjamin – a hundred and eighty thousand fighting men – to make war against Israel and to regain the kingdom for Rehoboam. ²But this word of the Lord came to Shemaiah the man of God: ³"Say to Rehoboam son of Solomon king of Judah and to all the Israelites in Judah and Benjamin, ⁴'This is what the Lord says: Do not go up to fight against your brothers. Go home, every one of you, for this is my doing.'" So they obeyed the words of the Lord and turned back from marching against Jeroboam.

For Thought and **Contemplation**

Careful words and moderate statements may cost a good deal in terms of self-denial and self-control, but they purchase great things. God's work has often been the casualty of unstudied remarks. Ask the Lord today to make you a peacemaker and not a piece-maker.

"Who is wise and understanding among you? Let him show it by his good life, by deeds done in the humility that comes from wisdom." (Jas. 3:13)

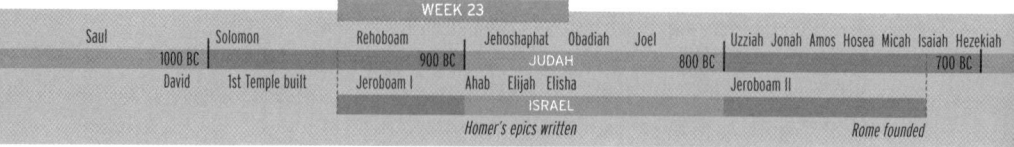

The Divided Kingdom

NORTHERN KINGDOM

Kings of the Northern Kingdom

Jeroboam I	Jehoahaz
Nadab	Jehoash
Baasha	Jeroboam II
Elah	Zechariah
Zimri	Shallum
Omri	Menahem
Ahab	Pekahiah
Ahaziah	Pekah
Joram	Hoshea
Jehu	

Saul, David and Solomon reigned over all Israel for 40 years each. After Solomon's reign and his unfaithfulness to God the united kingdom of Israel was split into two: the Northern Kingdom (which was still known as Israel), and the Southern Kingdom of Judah.

- Referred to as Israel and Ephraim
- Lasted 224 years: 945-721 BC
- Nineteen rulers in all – all unrighteous
- Composed of ten tribes
- Capital was Shechem, then Tirzah. Samaria established as capital from time of Omri onwards.
- No return from captivity.

SOUTHERN KINGDOM

Kings of the Southern Kingdom

Rehoboam	Ahaz
Abijah	Hezekiah
Asa	Manasseh
Jehoshaphat	Amon
Jehoram	Josiah
Ahaziah	Jehoahaz
Athaliah	Jehoiakim
Joash	Jehoiachin
Amaziah	Zedekiah
Uzziah	
Jotham	

- Referred to as Judah
- Lasted 359 years: 945-586 BC
- Twenty rulers in all – eight of them righteous
- Composed of two tribes
- Capital was Jerusalem
- Captured by the Babylonians in 586 BC
- Three separate returns from captivity

Map

Tribes and locations:
- DAN (North)
- ASHER
- NAPHTALI
- MANASSEH (East)
- ZEBULUN
- ISSACHAR
- MANASSEH (West)
- GAD
- EPHRAIM
- DAN (South)
- BENJAMIN
- JUDAH
- REUBEN

Cities:
- Samaria
- Tirzah
- Shechem
- Jerusalem

DAY 156 — Jeroboam and Rehoboam

Rehoboam's kingdom
2 Chronicles 11:5–12

Influence of spiritual people
2 Chronicles 11:13–14, 16–17

Judgment of a man of God
1 Kings 13:11–32

Rehoboam's family
2 Chronicles 11:18–23

His apostasy
2 Chronicles 12:1, 14, 1 Kings 14:22–24

Shishak invades Jerusalem
1 Kings 14:25–28, 2 Chronicles 12:2–12

Jeroboam's persistence in evil
1 Kings 13:33–34

Ahijah's prediction
1 Kings 14:1–18

Warfare
1 Kings 14:30, 1 Kings 15:6

Rehoboam's death
1 Kings 14:29, 31, 2 Chronicles 12:15–16

2 Chronicles 12:2–8

²Because they had been unfaithful to the Lord, Shishak king of Egypt attacked Jerusalem in the fifth year of King Rehoboam. ³With twelve hundred chariots and sixty thousand horsemen and the innumerable troops of Libyans, Sukkites and Cushites that came with him from Egypt, ⁴he captured the fortified cities of Judah and came as far as Jerusalem.
⁵Then the prophet Shemaiah came to Rehoboam and to the leaders of Judah who had assembled in Jerusalem for fear of Shishak, and he said to them, "This is what the Lord says: 'You have abandoned me; therefore I now abandon you to Shishak.'"
⁶The leaders of Israel and the king humbled themselves and said, "The Lord is just."
⁷When the Lord saw that they humbled themselves, this word of the Lord came to Shemaiah: "Since they have humbled themselves, I will not destroy them but will soon give them deliverance. My wrath will not be poured out on Jerusalem through Shishak. ⁸They will, however, become subject to him ..."

For Thought and **Contemplation**

The reason for Rehoboam's sins and errors is captured in these words, "he had not set his heart on seeking the Lord" (2 Chron. 12:14). When we fail to *seek* the Lord, then it follows as the night follows the day that we will not *serve* the Lord.

"I have set the Lord always before me. Because he is at my right hand, I shall not be shaken. Therefore my heart is glad and my tongue rejoices; my body also will rest secure." (Psa. 16:8–9)

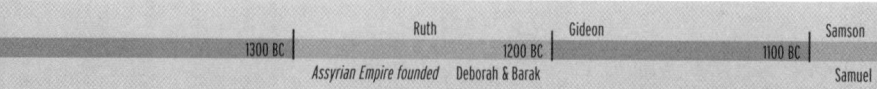

Evil and good kings

DAY 157

2 Chronicles 14:1–7

¹And Abijah rested with his fathers and was buried in the City of David. Asa his son succeeded him as king, and in his days the country was at peace for ten years. ²Asa did what was good and right in the eyes of the Lord his God. ³He removed the foreign altars and the high places, smashed the sacred stones and cut down the Asherah poles. ⁴He commanded Judah to seek the Lord, the God of their fathers, and to obey his laws and commands. ⁵He removed the high places and incense altars in every town in Judah, and the kingdom was at peace under him. ⁶He built up the fortified cities of Judah, since the land was at peace. No-one was at war with him during those years, for the Lord gave him rest. ⁷"Let us build up these towns," he said to Judah, "and put walls round them, with towers, gates and bars. The land is still ours, because we have sought the Lord our God; we sought him and he has given us rest on every side." So they built and prospered.

Abijah king of Judah	1 Kings 15:1–2, 2 Chronicles 13:1–2
War between Jeroboam and Abijah	2 Chronicles 13:3–19
Abijah's family	2 Chronicles 13:21
His evil life	1 Kings 15:3–4
His death	2 Chronicles 13:22, 1 Kings 15:7–8
Asa king of Judah	1 Kings 15:9–11, 2 Chronicles 14:1–5
Nadab	1 Kings 15:25–26
Jeroboam's death	2 Chronicles 13:20, 1 Kings 14:19–20
Asa's cities and army	2 Chronicles 14:6–8
Nadab's death	1 Kings 15:27–28,31
Baasha king of Israel	1 Kings 15:33–34, 29–30
Asa defeats Ethiopians	2 Chronicles 14:9–15
Comfort in distress	Psalm 77:1–20

For Thought and **Contemplation**

Do you have times when, like Asaph in Psalm 77, you feel God has forgotten to be merciful? (v.9) In such times, do as Asaph did, and remind yourself of the many blessings He has given you in the past (v.11). It will help you to keep things in perspective.

"Guide me in your truth and teach me, for you are God my Saviour, and my hope is in you all day long. Remember, O Lord, your great mercy and love, for they are from of old." (Psa. 25:5–6)

DAY 158

Asa's godly reign

Azariah's prophecy
2 Chronicles 15:1–7

Reforms in worship
2 Chronicles 15:8, 17–18,
1 Kings 15:12, 14–15

Covenant renewal
2 Chronicles 15:9–15

Asa removes his grandmother
1 Kings 15:13, 2 Chronicles 15:16

Time of peace
2 Chronicles 15:19

War between Baasha and Asa
1 Kings 15:16, 32

Asa defeats Israel
2 Chronicles 16:1–6, 1 Kings 15:17–22

Jehu's prophecy
1 Kings 16:1–4, 7

Hanani's warning
2 Chronicles 16:7–10

Baasha's death
1 Kings 16:5–6

Elah
1 Kings 16:8–10, 14

Zimri
1 Kings 16:11–13, 15–20

Omri and Tibni
1 Kings 16:21–28

Ahab
1 Kings 16:29–33, 21:25–26

Asa's feet diseased
1 Kings 15:23, 2 Chronicles 16:11–12

2 Chronicles 15:1–7

¹The Spirit of God came upon Azariah son of Oded. ²He went out to meet Asa and said to him, "Listen to me, Asa and all Judah and Benjamin. The Lord is with you when you are with him. If you seek him, he will be found by you, but if you forsake him, he will forsake you. ³For a long time Israel was without the true God, without a priest to teach and without the law. ⁴But in their distress they turned to the Lord, the God of Israel, and sought him, and he was found by them. ⁵In those days it was not safe to travel about, for all the inhabitants of the lands were in great turmoil. ⁶One nation was being crushed by another and one city by another, because God was troubling them with every kind of distress. ⁷But as for you, be strong and do not give up, for your work will be rewarded."

For Thought and **Contemplation**

Two years before he died, Asa's feet became diseased. Did God condemn him for seeking the help of physicians? No – God's condemnation was because he sought help *only* from the physicians and not from the Lord. We must never lose sight of the fact that a doctor can only prescribe: it is God who heals.

"... 'If you listen carefully to the voice of the Lord your God and do what is right in his eyes, if you pay attention to his commands and keep all his decrees, I will not bring on you any of the diseases I brought on the Egyptians, for I am the Lord, who heals you.'"
(Ex. 15:26)

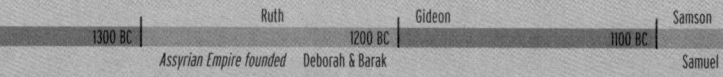

Elijah's early ministry

DAY **159**

1 Kings 17:1–6

¹Now Elijah the Tishbite, from Tishbe in Gilead, said to Ahab, "As the Lord, the God of Israel, lives, whom I serve, there will be neither dew nor rain in the next few years except at my word."
²Then the word of the Lord came to Elijah: ³"Leave here, turn eastward and hide in the Kerith Ravine, east of the Jordan. ⁴You will drink from the brook, and I have ordered the ravens to feed you there."
⁵So he did what the Lord had told him. He went to the Kerith Ravine, east of the Jordan, and stayed there. ⁶The ravens brought him bread and meat in the morning and bread and meat in the evening, and he drank from the brook.

Asa's death
1 Kings 15:24, 2 Chronicles 16:13–14

Rebuilding of Jericho
1 Kings 16:34

Elijah's ministry 882–868 BC

Persecution of prophets
1 Kings 18:4

Jehoshaphat
2 Chronicles 20:31–33,
1 Kings 22:41–43 & 46,
2 Chronicles 17:1–19, 18:1

Elijah's ministry begins
1 Kings 17:1–24

Obadiah and Ahab
1 Kings 18:1–3, 5–16

For Thought and **Contemplation**

Elijah had to learn to sit quietly before the Lord before he was called upon to engage in activity for Him. Have you learned that lesson yet? Many can work for Him, but are unable to remain quietly before Him. As the poet Milton said, "They also serve who only stand and wait."

"I waited patiently for the Lord;
he turned to me and heard my cry."
(Psa. 40:1)

WEEK 23

| Saul | Solomon | Rehoboam | Jehoshaphat | Obadiah | Joel | Uzziah | Jonah | Amos | Hosea | Micah | Isaiah | Hezekiah |

1000 BC | 900 BC | JUDAH | 800 BC | 700 BC

David | 1st Temple built | Jeroboam I | Ahab | Elijah | Elisha | Jeroboam II

ISRAEL

Homer's epics written | Rome founded

DAY 160 — God's care for Elijah

Contest on Mount Carmel
1 Kings 18:17–39

Prophets of Baal destroyed
1 Kings 18:40

Elijah prays for rain
1 Kings 18:41–46

God's care for Elijah
1 Kings 19:1–7

God speaks at Horeb
1 Kings 19:8–18

Elisha joins Elijah
1 Kings 19:19–21

Ben-Hadad besieges Samaria
1 Kings 20:1–12

His defeat
1 Kings 20:13–21

1 Kings 19:3–9a

³Elijah was afraid and ran for his life. When he came to Beersheba in Judah, he left his servant there, ⁴while he himself went a day's journey into the desert. He came to a broom tree, sat down under it and prayed that he might die. "I have had enough, Lord," he said. "Take my life; I am no better than my ancestors." ⁵Then he lay down under the tree and fell asleep.

All at once an angel touched him and said, "Get up and eat." ⁶He looked around, and there by his head was a cake of bread baked over hot coals, and a jar of water. He ate and drank and then lay down again.

⁷The angel of the Lord came back a second time and touched him and said, "Get up and eat, for the journey is too much for you." ⁸So he got up and ate and drank. Strengthened by that food, he travelled forty days and forty nights until he reached Horeb, the mountain of God. ⁹There he went into a cave and spent the night.

For Thought and **Contemplation**

When God chooses His servants for a special work, He looks for those who are focusing wholeheartedly on the task they have in hand. Elisha was *ploughing* when he received his call, and Peter was *fishing* when he received his. Fulfil your present tasks well, and God will give you even greater things to do.

"... 'Well done, good and faithful servant! You have been faithful with a few things; I will put you in charge of many things. Come and share your master's happiness!'" (Matt. 25:23)

Elijah

WHEN ISRAEL was sliding into some of its darkest days under Ahab, Elijah's impact was stunning. God's power was dramatically demonstrated to Elijah personally and publicly to the nation.

Elijah is mentioned over 30 times in the New Testament. Both John the Baptist and Jesus were thought to be Elijah come back again. He arrived on the scene of time declaring fiery judgment on the king and nation. He left it in a chariot of fire.

Elijah's prayers

Elijah's life was characterised by four great prayers:
1. For no more rain to fall: James 5:17
2. For the widow's dead son: 1 Kings 17:19–24
3. For fire to fall from heaven: 1 Kings 18:36–38
4. For rain to fall again: 1 Kings 18:41–46

There are three marks of Elijah's prayers:
1. He delighted in asking God for the impossible.
2. He believed that he would receive what he prayed for.
3. He didn't give up.

DAY 161 — Jehoshaphat and Ahab

Syrians again defeated
1 Kings 20:22–30

Ahab makes peace with Ben-Hadad
1 Kings 20:31–34

Ahab's sentence
1 Kings 20:35–43

Three years of peace
1 Kings 22:1

Ahab and Naboth
1 Kings 21:1–3

Jezebel causes Naboth's death
1 Kings 21:4–16

Elijah announces doom
1 Kings 21:17–24

Ahab's repentance
1 Kings 21:27–29

Jehoshaphat joins Ahab
1 Kings 22:2–4, 2 Chronicles 18:2–3

Prophets lie to Ahab
1 Kings 22:5–6, 10–12, 2 Chronicles 18:4–5, 9–11

2 Chronicles 18:2–5

²Some years later [Jehoshaphat] went down to visit Ahab in Samaria. Ahab slaughtered many sheep and cattle for him and the people with him and urged him to attack Ramoth Gilead. ³Ahab king of Israel asked Jehoshaphat king of Judah, "Will you go with me against Ramoth Gilead?"
Jehoshaphat replied, "I am as you are, and my people as your people; we will join you in the war." ⁴But Jehoshaphat also said to the king of Israel, "First seek the counsel of the Lord."
⁵So the king of Israel brought together the prophets – four hundred men – and asked them, "Shall we go to war against Ramoth Gilead, or shall I refrain?"
"Go," they answered, "for God will give it into the king's hand."

For Thought and **Contemplation**

Ahab's desire to possess what didn't belong to him led eventually to discontent, death and destruction. Envy and jealousy are weeds that, if not uprooted the moment they are discovered, will spread like cancer. Is your heart free from these twin evils?

"Let us behave decently, as in the daytime, not in orgies and drunkenness, not in sexual immorality and debauchery, not in dissension and jealousy. Rather, clothe yourselves with the Lord Jesus Christ, and do not think about how to gratify the desires of the sinful nature." (Rom. 13:13–14)

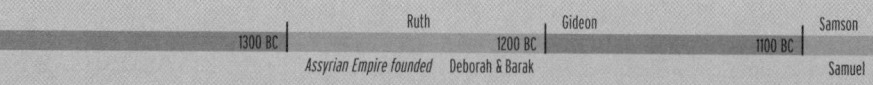

The godly Jehoshaphat

DAY **162**

2 Chronicles 19:1-7

¹When Jehoshaphat king of Judah returned safely to his palace in Jerusalem, ²Jehu the seer, the son of Hanani, went out to meet him and said to the king, "Should you help the wicked and love those who hate the Lord? Because of this, the wrath of the Lord is upon you. ³There is, however, some good in you, for you have rid the land of the Asherah poles and have set your heart on seeking God."
⁴Jehoshaphat lived in Jerusalem, and he went out again among the people from Beersheba to the hill country of Ephraim and turned them back to the Lord, the God of their fathers. ⁵He appointed judges in the land, in each of the fortified cities of Judah. ⁶He told them, "Consider carefully what you do, because you are not judging for man but for the Lord, who is with you whenever you give a verdict. ⁷Now let the fear of the Lord be upon you. Judge carefully, for with the Lord our God there is no injustice or partiality or bribery."

Micaiah summoned
1 Kings 22:7-9, 2 Chronicles 18:6-8

His true prophecy
1 Kings 22:13-28, 2 Chronicles 18:12-27

Ahab's death
1 Kings 22:29-40. 2 Chronicles 18:28-34

Jehoshaphat rebuked
2 Chronicles 19:1-7

God, the supreme Ruler
Psalm 82:1-8

Jehoshaphat restores order
2 Chronicles 19:8-11

For Thought and **Contemplation**

When Jehoshaphat was reproved by the prophet over his alliance with the ungodly Ahab, the king searched his heart and set about reforming his ways. How do you respond to the reproofs of God? With repentance – or with rebellion?

"'My son, do not make light of the Lord's discipline, and do not lose heart when he rebukes you, because the Lord disciplines those he loves, and he punishes everyone he accepts as a son'" (Heb. 12:5-6)

DAY 163 — Jehoshaphat's victory

Judah invaded
2 Chronicles 20:1–4

Jehoshaphat prays
2 Chronicles 20:5–13

A prayer for the defeat of enemies
Psalm 83:1–18

Jahaziel's prophecy
2 Chronicles 20:14–19

God is with us
Psalm 46:1–11

Singers appointed
2 Chronicles 20:20–21

The enemy destroyed
2 Chronicles 20:22–26

Judah rejoices
2 Chronicles 20:27–28

The city of God
Psalm 48:1–14

Judah's victory causes fear
2 Chronicles 20:29–30

Ahaziah and Moab
1 Kings 22:51–53, 2 Kings 3:4–5, 1:1–2

A brief alliance
2 Chronicles 20:35–37,
1 Kings 22:44, 47–49

2 Chronicles 20:22–26

²²As they began to sing and praise, the Lord set ambushes against the men of Ammon and Moab and Mount Seir who were invading Judah, and they were defeated. ²³The men of Ammon and Moab rose up against the men from Mount Seir to destroy and annihilate them. After they finished slaughtering the men from Seir, they helped to destroy one another.

²⁴When the men of Judah came to the place that overlooks the desert and looked towards the vast army, they saw only dead bodies lying on the ground; no-one had escaped. ²⁵So Jehoshaphat and his men went to carry off their plunder, and they found among them a great amount of equipment and clothing and also articles of value – more than they could take away. There was so much plunder that it took three days to collect it. ²⁶On the fourth day they assembled in the Valley of Beracah, where they praised the Lord. This is why it is called the Valley of Beracah to this day.

For Thought and **Contemplation**

Jehoshaphat's strategy of putting his singers at the forefront of his army as they went into battle is full of deep spiritual suggestiveness. Some battles are best approached in the spirit of praise, rather than in the spirit of prayer. This does not mean prayer is unimportant. It simply means that when prayer doesn't seem to bring victory – then try praise.

"Sing to the Lord a new song, for he has done marvellous things; his right hand and his holy arm have worked salvation for him." (Psa. 98:1)

a bird's eye view of **2 Kings**

Place in the Bible	**Main Characters**	**Special Features**
Twelfth Old Testament book; seventh book of history.	Elisha, Naaman, Hezekiah, Josiah.	The story of the two kingdoms continues. Israel is defeated by Assyria, its capital (Samaria) is destroyed, and its people taken into exile.

Elisha's ministry begins

DAY 164

2 Kings 2:9–12

⁹When they had crossed, Elijah said to Elisha, "Tell me, what can I do for you before I am taken from you?"

"Let me inherit a double portion of your spirit," Elisha replied.

¹⁰"You have asked a difficult thing," Elijah said, "yet if you see me when I am taken from you, it will be yours – otherwise not."

¹¹As they were walking along and talking together, suddenly a chariot of fire and horses of fire appeared and separated the two of them, and Elijah went up to heaven in a whirlwind. ¹²Elisha saw this and cried out, "My father! My father! The chariots and horsemen of Israel!" And Elisha saw him no more. Then he took hold of his own clothes and tore them apart.

Elijah calls down fire
2 Kings 1:3–15

Ahaziah's death
2 Kings 1:16–18

Elisha's ministry 868–808 BC

Joram
2 Kings 3:1–3

Elijah divides Jordan
2 Kings 2:1–8

Elijah is taken to heaven
2 Kings 2:9–12

Elisha gains mantle
2 Kings 2:13–18

The miracle of fresh water
2 Kings 2:19–22

Children destroyed
2 Kings 2:23–25

Jehoshaphat joins Joram
2 Kings 3:6–9

Elisha's promise
2 Kings 3:10–20

For Thought and **Contemplation**

It is often thought that Elisha wanted a ministry twice as great as Elijah's when he uttered the words: "let me inherit a double portion". Actually he was asking to carry on Elijah's ministry. Inheritance law assigned a double portion to the firstborn (see Deut. 21:17). How passionately do you long to continue in the style and character of your Master who walked on this earth?

"I want to know Christ and the power of his resurrection and the fellowship of sharing in his sufferings, becoming like him in his death, and so, somehow, to attain to the resurrection from the dead." (Phil. 3:10–11)

Jesus and the Book

The phrase "the word of the Lord" (or similar words) comes 24 times in this book. Jesus Christ is God's last word to us: "In the past God spoke to our forefathers through the prophets … but in these last days he has spoken to us by his Son …" (Heb. 1:1–2).

Teaching

1 and 2 Kings teach that rebellion against God is always a recipe for disaster. Yet the power and faithfulness of God shine out through the lives of prophets and kings who are true to Him.

A Verse to Remember

"O Lord, God of Israel … you alone are God over all the kingdoms of the earth. You have made heaven and earth" (2 Kings 19:15).

DAY 165 — Elisha and the Shunammite women

Defeat of the Moabites
2 Kings 3:21–27

The widow's oil
2 Kings 4:1–7

The Shunammite woman
2 Kings 4:8–17

Her son restored
2 Kings 4:18–37

Elisha predicts famine
2 Kings 8:1–2

Jehoram
2 Kings 8:16–17

Jehoshaphat's death
2 Chronicles 20:34, 1 Kings 22:45, 50, 2 Chronicles 21:1–3

Jehoram's evil life
2 Kings 8:18–19, 2 Chronicles 21:5–7, 11

Edom judged
Obadiah 1:1–9

Edom's great sin
Obadiah 1:10–14

2 Kings 4:8–17

⁸One day Elisha went to Shunem. And a well-to-do woman was there, who urged him to stay for a meal. So whenever he came by, he stopped there to eat. ⁹She said to her husband, "I know that this man who often comes our way is a holy man of God. ¹⁰Let's make a small room on the roof and put in it a bed and a table, a chair and a lamp for him. Then he can stay there whenever he comes to us."

¹¹One day when Elisha came, he went up to his room and lay down there. ¹²He said to his servant Gehazi ... ¹⁴"What can be done for her?" Elisha asked.

Gehazi said, "Well, she has no son and her husband is old."

¹⁵Then Elisha said, "Call her." So he called her, and she stood in the doorway. ¹⁶"About this time next year," Elisha said, "you will hold a son in your arms."

"No, my lord," she objected. "Don't mislead your servant, O man of God!"

¹⁷But the woman became pregnant, and the next year about that same time she gave birth to a son, just as Elisha had told her.

For Thought and **Contemplation**

For Elisha to receive the coveted mantle of power the condition was quite simple – he had to keep his eyes fixed on Elijah as his master was translated to heaven. The same principle applies in relation to the receiving of power in today's Church. You have to keep your eyes on Jesus.

"Let us fix our eyes on Jesus, the author and perfecter of our faith, who for the joy set before him endured the cross, scorning its shame, and sat down at the right hand of the throne of God." (Heb.12:2)

a bird's eye view of **Obadiah & Nahum**

Place in the Bible

Thirty-first and thirty-fourth Old Testament books; ninth and twelfth books of prophecy.

Jesus and the prophecy of Obadiah

Like the good news the messenger brought in verse 17 Jesus Christ came to tell people about the gospel of salvation.

Elisha's other miracles

DAY **166**

2 Kings 6:1–7

¹The company of the prophets said to Elisha, "Look, the place where we meet with you is too small for us. ²Let us go to the Jordan, where each of us can get a pole; and let us build a place there for us to live."

And he said, "Go."
³Then one of them said, "Won't you please come with your servants?"

"I will," Elisha replied. ⁴And he went with them.

They went to the Jordan and began to cut down trees. ⁵As one of them was cutting down a tree, the iron axe-head fell into the water. "Oh, my lord," he cried out, "it was borrowed!"

⁶The man of God asked, "Where did it fall?" When he showed him the place, Elisha cut a stick and threw it there, and made the iron float. ⁷"Lift it out," he said. Then the man reached out his hand and took it.

Elisha's other miracles	2 Kings 4:38–44
Condemnation of nations	Obadiah 1:15–16
Future kingdom	Obadiah 1:17–21
Revolt of Edom and Libnah	2 Kings 8:20–22, 2 Chronicles 21:8–10
Elijah's prophecy and Jehoram's death	2 Chronicles 21:12–20, 2 Kings 8:23–24
Healing of Naaman	2 Kings 5:1–19
Gehazi's punishment	2 Kings 5:20–27
Recovery of axe head	2 Kings 6:1–7

For Thought and **Contemplation**

When the axe-head was lost, no further work could be done as the tool had lost its cutting edge. But miraculously, and in response to a desperate cry, the axe-head returned from the deep. Have you lost the cutting edge in your Christian experience? Then cry out in repentance and desperation, and God will return it to you – today.

"Yet I hold this against you: You have forsaken your first love. Remember the height from which you have fallen! Repent and do the things you did at first ..." (Rev. 2:4–5)

Jesus and the prophecy of Nahum

After the celebrated verse from Nahum 1.15, "Look ... the feet of one who brings good news ..." the next mention of "good news" is in Matthew 4:23. Matthew describes the supreme bearer of good news: Jesus.

Teaching

In common with Israel's other enemies, Obadiah prophesied that Edom would be punished. Nahum's poems reflect the delight the Jews felt when Nineveh, the capital of their sworn enemy Assyria, fell.

A Verse to Remember

"The Lord is good, a refuge in times of trouble. He cares for those who trust in him ..." (Nahum 1:7)

DAY 167

The siege of Samaria

The Syrians' defeat
2 Kings 6:8–23

Ahaziah
2 Kings 9:29, 8:25

Siege of Samaria
2 Kings 6:24–33, 7:1–20

Shunammite land restored
2 Kings 8:3–6

Ahaziah's evil reign
2 Kings 8:26–27, 2 Chronicles 22:2–4

Ben-Hadad's death
2 Kings 8:7–15

2 Kings 7:8–11

⁸The men who had leprosy reached the edge of the camp and entered one of the tents. They ate and drank, and carried away silver, gold and clothes, and went off and hid them. They returned and entered another tent and took some things from it and hid them also.
⁹Then they said to each other, "We're not doing right. This is a day of good news and we are keeping it to ourselves. If we wait until daylight, punishment will overtake us. Let's go at once and report this to the royal palace."
¹⁰So they went and called out to the city gatekeepers and told them, "We went into the Aramean camp and not a man was there – not a sound of anyone – only tethered horses and donkeys, and the tents left just as they were." ¹¹The gatekeepers shouted the news, and it was reported within the palace.

For Thought and **Contemplation**

The four lepers of Samaria who came upon the abandoned food and supplies of the Syrian army knew instinctively that what they had discovered must be shared. "This is a day of good news and we are keeping it to ourselves." Do you long to share what you have miraculously received?

"Heal the sick, raise the dead, cleanse those who have leprosy, drive out demons. Freely you have received, freely give." (Matt. 10:8)

Elisha's Miracles

ELISHA'S PRAYER was that when Elijah was taken up to heaven, he would receive a double portion of his spirit (2 Kings 2:9).

1.	**Dividing of the Jordan**	2 Kings 2:14
2.	**The healing of the waters**	2 Kings 2:21–22
3.	**The judgment of irreverence**	2 Kings 2:23–24
4.	**Valleys filled with water, and defeat of the Moabite army**	2 Kings 3:9–24
5.	**Multiplying the widow's oil**	2 Kings 4:1–7
6.	**Raising of the Shunammite's son**	2 Kings 4:32–36
7.	**Poisonous stew made wholesome**	2 Kings 4:38–41
8.	**Feeding of the multitude**	2 Kings 4:42–44
9.	**Healing of Naaman**	2 Kings 5:1–14
10.	**Gehazi struck with leprosy**	2 Kings 5:26–27
11.	**The lost axe-head**	2 Kings 6:5–7
12.	**Syrians struck with blindness**	2 Kings 6:15–23
13.	**Prophecy of the Syrians' defeat and the death of the king's officer**	2 Kings Ch. 7
14.	**Resurrection life even after death**	2 Kings 13:20–21

DAY 168 — Royal killings

Ahaziah and Joram
2 Kings 8:28–29, 2 Chronicles 22:5–6

Jehu anointed king
2 Kings 9:1–13

Jehu slays Joram
2 Kings 9:14–26, 2 Chronicles 22:7

Princes slain
2 Kings 10:12–14, 2 Chronicles 22:8

Ahaziah's death
2 Kings 9:27–28, 2 Chronicles 22:9

Royal family slain
2 Kings 11:1, 2 Chronicles 22:10

Joash spared
2 Kings 11:2–3, 2 Chronicles 22:11–12

Jezebel
2 Kings 9:30–37

2 Chronicles 22:8–11

⁸While Jehu was executing judgment on the house of Ahab, he found the princes of Judah and the sons of Ahaziah's relatives, who had been attending Ahaziah, and he killed them. ⁹He then went in search of Ahaziah, and his men captured him while he was hiding in Samaria. He was brought to Jehu and put to death. They buried him, for they said, "He was a son of Jehoshaphat, who sought the Lord with all his heart." So there was no-one in the house of Ahaziah powerful enough to retain the kingdom.

¹⁰When Athaliah the mother of Ahaziah saw that her son was dead, she proceeded to destroy the whole royal family of the house of Judah. ¹¹But Jehosheba, the daughter of King Jehoram, took Joash son of Ahaziah and stole him away from among the royal princes who were about to be murdered and put him and his nurse in a bedroom. Because Jehosheba, the daughter of King Jehoram and wife of the priest Jehoiada, was Ahaziah's sister, she hid the child from Athaliah so that she could not kill him.

For Thought and **Contemplation**

It's sad, of course, when anyone is killed, but when a royal family is wiped out in this way, then it is very tragic. When did you last pray for the protection and safety of the royal family? Remember that, for a Christian, prayer for the royal family is not an option: it's a command.

"I urge, then, first of all, that requests, prayers, intercession and thanksgiving be made for everyone – for kings and all those in authority, that we may live peaceful and quiet lives in all godliness and holiness." (1 Tim. 2:1–2)

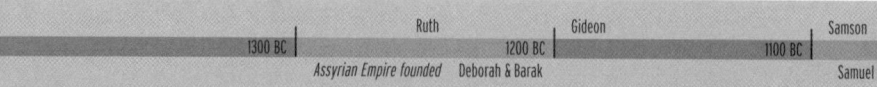

Jehu and Joash

DAY **169**

2 Kings 11:9–12

⁹The commanders of units of a hundred did just as Jehoiada the priest ordered. Each one took his men – those who were going on duty on the Sabbath and those who were going off duty – and came to Jehoiada the priest. ¹⁰Then he gave the commanders the spears and shields that had belonged to King David and that were in the temple of the Lord. ¹¹The guards, each with his weapon in his hand, stationed themselves round the king – near the altar and the temple, from the south side to the north side of the temple. ¹²Jehoiada brought out the king's son and put the crown on him; he presented him with a copy of the covenant and proclaimed him king. They anointed him, and the people clapped their hands and shouted, "Long live the king!"

Judgment on Ahab	2 Kings 10:1–11
Jehonadab spared	2 Kings 10:15–17
Jehu destroys Baal worship	2 Kings 10:18–28, 30
Joash becomes king	2 Kings 11:4–12, 2 Chronicles 23:1–11
Jehu's backsliding	2 Kings 10:29, 31–33
Athaliah executed	2 Kings 11:13–16, 2 Chronicles 23:12–15
Joash's good life	2 Chronicles 24:1–2, 2 Kings 11:21, 12:1–3

For Thought and **Contemplation**

Joash's concern to restore the temple of the Lord was highly commendable; the Lord's house must be kept in good repair (2 Chron. 24:4). Your body, too, is a temple of the Lord. How good a caretaker are you of the Lord's property?

"Do you not know that your body is a temple of the Holy Spirit, who is in you, whom you have received from God? You are not your own; you were bought at a price. Therefore honour God with your body." (1 Cor. 6:19–20)

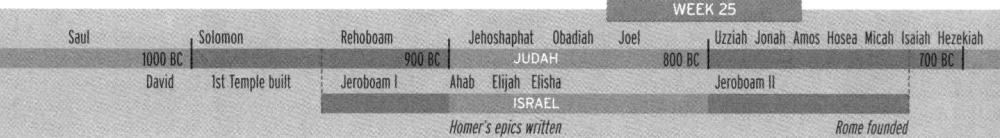

DAY 170

Joash's godly reign

Revival under Jehoiada
2 Kings 11:17–20, 2 Chronicles 23:16–21

Joash's family
2 Chronicles 24:3

Jehu's death
2 Kings 10:34–36

Faithless priests
2 Chronicles 24:4–7, 2 Kings 12:4–8

Jehoahaz
2 Kings 13:1–2

Syria's oppression
2 Kings 13:22, 3–7

Joash repairs temple
2 Kings 12:9–16, 2 Chronicles 24:8–14

Plague of insects
Joel 1:1–20

2 Chronicles 24:8–12

⁸At the king's command, a chest was made and placed outside, at the gate of the temple of the Lord. ⁹A proclamation was then issued in Judah and Jerusalem that they should bring to the Lord the tax that Moses the servant of God had required of Israel in the desert. ¹⁰All the officials and all the people brought their contributions gladly, dropping them into the chest until it was full. ¹¹Whenever the chest was brought in by the Levites to the king's officials and they saw that there was a large amount of money, the royal secretary and the officer of the chief priest would come and empty the chest and carry it back to its place. They did this regularly and collected a great amount of money. ¹²The king and Jehoiada gave it to the men who carried out the work required for the temple of the Lord. They hired masons and carpenters to restore the Lord's temple, and also workers in iron and bronze to repair the temple.

For Thought and **Contemplation**

Jehoiada's idea of placing an offering chest at the side of the altar was an inspired one (2 Kings 12:9); it underlined the fact that worship and giving are inseparably linked. You cannot worship God and money, but you can worship God with money.

"... No man should appear before the Lord empty-handed: Each of you must bring a gift in proportion to the way the Lord your God has blessed you." (Deut. 16:16–17)

a bird's eye view of **Joel**

Place in the Bible
Twenty-ninth Old Testament book; seventh book of prophecy.

Special feature:
A recent event, a devastating plague of locusts, is used by Joel for illustration.

Joel's prophecy

DAY 171

God's judgments
Joel 2:1–11

Exhortation to repent
Joel 2:12–17

Results of repentance
Joel 2:18–27

The great promise
Joel 2:28–32

Nations judged
Joel 3:1–17

Judah's restoration
Joel 3:18–21

Jehoiada's death
2 Chronicles 24:15–16

Princes backslide
2 Chronicles 24:17–19

Joash bribes Hazael
2 Kings 12:17–18

Jehoahaz's death
2 Kings 13:8–9

Jehoash
2 Kings 13:10

Jehoash's evil life
2 Kings 13:11

Zechariah slain
2 Chronicles 24:20–22

Judah defeated
2 Chronicles 24:23–24

Joash slain
2 Chronicles 24:25–27,
2 Kings 12:19–21

Joel 2:28–32

²⁸'And afterwards,
I will pour out my Spirit on all people.
Your sons and daughters will prophesy,
your old men will dream dreams,
your young men will see visions.
²⁹Even on my servants, both men and women,
I will pour out my Spirit in those days.
³⁰I will show wonders in the heavens and on the earth,
blood and fire and billows of smoke.
³¹The sun will be turned to darkness
and the moon to blood
before the coming of the great and dreadful day of the Lord.
³²And everyone who calls
on the name of the Lord will be saved ...

For Thought and **Contemplation**

Joel prophesied that one day the Spirit would come, not at special times and on special occasions, but that He would dwell in the hearts of God's people permanently and perpetually. The day of which Joel spoke is here! Aren't you glad?

"... this is what was spoken by the prophet Joel: 'In the last days, God says, I will pour out my Spirit on all people. Your sons and daughters will prophesy, your young men will see visions, your old men will dream dreams.'" (Acts 2:16–17)

Jesus and the Book

Jesus Christ enlarged on Joel's wonderful promises about the Holy Spirit in John 16:13, "But when he, the Spirit of truth, comes, he will guide you into all truth ..."

Teaching

God will intervene decisively in human history. God will then be seen to be who he is – King.

A Verse to Remember

"And afterwards, I will pour out my Spirit on all people. Your sons and daughters will prophesy, your old men will dream dreams, your young men will see visions." (Joel 2:28)

DAY **172**

Judah and Israel

Jehoash visits Elisha
2 Kings 13:14–19

Miracle in tomb
2 Kings 13:20–21

Amaziah
2 Chronicles 25:1–4, 2 Kings 14:1–6

Syria's defeat
2 Kings 13:23–25

Amaziah gathers army
2 Chronicles 25:5–10

Amaziah's victory
2 Kings 14:7, 2 Chronicles 25:11–12

Cities plundered
2 Chronicles 25:13

Amaziah's idolatry
2 Chronicles 25:14–16

Jerusalem plundered
2 Kings 14:8–14, 2 Chronicles 25:17–24

Uzziah (Azariah) becomes co-regent aged 16
2 Kings 15:2, 2 Chronicles 26:1, 3–5

Jehoash's death
2 Kings 13:12–13, 14:15–16

Amaziah's last years
2 Kings 14:17, 22,
2 Chronicles 25:25, 26:2

2 Kings 13:20–25

[20]Elisha died and was buried. Now Moabite raiders used to enter the country every spring. [21]Once while some Israelites were burying a man, suddenly they saw a band of raiders; so they threw the man's body into Elisha's tomb. When the body touched Elisha's bones, the man came to life and stood up on his feet. [22]Hazael king of Aram oppressed Israel throughout the reign of Jehoahaz. [23]But the Lord was gracious to them and had compassion and showed concern for them because of his covenant with Abraham, Isaac and Jacob. To this day he has been unwilling to destroy them or banish them from his presence. [24]Hazael king of Aram died, and Ben-Hadad his son succeeded him as king. [25]Then Jehoash son of Jehoahaz recaptured from Ben-Hadad son of Hazael the towns he had taken in battle from his father Jehoahaz. Three times Jehoash defeated him, and so he recovered the Israelite towns.

For Thought and **Contemplation**

Such was the power of God that rested on Elisha that it remained in his bones even after his death (2 Kings 13:21). Seems like there was more power in Elisha after he was dead than in many Christians when they are alive!

"And if the Spirit of him who raised Jesus from the dead is living in you, he who raised Christ from the dead will also give life to your mortal bodies through his Spirit, who lives in you." (Rom. 8:11)

a bird's eye view of **Hosea**

Place in the Bible	**Main Characters**	**Special Feature**
Twenty-eighth Old Testament book; sixth book of prophecy.	Hosea and Gomer.	Hosea uses the adultery of his wife to illustrate the theme of this book.

Hosea's message

DAY **173**

Hosea 3:1-5

¹The Lord said to me, "Go, show your love to your wife again, though she is loved by another and is an adulteress. Love her as the Lord loves the Israelites, though they turn to other gods and love the sacred raisin cakes." ²So I bought her for fifteen shekels of silver and about a homer and a lethek of barley. ³Then I told her, "You are to live with me for many days; you must not be a prostitute or be intimate with any man, and I will live with you."
⁴For the Israelites will live for many days without king or prince, without sacrifice or sacred stones, without ephod or idol. ⁵Afterwards the Israelites will return and seek the Lord their God and David their king. They will come trembling to the Lord and to his blessings in the last days.

Jeroboam	2 Kings 14:23-27
Amaziah's death	2 Kings 14:18-20, 2 Chronicles 25:26-28
Uzziah becomes sole ruler	2 Kings 15:1
Uzziah's success	2 Chronicles 26:6-15
Israel's future restoration	Amos 9:11-15
Israel rebuked	Hosea 1:1-2:5
God's judgments	Hosea 2:6-13
His promises	Hosea 2:14-23
Israel restored	Hosea 3:1-5

For Thought and **Contemplation**

Hosea may have been a minor prophet, but he was given a major task by God of demonstrating to Israel the kind of love that goes on loving even in the face of unfaithfulness. Is God asking the same of you at this moment? Then do as Hosea did – lean hard on the Lord. He will never fail.

"Love is patient, love is kind. It does not envy, it does not boast, it is not proud ... It always protects, always trusts, always hopes, always perseveres. Love never fails ..." (1 Cor. 13:4, 7 & 8)

Jesus and the Book

Jesus Christ quotes from Hosea 6:6: "It is not the healthy who need a doctor, but the sick. But go and learn what this means: 'I desire mercy, not sacrifice.' For I have not come to call the righteous, but sinners." (Matt. 9:12-13)

Teaching

Hosea depicts God's yearning and overflowing love for His people in the book, reaching breath-taking heights in chapter 14. Hosea shows how, despite Israel's unfaithfulness to God, God continually loves His people and desires them to return to Him.

A Verse to Remember

"I will heal their waywardness and love them freely, for my anger has turned away from them. I will be like the dew to Israel; he will blossom like a lily" (Hos. 14:4-5).

DAY **174** — Jonah

Jonah's disobedience
Jonah 1:1–11

Jonah in the fish
Jonah 1:12–17

Jonah's prayer
Jonah 2:1–9

His deliverance
Jonah 2:10

Jonah at Nineveh
Jonah 3:1–10

His strange reaction
Jonah 4:1–11

Judgments against nations
Amos 1:1–15, 2:1–3

Judgments against Israel and Judah
Amos 2:4–3:15

Jonah 2:1–7

¹From inside the fish Jonah prayed to the Lord his God. ²He said:
"In my distress I called to the Lord, and he answered me.
From the depths of the grave I called for help,
 and you listened to my cry.
³You hurled me into the deep,
 into the very heart of the seas,
 and the currents swirled about me;
all your waves and breakers
 swept over me.
⁴I said, 'I have been banished
 from your sight; yet I will look
again towards your holy temple.'
⁵The engulfing waters threatened me, the deep surrounded me;
 seaweed was wrapped around my head.
⁶To the roots of the mountains I sank down;
 the earth beneath barred me in for ever.
But you brought my life up from the pit,
 O Lord my God.
⁷When my life was ebbing away,
 I remembered you, Lord,
and my prayer rose to you,
 to your holy temple. ..."

For Thought and **Contemplation**

Jonah's greatest problem was his fear of being proved wrong (see Jonah 4:2). He thought more of himself than he did of God, or of the message he had been given by God. If you want to be used by God then you must be willing to put His message first, and your feelings second. Otherwise, like Jonah, you're heading for trouble.

"Yet when I preach the gospel, I cannot boast, for I am compelled to preach. Woe to me if I do not preach the gospel!" (1 Cor. 9:16)

a bird's eye view of **Jonah**

Place in the Bible

Thirty-second Old Testament book; tenth book of prophecy.

Amos' message

DAY **175**

Amos 5:1–6

¹Hear this word, O house of Israel,
this lament I take up concerning you:
²"Fallen is Virgin Israel,
 never to rise again,
deserted in her own land,
 with no-one to lift her up."
³This is what the Sovereign Lord says:
"The city that marches out a thousand strong for Israel
 will have only a hundred left;
the town that marches out a hundred strong
 will have only ten left."
⁴This is what the Lord says to the house of Israel:
"Seek me and live;
 ⁵do not seek Bethel,
do not go to Gilgal,
 do not journey to Beersheba.
For Gilgal will surely go into exile,
 and Bethel will be reduced to nothing."
⁶Seek the Lord and live,
 or he will sweep through the house of Joseph like a fire;
it will devour,
 and Bethel will have no-one
to quench it.

Israel is reproved	Amos 4:1–5
Their impenitence shown	Amos 4:6–13
The call to seek the Lord	Amos 5:1–6
Exhortations to repentance	Amos 5:7–17
Warnings of judgment	Amos 5:18–27
The danger of luxury	Amos 6:1–7
Punishments for sins	Amos 6:8–14
Amos' visions	Amos 7:1–9
Amos and Amaziah	Amos 7:10–17

For Thought and **Contemplation**

When Amos placed God's plumbline against Israel, the nation was found greatly wanting. What would happen if Amos was to pay you a visit today and set your life against God's plumbline? Would it measure up – or would it be found wanting?

"Blessed is the man who perseveres under trial, because when he has stood the test, he will receive the crown of life that God has promised to those who love him." (Jas. 1:12)

Jesus and the Book

Jesus Christ took Jonah's experience as an illustration of his own death and resurrection to life (Matt. 12:39–41).

Teaching

Nineveh, the capital of the hated Assyrians, was a byword for evil and cruelty. It is not surprising, then, that Jonah was reluctant to obey God's call to go there. Throughout this book God's great love for Gentiles is portrayed.

A Verse to Remember

"... I knew that you are a gracious and compassionate God, slow to anger and abounding in love." (Jonah 4:2)

DAY 176 — Evil kings

Another vision	Amos 8:1–3
Israel's doom	Amos 8:4–14
The Lord's judgments	Amos 9:1–10
Jeroboam's death	2 Kings 14:28–29
The Lord's accusation	Hosea 4:1–11
Pagan worship condemned	Hosea 4:12–19
Zechariah	2 Kings 15:8–12
Shallum	2 Kings 15:13–15
Menahem	2 Kings 15:16–18
Assyrian invasion	2 Kings 15:19–20
Uzziah's intrusion	2 Chronicles 26:16–18
Uzziah's leprosy	2 Chronicles 26:19–21, 2 Kings 15:5
Menahem's death	2 Kings 15:21–22
Pekahiah	2 Kings 15:23–24

2 Kings 15:8–12

⁸In the thirty-eighth year of Azariah king of Judah, Zechariah son of Jeroboam became king of Israel in Samaria, and he reigned for six months. ⁹He did evil in the eyes of the Lord, as his fathers had done. He did not turn away from the sins of Jeroboam son of Nebat, which he had caused Israel to commit. ¹⁰Shallum son of Jabesh conspired against Zechariah. He attacked him in front of the people, assassinated him and succeeded him as king. ¹¹The other events of Zechariah's reign are written in the book of the annals of the kings of Israel. ¹²So the word of the Lord spoken to Jehu was fulfilled: "Your descendants will sit on the throne of Israel to the fourth generation."

For Thought and Contemplation

Uzziah's sin was that he became proud and intruded upon the work of the priests by burning incense on God's altar – a task assigned only to the descendants of Aaron. As a result he was punished by becoming a leper and had to live in isolation. Those who covet forbidden honours often find they forfeit legitimate ones.

"For it is not the one who commends himself who is approved, but the one whom the Lord commends."
(2 Cor. 10:18)

a bird's eye view of **Amos**

Place in the Bible

Thirtieth Old Testament book; eighth book of prophecy.

Isaiah's message

DAY **177**

Isaiah 6:1–7

¹In the year that King Uzziah died, I saw the Lord seated on a throne, high and exalted, and the train of his robe filled the temple. ²Above him were seraphs, each with six wings: With two wings they covered their faces, with two they covered their feet, and with two they were flying. ³And they were calling to one another:
"Holy, holy, holy is the Lord Almighty;
 the whole earth is full of his glory."
⁴At the sound of their voices the doorposts and thresholds shook and the temple was filled with smoke.
⁵"Woe to me!" I cried. "I am ruined! For I am a man of unclean lips, and I live among a people of unclean lips, and my eyes have seen the King, the Lord Almighty."
⁶Then one of the seraphs flew to me with a live coal in his hand, which he had taken with tongs from the altar. ⁷With it he touched my mouth and said, "See, this has touched your lips; your guilt is taken away and your sin atoned for."

Pekahiah killed	2 Kings 15:25–26
Pekah	2 Kings 15:27–28
Uzziah's death	2 Kings 15:6–7, 2 Chronicles 26:22–23
Isaiah sees the Lord	Isaiah 6:1–13
Jotham	2 Chronicles 27:1, 2, 8, 2 Kings 15:32–35
The promise	Isaiah 2:1–5
Chastisement before blessing	Isaiah 2:6–3:26

For Thought and **Contemplation**

Isaiah said, "In the year that King Uzziah died, I saw the Lord." It was only when the prophet saw the earthly king in his coffin that he was able to see the heavenly King on His throne. How sad that God sometimes has to take something from us in order to focus our gaze on Himself.

"But as for me, I watch in hope for the Lord, I wait for God my Saviour; my God will hear me." (Mic. 7:7)

Jesus and the Book

Like Amos, Jesus Christ set His face implacably against all religious hypocrisy and spiritual humbug: see, for example, Matthew 23:23.

Teaching

Amos' hard hitting message starts by roundly condemning Israel's sinful neighbours, but then he homes in on Israel itself and teaches them about God's basic demands – social justice, and faithful worship.

A Verse to Remember

"But let justice roll on like a river, righteousness like a never-failing stream!" (Amos 5:24)

DAY 178 — Micah's message

Restoration of Jerusalem
Isaiah 4:1–6

Parable of vineyard
Isaiah 5:1–7

Six woes
Isaiah 5:8–30

Micah's message
Micah 1:1

The wrath of God
Micah 1:2–16

Israel's sins
Micah 2:1–5

The evil practices
Micah 2:6–11

A promise
Micah 2:12–13

Jotham's strength
2 Chronicles 27:3–6

Rezin joins Pekah
2 Kings 15:37

Jotham's death
2 Kings 15:36 & 38, 2 Chronicles 27:7 & 9

Micah 2:8–12

"… ⁸Lately my people have risen up
 like an enemy.
You strip off the rich robe
 from those who pass by without a care,
 like men returning from battle.
⁹You drive the women of my people
 from their pleasant homes.
You take away my blessing
 from their children for ever.
¹⁰Get up, go away!
 For this is not your resting place,
 because it is defiled,
 it is ruined, beyond all remedy.
¹¹If a liar and deceiver comes and says,
 'I will prophesy for you plenty of wine and beer,'
 he would be just the prophet for this people!
¹²I will surely gather all of you, O Jacob;
 I will surely bring together the remnant of Israel.
I will bring them together like sheep in a pen,
 like a flock in its pasture …"

For Thought and **Contemplation**

Micah shows that the game, "follow my leader", can be fine when the leaders are following the Lord. Who leads you spiritually? Are they people whose lives radiate the love of Christ? If not, then you need to re-examine your spiritual commitments.

"Be imitators of God, therefore, as dearly loved children and live a life of love, just as Christ loved us and gave himself up for us as a fragrant offering and sacrifice to God." (Eph. 5:1-2)

Place in the Bible
Twenty-third Old Testament book; first book of prophecy.

a bird's eye view of **Isaiah**

The coming Messiah

DAY 179

Isaiah 9:2–6

²The people walking in darkness
  have seen a great light;
on those living in the land of the shadow of death
  a light has dawned.
³You have enlarged the nation
  and increased their joy;
they rejoice before you
  as people rejoice at the harvest,
  as men rejoice
  when dividing the plunder.
⁴For as in the day of Midian's defeat,
  you have shattered
the yoke that burdens them,
  the bar across their shoulders,
  the rod of their oppressor.
⁵Every warrior's boot used in battle
  and every garment rolled in blood
  will be destined for burning,
  will be fuel for the fire.
⁶For to us a child is born,
  to us a son is given,
  and the government will be on his shoulders.
  And he will be called
  Wonderful Counsellor, Mighty God,
  Everlasting Father, Prince of Peace. ...

Ahaz	2 Kings 16:1–4, 2 Chronicles 28:1–4
Pekah's victory	2 Chronicles 28:5–8
Future hope	Isaiah 7:10–16
The future King	Isaiah 9:1–7
Judah will be invaded	Isaiah 7:17–25, 8:5–22
The coming chastisement	Isaiah 9:8–10:4
Oded's intercession	2 Chronicles 28:9–15

For Thought and **Contemplation**

It is only in recent times that it has become possible to determine the sex of a child in advance. Yet Isaiah, hundreds of years before Christ was born, predicts that a virgin would conceive and bear a son. You need have no worries about the accuracy of Scripture when it contains such unerring predictions.

"And we have the word of the prophets made more certain, and you will do well to pay attention to it, as to a light shining in a dark place ... For prophecy never had its origin in the will of man, but men spoke from God as they were carried along by the Holy Spirit."
(2 Pet. 1:19 & 21)

Jesus and the Book

Isaiah 52:13 to 53:12 ranks as the perfect commentary on the sacrificial death of Jesus for sinful men and women. As many as eighty-five quotes and allusions to Isaiah 53 have been counted in the New Testament.

Teaching

Isaiah's message is that God's salvation has come to His people, the Israelites, and to all nations. Isaiah teaches much about God, His righteousness, His holiness, His sovereignty, His Day (the Day of the Lord), His servant, His judgment, and His comfort.

A Verse to Remember

"We all, like sheep, have gone astray, each of us has turned to his own way; and the Lord has laid on him the iniquity of us all" (Isa. 53:6).

DAY 180 — Assyria's victories

The conspiracy
2 Kings 16:5–6, Isaiah 7:1–2

Israel to be broken
Isaiah 7:3–9

Judah invaded
2 Chronicles 28:17–19

True worship
Psalm 50:1–23

Damascus to be judged
Isaiah 8:1–4, 17:1–14

Assyria defeats Syria
2 Chronicles 28:16 & 21, 2 Kings 16:7–9

Eastern tribes deported
2 Kings 15:29, 1 Chronicles 5:25–26

Warning to Judah
Isaiah 1:2–20

Isaiah 8:1–4

¹The Lord said to me, "Take a large scroll and write on it with an ordinary pen: Maher-Shalal-Hash-Baz. ²And I will call in Uriah the priest and Zechariah son of Jeberekiah as reliable witnesses for me."

³Then I went to the prophetess, and she conceived and gave birth to a son. And the Lord said to me, "Name him Maher-Shalal-Hash-Baz. ⁴Before the boy knows how to say 'My father' or 'My mother,' the wealth of Damascus and the plunder of Samaria will be carried off by the king of Assyria."

For Thought and **Contemplation**

God will prune and purify His people even if He has to use an ungodly nation like Assyria to achieve it. Are you being plagued or harassed by a non-Christian source at the moment? Then ask the Lord to show you why. This may be the only way He can bring you into line with His will and purposes!

"These have come so that your faith – of greater worth than gold, which perishes even though refined by fire – may be proved genuine and may result in praise, glory and honour when Jesus Christ is revealed." (1 Pet. 1:7)

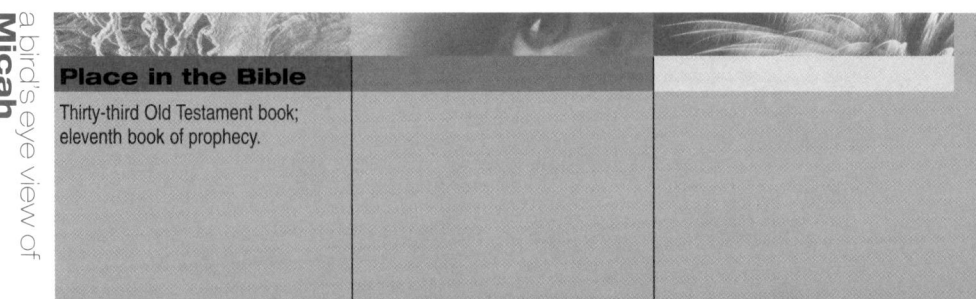

a bird's eye view of **Micah**

Place in the Bible
Thirty-third Old Testament book; eleventh book of prophecy.

Hezekiah's godly reign

DAY **181**

2 Kings 18:1–3, 5–6

¹In the third year of Hoshea son of Elah king of Israel, Hezekiah son of Ahaz king of Judah began to reign. ²He was twenty-five years old when he became king, and he reigned in Jerusalem for twenty-nine years. His mother's name was Abijah daughter of Zechariah. ³He did what was right in the eyes of the Lord, just as his father David had done. ...

⁵Hezekiah trusted in the Lord, the God of Israel. There was no-one like him among all the kings of Judah, either before him or after him. ⁶He held fast to the Lord and did not cease to follow him; he kept the commands the Lord had given Moses.

The sinful city
Isaiah 1:21–31

Jerusalem plundered
2 Kings 16:10–18,
2 Chronicles 28:20, 22–25

Pekah killed
2 Kings 15:31 & 30

Hoshea
2 Kings 17:1–2

Death of Ahaz
2 Kings 16:19–20, 2 Chronicles 28:26–27

Hezekiah
2 Kings 18:1–3, 5–6, 2 Chronicles 29:1–2

Temple reconsecrated and cleansed
2 Chronicles 29:3–19

Temple worship restored
2 Chronicles 29:20–36

For Thought and **Contemplation**

As soon as Hezekiah heard that the temple was ready for worship, he lost no time in making an offering for atonement – and, as the offering was laid on the altar, the Levites broke out in song. Be sure that your sorrow over sin does not prevent you, in due course, from praising God.

"We will shout for joy when you are victorious and will lift up our banners in the name of our God. May the Lord grant all your requests. (Psa. 20:5)

Jesus and the Book

Micah's prophecy in chapter 5:2, referred to in Matthew 2:5–6, is a clear reference to the birth of the Saviour of the world.

Teaching

Micah delivers God's call to repentance and social justice.

A Verse to Remember

"He has showed you, O man, what is good. And what does the Lord require of you? To act justly and to love mercy and to walk humbly with your God." (Mic. 6:8)

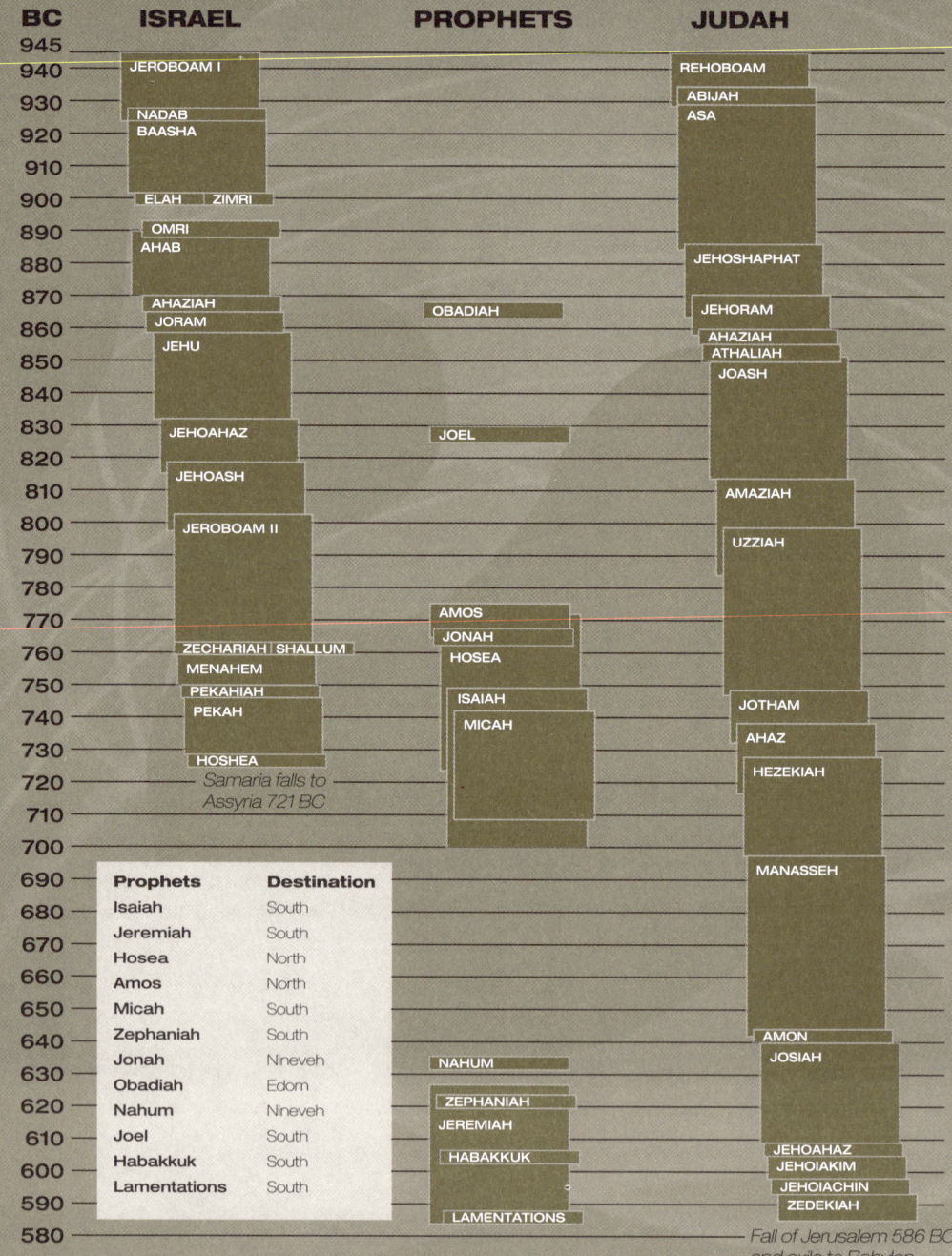

The Passover renewed

DAY 182

2 Chronicles 30:23-27

²³The whole assembly then agreed to celebrate the festival seven more days; so for another seven days they celebrated joyfully. ²⁴Hezekiah king of Judah provided a thousand bulls and seven thousand sheep and goats for the assembly, and the officials provided them with a thousand bulls and ten thousand sheep and goats. A great number of priests consecrated themselves. ²⁵The entire assembly of Judah rejoiced, along with the priests and Levites and all who had assembled from Israel, including the aliens who had come from Israel and those who lived in Judah. ²⁶There was great joy in Jerusalem, for since the days of Solomon son of David king of Israel there had been nothing like this in Jerusalem. ²⁷The priests and the Levites stood to bless the people, and God heard them, for their prayer reached heaven, his holy dwelling-place.

A warning
Isaiah 28:1-6

The drunken prophets of Judah
Isaiah 28:7-13

A cornerstone for Zion
Isaiah 28:14-22

God's wisdom
Isaiah 28:23-29

A warning against idolatry
Hosea 5:1-7

Judgment on Judah and Israel
Hosea 5:8-15

The people's insincere repentance
Hosea 6:1-11

Preparations for the Passover
2 Chronicles 30:1-12

The Passover is celebrated
2 Chronicles 30:13-22

A second celebration
2 Chronicles 30:23-27

For Thought and **Contemplation**

We ought never to think lightly of sin. Those who view the Passover as God simply overlooking human faults and errors are quite mistaken. God does not overlook sin; He "looks over" it to focus His gaze, not on the sinner and his sins, but on the substitutionary sacrifice. Forgiveness may be free, but it is never cheap.

"If we claim to be without sin, we deceive ourselves and the truth is not in us. If we confess our sins, he is faithful and just and will forgive us our sins and purify us from all unrighteousness." (1 Jn. 1:8-9)

Heart to Heart

Section 6

Excellent! You have read through half of the entire Bible. Some of you may have struggled to get this far and could be several days behind. Don't despair – encourage yourself by realising just how far you have already come. If you are behind why not use your day of worship to catch up.

Visit the web site: **www.cover2cover.org**

7

In this section

The Assyrian conquest of Israel
God's intervention in Hezekiah's life
Isaiah's messages of hope and victory
Josiah's programme of reform
The pleas of Jeremiah for repentance

DAY 183 — Hezekiah's reforms

A festival song
Psalm 81:1–16

Idols destroyed
2 Chronicles 31:1, 2 Kings 18:4

Hezekiah's further reforms
2 Chronicles 31:2–21

Israel's leaders denounced
Micah 3:1–12

Hoshea taken prisoner
2 Kings 17:3–4

Israel's wickedness
Hosea 7:1–2

Conspiracy in the palace
Hosea 7:3–7

Israel and the nations
Hosea 7:8–16

2 Chronicles 31:1–4

¹When all this had ended, the Israelites who were there went out to the towns of Judah, smashed the sacred stones and cut down the Asherah poles. They destroyed the high places and the altars throughout Judah and Benjamin and in Ephraim and Manasseh. After they had destroyed all of them, the Israelites returned to their own towns and to their own property. ²Hezekiah assigned the priests and Levites to divisions – each of them according to their duties as priests or Levites – to offer burnt offerings and fellowship offerings, to minister, to give thanks and to sing praises at the gates of the Lord's dwelling. ³The king contributed from his own possessions for the morning and evening burnt offerings and for the burnt offerings on the Sabbaths, New Moons and appointed feasts as written in the Law of the Lord. ⁴He ordered the people living in Jerusalem to give the portion due the priests and Levites so that they could devote themselves to the Law of the Lord ...

For Thought and **Contemplation**

Following the celebration of the Passover, great spiritual reforms took place in Israel. This is how it ought always to be. The benefits we receive through prayer, Holy Communion and the ministry of the Word in the house of God on Sundays ought to be worked out in our own house on Mondays. And Tuesdays. And Wednesdays ...

"... continue to work out your salvation with fear and trembling, for it is God who works in you to will and to act according to his good purpose." (Phil. 2:12–13)

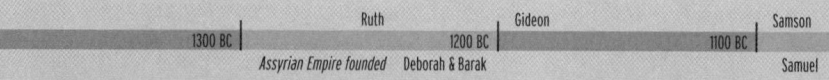

Israel's punishment

DAY **184**

Hosea 13:1–6

When Ephraim spoke, men trembled;
 he was exalted in Israel.
 But he became guilty of Baal worship and died.
²Now they sin more and more;
 they make idols for themselves from their silver,
 cleverly fashioned images,
 all of them the work of craftsmen.
 It is said of these people,
 "They offer human sacrifice and kiss the calf-idols."
³Therefore they will be like the morning mist,
 like the early dew that disappears,
 like chaff swirling from a threshing floor,
 like smoke escaping through a window.
⁴"But I am the Lord your God,
 [who brought you] out of Egypt.
 You shall acknowledge no God but me,
 no Saviour except me.
⁵I cared for you in the desert,
 in the land of burning heat.
⁶When I fed them, they were satisfied ..."

The Lord condemns Israel	Hosea 8:1–14
Hosea's announcement	Hosea 9:1–9
The consequences of Israel's sin	Hosea 9:10–14
The Lord's judgment	Hosea 9:15–16
The prophet speaks	Hosea 9:17, 10:1–8
The Lord pronounces judgment	Hosea 10:9–15
God's love	Hosea 11:1–11
Israel and Judah are condemned	Hosea 11:12, 12:1–6
Further words of judgment	Hosea 12:7–14
Final judgment on Israel	Hosea 13:1–8

For Thought and **Contemplation**

It is important to remember that God's judgment of His people's sins is not merely retributive, but remedial. He isn't against us for our sin, but for us against our sin. Think about it. It's a thought worth holding in our minds throughout the whole of this day.

"But God demonstrates his own love for us in this: While we were still sinners, Christ died for us." (Rom. 5:8)

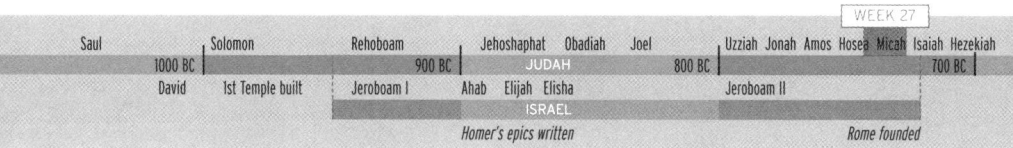

DAY 185 — Israel taken captive

Final judgment on Israel
Hosea 13:9–16

Hosea's plea
Hosea 14:1–3

Israel's restoration
Hosea 14:4–9

Samaria besieged
2 Kings 17:5, 18:9

Israel taken captive
2 Kings 17:6, 18:10–11

Reasons for Israel's downfall
2 Kings 17:7–23, 18:12

Prayer for Israel's restoration
Psalm 80:1–19

The Fall of Israel 721 BC

A vision of Babylon's fall
Isaiah 21:1–10

2 Kings 17:7–12

⁷All this took place because the Israelites had sinned against the Lord their God, who had brought them out of Egypt from under the power of Pharaoh king of Egypt. They worshipped other gods ⁸and followed the practices of the nations the Lord had driven out before them, as well as the practices that the kings of Israel had introduced. ⁹The Israelites secretly did things against the Lord their God that were not right. From watchtower to fortified city they built themselves high places in all their towns. ¹⁰They set up sacred stones and Asherah poles on every high hill and under every spreading tree. ¹¹At every high place they burned incense, as the nations whom the Lord had driven out before them had done. They did wicked things that provoked the Lord to anger. ¹²They worshipped idols, though the Lord had said, "You shall not do this." ...

For Thought and **Contemplation**

One of the greatest mysteries of life is why God uses ungodly people or nations to chastise His own children. Surely one answer must be that if we fail to examine our own hearts, then God must do it for us. And the "examination board" He uses may not always be to our liking!

"My son, do not despise the Lord's discipline and do not resent his rebuke, because the Lord disciplines those he loves, as a father the son he delights in." (Prov. 3:11–12)

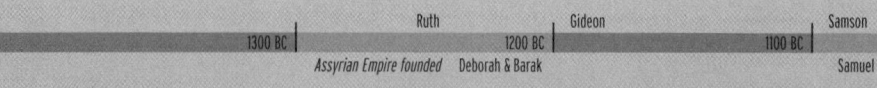

The nations judged

DAY 186

Isaiah 14:28-32

²⁸This oracle came in the year King Ahaz died:
²⁹Do not rejoice, all you Philistines,
 that the rod that struck you is broken;
 from the root of that snake will spring up a viper,
 its fruit will be a darting, venomous serpent.
³⁰The poorest of the poor will find pasture,
 and the needy will lie down in safety.
 But your root I will destroy by famine;
 it will slay your survivors.
³¹Wail, O gate! Howl, O city!
 Melt away, all you Philistines!
 A cloud of smoke comes from the north,
 and there is not a straggler in its ranks.
³²What answer shall be given
 to the envoys of that nation?
"The Lord has established Zion,
 and in her his afflicted people will find refuge."

A message about Edom	Isaiah 21:11–12
A message about Arabia	Isaiah 21:13–17
Judgment upon the Philistines	Isaiah 14:28–32
Judgment upon Moab	Isaiah 15:1–9
Moab's hopeless situation	Isaiah 16:1–14
Hezekiah defies Assyria	2 Kings 18:7–8
The Amalekites slain	1 Chronicles 4:39–43
Judgment against Ethiopia	Isaiah 18:1–7
Judgment against Egypt	Isaiah 19:1–15
Egypt will worship the Lord	Isaiah 19:16–25

For Thought and **Contemplation**

The theme of judgment, although very conspicuous in Old Testament times, is often missing from modern Christian thought. Yet make no mistake about it – judgment will come. As someone has said: "If God will not judge the nations for their sins, then He will surely have to apologise to Sodom and Gomorrah."

" ... the Lord ... comes to judge the earth. He will judge the world in righteousness and the peoples in his truth." (Psa. 96:13)

WEEK 27

Saul	Solomon	Rehoboam	Jehoshaphat Obadiah Joel	Uzziah Jonah Amos Hosea Micah Isaiah Hezekiah
1000 BC		900 BC	JUDAH 800 BC	700 BC
David	1st Temple built	Jeroboam I	Ahab Elijah Elisha	Jeroboam II	Fall of Samaria
			ISRAEL	
			Homer's epics written	Rome founded

DAY 187 — Assyria's coming destruction

The sign to Egypt and Ethiopia
Isaiah 20:1–6

Judgment against Tyre
Isaiah 23:1–18

Assyria, God's instrument
Isaiah 10:5–19

Remnant of Israel to be saved
Isaiah 10:20–23

Judgment against Assyria
Isaiah 10:24–27

The invader attacks
Isaiah 10:28–34

The peaceful kingdom
Isaiah 11:1–9

The exiles will return
Isaiah 11:10–16

Hymn of thanksgiving
Isaiah 12:1–6

Isaiah 10:28–34

²⁸They enter Aiath;
  they pass through Migron;
  they store supplies at Michmash.
²⁹They go over the pass, and say,
  "We will camp overnight at Geba."
  Ramah trembles;
  Gibeah of Saul flees.
³⁰Cry out, O Daughter of Gallim!
  Listen, O Laishah!
  Poor Anathoth!
³¹Madmenah is in flight;
  the people of Gebim take cover.
³²This day they will halt at Nob;
  they will shake their fist
  at the mount of the Daughter of Zion,
  at the hill of Jerusalem.
³³See, the Lord, the Lord Almighty,
  will lop off the boughs with great power.
  The lofty trees will be felled,
  the tall ones will be brought low.
³⁴He will cut down the forest thickets with an axe;
  Lebanon will fall before the Mighty One.

For Thought and **Contemplation**

This point must never be forgotten: when God allows His people to fall into trouble, it is to humble them and bring their sin to remembrance. The ultimate end of all God's judgments, as they relate to His people, is the putting away of sin. He upsets us in order to set us up.

"The eyes of the arrogant man will be humbled and the pride of men brought low; the Lord alone will be exalted in that day." (Isa. 2:11)

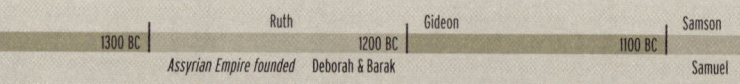

The Lord's judgments

DAY **188**

Isaiah 14:22–26

²²"I will rise up against them,"
 declares the Lord Almighty.
"I will cut off from Babylon her name and survivors,
 her offspring and descendants,"
 declares the Lord.
²³"I will turn her into a place for owls
 and into swampland;
I will sweep her with the broom of destruction,"
 declares the Lord Almighty.
²⁴The Lord Almighty has sworn,
"Surely, as I have planned, so it will be,
 and as I have purposed, so it will stand.
²⁵I will crush the Assyrian in my land;
 on my mountains I will trample him down.
His yoke will be taken from my people,
 and his burden removed from their shoulders."
²⁶This is the plan determined for the whole world;
 this is the hand stretched out over all nations. ...

Judgment upon Babylon	Isaiah 13:1–16
The return from exile	Isaiah 14:1–3
The king of Babylon's fall	Isaiah 14:4–11, 18–21
God will destroy Babylon	Isaiah 14:22–23
God will destroy the Assyrians	Isaiah 14:24–27
Judgment upon the world	Isaiah 24:1–23
A hymn of praise	Isaiah 25:1–5
God prepares a banquet	Isaiah 25:6–9
God will punish Moab	Isaiah 25:10–12
God's victorious people	Isaiah 26:1–11

For Thought and **Contemplation**

More and more judgment! When will God stop? The answer surely is – when men turn from their sin and follow the path of righteousness. And those who obey the divine command to cease from sin discover this encouraging truth – the Almighty is as great in mercy as He is in judgment. Hallelujah!

" ... unless you repent, you too will all perish." (Lk. 13:3)

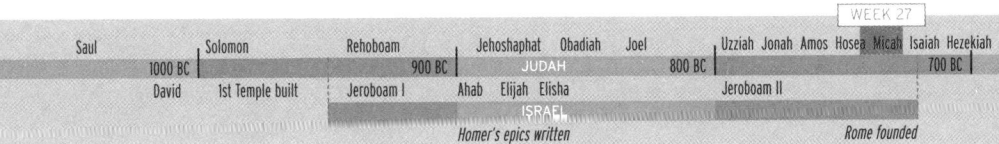

DAY 189 — The way of holiness

God's victorious people
Isaiah 26:12–19

Judgment and restoration
Isaiah 26:20–21, 27:1–13

The coming siege
Isaiah 22:1–14

God will punish His enemies
Isaiah 34:1–17

The coming victory
Isaiah 35:1–10

Hezekiah's divine healing
2 Kings 20:1–11

Hezekiah's pride
2 Chronicles 32:24–26

Isaiah 35:1–6

¹The desert and the parched land will be glad;
 the wilderness will rejoice and blossom.
 Like the crocus,
²it will burst into bloom;
 it will rejoice greatly and shout for joy.
 The glory of Lebanon will be given to it,
 the splendour of Carmel and Sharon;
 they will see the glory of the Lord,
 the splendour of our God.
³Strengthen the feeble hands,
 steady the knees that give way;
⁴say to those with fearful hearts,
 "Be strong, do not fear;
your God will come,
 he will come with vengeance;
with divine retribution
 he will come to save you."
⁵Then will the eyes of the blind be opened
 and the ears of the deaf unstopped.
⁶Then will the lame leap like a deer,
 and the mute tongue shout for joy ...

For Thought and **Contemplation**

Never let it be forgotten that God's way is a way of holiness. Did you know that the root meaning of "holiness" is "healthiness"? Perhaps this is a good moment to check your spiritual health. When we are unholy, we are unhealthy. How "healthy" are you at this present moment?

"Consecrate yourselves and be holy, because I am the Lord your God." (Lev. 20:7)

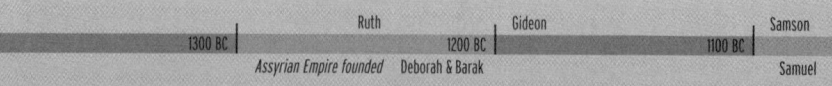

The incomparable God

DAY **190**

Isaiah 40:12–15

¹²Who has measured the waters in the hollow of his hand,
  or with the breadth of his hand marked off the heavens?
 Who has held the dust of the earth in a basket,
  or weighed the mountains on the scales
  and the hills in a balance?
¹³Who has understood the mind of the Lord,
  or instructed him as his counsellor?
¹⁴Whom did the Lord consult to enlighten him,
  and who taught him the right way?
 Who was it that taught him knowledge
  or showed him the path of understanding?
¹⁵Surely the nations are like a drop in a bucket;
  they are regarded as dust on the scales;
  he weighs the islands as though they were fine dust ...

Hezekiah's illness and healing
Isaiah 38:1–8, 21–22

Hezekiah is thankful
Isaiah 38:9–20

Words of hope
Isaiah 40:1–9

God's care and protection
Isaiah 40:10–11

Israel's incomparable God
Isaiah 40:12–26

God reassures His people
Isaiah 40:27–31

God's promise to Israel
Isaiah 41:1–20

The Lord's challenge
Isaiah 41:21–29

For Thought and **Contemplation**

It's worth reflecting on the fact that our spiritual progress is largely determined by our view of God. If we hold in our hearts a limited or inadequate picture of Him, this will mirror itself in how we live, and what we ask of Him. Isaiah saw God as not just mighty but *almighty*. Do you?

"For by him all things were created: things in heaven and on earth, visible and invisible, whether thrones or powers or rulers or authorities; all things were created by him and for him." (Col. 1:16)

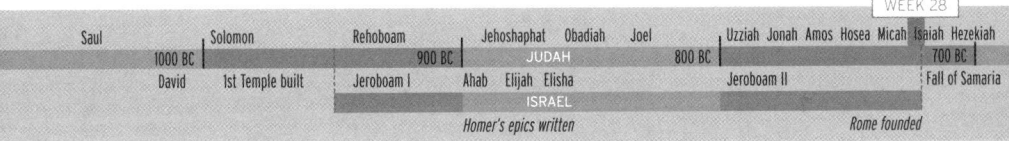

DAY 191

Israel: God's witness

The Lord's servant
Isaiah 42:1–9

A song of praise
Isaiah 42:10–13

God promises His help
Isaiah 42:14–17

Israel's failure to learn
Isaiah 42:18–25

God's promised rescue
Isaiah 43:1–7

Israel is God's witness
Isaiah 43:8–13

Escape from Babylon
Isaiah 43:14–21

Israel's sin
Isaiah 43:22–28

The only God
Isaiah 44:1–8

Idolatry ridiculed
Isaiah 44:9–20

The Creator and Saviour
Isaiah 44:21–28

Isaiah 43:8–12

⁸Lead out those who have eyes but are blind,
  who have ears but are deaf.
⁹All the nations gather together
  and the peoples assemble.
Which of them foretold this
  and proclaimed to us the former things?
Let them bring in their witnesses to prove they were right,
  so that others may hear and say, "It is true."
¹⁰"You are my witnesses," declares the Lord,
  "and my servant whom I have chosen,
  so that you may know and believe me
  and understand that I am he.
Before me no god was formed,
  nor will there be one after me.
¹¹I, even I, am the Lord,
  and apart from me there is no saviour.
¹²I have revealed and saved and proclaimed –
  I, and not some foreign god among you.
You are my witnesses," declares the Lord, "that I am God …"

For Thought and **Contemplation**

Throughout time, God has always sought to maintain in His creation a witness to His honour and to His Name. In the Old Testament age, God's chief witness was Israel. In the New Testament age, His chief witness is the Church. Israel failed miserably. Do we?

"But you will receive power when the Holy Spirit comes on you; and you will be my witnesses in Jerusalem, and in all Judea and Samaria, and to the ends of the earth." (Acts 1:8)

Prophecies Concerning
Gentile Nations in Isaiah

Mediterranean

Assyria *(14:24–27)*
To be crushed upon the mountains of Israel

Syria-Damascus *(17)*
To be defeated by Shalmaneser, Assyrian king

● Damascus

Tyre *(23)*
To suffer a seventy-year Babylonian captivity.

Babylon ●

Babylon *(13, 14, 21)*
To be destroyed by the Medes. To become desolate

Philistia *(14:28–32)*
To suffer defeat by Sargon, the Assyrian king

Jerusalem

Moab *(15, 16)*
Chief cities to be destroyed in one night by Assyrians

Egypt *(19, 20)*
To be ruled harshly by her enemies.

Edom *(21:11, 12)*
To be destroyed by the Medes

Arabia *(21:13–17)*
To have its armies decimated

Ethiopia *(18)*
Fallen armies to become food for animals and birds

Red Sea

DAY 192

Lord of all

Cyrus, a chosen vessel
Isaiah 45:1–8

The Lord of creation and history
Isaiah 45:9–17, 19

Lord of all
Isaiah 45:20–25

Deliverance from Babylon
Isaiah 46:1–13

Judgment on Babylon
Isaiah 47:1–15

God is Lord of the future
Isaiah 48:1–11

Cyrus, the Lord's chosen leader
Isaiah 48:12–16

The Lord's plan for His people
Isaiah 48:17–22

Isaiah 45:20–24

²⁰"Gather together and come;
  assemble, you fugitives from the nations.
 Ignorant are those who carry about idols of wood,
  who pray to gods that cannot save.
²¹Declare what is to be, present it –
  let them take counsel together.
 Who foretold this long ago,
  who declared it from the distant past?
 Was it not I, the Lord?
 And there is no God apart from me,
  a righteous God and a Saviour;
  there is none but me.
²²Turn to me and be saved,
  all you ends of the earth;
  for I am God, and there is no other.
²³By myself I have sworn,
  my mouth has uttered in all integrity
 a word that will not be revoked:
 Before me every knee will bow;
  by me every tongue will swear.
²⁴They will say of me, 'In the Lord alone are righteousness and strength.'" ...

For Thought and **Contemplation**

His-story. Men, though unaware of it, are girded and guided by the divine hand. So remember this – behind every nation is a leader, and behind every leader is God. And God, not men, will have the last word in the nation's affairs. It's God, our God, who *reigns!*

"Everyone must submit himself to the governing authorities, for there is no authority except that which God has established. The authorities that exist have been established by God." (Rom. 13:1)

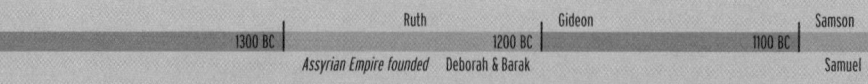

The restoration of Jerusalem

DAY 193

Isaiah 49:8–11

⁸This is what the Lord says:
"In the time of my favour I will answer you,
 and in the day of salvation I will help you;
I will keep you and will make you
 to be a covenant for the people,
to restore the land
 and to reassign its desolate inheritances,
⁹to say to the captives, 'Come out,'
 and to those in darkness, 'Be free!'
They will feed beside the roads
 and find pasture on every barren hill.
¹⁰They will neither hunger nor thirst,
 nor will the desert heat or the sun beat upon them.
He who has compassion on them will guide them
 and lead them beside springs of water.
¹¹I will turn all my mountains into roads,
 and my highways will be raised up. ..."

Israel, a light to the nations	Isaiah 49:1–7
Restoration of Jerusalem	Isaiah 49:8–26, 50:1–3
Obedience of the Lord's servant	Isaiah 50:4–11
The faithful encouraged	Isaiah 51:1–16
The end of Jerusalem's suffering	Isaiah 51:17–23
God will rescue Jerusalem	Isaiah 52:1–12
The suffering servant	Isaiah 52:13–15

For Thought and **Contemplation**

When God's people repent and confess their sins, the inevitable consequence is restoration and revival. Can you imagine what would happen if God's people throughout the world would seek His face in earnest confession and repentance? The restoration of Jerusalem would be as nothing compared to the glory and power that would flow through His Church.

"If my people, who are called by my name, will humble themselves and pray and seek my face and turn from their wicked ways, then will I hear from heaven and will forgive their sin and will heal their land." (2 Chron. 7:14)

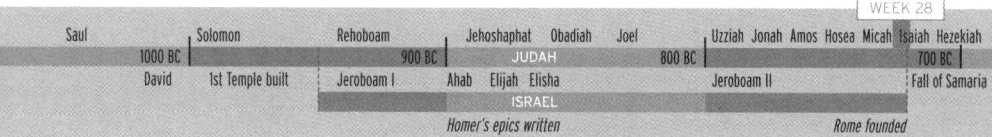

DAY 194 — God's people comforted

Christ, the sinbearer
Isaiah 53:1–12

The Lord's never-ending love
Isaiah 54:1–10

The future Jerusalem
Isaiah 54:11–17

God's offer of mercy
Isaiah 55:1–13

God's worldwide invitation
Isaiah 56:1–8

Israel's leaders condemned
Isaiah 56:9–12

Israel's idolatry condemned
Isaiah 57:1–13

God's promise of help and healing
Isaiah 57:14–21

Isaiah 54:11–17

¹¹"'O afflicted city, lashed by storms and not comforted,
  I will build you with stones of turquoise,
  your foundations with sapphires.
¹²I will make your battlements of rubies,
  your gates of sparkling jewels,
  and all your walls of precious stones.
¹³All your sons will be taught by the Lord,
  and great will be your children's peace.
¹⁴In righteousness you will be established:
 Tyranny will be far from you;
  you will have nothing to fear.
 Terror will be far removed;
  it will not come near you.
¹⁵If anyone does attack you, it will not be my doing;
  whoever attacks you will surrender to you.
¹⁶See, it is I who created the blacksmith
  who fans the coals into flame
  and forges a weapon fit for its work.
 And it is I who have created the destroyer to work havoc;
¹⁷no weapon forged against you will prevail ..."

For Thought and **Contemplation**

Let your thoughts linger today on Isaiah 53:5 – what someone has called the greatest verse of the Old Testament. It will only have meaning for you, however, if you have personalised it by faith. Can you say, "He was wounded for *my* transgressions ... bruised for *my* iniquities" (AV)? If you have not yet done so, receive the Lord Jesus Christ into your heart and life right now.

"For Christ died for sins once for all, the righteous for the unrighteous, to bring you to God. He was put to death in the body but made alive by the Spirit." (1 Pet. 3:18)

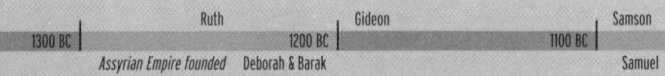

Jerusalem's future greatness

DAY **195**

Isaiah 60:1–5

¹"Arise, shine, for your light has come,
 and the glory of the Lord rises upon you.
²See, darkness covers the earth
 and thick darkness is over the peoples,
 but the Lord rises upon you
 and his glory appears over you.
³Nations will come to your light,
 and kings to the brightness of your dawn.
⁴Lift up your eyes and look about you:
 All assemble and come to you;
 your sons come from afar,
 and your daughters are carried on the arm.
⁵Then you will look and be radiant,
 your heart will throb and swell with joy;
 the wealth on the seas will be brought to you,
 to you the riches of the nations will come. ..."

True worship	Isaiah 58:1–12
Reward for keeping the Sabbath	Isaiah 58:13–14
The people's sins condemned	Isaiah 59:1–8
The people's confession	Isaiah 59:9–15
The coming of Christ	Isaiah 59:16–21
Jerusalem's future glory	Isaiah 60:1–5
All nations to honour God's people	Isaiah 60:6–9
God's favour and mercy	Isaiah 60:10–22
Good news of deliverance	Isaiah 61:1–11

For Thought and **Contemplation**

When God's people forsake their evil ways and turn back to Him, the future is bright indeed! That applies not only to the people of "natural" Jerusalem – the Jews – but also to those who belong to the "spiritual" Jerusalem – the Church. For all people, repentance before God is the key to everlasting joy.

"Repent, then, and turn to God, so that your sins may be wiped out, that times of refreshing may come from the Lord." (Acts 3:19)

WEEK 28

Saul		Solomon		Rehoboam		Jehoshaphat	Obadiah	Joel		Uzziah	Jonah	Amos	Hosea	Micah	Isaiah	Hezekiah
1000 BC					900 BC		JUDAH		800 BC						700 BC	
	David		1st Temple built		Jeroboam I	Ahab	Elijah	Elisha				Jeroboam II				Fall of Samaria
							ISRAEL									
						Homer's epics written							Rome founded			

DAY 196 — The Lord's mercy

God's care
Isaiah 62:1–5

The faithful watchmen
Isaiah 62:6–9

Announcement of salvation
Isaiah 62:10–12

Christ's victory
Isaiah 63:1–6

His mercy to Israel
Isaiah 63:7–14

Prayer of intercession
Isaiah 63:15–19, 64:1–5

A confession of sin
Isaiah 64:6–12

The calling of the Gentiles
Isaiah 65:1–7

Remnant preserved
Isaiah 65:8–10

Judgments on the wicked
Isaiah 65:11–16

The new Jerusalem
Isaiah 65:17–25

Isaiah 62:1–5

¹For Zion's sake I will not keep silent,
  for Jerusalem's sake I will not remain quiet,
till her righteousness shines out like the dawn,
  her salvation like a blazing torch.
²The nations will see your righteousness,
  and all kings your glory;
you will be called by a new name
  that the mouth of the Lord will bestow.
³You will be a crown of splendour in the Lord's hand,
  a royal diadem in the hand of your God.
⁴No longer will they call you Deserted,
  or name your land Desolate.
But you will be called Hephzibah,
  and your land Beulah;
for the Lord will take delight in you,
  and your land will be married.
⁵As a young man marries a maiden,
  so will your sons marry you;
as a bridegroom rejoices over his bride,
  so will your God rejoice over you.

For Thought and **Contemplation**

Here's a threefold truth that ought to stimulate your spiritual digestive system! Think about it every spare moment of this day: When the Messiah, the light of Jerusalem, comes (60:1) then righteousness will shine forth to the nations of the world (62:1) and Jerusalem shall be "a praise in the earth" (62:7).

"You are the light of the world. A city on a hill cannot be hidden." (Matt. 5:14)

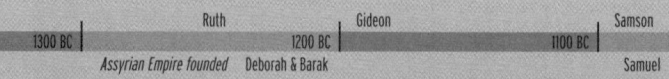

Micah's prophecies

DAY **197**

Micah 4:9-13

⁹Why do you now cry aloud –
have you no king?
Has your counsellor perished,
 that pain seizes you like that of
a woman in labour?
¹⁰Writhe in agony, O Daughter of Zion,
 like a woman in labour,
for now you must leave the city
 to camp in the open field.
You will go to Babylon;
 there you will be rescued.
There the Lord will redeem you
 out of the hand of your enemies.
¹¹But now many nations
 are gathered against you.
They say, "Let her be defiled,
 let our eyes gloat over Zion!"
¹²But they do not know
 the thoughts of the Lord;
they do not understand his plan,
 he who gathers them like
sheaves to the threshing-floor.
¹³"Rise and thresh, O Daughter
of Zion,
 for I will give you horns of iron;
I will give you hoofs of bronze
 and you will break to pieces
many nations."
You will devote their ill-gotten
gains to the Lord,
 their wealth to the Lord of all
the earth.

Vengeance is threatened
Isaiah 66:1–4

Jerusalem's future glory
Isaiah 66:5–14

Final ruin of the ungodly
Isaiah 66:15–24

A kingdom of peace
Micah 4:1–8

Final triumph of Israel
Micah 4:9–13

Christ's birth prophesied
Micah 5:1–6

Deliverance and punishment
Micah 5:7–15

God's controversy with Israel
Micah 6:1–5

The duties God requires
Micah 6:6–8

The wickedness of Israel
Micah 6:9–16

For Thought and **Contemplation**

The Old Testament prophets lived in eager anticipation of their coming Messiah. Do you? Someone has said: "The degree to which we desire Christ's coming is the degree to which we are experiencing His presence in our lives." The one is the natural outcome of the other.

"He who testifies to these things says, 'Yes, I am coming soon.' Amen. Come, Lord Jesus." (Rev. 22:20)

DAY 198 — Jerusalem threatened

Israel's moral corruption
Micah 7:1–7

The Lord brings salvation
Micah 7:8–13

The Lord's compassion
Micah 7:14–20

Sennacherib and Hezekiah
2 Chronicles 32:1, Isaiah 36:1,
2 Kings 18:13–16

Jerusalem's defence prepared
2 Chronicles 32:2–8

Sennacherib threatens Jerusalem
2 Kings 18:17–26, 2 Chronicles 32:9–14,
Isaiah 36:2–11

Rabshakeh's defiance
2 Kings 18:27–35,
2 Chronicles 32:15–16, 18–19

Micah 7:8–12

⁸Do not gloat over me, my enemy!
Though I have fallen, I will rise.
Though I sit in darkness,
  the Lord will be my light.
⁹Because I have sinned against him,
I will bear the Lord's wrath,
  until he pleads my case
  and establishes my right.
He will bring me out into the light;
  I will see his righteousness.
¹⁰Then my enemy will see it
  and will be covered with shame,
she who said to me,
  "Where is the Lord your God?"
My eyes will see her downfall;
  even now she will be trampled underfoot
  like mire in the streets.
¹¹The day for building your walls will come,
  the day for extending your boundaries.
¹²In that day people will come to you
  from Assyria and the cities of Egypt ...

For Thought and **Contemplation**

The history of Israel is a series of ups and downs. One day repentant – the next day recalcitrant. Yet God loved them too much to let them get away with anything. Never forget that love is the reason for His discipline, not His discipline the reason for His love.

"Keep yourselves in God's love as you wait for the mercy of our Lord Jesus Christ to bring you to eternal life."
(Jude v. 21)

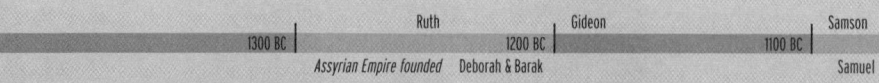

Israel seeks help

DAY 199

Isaiah 31:4-8

⁴This is what the Lord says to me:
"As a lion growls,
 a great lion over his prey –
 and though a whole band of shepherds
 is called together against him,
 he is not frightened by their shouts
 or disturbed by their clamour –
so the Lord Almighty will come down
 to do battle on Mount Zion and on its heights.
⁵Like birds hovering overhead,
 the Lord Almighty will shield Jerusalem;
 he will shield it and deliver it,
 he will 'pass over' it and will rescue it."
⁶Return to him you have so greatly revolted against, O Israelites. ⁷For in that day every one of you will reject the idols of silver and gold your sinful hands have made.
⁸"Assyria will fall by a sword that is not of man;
 a sword, not of mortals, will devour them.
 They will flee before the sword
 and their young men will be put to forced labour. …"

Rabshakeh's defiance
Isaiah 36:12–20

Siege of Jerusalem prophesied
Isaiah 29:1–8

The Jews' hypocrisy
Isaiah 29:9–16

Future blessings
Isaiah 29:17–24

The Jews reproved
Isaiah 30:1–7

The disobedient people
Isaiah 30:8–17

God's mercies
Isaiah 30:18–26

Final ruin of the Assyrians
Isaiah 30:27–33

The folly of seeking help
Isaiah 31:1–3

God's care for Jerusalem
Isaiah 31:4–9

For Thought and **Contemplation**

The leaders of Judah were upset that Isaiah lectured them like children: "precept upon precept, line upon line …" (Isa. 28:9-11, AV), and they completely ignored his warnings. Instead they had to listen to the stronger voice of their Assyrian conquerors. Beware of failing to heed the gentle reproofs of the Spirit, or else you may well be forced to heed the stronger voice of circumstances.

"You stiff-necked people, with uncircumcised hearts and ears! You are just like your fathers: You always resist the Holy Spirit!" (Acts 7:51)

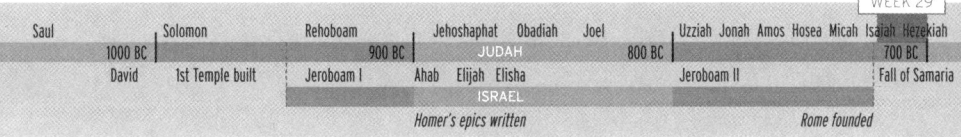

Seasons in Israel

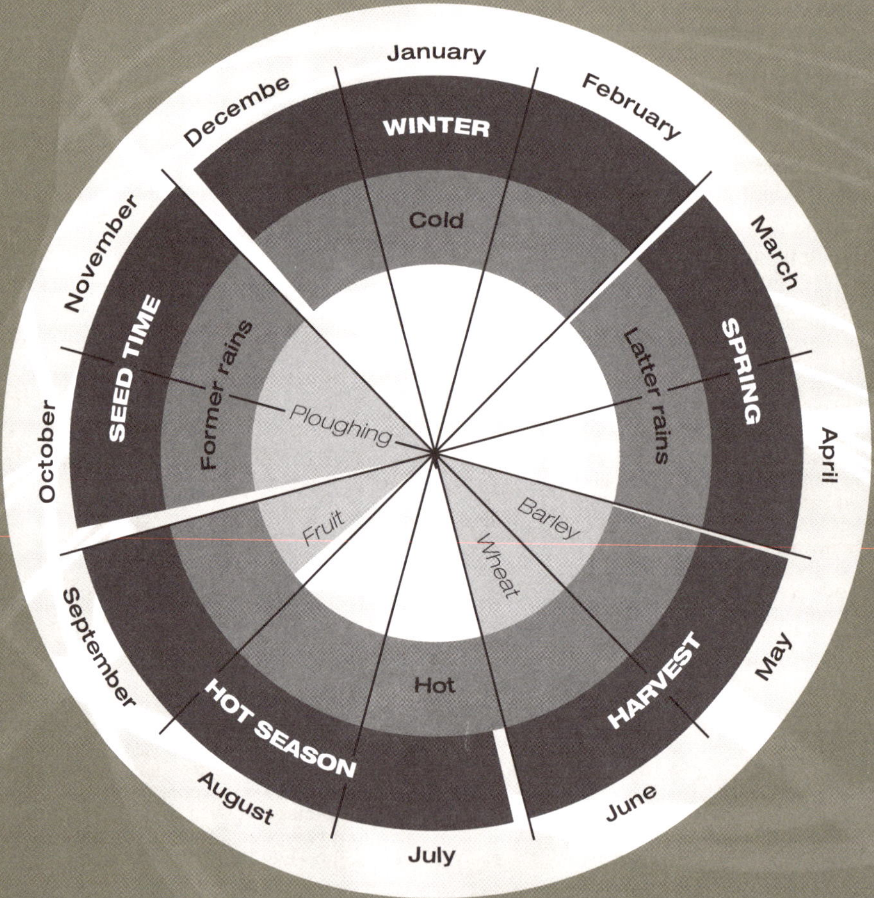

Hezekiah's consultation

DAY 200

2 Kings 19:2–7

²He [Hezekiah] sent Eliakim the palace administrator, Shebna the secretary and the leading priests, all wearing sackcloth, to the prophet Isaiah son of Amoz. ³They told him, "This is what Hezekiah says: This day is a day of distress and rebuke and disgrace, as when children come to the point of birth and there is no strength to deliver them. ⁴It may be that the Lord your God will hear all the words of the field commander, whom his master, the king of Assyria, has sent to ridicule the living God, and that he will rebuke him for the words the Lord your God has heard. Therefore pray for the remnant that still survives."

⁵When King Hezekiah's officials came to Isaiah, ⁶Isaiah said to them, "Tell your master, 'This is what the Lord says: Do not be afraid of what you have heard – those words with which the underlings of the king of Assyria have blasphemed me. ⁷Listen! I am going to put such a spirit in him that when he hears a certain report, he will return to his own country, and there I will have him cut down with the sword.'"

Time of peace	Isaiah 32:1–8
Time of trouble	Isaiah 32:9–14
Time of blessing	Isaiah 32:15–20
A prayer for help	Isaiah 33:1–9
The Lord's warning	Isaiah 33:10–16
The glorious future	Isaiah 33:17–24
Hezekiah humbles himself	2 Kings 18:36–37, 19:1, Isaiah 36:21–22, 37:1
Hezekiah consults Isaiah	2 Kings 19:2–7, Isaiah 37:2–7
A prayer for protection	Psalm 44:1–26

For Thought and **Contemplation**

How extremely comforting it must have been for Hezekiah when, concerned about the dishonour done to God by Rabshakeh's blasphemy, he was able to share his burden with the godly Isaiah. Do you have a prayer partner in whom you can confide? If not, ask God today to give you one.

"Then Daniel returned to his house and explained the matter to his friends Hananiah, Mishael and Azariah. He urged them to plead for mercy from the God of heaven concerning this mystery, so that he and his friends might not be executed with the rest of the wise men of Babylon." (Daniel 2:17–18)

WEEK 29

Saul		Solomon		Rehoboam		Jehoshaphat	Obadiah	Joel		Uzziah Jonah Amos Hosea Micah Isaiah Hezekiah
1000 BC				900 BC		JUDAH			800 BC	700 BC
	David	1st Temple built		Jeroboam I		Ahab Elijah Elisha			Jeroboam II	Fall of Samaria
						ISRAEL				
					Homer's epics written				Rome founded	

DAY 201 — Hezekiah's prayer answered

Sennacherib's letters
2 Chronicles 32:17

He defies God
2 Kings 19:8–13, Isaiah 37:8–13

Hezekiah's prayer
2 Chronicles 32:20, 2 Kings 19:14–19, Isaiah 37:14–20

The psalmist's temptation
Psalm 73:1–14

How he gained victory
Psalm 73:15–20

How he profited by it
Psalm 73:21–28

Isaiah's response to Hezekiah
2 Kings 19:20–34, Isaiah 37:21–35

Isaiah 37:14–20

¹⁴Hezekiah received the letter from the messengers and read it. Then he went up to the temple of the Lord and spread it out before the Lord. ¹⁵And Hezekiah prayed to the Lord: ¹⁶"O Lord Almighty, God of Israel, enthroned between the cherubim, you alone are God over all the kingdoms of the earth. You have made heaven and earth. ¹⁷Give ear, O Lord, and hear; open your eyes, O Lord, and see; listen to all the words Sennacherib has sent to insult the living God. ¹⁸It is true, O Lord, that the Assyrian kings have laid waste all these peoples and their lands. ¹⁹They have thrown their gods into the fire and destroyed them, for they were not gods but only wood and stone, fashioned by human hands. ²⁰Now, O Lord our God, deliver us from his hand, so that all kingdoms on earth may know that you alone, O Lord, are God."

For Thought and **Contemplation**

Hezekiah's plea to God through Isaiah was not only heard, but answered. God not only listened but responded. Some think that prayer is merely talking to God. It's much more than that. Prayer is *conversation*; you talking to God and God talking to you. Is that the way it is in your prayer life?

"Come near to God and he will come near to you ..." (Jas. 4:8)

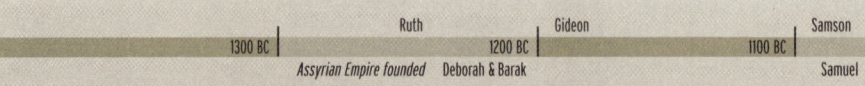

Hezekiah's last days

DAY **202**

Psalm 75:1–7

¹We give thanks to you, O God,
  we give thanks, for your Name is near;
  men tell of your wonderful deeds.
²You say, "I choose the appointed time;
  it is I who judge uprightly.
³When the earth and all its people quake,
  it is I who hold its pillars firm.
                    Selah
⁴To the arrogant I say, 'Boast no more,'
  and to the wicked, 'Do not lift up your horns.
⁵Do not lift your horns against heaven;
  do not speak with outstretched neck.'"
⁶No-one from the east or the west
  or from the desert can exalt a man.
⁷But it is God who judges:
  He brings one down, he exalts another.

Assyrian army destroyed	2 Kings 19:35–36, 2 Chronicles 32:21–22, Isaiah 37:36–37
God the Judge	Psalm 75:1–10
God the Victor	Psalm 76:1–12
Hezekiah's prosperity	2 Chronicles 32:23, 27–30, 2 Kings 20:20
The Babylonian ambassadors	2 Kings 20:12–19, Isaiah 39:1–8, 2 Chronicles 32:31
Hezekiah's death	2 Kings 20:21, 2 Chronicles 32:32–33
Assyrians settle in Samaria	2 Kings 17:24–41

For Thought and **Contemplation**

God extended Hezekiah's life by fifteen years but, regrettably, Hezekiah used those years for his own selfish endeavours rather than for God's glory. How sad when divine favour is prostituted and used for self-centred ends.

"When you ask, you do not receive, because you ask with wrong motives, that you may spend what you get on your pleasures." (Jas. 4:3)

DAY 203 — Manasseh turns to God

Manasseh's sinful ways
2 Kings 21:1–9, 2 Chronicles 33:1–9

God's displeasure
2 Kings 21:10–15, 2 Chronicles 33:10

Warning to Shebna
Isaiah 22:15–25

Sennacherib's death
2 Kings 19:37, Isaiah 37:38

Manasseh's sin and repentance
2 Kings 21:16, 2 Chronicles 33:11–13

His reforms
2 Chronicles 33:14–17

His death
2 Kings 21:17–18, 2 Chronicles 33:18–20

Amon's evil life and death
2 Kings 21:19–23, 26,
2 Chronicles 33:21–24,

Josiah becomes king
2 Kings 21:24, 2 Chronicles 33:25

2 Chronicles 33:11–15

¹¹"So the Lord brought against them the army commanders of the king of Assyria, who took Manasseh prisoner, put a hook in his nose, bound him with bronze shackles and took him to Babylon. ¹²In his distress he sought the favour of the Lord his God and humbled himself greatly before the God of his fathers. ¹³And when he prayed to him, the Lord was moved by his entreaty and listened to his plea; so he brought him back to Jerusalem and to his kingdom. Then Manasseh knew that the Lord is God.

¹⁴Afterwards he rebuilt the outer wall of the City of David, west of the Gihon spring in the valley, as far as the entrance of the Fish Gate and encircling the hill of Ophel; he also made it much higher. He stationed military commanders in all the fortified cities in Judah.

¹⁵He got rid of the foreign gods and removed the image from the temple of the Lord, as well as all the altars he had built on the temple hill and in Jerusalem; and he threw them out of the city ..."

For Thought and **Contemplation**

Manasseh and Amon were two of the most evil men who ever lived. One wonders why God allowed such rulers to hold sway over His people. One thing, however, is sure – all will ultimately perish who refuse to walk in God's ways.

"Therefore the wicked will not stand in the judgment, nor sinners in the assembly of the righteous. For the Lord watches over the way of the righteous, but the way of the wicked will perish." (Psa. 1:5–6)

The fall of Nineveh

DAY **204**

Nahum 1:1–5

¹An oracle concerning Nineveh. The book of the vision of Nahum the Elkoshite.
²The Lord is a jealous and avenging God;
  the Lord takes vengeance and is filled with wrath.
 The Lord takes vengeance on his foes
  and maintains his wrath against his enemies.
³The Lord is slow to anger and great in power;
  the Lord will not leave the guilty unpunished.
 His way is in the whirlwind and the storm,
  and clouds are the dust of his feet.
⁴He rebukes the sea and dries it up;
  he makes all the rivers run dry.
 Bashan and Carmel wither
  and the blossoms of Lebanon fade.
⁵The mountains quake before him and the hills melt away.
 The earth trembles at his presence,
  the world and all who live in it.

Josiah's godly character
2 Chronicles 34:1–2, 2 Kings 22:1–2, 23:25

God's justice and power
Nahum 1:1–8

The Assyrians overthrown
Nahum 1:9–15

Nineveh's destruction foretold
Nahum 2:1–10

The cause
Nahum 2:11–13

The fall of Nineveh
Nahum 3:1–19

Josiah's early reforms
2 Chronicles 34:3–7

Jeremiah's ministry begins 628 BC

Jeremiah's call and early vision
Jeremiah 1:1–19

For Thought and **Contemplation**

When a nation comes under the judgment of God then the mightiest defences are of no avail. It's a sobering thought that one day God will judge the nations of the world for their disobedience to His commands. And when He does, the most powerful nuclear defence strategy will be powerless to stand against His wrath.

"But they will have to give account to him who is ready to judge the living and the dead." (1 Pet. 4:5)

Zerubbabel and main party return	Iron Age begins in Britain	Ezra returns	Malachi	
500 BC				400 BC
Cyrus	Zechariah Haggai 2nd Temple built		Nehemiah rebuilds walls of Jerusalem	

DAY 205 — Jeremiah's first message

Israel's early love for God
Jeremiah 2:1–3

The sin of Israel's leaders
Jeremiah 2:4–8

The Lord's plea
Jeremiah 2:9–13

The results of unfaithfulness
Jeremiah 2:14–19

The sins of Judah
Jeremiah 2:20–28

Their false confidence
Jeremiah 2:29–37

Exhortations to repentance
Jeremiah 3:1–5

The coming of judgment
Zephaniah 1:1–18

A plea for repentance
Zephaniah 2:1–3

Judgment against the nations
Zephaniah 2:4–15

Jeremiah 2:4–8

⁴Hear the word of the Lord, O house of Jacob,
  all you clans of the house of Israel.
⁵This is what the Lord says:
"What fault did your fathers find in me,
  that they strayed so far from me?
They followed worthless idols
  and became worthless themselves.
⁶They did not ask, 'Where is the Lord,
  who brought us up out of Egypt
and led us through the barren wilderness, through a land of deserts and rifts,
  a land of drought and darkness,
  a land where no-one travels and no-one lives?'
⁷I brought you into a fertile land
  to eat its fruit and rich produce.
But you came and defiled my land
  and made my inheritance detestable.
⁸The priests did not ask,
  'Where is the Lord?'
Those who deal with the law did not know me;
  the leaders rebelled against me ...

For Thought and **Contemplation**

"I'll do it if I feel like it." Unfortunately many Christians adopt this attitude to God's commands. If Jeremiah had done that, then it would have changed a whole section of Old Testament history. Are you fighting the "God-said-it-but-I-don't-feel-like-it" battle? Then decide right now to do what God asks – *whether you feel like it or not.*

"If you love me, you will obey what I command." (Jn 14:15)

WEEK 30

700 BC		Nahum Zephaniah Josiah Nebuchadnezzar	Jerusalem destroyed
		600 BC	FALL OF JUDAH
Assyrians besiege Jerusalem		Daniel taken to Babylon	Ezekiel
		Jeremiah Habakkuk	Exile in Babylon

Prophecies of Jeremiah

1. **Fall of Jerusalem**
   (1:14–16, 4:5–9, 5:15–17, 6:1–6, 32:2–3, 38:17–18)

2. **Destruction of the Temple** (7:11–15, 26:6–9)

3. **Death of deposed King Jehoahaz in Egypt**
   (22:10–12)

4. **Unlamented death of King Jehoiakim** (36:27–30)

5. **Cutting of the royal line of King Jehoiachin**
   (22:24–30)

6. **Death of two false prophets and punishment of another – all three living in Babylon** (29:20–32)

7. **Death of a false Jerusalem prophet** (28:13–17)

8. **Capture and exile of a friend named Seraiah**
   (51:59)

9. **Failure of the Egyptian-Judean military alliance against Babylon** (37:5–10)

10. **Defeat of Egypt by Babylon at Carchemish**
    (46:1–12)

11. **Babylonian occupation of Egypt** (43:9–13)

12. **Seventy-year captivity of Judah in Babylon**
    (25:11, 29:10)

13. **Restoration to Jerusalem after the seventy years**
    (27:19–22; 30:3, 10–11, 18–21; 31:9, 12, 38–39; 33:3–9)

14. **Defeat of Babylon after the seventy years**
    (25:12, 27:7)

15. **Capture of Zedekiah** (21:3–7, 34:1–5, 37:17)

16. **Kindly treatment of the godly exiles in Babylon**
    (24:1–7)

17. **Final regathering of people of Israel**
    (30:3, 10; 31:8–12)

18. **Final rebuilding of the land of Israel**
    (30:18–21, 31:38–39, 33:7–9)

DAY **206**

Josiah's godly reign

Further reproofs for sin
Zephaniah 3:1–7

God's mercy
Zephaniah 3:8–13

Restoration of Israel and Jerusalem
Zephaniah 3:14–20

Josiah repairs the temple
2 Kings 22:3–7, 2 Chronicles 34:8–13

The Book of the Law is found
2 Kings 22:8–10, 2 Chronicles 34:14–18

Josiah consults Huldah
2 Kings 22:11–20, 2 Chronicles 34:19–28

The king's covenant
2 Kings 23:1–3, 2 Chronicles 34:29–32

2 Chronicles 34:29–32
²⁹Then the king called together all the elders of Judah and Jerusalem. ³⁰He went up to the temple of the Lord with the men of Judah, the people of Jerusalem, the priests and the Levites – all the people from the least to the greatest. He read in their hearing all the words of the Book of the Covenant, which had been found in the temple of the Lord. ³¹The king stood by his pillar and renewed the covenant in the presence of the Lord – to follow the Lord and keep his commands, regulations and decrees with all his heart and all his soul, and to obey the words of the covenant written in this book.
³²Then he had everyone in Jerusalem and Benjamin pledge themselves to it; the people of Jerusalem did this in accordance with the covenant of God, the God of their fathers.

For Thought and **Contemplation**

Question: Why did some of Israel's kings turn out to be evil and wicked men while others were righteous? *Answer:* It depended not merely on their upbringing, their temperament or their view of life, but on their *willingness* to obey the word of the Lord. The will is a crucial issue in the battle between sin and evil. So ask yourself at this moment: How willing am I to obey the divine will?

"Whether it is favourable or unfavourable, we will obey the Lord our God, to whom we are sending you, so that it will go well with us, for we will obey the Lord our God." (Jer. 42:6)

a bird's eye view of **Zephaniah**

Place in the Bible
Thirty-sixth Old Testament book; fourteenth book of prophecy.

Special feature
The prominence of "The Day of the Lord"

Jeremiah's second message

DAY **207**

Jeremiah 4:1–4

¹"If you will return, O Israel,
  return to me,"
  declares the Lord.
"If you put your detestable idols
out of my sight
  and no longer go astray,
²and if in a truthful, just and
righteous way
  you swear, 'As surely as the
Lord lives,'
  then the nations will be blessed
by him
  and in him they will glory."
³This is what the Lord says to the
men of Judah and to Jerusalem:
"Break up your unploughed
ground
  and do not sow among thorns.
⁴Circumcise yourselves to the
Lord,
  circumcise your hearts,
  you men of Judah and people
of Jerusalem,
  or my wrath will break out and
burn like fire
  because of the evil you have
done –
  burn with no-one to quench it."

Israel better than Judah	Jeremiah 3:6–11
Pardon is promised	Jeremiah 3:12–20
Israel's repentance	Jeremiah 3:21–25
A call to repentance	Jeremiah 4:1–4
Judah is threatened	Jeremiah 4:5–12
Judah is surrounded	Jeremiah 4:13–18
Jeremiah's sorrow	Jeremiah 4:19–22
His vision	Jeremiah 4:23–31
Jerusalem's sin	Jeremiah 5:1–11
Israel's enemies	Jeremiah 5:12–19
God's warning	Jeremiah 5:20–31

For Thought and **Contemplation**

Many of God's people are spiritually shipwrecked because they believe that God will not be as strict as His Word suggests. Adam and Eve failed because of this. And, as our present reading shows, so did the people of Israel. Ask yourself right now: is this same attitude to be found in me?

"'Is not my word like fire,' declares the Lord, 'and like a hammer that breaks a rock in pieces?'" (Jeremiah 23:29)

Jesus and the Book

Jesus Christ often spoke about His second coming, which is closely linked in the Bible to Zephaniah's message of the Day of the Lord: see Matthew 24:42, "Therefore keep watch, because you do not know on what day your Lord will come."

Teaching

Zephaniah insists that the Day of the Lord, God's day of judgment, will come to Jerusalem. Like other prophets his message is that God must punish sin, especially idol worship, but for those who trust in God there will be mercy and rejoicing.

A Verse to Remember

"Seek the Lord, all you humble of the land, you who do what he commands. Seek righteousness, seek humility ..." (Zeph. 2:3)

DAY 208 — The Passover is kept

The invasion of Jerusalem
Jeremiah 6:1–8

Rebellious Israel
Jeremiah 6:9–15

Israel's rejection of God's way
Jeremiah 6:16–21

Invasion from the north
Jeremiah 6:22–30

Josiah celebrates the Passover
2 Kings 23:21–23, 26–27,
2 Chronicles 35:1–19

Josiah's further reforms
2 Kings 23:4–14

2 Chronicles 35:1–6

¹Josiah celebrated the Passover to the Lord in Jerusalem, and the Passover lamb was slaughtered on the fourteenth day of the first month. ²He appointed the priests to their duties and encouraged them in the service of the Lord's temple. ³He said to the Levites, who instructed all Israel and who had been consecrated to the Lord: "Put the sacred ark in the temple that Solomon son of David king of Israel built. It is not to be carried about on your shoulders. Now serve the Lord your God and his people Israel. ⁴Prepare yourselves by families in your divisions, according to the directions written by David king of Israel and by his son Solomon.

⁵"Stand in the holy place with a group of Levites for each sub-division of the families of your fellow countrymen, the lay people. ⁶Slaughter the Passover lambs, consecrate yourselves and prepare [the lambs] for your fellow countrymen, doing what the Lord commanded through Moses."

For Thought and Contemplation

Josiah's decision to celebrate the Passover – an ordinance that had been neglected in previous reigns – brought joy to God and delight to the people. The Almighty rewarded their commitment with evidences of His approval and favour. When we draw near to Him, He never fails to draw near to us.

"Let us draw near to God with a sincere heart in full assurance of faith, having our hearts sprinkled to cleanse us from a guilty conscience and having our bodies washed with pure water." (Heb. 10:22)

a bird's eye view of **Jeremiah**

Place in the Bible
Twenty-fourth Old Testament book; second book of prophecy.

Special Features
Autobiographical style.

Jeremiah's third message

DAY **209**

Jeremiah 8:18–22

¹⁸O my Comforter in sorrow,
  my heart is faint within me.
¹⁹Listen to the cry of my people
  from a land far away:
"Is the Lord not in Zion?
  Is her King no longer there?"
"Why have they provoked me
to anger with their images,
  with their worthless foreign idols?"
²⁰"The harvest is past,
  the summer has ended,
  and we are not saved."
²¹Since my people are crushed,
I am crushed;
  I mourn, and horror grips me.
²²Is there no balm in Gilead?
  Is there no physician there?
Why then is there no healing
  for the wound of my people?

| Josiah's reforms |
| 2 Kings 23:15–20, 2 Chronicles 34:33 |
| Jeremiah preaches in the temple |
| Jeremiah 7:1–15 |
| **Birth of Ezekiel 622 BC** |
| The people's disobedience |
| Jeremiah 7:16–29 |
| Vengeance threatened |
| Jeremiah 7:30–34 |
| Bones to remain unburied |
| Jeremiah 8:1–3 |
| The people's stupidity |
| Jeremiah 8:4–13 |
| The alarm of invasion |
| Jeremiah 8:14–17 |
| Jeremiah's lamentation |
| Jeremiah 8:18–22 |

For Thought and **Contemplation**

Israel's greatest sin was that of idolatry – replacing the true object of worship with one which made lesser demands. But God will brook no rival in His universe, and therefore idolatry *must* be removed. If we don't get rid of the idols in our lives by our own volition, then we give God no other option than to topple them Himself.

"The acts of the sinful nature are obvious ... idolatry and witchcraft ..." (Gal. 5:19–20)

Jesus and the Book

Jeremiah looked towards the time when there would be a "new covenant" (Jer. 31:31–34), the covenant inaugurated by Jesus' death, which He spoke about at the Last Supper when He told His disciples: "This is my blood of the covenant ..." (Matt. 26:27–28).

Teaching

Jeremiah's prescription for Israel's sins of immorality and idolatry was to return to God in repentance. He insisted that this was much more important than relying on a foreign army to deliver them from the siege of Jerusalem.

A Verse to Remember

"This is the covenant that I will make with the house of Israel after that time," declares the Lord. "I will put my law in their minds and write it on their hearts. I will be their God, and they will be my people" (Jer. 31:33).

DAY 210

A further message

The people are corrected
Jeremiah 9:1–11

The captives suffer
Jeremiah 9:12–22

God's loving-kindness
Jeremiah 9:23–24

Punishment of the unrighteous
Jeremiah 9:25–26

Idolatry and true worship
Jeremiah 10:1–11

A hymn of praise
Jeremiah 10:12–16

The coming exile
Jeremiah 10:17–25

Disobedient Jews reproved
Jeremiah 11:1–10

Their utter ruin
Jeremiah 11:11–17

A plot against Jeremiah's life
Jeremiah 11:18–23

Jeremiah 10:12–16

¹²But God made the earth by his power;
  he founded the world by his wisdom
  and stretched out the heavens by his understanding.
¹³When he thunders, the waters in the heavens roar;
  he makes clouds rise from the ends of the earth.
 He sends lightning with the rain
  and brings out the wind from his storehouses.
¹⁴Everyone is senseless and without knowledge;
  every goldsmith is shamed by his idols.
 His images are a fraud;
  they have no breath in them.
¹⁵They are worthless, the objects of mockery;
  when their judgment comes, they will perish.
¹⁶He who is the Portion of Jacob is not like these,
  for he is the Maker of all things,
  including Israel, the tribe of his inheritance –
  the Lord Almighty is his name.

For Thought and **Contemplation**

How do you feel when you see God's hand of discipline on someone you know and love? Do you ignore it or do you "weep" over it as did Jeremiah? Pause for a moment to see if God wants you to intercede on behalf of an erring brother and sister. Let Jeremiah's deep concern be your example.

"Brothers, if someone is caught in a sin, you who are spiritual should restore him gently. But watch yourself, or you also may be tempted." (Gal. 6:1)

The sign of the ox yoke

DAY 211

Jeremiah 27:1-7

¹Early in the reign of Zedekiah son of Josiah king of Judah, this word came to Jeremiah from the Lord: ²This is what the Lord said to me: "Make a yoke out of straps and crossbars and put it on your neck. ³Then send word to the kings of Edom, Moab, Ammon, Tyre and Sidon through the envoys who have come to Jerusalem to Zedekiah king of Judah. ⁴Give them a message for their masters and say, 'This is what the Lord Almighty, the God of Israel, says: "Tell this to your masters: ⁵With my great power and outstretched arm I made the earth and its people and the animals that are on it, and I give it to anyone I please. ⁶Now I will hand all your countries over to my servant Nebuchadnezzar king of Babylon; I will make even the wild animals subject to him. ⁷All nations will serve him and his son and his grandson until the time for his land comes; then many nations and great kings will subjugate him. ..."

Jeremiah's questions and God's answer
Jeremiah 12:1–6

The Lord's sorrow
Jeremiah 12:7–13

Babylon: the world power 612–539 BC

His promise
Jeremiah 12:14–17

Josiah slain
2 Kings 23:28–30, 2 Chronicles 35:20–24

Lamentation for Josiah
2 Chronicles 35:25–27

Jehoahaz' evil life
2 Kings 23:31–32, 2 Chronicles 36:1–2

Judah pays tribute
2 Kings 23:33, 2 Chronicles 36:3

Jehoahaz' death
2 Kings 23:34, Jeremiah 22:10–12

Jehoiakim made king
2 Kings 23:36–37 & 35, 2 Chronicles 36:5

The sign of the yoke
Jeremiah 27:1–11

Jeremiah in the temple court
Jeremiah 26:1–7

For Thought and **Contemplation**

Jeremiah's sign of the ox alerted the people to the fact that soon they would become subservient to the king of Babylon. He urges them to submit with meekness to this hard and humbling turn of providence in the sure knowledge that, in the lives of His people, God only allows what He can use.

"And we know that in all things God works for the good of those who love him, who have been called according to his purpose." (Rom. 8:28)

Zerubbabel and main party return	Iron Age begins in Britain	Ezra returns	Malachi
500 BC			400 BC
Cyrus Zechariah Haggai 2nd Temple built		Nehemiah rebuilds walls of Jerusalem	

DAY 212 — Habakkuk's message

Jeremiah proclaimed a traitor
Jeremiah 26:8–19

Habakkuk complains of injustice
Habakkuk 1:1–4

The Lord's reply
Habakkuk 1:5–11

Habakkuk's further complaint
Habakkuk 1:12–17

Habakkuk must wait
Habakkuk 2:1–4

Judgments on the unrighteous
Habakkuk 2:5–20

Habakkuk's plea
Habakkuk 3:1–2

His prayer and praise
Habakkuk 3:3–19

Habakkuk 2:1–4

I will stand at my watch
  and station myself on the ramparts;
 I will look to see what he will say to me,
  and what answer I am to give to this complaint.
²Then the Lord replied:
 "Write down the revelation
  and make it plain on tablets
  so that a herald may run with it.
 ³For the revelation awaits an appointed time;
  it speaks of the end
  and will not prove false.
 Though it linger, wait for it;
  it will certainly come and will not delay.
 ⁴See, he is puffed up;
  his desires are not upright –
  but the righteous will live by his faith – ..."

For Thought and **Contemplation**

Almost all of the Old Testament prophets confessed to being confused by the ways and designs of God. But as they waited before Him, the confusion gave way to confidence. The secret of understanding God's ways is to "wait". Finally, the answer always comes.

"'For my thoughts are not your thoughts, neither are your ways my ways,' declares the Lord. 'As the heavens are higher than the earth, so are my ways higher than your ways and my thoughts than your thoughts.'" (Isa. 55:8–9)

a bird's eye view of Habakkuk

Place in the Bible
Thirty-fifth Old Testament book; thirteenth book of prophecy.

Special Features
Two rounds of questions and answers.

The first deportation

DAY **213**

Jeremiah 36:1–7

¹In the fourth year of Jehoiakim son of Josiah king of Judah, this word came to Jeremiah from the Lord: ²"Take a scroll and write on it all the words I have spoken to you concerning Israel, Judah and all the other nations from the time I began speaking to you in the reign of Josiah till now. ³Perhaps when the people of Judah hear about every disaster I plan to inflict on them, each of them will turn from his wicked way; then I will forgive their wickedness and their sin."
⁴So Jeremiah called Baruch son of Neriah, and while Jeremiah dictated all the words the Lord had spoken to him, Baruch wrote them on the scroll. ⁵Then Jeremiah told Baruch, "I am restricted; I cannot go to the Lord's temple. ⁶So you go to the house of the Lord on a day of fasting and read to the people from the scroll the words of the Lord that you wrote as I dictated. Read them to all the people of Judah who come in from their towns. ⁷Perhaps they will bring their petition before the Lord, and each will turn from his wicked ways …"

Obedience of the Recabites
Jeremiah 35:1–11

The Jews' disobedience
Jeremiah 35:12–19

Jerusalem's 20-year siege begins 606 BC

The wine cup of wrath
Jeremiah 25:15–38

Nebuchadnezzar besieges Jerusalem
Daniel 1:1

Some Israelites deported
Daniel 1:2–3

Prophecy concerning Israel's captivity
Jeremiah 25:1–11

Prophecies to be written
Jeremiah 36:1–8

God's promise to Baruch
Jeremiah 45:1–5

For Thought and **Contemplation**

Why would God allow His people to be deported and sent into exile? There could be only one reason: if they would not heed God's tender disciplines as given through the word of His prophets, then they must submit to His terrible disciplines as brought about through difficult circumstances. Got the point?

"These things happened to them as examples and were written down as warnings for us, on whom the fulfilment of the ages has come." (1 Cor. 10:11)

Jesus and the Book

Habakkuk states that God is his Saviour (3:18). The name "Jesus" means "The Lord saves". Jesus is the Saviour of the world: "… you are to give him the name Jesus, because he will save his people from their sins." (Matt. 1:21).

Teaching

Habakkuk observes unjust suffering, and God reveals that something even worse is in store for Judah – being crushed by the Babylonians. God shows Habakkuk that the only way a righteous person can survive is by being faithful to God.

A Verse to Remember

"I will rejoice … in God my Saviour" (Hab. 3:18).

Heart to Heart

Section 7

Many of you are now experiencing the heat of summer when we really enjoy a cold refreshing drink. As you read God's Word allow it to refresh and encourage you. Reading through the Bible is not meant to be a business project but a life-refreshing and transforming experience. God gave His Word for our heart and spirit not just our intellect.

Visit the web site: **www.cover2cover.org**

In this section

The Babylonian invasion of Judah
Exile in Babylon
Laments for Jerusalem
Daniel's rise to power
Ezekiel's prophecies of new life

DAY 214

Daniel tested

Egypt's defeat
Jeremiah 46:1–12

Nebuchadnezzar's conquests
2 Kings 24:7

Daniel, Hananiah, Mishael and Azariah
Daniel 1:4–7

Their refusal
Daniel 1:8–16

Their improvement in wisdom
Daniel 1:17–20

Uriah martyred
Jeremiah 26:20–24

Jeremiah's lament
Jeremiah 22:13–19

A fast proclaimed
Jeremiah 36:9

Nebuchadnezzar's dream
Daniel 2:1–13

The dream revealed to Daniel
Daniel 2:14–35

Daniel 1:17–20

¹⁷To these four young men God gave knowledge and understanding of all kinds of literature and learning. And Daniel could understand visions and dreams of all kinds. ¹⁸At the end of the time set by the king to bring them in, the chief official presented them to Nebuchadnezzar. ¹⁹The king talked with them, and he found none equal to Daniel, Hananiah, Mishael and Azariah; so they entered the king's service. ²⁰In every matter of wisdom and understanding about which the king questioned them, he found them ten times better than all the magicians and enchanters in his whole kingdom.

For Thought and **Contemplation**

Daniel endured three great tests in Babylon: (1) the test of *food*, proving his obedience to God's law. (2) The test of the *dream*, proving his willingness to trust God's provision. (3) The test of the *lions' den*, proving his allegiance to God's Word. Could you have passed all three tests?

"These have come so that your faith – of greater worth than gold, which perishes even though refined by fire – may be proved genuine and may result in praise, glory and honour when Jesus Christ is revealed." (1 Pet. 1:7)

a bird's eye view of **Daniel**

Place in the Bible	**Main Characters**	**Special Features**
Twenty-seventh Old Testament book; fifth book of prophecy.	Daniel, Nebuchadnezzar.	Dreams and visions.

The sign of the linen girdle — DAY **215**

Jeremiah 36:27–31

²⁷After the king burned the scroll containing the words that Baruch had written at Jeremiah's dictation, the word of the Lord came to Jeremiah: ²⁸"Take another scroll and write on it all the words that were on the first scroll, which Jehoiakim king of Judah burned up. ²⁹Also tell Jehoiakim king of Judah, 'This is what the Lord says: You burned that scroll and said, "Why did you write on it that the king of Babylon would certainly come and destroy this land and cut off both men and animals from it?" ³⁰Therefore, this is what the Lord says about Jehoiakim king of Judah: He will have no-one to sit on the throne of David; his body will be thrown out and exposed to the heat by day and the frost by night. ³¹I will punish him and his children and his attendants for their wickedness; I will bring on them and those living in Jerusalem and the people of Judah every disaster I pronounced against them, because they have not listened.'"

Daniel's interpretation	Daniel 2:36–45
The king rewards Daniel	Daniel 2:46–49
The Word of God is read	Jeremiah 36:10–19
The king destroys the scroll	Jeremiah 36:20–26
Jeremiah replaces it	Jeremiah 36:27–32
The sign of the linen girdle	Jeremiah 13:1–11
The wine jar	Jeremiah 13:12–14
Jeremiah's warning	Jeremiah 13:15–27
The drought	Jeremiah 14:1–12

For Thought and **Contemplation**

Jeremiah's sign of the linen girdle was meant to show that Israel had corrupted themselves by their idolatry, so much that they were good for nothing. What an indictment! What sign, do you think, would Jeremiah give us if he were alive today, and wanted to indicate the true condition of the contemporary Christian Church?

"For it is time for judgment to begin with the family of God; and if it begins with us, what will the outcome be for those who do not obey the gospel of God?" (1 Pet. 4:17)

Jesus and the Book

Both Daniel and Jesus Christ prophesy of the end times. (See Mark chapter 13:26–27.)

Teaching

Daniel, a prisoner-of-war, shows his faith in God – as seen in the well known lions' den incident and in his interpreting dreams – and so taught his captors, and teaches us today, that true wisdom and ultimate power belong only to God.

A Verse to Remember

"Praise be to the name of God for ever and ever; wisdom and power are his. He changes times and seasons; he sets up kings and deposes them. He gives wisdom to the wise and knowledge to the discerning" (Dan. 2:20–22).

DAY 216 — Punishment for sin

False prophets
Jeremiah 14:13–18

The people's plea
Jeremiah 14:19–22

The destruction of the wicked
Jeremiah 15:1–9

Jeremiah's complaint
Jeremiah 15:10–18

The Lord's reply
Jeremiah 15:19–21

The Lord's will for Jeremiah
Jeremiah 16:1–9

Return from exile prophesied
Jeremiah 16:10–15

The coming punishment
Jeremiah 16:16–18

Jeremiah's prayer
Jeremiah 16:19–21

The sin and punishment of Judah
Jeremiah 17:1–13

Jeremiah 16:19–21

¹⁹O Lord, my strength and my fortress,
 my refuge in time of distress,
to you the nations will come
 from the ends of the earth
and say,
 "Our fathers possessed nothing but false gods,
 worthless idols that did them no good.
²⁰Do men make their own gods?
 Yes, but they are not gods!"
²¹"Therefore I will teach them –
 this time I will teach them
 my power and might.
Then they will know
 that my name is the Lord."

For Thought and **Contemplation**

We are indebted to Jeremiah for reminding us that the heart of human problems is the problem of the heart (17:9). And what is the solution? This: "I the Lord search the heart" (17:10). Let God apply the searchlight of His Spirit today to those areas of your life where you have trouble trusting Him.

"Create in me a pure heart, O God, and renew a steadfast spirit within me." (Psa. 51:10)

WEEK 31

700 BC | Assyrians besiege Jerusalem | Nahum Zephaniah Josiah Nebuchadnezzar | 600 BC | Daniel taken to Babylon | Jeremiah Habakkuk | FALL OF JUDAH | Ezekiel | Jerusalem destroyed | Exile in Babylon

Babylon

THE ASSYRIAN empire was replaced by the Babylonian. Nebuchadnezzar, its most famous king, conquered Judah in 597 BC, when Judah's king and skilled artisans were deported to Babylon. The city of Babylon was described by Herodotus as occupying about 200 square miles. It had eight ornamental gates, magnificent buildings and wide, tree-lined streets and double defensive walls. Its "hanging gardens", built by Nebuchadnezzar for his wife, were one of the wonders of the ancient world. The prophecy concerning Babylon in Isaiah 13 has been literally fulfilled. Its ruins are uninhabited except by wild animals. The region, once fertile, is now mostly barren marshland. There have been many excavations, and a few buildings have been reconstructed, but it has never been rebuilt.

DAY 217 — Further signs

Jeremiah's prayer
Jeremiah 17:14–18

The Sabbath
Jeremiah 17:19–27

The sign of the potter's vessel
Jeremiah 18:1–10

The people's rejection
Jeremiah 18:11–17

A plot against Jeremiah
Jeremiah 18:18–23

The broken jar
Jeremiah 19:1–13

Jeremiah's conflict with Pashhur
Jeremiah 19:14–15, 20:1–6

His complaint
Jeremiah 20:7–18

Jehoiakim's rebellion
2 Kings 24:1

Message against Philistia
Jeremiah 47:1–7

Jeremiah 17:14–18

¹⁴Heal me, O Lord, and I shall be healed;
  save me and I shall be saved,
  for you are the one I praise.
¹⁵They keep saying to me,
  "Where is the word of the Lord?
  Let it now be fulfilled!"
¹⁶I have not run away from being your shepherd;
  you know I have not desired the day of despair.
  What passes my lips is open before you.
¹⁷Do not be a terror to me;
  you are my refuge in the day of disaster.
¹⁸Let my persecutors be put to shame,
  but keep me from shame;
  let them be terrified,
  but keep me from terror.
  Bring on them the day of disaster;
  destroy them with double destruction.

For Thought and **Contemplation**

Do you feel a failure in your Christian life? A broken and defiled vessel? Then take note of what Jeremiah learned in the potter's house – namely, that God can refashion you into a new and glorious vessel. Ask Him to make you anew right now, and stay still under His touch as He puts you back on to the wheel of His purpose this very day.

"He restores my soul. He guides me in paths of righteousness for his name's sake." (Psa. 23:3)

The Lord's judgments

DAY **218**

Jeremiah 49:23–27

²³Concerning Damascus:
"Hamath and Arpad are dismayed,
  for they have heard bad news.
They are disheartened,
  troubled like the restless sea.
²⁴Damascus has become feeble,
  she has turned to flee
and panic has gripped her;
  anguish and pain have seized her,
  pain like that of a woman in labour.
²⁵Why has the city of renown not been abandoned,
  the town in which I delight?
²⁶Surely, her young men will fall in the streets;
  all her soldiers will be silenced in that day,"
    declares the Lord Almighty.
²⁷"I will set fire to the walls of Damascus;
  it will consume the fortresses of Ben-Hadad."

The destruction of Moab	Jeremiah 48:1–10
Cities of Moab destroyed	Jeremiah 48:11–25
Moab will be humbled	Jeremiah 48:26–39
No escape for Moab	Jeremiah 48:40–47
The Lord's judgment on Ammon	Jeremiah 49:1–6
His judgment of Edom	Jeremiah 49:7–22
His judgment on Damascus	Jeremiah 49:23–27
His judgment on Kedar and Hazor	Jeremiah 49:28–33
His judgment of Elam	Jeremiah 49:34–39

For Thought and **Contemplation**

Just as the New Testament shows how marvellous is God's mercy, so the Old Testament shows how terrible He is in judgment. Without judgment, grace would be sickly and sentimental, and without mercy, judgment would be terrifying and overwhelming. God needs to be seen in both aspects if He is really to be properly served and understood.

"It does not, therefore, depend on man's desire or effort, but on God's mercy." (Rom. 9:16)

Zerubbabel and main party return	Iron Age begins in Britain	Ezra returns	Malachi	
500 BC				400 BC
Cyrus Zechariah Haggai 2nd Temple built			Nehemiah rebuilds walls of Jerusalem	

DAY 219 — Second and third deportations: 598 BC

Jehoiakim's enemies
2 Kings 24:2–4

Second deportation: 3,023 captives
2 Chronicles 36:6–7, Jeremiah 52:28

Jehoiakim's death
2 Kings 24:5–6, 2 Chronicles 36:8

Jehoiachin
2 Kings 24:8–9, 2 Chronicles 36:9

His captivity foretold
Jeremiah 22:24–30

Third deportation: 10,000 captives
2 Kings 24:10–16,
2 Chronicles 36:10, Esther 2:6

Zedekiah
2 Kings 24:17–20, 2 Chronicles 36:11–16,
Jeremiah 37:1–2, 52:1–2

Israel's captivity foretold
Jeremiah 21:1–14

Jeremiah's message to the king
Jeremiah 22:1–9, 20–23

2 Chronicles 36:11–16

¹¹Zedekiah was twenty-one years old when he became king, and he reigned in Jerusalem for eleven years. ¹²He did evil in the eyes of the Lord his God and did not humble himself before Jeremiah the prophet, who spoke the word of the Lord. ¹³He also rebelled against King Nebuchadnezzar, who had made him take an oath in God's name. He became stiff-necked and hardened his heart and would not turn to the Lord, the God of Israel. ¹⁴Furthermore, all the leaders of the priests and the people became more and more unfaithful, following all the detestable practices of the nations and defiling the temple of the Lord, which he had consecrated in Jerusalem.

¹⁵The Lord, the God of their fathers, sent word to them through his messengers again and again, because he had pity on his people and on his dwelling-place. ¹⁶But they mocked God's messengers, despised his words and scoffed at his prophets until the wrath of the Lord was aroused against his people and there was no remedy.

For Thought and **Contemplation**

Ancient Israel is seen by many as being haughty in times of peace, fearful in time of trouble, downcast under the yoke of oppression, and unwilling to break with sin and idolatry until the last possible moment. Is this a description of many in today's Church? What do you think?

"See to it, brothers, that none of you has a sinful, unbelieving heart that turns away from the living God." (Heb. 3:12)

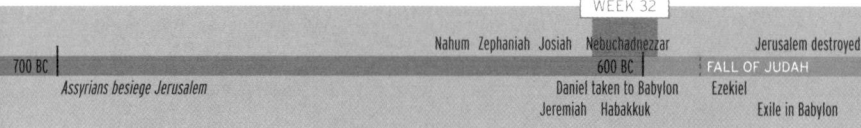

Good and bad figs

DAY **220**

Jeremiah 23:5–8

⁵"The days are coming," declares the Lord,
"when I will raise up to David a righteous Branch,
 a King who will reign wisely
 and do what is just and right in the land.
⁶In his days Judah will be saved
 and Israel will live in safety.
This is the name by which he will be called:
 The Lord Our Righteousness.
⁷"So then, the days are coming," declares the Lord, "when people will no longer say, 'As surely as the Lord lives, who brought the Israelites up out of Egypt,' ⁸but they will say, 'As surely as the Lord lives, who brought the descendants of Israel up out of the land of the north and out of all the countries where he had banished them.' Then they will live in their own land."

Faithless shepherds rebuked
Jeremiah 23:1–4

Israel's future restoration
Jeremiah 23:5–8

Message to prophets
Jeremiah 23:9–32

The Lord's burden
Jeremiah 23:33–40

Two baskets of figs
Jeremiah 24:1–10

Jeremiah's advice to Zedekiah
Jeremiah 27:12–22

Jeremiah's letter to the exiles
Jeremiah 29:1–14

Message to those who remained
Jeremiah 29:16–19

For Thought and **Contemplation**

Just as in Israel, so in today's Church there are "good and bad figs". The "good figs" are those who learn from corrective discipline, and the "bad figs" are those who continue in their wilfulness. In which basket do you think God might place you?

"Endure hardship as discipline; God is treating you as sons. For what son is not disciplined by his father?" (Heb. 12:7)

Zerubbabel and main party return | Iron Age begins in Britain | Ezra returns | Malachi
500 BC | | | 400 BC
Cyrus | Zechariah Haggai | | Nehemiah rebuilds walls of Jerusalem
     | 2nd Temple Built

DAY 221

Israel's bright future

Jeremiah's letter to the exiles
Jeremiah 29:20, 15, 21–23

Message to Shemaiah
Jeremiah 29:24–28

Shemaiah's punishment
Jeremiah 29:30–32

Coming trouble
Jeremiah 30:1–7

The Lord's promises
Jeremiah 30:8–17

Future restoration
Jeremiah 30:18–24

Israel's return home
Jeremiah 31:1–14

The Lord's mercy
Jeremiah 31:15–22

Future prosperity
Jeremiah 31:23–30

God's new covenant with Israel
Jeremiah 31:31–34

His everlasting mercy
Jeremiah 31:35–40

Jeremiah 31:31–34

[31]"The time is coming," declares the Lord,
"when I will make a new covenant with the house of Israel
and with the house of Judah.
[32]It will not be like the covenant I made with their forefathers
when I took them by the hand to lead them out of Egypt,
because they broke my covenant, though I was a husband to them,"
declares the Lord.
[33]"This is the covenant that I will make with the house of Israel
after that time," declares the Lord.
"I will put my law in their minds and write it on their hearts.
I will be their God, and they will be my people.
[34]No longer will a man teach his neighbour,
or a man his brother, saying, 'Know the Lord,'
because they will all know me, from the least of them to the greatest,"
    declares the Lord.
"For I will forgive their wickedness and will remember their sins no more."

For Thought and **Contemplation**

It is characteristic of the Almighty that once His people are purified by oppression and exile, He acts at once to re-establish them and bring about their restoration. What would happen, do you think, if God's Church broke with all forms of idolatry, lukewarmness and indolence, and sought His face? There can only be one answer – *revival*.

"Restore to me the joy of your salvation and grant me a willing spirit, to sustain me. Then I will teach transgressors your ways, and sinners will turn back to you." (Psa. 51:12–13)

a bird's eye view of **Ezekiel**

Place in the Bible

Twenty-sixth Old Testament book; fourth book of prophecy.

Special Features

Visions are the characteristic feature of this book.

Ezekiel's vision

DAY 222

Ezekiel 1:22-28

²²Spread out above the heads of the living creatures was what looked like an expanse, sparkling like ice, and awesome. ²³Under the expanse their wings were stretched out one towards the other, and each had two wings covering its body. ²⁴When the creatures moved, I heard the sound of their wings, like the roar of rushing waters, like the voice of the Almighty, like the tumult of an army. When they stood still, they lowered their wings.
²⁵Then there came a voice from above the expanse over their heads as they stood with lowered wings. ²⁶Above the expanse over their heads was what looked like a throne of sapphire, and high above on the throne was a figure like that of a man. ²⁷I saw that from what appeared to be his waist up he looked like glowing metal, as if full of fire, and that from there down he looked like fire; and brilliant light surrounded him. ²⁸Like the appearance of a rainbow in the clouds on a rainy day, so was the radiance around him.
This was the appearance of the likeness of the glory of the Lord. ...

Hananiah's false prophecy	Jeremiah 28:1-16
His death	Jeremiah 28:17
Seraiah and Zedekiah visit Babylon	Jeremiah 51:59
Ezekiel's preparation	Ezekiel 1:1
His vision of God	Ezekiel 1:2-14
The four wheels	Ezekiel 1:15-21
God's throne	Ezekiel 1:22-28
Filled with the Spirit	Ezekiel 2:1-2
Ezekiel's commission as prophet	Ezekiel 2:3-10, 3:1-9

For Thought and **Contemplation**

Jeremiah prophesied to the remaining Jews in Jerusalem, while Ezekiel prophesied to the exiles in Babylon. Although God has one message, He uses many different messengers. If you run from the word of the Lord in your own church, then you will find the same message facing you in another. Worth pondering – don't you think?

"Where can I go from your Spirit? Where can I flee from your presence?" (Psa. 139:7)

Jesus and the Book

In chapter 34 Ezekiel contrasts faithful shepherds with uncaring shepherds, and in John 10:11 Jesus described himself as the "good shepherd" caring, leading and giving life to His followers.

Teaching

Through the six visions, six parables and ten signs Ezekiel comforted the downcast Jews, in exile in Babylon. He taught the Israelites how God had to punish sin, and also how God promised a new life through the activity of His Spirit.

A Verse to Remember

"I will give you a new heart and put a new spirit in you; I will remove from you your heart of stone and give you a heart of flesh. And I will put my Spirit in you ..." (Ezek. 36:26-27).

DAY 223 — Ezekiel portrays the siege

Ezekiel appointed watchman
Ezekiel 3:10–21

God's glory
Ezekiel 3:22–23

Filled with the Spirit again
Ezekiel 3:24–27

The sign of the tile
Ezekiel 4:1–17

The sign of the sharp knife
Ezekiel 5:1–17

Idolatry condemned
Ezekiel 6:1–7

Remnant to be spared
Ezekiel 6:8–10

Desolation to come
Ezekiel 6:11–14

Ezekiel 3:24–27

²⁴Then the Spirit came into me and raised me to my feet. He spoke to me and said: "Go, shut yourself inside your house. ²⁵And you, son of man, they will tie with ropes; you will be bound so that you cannot go out among the people. ²⁶I will make your tongue stick to the roof of your mouth so that you will be silent and unable to rebuke them, though they are a rebellious house. ²⁷But when I speak to you, I will open your mouth and you shall say to them, 'This is what the Sovereign Lord says.' Whoever will listen let him listen, and whoever will refuse let him refuse; for they are a rebellious house.

For Thought and **Contemplation**

There are two essential prerequisites to an effective ministry for God. They are: (1) an overwhelming vision of God's power and greatness and (2) an understanding of where one fits into God's programme for the world. Ezekiel knew something of both these factors. Do you?

"Brothers, think of what you were when you were called. Not many of you were wise by human standards; not many were influential; not many were of noble birth. But God chose the foolish things of the world to shame the wise; God chose the weak things of the world to shame the strong." (1 Cor. 1:26–27)

WEEK 32

700 BC — Nahum Zephaniah Josiah Nebuchadnezzar — 600 BC — Jerusalem destroyed — FALL OF JUDAH

Assyrians besiege Jerusalem · Daniel taken to Babylon · Ezekiel · Exile in Babylon
Jeremiah Habakkuk

Ezekiel's second vision

DAY 224

Ezekiel 8:1–6

¹In the sixth year, in the sixth month on the fifth day, while I was sitting in my house and the elders of Judah were sitting before me, the hand of the Sovereign Lord came upon me there. ²I looked, and I saw a figure like that of a man. From what appeared to be his waist down he was like fire, and from there up his appearance was as bright as glowing metal. ³He stretched out what looked like a hand and took me by the hair of my head. The Spirit lifted me up between earth and heaven and in visions of God he took me to Jerusalem, to the entrance to the north gate of the inner court, where the idol that provokes to jealousy stood. ⁴And there before me was the glory of the God of Israel, as in the vision I had seen in the plain.
⁵Then he said to me, "Son of man, look towards the north." So I looked, and in the entrance north of the gate of the altar I saw this idol of jealousy.
⁶And he said to me, "Son of man, do you see what they are doing – the utterly detestable things the house of Israel is doing here …"

The desolation of the land
Ezekiel 7:1–15

The distress of the few
Ezekiel 7:16–22

The captivity
Ezekiel 7:23–27

Idolatry in Jerusalem
Ezekiel 8:1–6

The hole in the wall
Ezekiel 8:7–12

Mourning for Tammuz
Ezekiel 8:13–14

The sun worshippers
Ezekiel 8:15–16

The Lord's response
Ezekiel 8:17–18

Marked men
Ezekiel 9:1–11

The Lord's departure
Ezekiel 10:1–15

For Thought and **Contemplation**

What foolishness was manifested by the elders of Israel in thinking that what they did in the dark could not be seen by the Lord. Someone has said that sin is the greatest of detectives. "Be sure your sin will find you out."

"Therefore judge nothing before the appointed time; wait till the Lord comes. He will bring to light what is hidden in darkness and will expose the motives of men's hearts. At that time each will receive his praise from God." (1 Cor. 4:5)

Zerubbabel and main party return	Iron Age begins in Britain	Ezra returns	Malachi	
500 BC				400 BC
Cyrus	Zechariah Haggai 2nd Temple built		Nehemiah rebuilds walls of Jerusalem	

DAY 225 — The Lord's condemnation

The Lord's departure
Ezekiel 10:16–22

Jerusalem is condemned
Ezekiel 11:1–13

God's promise to the exiles
Ezekiel 11:14–21

God's glory leaves Jerusalem
Ezekiel 11:22–25

Ezekiel the refugee
Ezekiel 12:1–7

The approaching captivity
Ezekiel 12:8–12, 15–16

The sign of the trembling prophet
Ezekiel 12:17–20

Objections answered
Ezekiel 12:21–28

False male prophets condemned
Ezekiel 13:1–16

False female prophets condemned
Ezekiel 13:17–23

Ezekiel 11:14–19

[14] The word of the Lord came to me: [15] "Son of man, your brothers – your brothers who are your blood-relatives and the whole house of Israel – are those of whom the people of Jerusalem have said, 'They are far away from the Lord; this land was given to us as our possession.'

[16] Therefore say: 'This is what the Sovereign Lord says: Although I sent them far away among the nations and scattered them among the countries, yet for a little while I have been a sanctuary for them in the countries where they have gone.'

[17] Therefore say: 'This is what the Sovereign Lord says: I will gather you from the nations and bring you back from the countries where you have been scattered, and I will give you back the land of Israel again.'

[18] They will return to it and remove all its vile images and detestable idols. [19] I will give them an undivided heart and put a new spirit in them; I will remove from them their heart of stone and give them a heart of flesh."

For Thought and **Contemplation**

Much of Israel's downfall was due to the failure of her shepherds (i.e. leaders) – those who *plundered* rather than *protected* the flock. How true is the saying that it takes dedicated leaders to produce dedicated followers. Pray for your spiritual shepherd today.

"Obey your leaders and submit to their authority. They keep watch over you as men who must give an account. Obey them so that their work will be a joy, not a burden, for that would be of no advantage to you." (Heb. 13:17)

WEEK 33

700 BC — Assyrians besiege Jerusalem — Nahum Zephaniah Josiah Nebuchadnezzar — 600 BC — Daniel taken to Babylon — Jeremiah Habakkuk — FALL OF JUDAH — Ezekiel — Jerusalem destroyed — Exile in Babylon

Jerusalem's adultery

DAY **226**

Ezekiel 16:9–14

⁹"'I bathed you with water and washed the blood from you and put ointments on you. ¹⁰I clothed you with an embroidered dress and put leather sandals on you. I dressed you in fine linen and covered you with costly garments. ¹¹I adorned you with jewellery: I put bracelets on your arms and a necklace around your neck, ¹²and I put a ring on your nose, ear-rings on your ears and a beautiful crown on your head. ¹³So you were adorned with gold and silver; your clothes were of fine linen and costly fabric and embroidered cloth. Your food was fine flour, honey and olive oil. You became very beautiful and rose to be a queen. ¹⁴And your fame spread among the nations on account of your beauty, because the splendour I had given you made your beauty perfect, declares the Sovereign Lord.

Hypocrites threatened
Ezekiel 14:1–11

God's punishment
Ezekiel 14:12–23

Parable of the vine
Ezekiel 15:1–8

The Lord's covenant
Ezekiel 16:1–8

God's blessings
Ezekiel 16:9–14

Jerusalem's unfaithfulness
Ezekiel 16:15–22

Her adultery
Ezekiel 16:23–34

God's judgment on Jerusalem
Ezekiel 16:35–43

For Thought and **Contemplation**

Spend a few moments comparing the vine in Ezekiel with the vine in John 15. Remember that, in both cases, the only value of a vine is in the fruit it produces; its wood is quite useless (Ezek. 15:3). How much fruit is growing on your vine?

"I am the vine; you are the branches. If a man remains in me and I in him, he will bear much fruit; apart from me you can do nothing." (Jn. 15:5)

Zerubbabel and main party return	Iron Age begins in Britain	Ezra returns	Malachi	
500 BC				400 BC
Cyrus	Zechariah Haggai 2nd Temple built		Nehemiah rebuilds walls of Jerusalem	

DAY 227 — A parable explained

Like mother, like daughter
Ezekiel 16:44–45

Judah worse than Sodom and Samaria
Ezekiel 16:46–52

Sodom and Samaria's future prosperity
Ezekiel 16:53–58

The renewed covenant
Ezekiel 16:59–63

Parable of the eagles and the vine
Ezekiel 17:1–10

The parable explained
Ezekiel 17:11–21

God's promise
Ezekiel 17:22–24

No respecter of persons
Ezekiel 18:1–20

The Lord's vindication
Ezekiel 18:21–29

Invitation to repent
Ezekiel 18:30–32

Ezekiel 18:30–32

³⁰"Therefore, O house of Israel, I will judge you, each one according to his ways, declares the Sovereign Lord. Repent! Turn away from all your offences; then sin will not be your downfall. ³¹Rid yourselves of all the offences you have committed, and get a new heart and a new spirit. Why will you die, O house of Israel? ³²For I take no pleasure in the death of anyone, declares the Sovereign Lord. Repent and live!

For Thought and Contemplation

There is only one word to describe the act of playing fast and loose with spiritual things – *prostitution*. It's a grim and horrifying word, but how else can God view the condition of those who pledge their fidelity to Him and then renege on their commitment?

"Now it is required that those who have been given a trust must prove faithful" (1 Cor. 4:2)

The Lord's reminder

DAY **228**

Ezekiel 20:27–31

²⁷"Therefore, son of man, speak to the people of Israel and say to them, 'This is what the Sovereign Lord says: In this also your fathers blasphemed me by forsaking me: ²⁸When I brought them into the land I had sworn to give them and they saw any high hill or any leafy tree, there they offered their sacrifices, made offerings that provoked me to anger, presented their fragrant incense and poured out their drink offerings. ²⁹Then I said to them: What is this high place you go to?'" (It is called Bamah to this day.)

³⁰"Therefore say to the house of Israel: 'This is what the Sovereign Lord says: Will you defile yourselves the way your fathers did and lust after their vile images? ³¹When you offer your gifts – the sacrifice of your sons in the fire – you continue to defile yourselves with all your idols to this day. Am I to let you enquire of me, O house of Israel? As surely as I live, declares the Sovereign Lord, I will not let you enquire of me.'"

	A lament for Israel's princes
	Ezekiel 19:1–9
	Another lament
	Ezekiel 19:10–14
	A reminder to the leaders
	Ezekiel 20:1–9
	In the wilderness
	Ezekiel 20:10–26
	In Canaan
	Ezekiel 20:27–32
	Pardon and restoration
	Ezekiel 20:33–44
	Prophecy against Jerusalem
	Ezekiel 20:45–49
	The Lord's sword
	Ezekiel 21:1–7

For Thought and **Contemplation**

Why is it that we have to learn things the *hard* way? Israel had received so many warnings from God, yet they persisted in following their own stubborn and wilful ways. Know anyone else like that?

"We must pay more careful attention, therefore, to what we have heard, so that we do not drift away." (Heb. 2:1)

Zerubbabel and main party return	Iron Age begins in Britain	Ezra returns	Malachi	
500 BC				400 BC
Cyrus	Zechariah Haggai		Nehemiah rebuilds walls of Jerusalem	
	2nd Temple built			

DAY 229 — God's refinery

Judgment by the sword
Ezekiel 21:8-17

The king of Babylon's approach
Ezekiel 21:18-27

The Ammonites' destruction
Ezekiel 21:28-32

The sins of Jerusalem
Ezekiel 22:1-16

God's furnace
Ezekiel 22:17-22

The sins of Israel's leaders
Ezekiel 22:23-31

The lustful sisters
Ezekiel 23:1-21

Ezekiel 22:17-22

¹⁷Then the word of the Lord came to me: ¹⁸"Son of man, the house of Israel has become dross to me; all of them are the copper, tin, iron and lead left inside a furnace. They are but the dross of silver. ¹⁹Therefore this is what the Sovereign Lord says: 'Because you have all become dross, I will gather you into Jerusalem. ²⁰As men gather silver, copper, iron, lead and tin into a furnace to melt it with a fiery blast, so will I gather you in my anger and my wrath and put you inside the city and melt you. ²¹I will gather you and I will blow on you with my fiery wrath, and you will be melted inside her. ²²As silver is melted in a furnace, so you will be melted inside her, and you will know that I the Lord have poured out my wrath upon you.'"

For Thought and **Contemplation**

Israel spent much of their time in God's refinery. This was because, as we have seen, they failed to heed His Word. Ever been in God's refinery? Perhaps you are there right now. The heat is intense and the pressure is relentless, but the results are well worth the cost. You'll see.

"For you, O God, tested us; you refined us like silver." (Psa. 66:10)

The Diaspora

The term "Diaspora" refers to Jews who live outside of Palestine (now Israel). Moses had warned the Israelites that they would be scattered among the Gentiles if they deserted the true God and worshipped idols. This scattering began through the Assyrian and Babylonian captivities, and became worldwide after the destruction of Jerusalem and the Temple in AD 70.

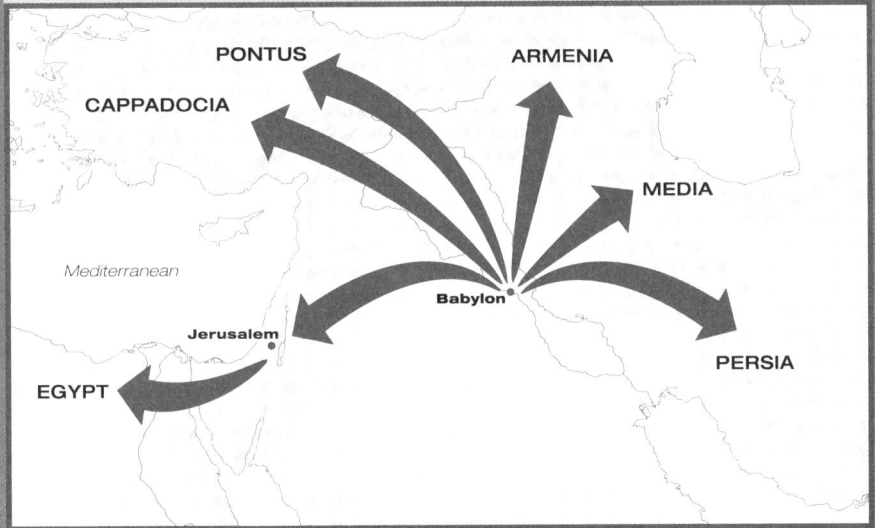

Famous sayings of Jeremiah

"Is there no balm in Gilead? Is there no physician there? Why then is there no healing for the wound of my people?" (8:22)

"Can the Ethiopian change his skin or the leopard its spots? Neither can you do good who are accustomed to doing evil." (13:23)

"The heart is deceitful above all things and beyond cure. Who can understand it?" (17:9)

"Is not my word like fire ... and like a hammer that breaks a rock in pieces?" (23:29)

"Call to me and I will answer you and tell you great and unsearchable things you do not know." (33:3)

DAY 230 — The fourth deportation: 588 BC

God's judgment on Oholibah
Ezekiel 23:22–35

God's judgment on Oholah and Oholibah
Ezekiel 23:36–49

The boiling cauldron
Ezekiel 24:1–14, 19–27

City's capture approaches
Jeremiah 52:3–5, 39:1, 2 Kings 25:1–2

Ezekiel's wife dies
Ezekiel 24:15–18

832 captives taken
Jeremiah 52:29

Jeremiah's first imprisonment
Jeremiah 32:1–5

Deceitful treatment of slaves
Jeremiah 34:8–11

Jeremiah 32:1–5

¹This is the word that came to Jeremiah from the Lord in the tenth year of Zedekiah king of Judah, which was the eighteenth year of Nebuchadnezzar. ²The army of the king of Babylon was then besieging Jerusalem, and Jeremiah the prophet was confined in the courtyard of the guard in the royal palace of Judah. ³Now Zedekiah king of Judah had imprisoned him there, saying, "Why do you prophesy as you do? You say, 'This is what the Lord says: I am about to hand this city over to the king of Babylon, and he will capture it. ⁴Zedekiah king of Judah will not escape out of the hands of the Babylonians but will certainly be handed over to the king of Babylon, and will speak with him face to face and see him with his own eyes. ⁵He will take Zedekiah to Babylon, where he will remain until I deal with him, declares the Lord. If you fight against the Babylonians, you will not succeed.'"

For Thought and **Contemplation**

By now the message that we either "take God's way or take the consequences" will undoubtedly have got home to you. Isolate one area of your life where you are going your own way, and draw up an alternative plan – God's plan. Then keep a diary of your progress and watch how things work out.

"In all your ways acknowledge him, and he will make your paths straight. Do not be wise in your own eyes; fear the Lord and shun evil." (Prov. 3:6–7)

The overthrow of Tyre — DAY **231**

Ezekiel 26:7–14

⁷"For this is what the Sovereign Lord says: From the north I am going to bring against Tyre Nebuchadnezzar king of Babylon ... ⁹He will direct the blows of his battering-rams against your walls and demolish your towers with his weapons. ¹⁰His horses will be so many that they will cover you with dust. Your walls will tremble at the noise of the war horses, wagons and chariots when he enters your gates as men enter a city whose walls have been broken through. ¹¹The hoofs of his horses will trample all your streets; he will kill your people with the sword, and your strong pillars will fall to the ground. ¹²They will plunder your wealth and loot your merchandise; they will break down your walls and demolish your fine houses and throw your stones, timber and rubble into the sea. ¹³I will put an end to your noisy songs, and the music of your harps will be heard no more. ¹⁴I will make you a bare rock, and you will become a place to spread fish-nets. You will never be rebuilt, for I the Lord have spoken, declares the Sovereign Lord."

Dishonourable treatment punished
Jeremiah 34:12–22

Prophecy against Egypt
Ezekiel 29:1–7

The desolation of Egypt
Ezekiel 29:8–16

Tyre's rejoicing
Ezekiel 26:1–2

Tyre's enemy
Ezekiel 26:3–6

Tyre's attacker
Ezekiel 26:7–8

Tyre's destruction
Ezekiel 26:9–14

A terrifying example
Ezekiel 26:15–21

Tyre's funeral song
Ezekiel 27:1–25

For Thought and **Contemplation**

One of the greatest dangers we face in life is prosperity – whether it be financial, social or spiritual. It's the successful person who is in danger of forgetting their dependency on God. Self-sufficiency brought Tyre down to ruins. Watch that it doesn't do the same to you.

"So, if you think you are standing firm, be careful that you don't fall!"
(1 Cor. 10:12)

Zerubbabel and main party return	*Iron Age begins in Britain*	Ezra returns	Malachi
	500 BC		400 BC
Cyrus	Zechariah Haggai		Nehemiah rebuilds walls of Jerusalem
	2nd Temple built		

DAY **232** — Further prophecies

Tyre's funeral song
Ezekiel 27:26–36

The fall of the king of Tyre
Ezekiel 28:1–12, 19

Prophecy against Pharaoh
Ezekiel 30:20–26

Further prophecy against Egypt
Ezekiel 31:1–18

Jeremiah's advice sought
Jeremiah 37:3–4

Egyptian intervention
Jeremiah 37:5

Egyptian army to return home
Jeremiah 37:6–10

Jeremiah arrested, then released
Jeremiah 37:11–21

Jeremiah 37:6–10

⁶Then the word of the Lord came to Jeremiah the prophet: ⁷"This is what the Lord, the God of Israel, says: Tell the king of Judah, who sent you to enquire of me, 'Pharaoh's army, which has marched out to support you, will go back to its own land, to Egypt. ⁸Then the Babylonians will return and attack this city; they will capture it and burn it down.' ⁹This is what the Lord says: Do not deceive yourselves, thinking, 'The Babylonians will surely leave us.' They will not! ¹⁰Even if you were to defeat the entire Babylonian army that is attacking you and only wounded men were left in their tents, they would come out and burn this city down."

For Thought and **Contemplation**

Ever heard the statement: Cheer up, things could be worse. So you cheered up, and sure enough – things got worse! Jeremiah could have identified with that. How did he cope? By living above his circumstances rather than under them! Have you learned that secret yet?

"But he said to me, 'My grace is sufficient for you, for my power is made perfect in weakness.' Therefore I will boast all the more gladly about my weaknesses, so that Christ's power may rest on me." (2 Cor. 12:9)

The promised Messiah

DAY 233

Jeremiah 33:14–18

[14] "'The days are coming,' declares the Lord, 'when I will fulfil the gracious promise I made to the house of Israel and to the house of Judah.
[15] In those days and at that time
  I will make a righteous Branch sprout from David's line;
  he will do what is just and right in the land.
[16] In those days Judah will be saved and Jerusalem will live in safety. This is the name by which it will be called:
  The Lord Our Righteousness.'
[17] For this is what the Lord says: 'David will never fail to have a man to sit on the throne of the house of Israel, [18] nor will the priests, who are Levites, ever fail to have a man to stand before me continually to offer burnt offerings, to burn grain offerings and to present sacrifices.'"

Jeremiah buys a field
Jeremiah 32:6–15

Jeremiah's prayer
Jeremiah 32:16–25

The Lord's answer
Jeremiah 32:26–35

The Lord's promise
Jeremiah 32:36–44

The restoration of the Jews
Jeremiah 33:1–13

The promised Messiah
Jeremiah 33:14–26

A message for Zedekiah
Jeremiah 34:1–7

Jeremiah in the well
Jeremiah 38:1–13

For Thought and **Contemplation**

Has life's circumstances cast you, like Jeremiah, into a well? Figuratively, we mean. Well, look up, for we are told that even in the daytime one can see the stars shining from the bottom of a well. And what do they say? "God's in His heaven – all's right with the world."

"Consider it pure joy, my brothers, whenever you face trials of many kinds, because you know that the testing of your faith develops perseverance. Perseverance must finish its work so that you may be mature and complete, not lacking anything." (Jas. 1:2–4)

Zerubbabel and main party return	Iron Age begins in Britain	Ezra returns	Malachi
500 BC			400 BC
Cyrus	Zechariah Haggai 2nd Temple built		Nehemiah rebuilds walls of Jerusalem

DAY 234 — The fall of Jerusalem

Zedekiah seeks advice
Jeremiah 38:14–27

Message to Ebed-Melech
Jeremiah 39:15–18

The fall of Jerusalem
Jeremiah 38:28

The famine
2 Kings 25:3, Jeremiah 52:6

Fall of Judah 586 BC

The Babylonian princes
Jeremiah 39:2–3

Zedekiah's flight and capture
2 Kings 25:4–5, Jeremiah 39:4–5, 52:7–8

The slaughter
2 Chronicles 36:17

Zedekiah's sons slain
Jeremiah 52:9–10, 39:6

His blindness
Ezekiel 12:13–14, 2 Kings 25:6–7, Jeremiah 39:7, 52:11

Temple and walls destroyed
2 Kings 25:8–10, 2 Chronicles 36:19, Jeremiah 39:8, 52:12–14

Jeremiah 39:15–18

¹⁵While Jeremiah had been confined in the courtyard of the guard, the word of the Lord came to him: ¹⁶"Go and tell Ebed-Melech the Cushite, 'This is what the Lord Almighty, the God of Israel, says: I am about to fulfil my words against this city through disaster, not prosperity. At that time they will be fulfilled before your eyes. ¹⁷But I will rescue you on that day, declares the Lord; you will not be handed over to those you fear. ¹⁸I will save you; you will not fall by the sword but will escape with your life, because you trust in me, declares the Lord.'"

For Thought and **Contemplation**

Sad though the fall of Jerusalem was, it is important to remember that from God's point of view, those walls were ever upright before Him (Isa. 49:16). God sees with a double vision. He sees things, not only as they are, but as they will be. Our hope must be His hope.

"Remember the former things, those of long ago; I am God, and there is no other; I am God, and there is none like me. I make known the end from the beginning, from ancient times, what is still to come. I say: My purpose will stand, and I will do all that I please." (Isa. 46:9–10)

a bird's eye view of **Lamentations**

Place in the Bible
Twenty-fifth Old Testament book; third book of prophecy.

Special features
Laments.

The fifth and sixth deportations

DAY **235**

Psalm 94:1-7

¹O Lord, the God who avenges,
  O God who avenges, shine forth.
²Rise up, O Judge of the earth;
  pay back to the proud what they deserve.
³How long will the wicked, O Lord,
  how long will the wicked be jubilant?
⁴They pour out arrogant words;
  all the evildoers are full of boasting.
⁵They crush your people, O Lord;
  they oppress your inheritance.
⁶They slay the widow and the alien;
  they murder the fatherless.
⁷They say, "The Lord does not see;
  the God of Jacob pays no heed." ...

Fifth deportation: the poor left behind
2 Kings 25:11-12, 2 Chronicles 36:20-21, Jeremiah 39:9-10, 52:15-16

God the judge of all
Psalm 94:1-23

The Temple looted
2 Kings 25:13-17, 2 Chronicles 36:18, Jeremiah 52:17-23

Priests deported
2 Kings 25:18, Jeremiah 52:24

Prayer for nation's deliverance
Psalm 74:1-23, 79:1-13

Important men killed
2 Kings 25:19-21, Jeremiah 52:25-27

For Thought and **Contemplation**

In the midst of desolation and catastrophe, where can one turn? Thankfully, those who know the Lord can lean hard upon His breast (Psalm 74). The old adage, though a cliché, is still reassuring: when the outlook is dark and depressing, try the uplook!

"God is our refuge and strength, an ever-present help in trouble. Therefore we will not fear, though the earth give way and the mountains fall into the heart of the sea ..." (Psa. 46:1-2)

Jesus and the Book

The opening poem of Lamentations depicts Jerusalem mourning over the destruction of its city and its temple. Jesus also wept over Jerusalem, reflecting His heartfelt love for the rebellious people of Jerusalem (Matt. 23:37-38).

Teaching

For the Jews the capture of Jerusalem in 586 BC was the ultimate disaster. They no longer had their land, their city or their temple. It was as if they no longer had God! But there is a shaft of light in chapter 3:22-24.

A Verse to Remember

"Because of the Lord's great love we are not consumed, for his compassions never fail. They are new every morning; great is your faithfulness" (Lam. 3:22-23).

DAY 236 — Jeremiah laments Jerusalem's fate

Jerusalem's miserable state
Lamentations 1:1–11

Jerusalem's sorrow
Lamentations 1:12–22

The Lord's terrible punishment
Lamentations 2:1–10

Jeremiah's deep sorrow
Lamentations 2:11–22

His suffering
Lamentations 3:1–20

His hope
Lamentations 3:21–30

The Lord's mercy
Lamentations 3:31–36

Lamentations 3:31–36

³¹For men are not cast off
   by the Lord for ever.
³²Though he brings grief, he will
show compassion,
   so great is his unfailing love.
³³For he does not willingly bring affliction
   or grief to the children of men.
³⁴To crush underfoot
   all prisoners in the land,
³⁵to deny a man his rights
   before the Most High,
³⁶to deprive a man of justice –
   would not the Lord see
such things?

For Thought and **Contemplation**

The more Jeremiah looked at the troubles of Israel, the more he was grieved. The more he looked on God's mercy, however, the more his spirit revived. It's not wrong to look at your difficulties and your problems, but it is wrong to look *only* at them. Do as one great saint said: "I glance at my difficulties, but I *gaze* at God."

"What, then, shall we say in response to this? If God is for us, who can be against us?" (Rom. 8:31)

Unexpected kindness

DAY **237**

Jeremiah 40:1–4

¹The word came to Jeremiah from the Lord after Nebuzaradan commander of the imperial guard had released him at Ramah. He had found Jeremiah bound in chains among all the captives from Jerusalem and Judah who were being carried into exile to Babylon. ²When the commander of the guard found Jeremiah, he said to him, "The Lord your God decreed this disaster for this place. ³And now the Lord has brought it about; he has done just as he said he would. All this happened because you people sinned against the Lord and did not obey him. ⁴But today I am freeing you from the chains on your wrists. Come with me to Babylon, if you like, and I will look after you; but if you do not want to, then don't come. Look, the whole country lies before you; go wherever you please."

Jeremiah's plea
Lamentations 3:37–66

Jerusalem after the fall
Lamentations 4:1–22

A prayer for mercy
Lamentations 5:1–22

Gedaliah becomes governor
2 Kings 25:22–24

Kindness shown to Jeremiah
Jeremiah 39:11–13

Jeremiah stays with Gedaliah
Jeremiah 39:14, 40:1–5

The captivity 586–516 BC

Gedaliah's care for the poor
Jeremiah 40:6–12

For Thought and **Contemplation**

When Jeremiah was in need of help he found it, not through his own people, but through Nebuzaradan, one of the oppressors of his people. It's a sad and sobering thought, that often God's people meet with more kindness from unbelievers than they do from their Christian brothers and sisters. Ought not this to be a matter of great prayer and concern?

"Carry each other's burdens, and in this way you will fulfil the law of Christ." (Gal. 6:2)

Zerubbabel and main party return	Iron Age begins in Britain	Ezra returns	Malachi	
500 BC				400 BC
Cyrus	Zechariah Haggai 2nd Temple built		Nehemiah rebuilds walls of Jerusalem	

DAY 238

No help in Egypt

Gedaliah killed
Jeremiah 40:13–16, 41:1–9, 2 Kings 25:25

Ishmael's escape
Jeremiah 41:10–15

The exodus to Egypt
2 Kings 25:26, Jeremiah 41:16–18

Jeremiah's assistance requested
Jeremiah 42:1–6

Safety in Judah
Jeremiah 42:7–12

Destruction in Egypt
Jeremiah 42:13–22

Jeremiah taken to Egypt
Jeremiah 43:1–7

Conquest of Egypt foretold
Jeremiah 43:8–13

Jeremiah 42:1–6

¹Then all the army officers, including Johanan son of Kareah and Jezaniah son of Hoshaiah, and all the people from the least to the greatest approached ²Jeremiah the prophet and said to him, "Please hear our petition and pray to the Lord your God for this entire remnant. For as you now see, though we were once many, now only a few are left. ³Pray that the Lord your God will tell us where we should go and what we should do."

⁴"I have heard you," replied Jeremiah the prophet. "I will certainly pray to the Lord your God as you have requested; I will tell you everything the Lord says and will keep nothing back from you."

⁵Then they said to Jeremiah, "May the Lord be a true and faithful witness against us if we do not act in accordance with everything the Lord your God sends you to tell us. ⁶Whether it is favourable or unfavourable, we will obey the Lord our God, to whom we are sending you, so that it will go well with us, for we will obey the Lord our God."

For Thought and **Contemplation**

Jeremiah's message could be summed up in these words: "Don't flee to Egypt. Stand your ground against the Babylonians, face them with the truth and you will be spared." Are you running from something at this moment? Then Stop. Face your problem in God's strength. Jer. 42:11 is God's special word to you today.

"He gives strength to the weary and increases the power of the weak. Even youths grow tired and weary, and young men stumble and fall; but those who hope in the Lord will renew their strength. They will soar on wings like eagles; they will run and not grow weary, they will walk and not be faint." (Isa. 40:29–31)

The Jews in Egypt

DAY **239**

Jeremiah 46:27-28

²⁷"Do not fear, O Jacob my servant;
   do not be dismayed, O Israel.
I will surely save you out of a distant place,
   your descendants from the land of their exile.
Jacob will again have peace and security,
   and no-one will make him afraid.
²⁸Do not fear, O Jacob my servant,
   for I am with you," declares the Lord.
"Though I completely destroy all the nations
   among which I scatter you,
I will not completely destroy you.
I will discipline you but only with justice;
   I will not let you go entirely unpunished."

The coming of Nebuchadnezzar
Jeremiah 46:13

The Lord's message to Jeremiah
Jeremiah 46:14-18

Egypt's overthrow
Jeremiah 46:19-26

God's promise to the Jews
Jeremiah 46:27-28

Their idolatry in Egypt
Jeremiah 44:1-14

Their refusal to reform
Jeremiah 44:15-19

Jeremiah's denouncement
Jeremiah 44:20-30

Ezekiel hears of Jerusalem's fall
Ezekiel 33:21-33

For Thought and **Contemplation**

Israel was plagued with "rabbititis". It is a condition that affects many people and makes them believe that there is no problem so big or complicated that it can't be run away from. We learned yesterday that running away from problems never solves them. Look again at Jer. 44:1-14 and you'll see why.

No temptation has seized you except what is common to man. And God is faithful; he will not let you be tempted beyond what you can bear. But when you are tempted, he will also provide a way out so that you can stand up under it." (1 Cor. 10:13)

Zerubbabel and main party return	Iron Age begins in Britain	Ezra returns	Malachi	
	500 BC			400 BC
Cyrus	Zechariah Haggai 2nd Temple built		Nehemiah rebuilds walls of Jerusalem	

DAY 240 — The seventh deportation: 582 BC

Prophecy against Ammon
Ezekiel 25:1–7

Prophecy against Moab
Ezekiel 25:8–11

Prophecy against Edom
Ezekiel 25:12–14

Prophecy against Philistia
Ezekiel 25:15–17

Prophecy against Sidon
Ezekiel 28:20–23

Blessing for Israel
Ezekiel 28:24–26

The fall of Egypt
Ezekiel 32:1–16

The world of the dead
Ezekiel 32:17–32

745 more captives taken
Jeremiah 52:30

Nebuchadnezzar's golden image
Daniel 3:1–7

Ezekiel 28:24–26

²⁴"'No longer will the people of Israel have malicious neighbours who are painful briers and sharp thorns. Then they will know that I am the Sovereign Lord. ²⁵This is what the Sovereign Lord says: When I gather the people of Israel from the nations where they have been scattered, I will show myself holy among them in the sight of the nations. Then they will live in their own land, which I gave to my servant Jacob. ²⁶They will live there in safety and will build houses and plant vineyards; they will live in safety when I inflict punishment on all their neighbours who maligned them. Then they will know that I am the Lord their God.'"

For Thought and **Contemplation**

Have you noticed how, in every setting of human failure, God breaks through with a heartening promise? But what is more to the point, have you learned to look for God's promises in the midst of your own failures and circumstances? They're always there – just keep on looking.

"Through these he has given us his very great and precious promises, so that through them you may participate in the divine nature and escape the corruption in the world caused by evil desires." (2 Pet. 1:4)

The fiery furnace

DAY **241**

Ezekiel 34:11–16

¹¹"'For this is what the Sovereign Lord says: I myself will search for my sheep and look after them. ¹²As a shepherd looks after his scattered flock when he is with them, so will I look after my sheep. I will rescue them from all the places where they were scattered on a day of clouds and darkness. ¹³I will bring them out from the nations and gather them from the countries, and I will bring them into their own land. I will pasture them on the mountains of Israel, in the ravines and in all the settlements in the land. ¹⁴I will tend them in a good pasture, and the mountain heights of Israel will be their grazing land. There they will lie down in good grazing land, and there they will feed in a rich pasture on the mountains of Israel. ¹⁵I myself will tend my sheep and have them lie down, declares the Sovereign Lord. ¹⁶I will search for the lost and bring back the strays. I will bind up the injured and strengthen the weak, but the sleek and the strong I will destroy. I will shepherd the flock with justice.' "

Shadrach, Meshach and Abednego
Daniel 3:8–18

The fiery furnace
Daniel 3:19–25

Nebuchadnezzar acknowledges God
Daniel 3:26–30

His proclamation
Daniel 4:1–3

The watchman
Ezekiel 33:1–9

Individual responsibility
Ezekiel 33:10–20

Message to faithless shepherds
Ezekiel 34:1–10

The Good Shepherd
Ezekiel 34:11–16

The flock judged
Ezekiel 34:17–19

For Thought and **Contemplation**

The faith of Daniel and his friends was of a special quality. It has been called "the 'if not' faith". They said: "Our God is able to deliver us ... BUT IF NOT ... we will still refuse to bow." They believed in the rightness of their stand, irrespective of whether God delivered them or not. Ask God to give you that kind of faith. There is nothing higher.

"Now faith is being sure of what we hope for and certain of what we do not see." (Heb. 11:1)

Zerubbabel and main party return		Iron Age begins in Britain	Ezra returns	Malachi	
	500 BC				400 BC
Cyrus	Zechariah Haggai			Nehemiah rebuilds walls of Jerusalem	
	2nd Temple built				

The Bad and the Good Shepherd

The many false shepherds in Ezekiel

They fed themselves instead of the flock (34:2,3)

They had not taken care of the weak, tended the sick, bound up the broken bones, nor sought the lost (34:4)

The sheep were then scattered, having no shepherd (34:5)

Therefore, the shepherds would be punished (34:10)

They would be removed from their position as shepherds (34:10)

They would not themselves be fed by the Great Shepherd (34:10)

The Good Shepherd in Ezekiel

He would search out the lost sheep (34:11)

He would deliver them from their enemies (34:12)

He would gather them from all nations (34:13)

He would feed them upon the mountains of Israel (34:14)

He would give them rest in green pastures (34:15)

He would put splints and bandages upon their broken limbs (34:16)

He would heal the sick (34:16)

He would make an eternal pact with them (34:25)

He would guarantee their safety and place them in a perfect paradise (34:25–28)

New life

DAY 242

Ezekiel 37:1-6

¹The hand of the Lord was upon me, and he brought me out by the Spirit of the Lord and set me in the middle of a valley; it was full of bones. ²He led me to and fro among them, and I saw a great many bones on the floor of the valley, bones that were very dry. ³He asked me, "Son of man, can these bones live?"

I said, "O Sovereign Lord, you alone know."

⁴Then he said to me, "Prophesy to these bones and say to them, 'Dry bones, hear the word of the Lord! ⁵This is what the Sovereign Lord says to these bones: I will make breath enter you, and you will come to life. ⁶I will attach tendons to you and make flesh come upon you and cover you with skin; I will put breath in you, and you will come to life. Then you will know that I am the Lord.'"

The Lord's flock
Ezekiel 34:20–31

Prophecy against Edom
Ezekiel 35:1–15

God's blessing on Israel
Ezekiel 36:1–15

Israel's former sins
Ezekiel 36:16–23

Israel's new life
Ezekiel 36:24–32

A witness to neighbouring nations
Ezekiel 36:33–38

The valley of dry bones
Ezekiel 37:1–14

For Thought and **Contemplation**

When God's people are in right standing before the Lord, the blessings that flow from this are innumerable. Some of them can be seen in Ezek. 36:24–31. How many can you find? There are at least ten.

"The blessing of the Lord brings wealth, and he adds no trouble to it."
(Prov. 10:22)

WEEK 35

700 BC	Nahum Zephaniah Josiah Nebuchadnezzar	Jerusalem destroyed
	600 BC	FALL OF JUDAH
Assyrians besiege Jerusalem	Daniel taken to Babylon	Ezekiel
	Jeremiah Habakkuk	Exile in Babylon

DAY **243**

The destruction of Gog

The sign of the two sticks
Ezekiel 37:15–19

Judah and Israel to be one nation
Ezekiel 37:20–28

The malice of Gog
Ezekiel 38:1–13

God's punishment of Gog
Ezekiel 38:14–23

The defeat of Gog
Ezekiel 39:1–10

The burial of Gog
Ezekiel 39:11–20

Israel's restoration
Ezekiel 39:21–29

Ezekiel 37:24–28

²⁴"'My servant David will be king over them, and they will all have one shepherd. They will follow my laws and be careful to keep my decrees. ²⁵They will live in the land I gave to my servant Jacob, the land where your fathers lived. They and their children and their children's children will live there for ever, and David my servant will be their prince for ever. ²⁶I will make a covenant of peace with them; it will be an everlasting covenant. I will establish them and increase their numbers, and I will put my sanctuary among them for ever. ²⁷My dwelling-place will be with them; I will be their God, and they will be my people. ²⁸Then the nations will know that I the Lord make Israel holy, when my sanctuary is among them for ever.'"

For Thought and **Contemplation**

Many believe that the restoring of the nation of Israel, as predicted by Ezekiel, is taking place right before our eyes. What will happen next? Keep your finger on Ezekiel 38. This chapter may bear more relation to the events of this generation than we think.

"Pray for the peace of Jerusalem: 'May those who love you be secure. May there be peace within your walls and security within your citadels.'" (Psa. 122:6–7)

Vision of future Temple

DAY **244**

Ezekiel 40:1–4

¹In the twenty-fifth year of our exile, at the beginning of the year, on the tenth of the month, in the fourteenth year after the fall of the city – on that very day the hand of the Lord was upon me and he took me there. ²In visions of God he took me to the land of Israel and set me on a very high mountain, on whose south side were some buildings that looked like a city. ³He took me there, and I saw a man whose appearance was like bronze; he was standing in the gateway with a linen cord and a measuring rod in his hand. ⁴The man said to me, "Son of man, look with your eyes and hear with your ears and pay attention to everything I am going to show you, for that is why you have been brought here. Tell the house of Israel everything you see."

Ezekiel's vision
Ezekiel 40:1–4

The East Gate
Ezekiel 40:5–16

The Outer Courtyard
Ezekiel 40:17–19

The North and South Gates
Ezekiel 40:20–27

The Inner Courtyard
Ezekiel 40:28–37

Buildings near the North Gate
Ezekiel 40:38–47

The Temple Porch
Ezekiel 40:48–49

The Most Holy Place
Ezekiel 41:1–4

The rooms
Ezekiel 41:5–12

The total measurements and details of the Temple building
Ezekiel 41:13–26

For Thought and **Contemplation**

The attention to detail which God displays in relation to His mighty works is just as evident, if you could but see it, in His personal plan for your life. Remember that the next time you are tempted to think that God might not be interested in the "little" things that go on in your life.

"Are not two sparrows sold for a penny? Yet not one of them will fall to the ground apart from the will of your Father. And even the very hairs of your head are all numbered. So don't be afraid; you are worth more than many sparrows." (Matt. 10:29–31)

Zerubbabel and main party return	Iron Age begins in Britain	Ezra returns	Malachi
500 BC			400 BC
Cyrus Zechariah Haggai 2nd Temple built		Nehemiah rebuilds walls of Jerusalem	

Heart to Heart

Section 8

Marathon runners talk of hitting the wall when they feel too exhausted to complete the course but often another competitor will encourage them to keep going. You have done so well to reach this far but if you are feeling exhausted seek encouraging prayer from a friend that you may be a faithful servant finishing what you have started.

Visit the web site: **www.cover2cover.org**

In this section

The return to Jerusalem
The rebuilding of the Temple
The roles played by Ezra and Nehemiah
Esther's prevention of a massacre

DAY 245 — The Lord's return

Two buildings near the Temple
Ezekiel 42:1–14

Measurements
of the Temple area
Ezekiel 42:15–20

The Lord returns to the Temple
Ezekiel 43:1–12

The Altar
Ezekiel 43:13–17

Consecration of Altar
Ezekiel 43:18–27

Use of the East Gate
Ezekiel 44:1–3

Rules for admission to Temple
Ezekiel 44:4–9

The Levites are excluded
Ezekiel 44:10–14

The priests
Ezekiel 44:15–31

Ezekiel 43:1–9

¹Then the man brought me to the gate facing east, ²and I saw the glory of the God of Israel coming from the east. His voice was like the roar of rushing waters, and the land was radiant with his glory. ³The vision I saw was like the vision I had seen when he came to destroy the city and like the visions I had seen by the Kebar River, and I fell face down. ⁴The glory of the Lord entered the temple through the gate facing east. ⁵Then the Spirit lifted me up and brought me into the inner court, and the glory of the Lord filled the temple.
⁶While the man was standing beside me, I heard someone speaking to me from inside the temple. ⁷He said: "Son of man, this is the place of my throne and the place for the soles of my feet. This is where I will live among the Israelites for ever. The house of Israel will never again defile my holy name – neither they nor their kings – by their prostitution and the lifeless idols of their kings at their high places. ...

For Thought and **Contemplation**

Make a point today of reflecting that, in these New Testament times, God's glory does not dwell in temples made with hands, but in the hearts of those who truly own Him as Lord. Are you one of them?

"Do you not know that your body is a temple of the Holy Spirit, who is in you, whom you have received from God? You are not your own; you were bought at a price. Therefore honour God with your body." (1 Cor. 6:19–20)

Temple worship

DAY **246**

Ezekiel 45:1-6

¹ "'When you allot the land as an inheritance, you are to present to the Lord a portion of the land as a sacred district, 25,000 cubits long and 20,000 cubits wide; the entire area will be holy. ²Of this, a section 500 cubits square is to be for the sanctuary, with 50 cubits around it for open land. ³In the sacred district, measure off a section 25,000 cubits long and 10,000 cubits wide. In it will be the sanctuary, the Most Holy Place. ⁴It will be the sacred portion of the land for the priests, who minister in the sanctuary and who draw near to minister before the Lord. It will be a place for their houses as well as a holy place for the sanctuary. ⁵An area 25,000 cubits long and 10,000 cubits wide will belong to the Levites, who serve in the temple, as their possession for towns to live in.
⁶You are to give the city as its property an area 5,000 cubits wide and 25,000 cubits long, adjoining the sacred portion; it will belong to the whole house of Israel.' "

The Lord's portion of the land	Ezekiel 45:1–6
The prince's portion	Ezekiel 45:7–8
Weights and measures	Ezekiel 45:9–15
The prince's duty	Ezekiel 45:16–17
The Festivals	Ezekiel 45:18–25
Rules regarding worship	Ezekiel 46:1–12
The daily offering	Ezekiel 46:13–15
The prince's land	Ezekiel 46:16–18
Place for boiling the offerings	Ezekiel 46:19–24
The stream flowing from the Temple	Ezekiel 47:1–12

For Thought and **Contemplation**

"Where do you worship?" asked one Christian of another. The reply he got quite startled him. "I worship in Woolworth's, in the High Street, in the bus, in the train, in the office, in my house ... anywhere and everywhere." If you can't worship God everywhere, then you won't worship Him anywhere.

"God is spirit, and his worshippers must worship in spirit and in truth." (Jn. 4:24)

Zerubbabel and main party return	Iron Age begins in Britain	Ezra returns	Malachi
500 BC			400 BC
Cyrus — Zechariah Haggai / 2nd Temple built			Nehemiah rebuilds walls of Jerusalem

305

DAY 247 — Division of land

The land's boundaries
Ezekiel 47:13–23

Division of land among the tribes
Ezekiel 48:1–9

The priests' and Levites' section
Ezekiel 48:10–20

The prince's section
Ezekiel 48:21–22

Land for the other tribes
Ezekiel 48:23–29

The gates of Jerusalem
Ezekiel 48:30–35

More prophecy against Egypt
Ezekiel 29:17–21, 30:1–19

Ezekiel 48:30–35

³⁰"These will be the exits of the city: Beginning on the north side, which is 4,500 cubits long, ³¹the gates of the city will be named after the tribes of Israel. The three gates on the north side will be the gate of Reuben, the gate of Judah and the gate of Levi.
³²On the east side, which is 4,500 cubits long, will be three gates: the gate of Joseph, the gate of Benjamin and the gate of Dan.
³³On the south side, which measures 4,500 cubits, will be three gates: the gate of Simeon, the gate of Issachar and the gate of Zebulun.
³⁴On the west side, which is 4,500 cubits long, will be three gates: the gate of Gad, the gate of Asher and the gate of Naphtali.
³⁵The distance all around will be 18,000 cubits.
And the name of the city from that time on will be:
    THE LORD IS THERE."

For Thought and **Contemplation**

In the divine order of things, worship must always precede work. First comes God's command to worship, then the command to divide and resettle the land. Which takes precedence in your life? Work, or worship? We are worshippers first and workers second. Reverse the order and you will end up spiritually bankrupt.

"Therefore, I urge you, brothers, in view of God's mercy, to offer your bodies as living sacrifices, holy and pleasing to God – this is your spiritual act of worship." (Rom. 12:1)

WEEK 36

700 BC | Assyrians besiege Jerusalem | Nahum Zephaniah Josiah Nebuchadnezzar | 600 BC | Daniel taken to Babylon | Jeremiah Habakkuk | Jerusalem destroyed | FALL OF JUDAH | Ezekiel | Exile in Babylon

God's dealings with Nebuchadnezzar — DAY **248**

Daniel 4:34–37

³⁴At the end of that time, I, Nebuchadnezzar, raised my eyes towards heaven, and my sanity was restored. Then I praised the Most High; I honoured and glorified him who lives for ever.

His dominion is an eternal dominion;
  his kingdom endures from generation to generation.
³⁵All the peoples of the earth
  are regarded as nothing.
He does as he pleases
  with the powers of heaven
  and the peoples of the earth.
No-one can hold back his hand
  or say to him: "What have you done?"

³⁶At the same time that my sanity was restored, my honour and splendour were returned to me for the glory of my kingdom. My advisers and nobles sought me out, and I was restored to my throne and became even greater than before. ³⁷Now I, Nebuchadnezzar, praise and exalt and glorify the King of heaven, because everything he does is right and all his ways are just. And those who walk in pride he is able to humble.

Nebuchadnezzar's second dream	Daniel 4:4–18
Daniel's explanation	Daniel 4:19–27
Nebuchadnezzar's seven years of madness	Daniel 4:28–33
Death of Jeremiah 570 BC	
Nebuchadnezzar is restored and praises God	Daniel 4:34–37
Release of Jehoiachin	2 Kings 25:27–30, Jeremiah 52:31–34
Daniel's vision of the four beasts	Daniel 7:1–8
His vision of the eternal God	Daniel 7:9–14

For Thought and **Contemplation**

How true is the Scripture that says: "Pride goes before destruction, a haughty spirit before a fall" (Proverbs 16:18). Lucifer's pride cost him his place in heaven, and the prospect of eternal judgment. Nebuchadnezzar's pride cost him his throne for seven years. How much is pride costing you?

"... That is why Scripture says: 'God opposes the proud but gives grace to the humble.' Submit yourselves, then, to God. Resist the devil, and he will flee from you." (Jas. 4:6–7)

Zerubbabel and main party return | Iron Age begins in Britain | Ezra returns | Malachi
500 BC | | | 400 BC
Cyrus | Zechariah Haggai | | Nehemiah rebuilds walls of Jerusalem
       | 2nd Temple built | |

DAY 249 — Psalms of the captivity

The meaning of the visions
Daniel 7:15–28

**Captivity psalms:
A song of thanksgiving**
Psalm 67:1–7

A prayer for mercy
Psalm 123:1–4

A prayer for help
Psalm 130:1–8

The Israelites' lament
Psalm 137:1–9

Daniel's vision of a ram and a goat
Daniel 8:1–14

The vision explained
Daniel 8:15–27

Fall of Babylon prophesied
Isaiah 13:17–22,
Jeremiah 25:12–14, 50:1–8

Psalm 123:1–4

¹I lift up my eyes to you,
 to you whose throne is in heaven.
²As the eyes of slaves look to the hand of their master,
 as the eyes of a maid look to the hand of her mistress,
 so our eyes look to the Lord our God,
 till he shows us his mercy.
³Have mercy on us, O Lord, have mercy on us,
 for we have endured much contempt.
⁴We have endured much ridicule from the proud,
 much contempt from the arrogant.

For Thought and **Contemplation**

Some of the greatest psalms came out of the greatest distresses. Are you in distress at this moment? Then follow the example of the psalmists who, though they began by focusing on their problems, finished by focusing on God. This will help you, too, to turn your pain into a paean of praise.

"God is our refuge and strength, an ever-present help in trouble. ... The Lord Almighty is with us; the God of Jacob is our fortress." (Psa. 46:1 & 11)

The Two Covenants

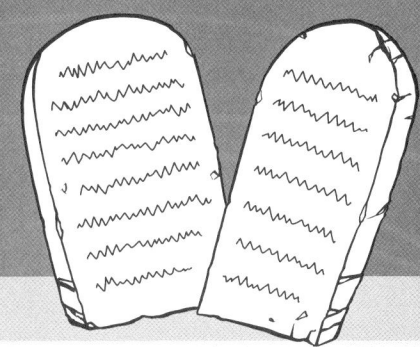

The old covenant

- **a.** It was mediated by Moses (Ex. 19; Jn. 1:17; Gal. 3:19)
- **b.** It was conditional (Deut. 28)
- **c.** It could not produce righteousness (Heb. 8:8)
- **d.** It was written on stone tablets (Ex. 32:15)

The new covenant

- **a.** Mediated by Christ (Heb. 9:15; Jn. 1:17)
- **b.** It is unconditional (Heb. 8:9)
- **c.** It can produce the necessary righteousness (Heb. 8:11)
- **d.** It is written on living hearts (Heb. 8:10)

DAY 250 — The judgment of Babylon

Babylon's fall prophesied
Jeremiah 50:9–16

Israel's return prophesied
Jeremiah 50:17–20

God's judgment on Babylon
Jeremiah 50:21–46

Further judgment on Babylon
Jeremiah 51:1–14

A hymn of praise to God
Jeremiah 51:15–19

The Lord's hammer
Jeremiah 51:20–23

Babylon's punishment
Jeremiah 51:24–35

Jeremiah 50:17–20

[17]"Israel is a scattered flock
  that lions have chased away.
The first to devour him
  was the king of Assyria;
the last to crush his bones
  was Nebuchadnezzar king of Babylon."
[18]Therefore this is what the Lord Almighty, the God of Israel, says:
"I will punish the king of Babylon and his land
  as I punished the king of Assyria.
[19]But I will bring Israel back to his own pasture
  and he will graze on Carmel and Bashan;
  his appetite will be satisfied
  on the hills of Ephraim and Gilead.
[20]In those days, at that time,"
  declares the Lord,
"search will be made for Israel's guilt,
  but there will be none,
and for the sins of Judah,
  but none will be found,
  for I will forgive the remnant I spare."

For Thought and **Contemplation**

Ever found yourself wondering why God allows sin and godlessness such freedom? Then remind yourself also of this – that every nation that rises up against God will one day fall. What happened to Babylon will happen to the godless nations of our own day. Learn to be patient with the patience of God.

"Blessed is the man who does not walk in the counsel of the wicked or stand in the way of sinners or sit in the seat of mockers. But his delight is in the law of the Lord, and on his law he meditates day and night." (Psa. 1:1–2)

WEEK 36

700 BC	Nahum Zephaniah Josiah Nebuchadnezzar	Jerusalem destroyed
	600 BC	FALL OF JUDAH
Assyrians besiege Jerusalem	Daniel taken to Babylon	Ezekiel
	Jeremiah Habakkuk	Exile in Babylon

Belshazzar's feast

DAY 251

Daniel 5:13–16

¹³So Daniel was brought before the king, and the king said to him, "Are you Daniel, one of the exiles my father the king brought from Judah? ¹⁴I have heard that the spirit of the gods is in you and that you have insight, intelligence and outstanding wisdom. ¹⁵The wise men and enchanters were brought before me to read this writing and tell me what it means, but they could not explain it. ¹⁶Now I have heard that you are able to give interpretations and to solve difficult problems. If you can read this writing and tell me what it means, you will be clothed in purple and have a gold chain placed around your neck, and you will be made the third highest ruler in the kingdom."

Help for Israel	Jeremiah 51:36–40
Babylon's fate	Jeremiah 51:41–49
God's message	Jeremiah 51:50–53
Complete destruction of Babylon	Jeremiah 51:54–58, 60–64
Persia the world power 539–333 BC	
Belshazzar's feast	Daniel 5:1–4
The handwriting on the wall	Daniel 5:5–12
Belshazzar calls for Daniel	Daniel 5:13–16
Daniel's interpretation	Daniel 5:17–29
Darius takes over	Daniel 5:30–31
Reigns of Cyrus and Darius	Isaiah 44:28, Daniel 1:21, 11:1

For Thought and **Contemplation**

There are three occasions in Scripture when God wrote with His finger a special message to men. Can you think of them? One, of course, is found here in the story of Belshazzar's feast. The other two can be found in Exodus 31:18 and John 8:6. Look them up right now.

"'This is the covenant I will make with them after that time, says the Lord. I will put my laws in their hearts, and I will write them on their minds.' Then he adds: 'Their sins and lawless acts I will remember no more.'" (Heb. 10:16–17)

Zerubbabel and main party return	Iron Age begins in Britain	Ezra returns	Malachi	
500 BC				400 BC
Cyrus Zechariah Haggai 2nd Temple built			Nehemiah rebuilds walls of Jerusalem	

DAY 252 — The command to rebuild the Temple

Daniel's prayer
Daniel 9:1–19

Gabriel's explanation
Daniel 9:20–27

The prayer of a troubled young man
Psalm 102:1–28

People challenged to rebuild the Temple
Ezra 5:13, 2 Chronicles 36:22–23, Ezra 1:1–4

A prayer for deliverance
Psalm 126:1–6

A prayer for the nation's welfare
Psalm 85:1–13

The people's response to the challenge
Ezra 1:5–6

Ezra 1:1–4

¹ In the first year of Cyrus king of Persia, in order to fulfil the word of the Lord spoken by Jeremiah, the Lord moved the heart of Cyrus king of Persia to make a proclamation throughout his realm and to put it in writing:

² "This is what Cyrus king of Persia says:

'The Lord, the God of heaven, has given me all the kingdoms of the earth and he has appointed me to build a temple for him at Jerusalem in Judah. ³Anyone of his people among you – may his God be with him, and let him go up to Jerusalem in Judah and build the temple of the Lord, the God of Israel, the God who is in Jerusalem. ⁴And the people of any place where survivors may now be living are to provide him with silver and gold, with goods and livestock, and with freewill offerings for the temple of God in Jerusalem.'"

For Thought and **Contemplation**

If there is one truth that is underlined in reading through the Old Testament, it is the truth of God's great patience and everlasting mercy. Though time and time again He is disappointed with His people, He does not cast them off. And what He was He is, and always will be. Hallelujah!

"But because of his great love for us, God, who is rich in mercy, made us alive with Christ even when we were dead in transgressions – it is by grace you have been saved." (Eph. 2:4–5)

a bird's eye view of **Ezra & Nehemiah**

Place in the Bible	**Main Characters**	**Special Features**
Fifteenth and sixteenth Old Testament books; tenth and eleventh books of history.	Ezra, Nehemiah	In fulfilment of God's promise some Jews return to Jerusalem to rebuild the Temple. Later, Ezra calls the community to wholehearted obedience to God's laws, and Nehemiah, 14 years afterward, leads the rebuilding of the city walls.

Daniel in the lions' den

DAY **253**

Daniel 6:25–28

²⁵Then King Darius wrote to all the peoples, nations and men of every language throughout the land:

"May you prosper greatly! ²⁶I issue a decree that in every part of my kingdom people must fear and reverence the God of Daniel.

For he is the living God
  and he endures for ever;
his kingdom will not be destroyed,
  his dominion will never end.
²⁷He rescues and he saves;
  he performs signs and wonders
in the heavens and on the earth.
He has rescued Daniel
  from the power of the lions."

²⁸So Daniel prospered during the reign of Darius and the reign of Cyrus the Persian.

	The Temple's vessels returned
	Ezra 1:7–11, 5:14–16
	Cyrus' decree
	Ezra 6:3–5
	Daniel thrown to the lions
	Daniel 6:1–18
	His deliverance and its result
	Daniel 6:19–28
	Daniel's three weeks of mourning
	Daniel 10:1–3
	His vision by the River Tigris
	Daniel 10:4–20
	Revelation promised
	Daniel 10:21
	Revelation of future kingdom
	Daniel 11:2–4

For Thought and **Contemplation**

You may not have to face the prospect of spending a night in a lions' den, but no doubt you have encountered that "roaring lion" who goes about "looking for someone to devour" (1 Pet. 5:8). Take heart – what God did for Daniel, He will do for you.

"... in all these things we are more than conquerors through him who loved us." (Rom. 8:37)

Jesus and the Books

Nehemiah faced ridicule and great opposition as he rebuilt Jerusalem. Jesus' followers too must expect opposition: "Blessed are you when people insult you, persecute you and falsely say all kinds of evil against you because of me" (Matt. 5:11).

Teaching

Ezra and Nehemiah are about building for God. Ezra the priest teaches the returned exiles about true worship, holiness and entire obedience to God. Nehemiah is an example of how diligent work and constant prayer go hand in hand in God's service.

A Verse to Remember

"'Blessed be your glorious name, and may it be exalted above all blessing and praise. You alone are the Lord. You made the heavens, ... the earth ... the seas ... You give life to everything, and the multitudes of heaven worship you.'" (Neh. 9:5–6)

DAY **254**

The end times

The kingdoms of Egypt and Syria
Daniel 11:5–20

The evil king of Syria
Daniel 11:21–24

He will invade Egypt
Daniel 11:25–30

Remnant returns (49,897) 536 BC

The abomination that causes desolation
Daniel 11:31–35

Prophecy of the Antichrist
Daniel 11:36–39

His final hour
Daniel 11:40–45

The end times
Daniel 12:1–13

The list of the returning exiles: the men of Israel
Ezra 2:1–20

Those from various towns
Ezra 2:21–35

The priests
Ezra 2:36–39

Daniel 11:36–39

³⁶"The king will do as he pleases. He will exalt and magnify himself above every god and will say unheard-of things against the God of gods. He will be successful until the time of wrath is completed, for what has been determined must take place. ³⁷He will show no regard for the gods of his fathers or for the one desired by women, nor will he regard any god, but will exalt himself above them all. ³⁸Instead of them, he will honour a god of fortresses; a god unknown to his fathers he will honour with gold and silver, with precious stones and costly gifts. ³⁹He will attack the mightiest fortresses with the help of a foreign god and will greatly honour those who acknowledge him. He will make them rulers over many people and will distribute the land at a price."

For Thought and **Contemplation**

Someone has pointed out that Daniel is one of the few people in the Bible about whom nothing negative is written. What was the secret of his wonderful life? There are many reasons, not the least being his prowess in prayer. Are you satisfied with your prayer life? If not, then decide now to do something positive about it.

"This is the confidence we have in approaching God: that if we ask anything according to his will, he hears us. And if we know that he hears us – whatever we ask – we know that we have what we asked of him."
(1 Jn. 5:14–15)

WEEK 37

Zerubbabel and main party return	Iron Age begins in Britain	Ezra returns	Malachi
	500 BC		400 BC
Cyrus	Zechariah Haggai 2nd Temple built		Nehemiah rebuilds walls of Jerusalem

The Return

DURING THE FIRST YEAR of Cyrus' reign in Babylon (539 BC), he issued the decree which permitted the Jews to return and rebuild the temple at Jerusalem.

Jeremiah had predicted the length of the captivity (see Jeremiah 25:11, 12; 29:10).

Isaiah had prophesied, 170 years before, that Cyrus would act in this way. (See Isa. 44:28; 45:1.)

There were three separate returns by the Jewish remnant: Zerubbabel led the first in 536 BC; Ezra led the second in 458 BC; and Nehemiah led the third in 445 BC.

In 535 BC the construction of the Temple began but it faced bitter opposition and so the prophets Haggai and Zechariah ministered to the discouraged remnant.

DAY 255

Nehemiah checks the list

The Levites, singers and gatekeepers
Ezra 2:40–42

The Temple servants and children of Solomon's servants
Ezra 2:43–58

No proof of ancestry
Ezra 2:59–63

The exiles' arrival at the Temple
Ezra 2:64–70

Nehemiah checks the family records
Nehemiah 7:5–7

Another list of the exiles
Nehemiah 7:8–69

Many contribute to the cost of restoring the Temple
Nehemiah 7:70–72

List of priests and Levites
Nehemiah 12:1–23

Assignment of duties
Nehemiah 12:24–26

Nehemiah 7:5–18

⁵So my God put it into my heart to assemble the nobles, the officials and the common people for registration by families. I found the genealogical record of those who had been the first to return. This is what I found written there: ⁶These are the people of the province who came up from the captivity of the exiles whom Nebuchadnezzar king of Babylon had taken captive (they returned to Jerusalem and Judah, each to his own town, ⁷in company with Zerubbabel, Jeshua, Nehemiah, Azariah, Raamiah, Nahamani, Mordecai, Bilshan, Mispereth, Bigvai, Nehum and Baanah):
The list of the men of Israel:
⁸the descendants

of Parosh	2,172
⁹of Shephatiah	372
¹⁰of Arah	652
¹¹of Pahath-Moab (through the line of Jeshua and Joab)	2,818
¹²of Elam	1,254
¹³of Zattu	845
¹⁴of Zaccai	760
¹⁵of Binnui	648
¹⁶of Bebai	628
¹⁷of Azgad	2,322
¹⁸of Adonikam	667 ...

For Thought and **Contemplation**

Nehemiah made certain that all who came to live in Jerusalem were there by divine right – hence the painstaking procedure of checking every name. How will it be with you when the time comes for you to enter the "New Jerusalem"? Is your name written there?

"... do not rejoice that the spirits submit to you, but rejoice that your names are written in heaven." (Lk. 10:20)

Rebuilding programme begins

DAY **256**

Ezra 3:10–13

¹⁰When the builders laid the foundation of the temple of the Lord, the priests in their vestments and with trumpets, and the Levites (the sons of Asaph) with cymbals, took their places to praise the Lord, as prescribed by David king of Israel. ¹¹With praise and thanksgiving they sang to the Lord:
"He is good;
  his love to Israel endures for ever."
And all the people gave a great shout of praise to the Lord, because the foundation of the house of the Lord was laid. ¹²But many of the older priests and Levites and family heads, who had seen the former temple, wept aloud when they saw the foundation of this temple being laid, while many others shouted for joy. ¹³No-one could distinguish the sound of the shouts of joy from the sound of weeping, because the people made so much noise. And the sound was heard far away.

The exiles rebuild the altar
Ezra 3:1–7

In praise of Jerusalem
Psalm 87:1–7

Rebuilding of the Temple begins
Ezra 3:8–9

The priests and Levites praise the Lord
Ezra 3:10–13

Longing for God's house
Psalm 84:1–12

In praise of God's goodness
Psalm 107:1–43

A song of praise and thanksgiving
Psalm 66:1–20

For Thought and **Contemplation**

The first thing the children of Israel did when they returned to Jerusalem was to build an altar. Worship, they realised, must come before work. Make a list of the things you have to do today, and before you do them, commit each item to God. You will find life runs better this way.

"Come, let us bow down in worship, let us kneel before the Lord our Maker; for he is our God and we are the people of his pasture, the flock under his care." (Psa. 95:6–7)

WEEK 37

	Zerubbabel and main party return	Iron Age begins in Britain	Ezra returns	Malachi	
	500 BC				400 BC
Cyrus	Zechariah Haggai 2nd Temple built			Nehemiah rebuilds walls of Jerusalem	

DAY 257 — Opposition to the work

Samaritan interference
Ezra 4:1–5

The security of God's people
Psalm 125:1–5

Letters of accusation
Ezra 4:6–16

Artaxerxes' answer
Ezra 4:17–22

Work suspended for seven years
Ezra 4:23–24

A prayer against Israel's enemies
Psalm 129:1–8

Haggai and Zechariah
Ezra 5:1

People reproached for neglect of Temple
Haggai 1:1–10

Zerubbabel and Joshua
Ezra 5:2, Haggai 1:11–15

The splendour of the future Temple
Haggai 2:1–9

Zechariah's plea
Zechariah 1:1–6

Psalm 125:1–5

¹Those who trust in the Lord
are like Mount Zion,
 which cannot be shaken but
endures for ever.
²As the mountains surround Jerusalem,
 so the Lord surrounds his people
 both now and for evermore.
³The sceptre of the wicked will not remain
 over the land allotted to the righteous,
 for then the righteous might use
 their hands to do evil.
⁴Do good, O Lord, to those who are good,
 to those who are upright in heart.
⁵But those who turn to crooked ways
 the Lord will banish with the evildoers.
 Peace be upon Israel.

For Thought and **Contemplation**

No work of God is ever established without opposition. Perhaps you are finding this to be true in your own life at this very moment. Be encouraged; opposition may seem to work against you – but it really works *for* you. It makes you less dependent on yourself and more dependent on God.

"But the Lord stood at my side and gave me strength, so that through me the message might be fully proclaimed and all the Gentiles might hear it. And I was delivered from the lion's mouth." (2 Timothy 4:17)

Place in the Bible

Thirty-seventh and thirty-eighth Old Testament books; fifteenth and sixteenth books of prophecy.

Jesus and the Books

Haggai was clear that the Lord has chosen the Jews to be His people, just as Christ called and chose people to be His followers: "You did not choose me, but I chose you ..." (John 15:16).
Zechariah has numerous references

Zechariah's visions

DAY 258

Zechariah 4:6–10

⁶So he said to me, "This is the word of the Lord to Zerubbabel: 'Not by might nor by power, but by my Spirit,' says the Lord Almighty. ⁷What are you, O mighty mountain? Before Zerubbabel you will become level ground. Then he will bring out the capstone to shouts of 'God bless it! God bless it!'"

⁸Then the word of the Lord came to me: ⁹"'The hands of Zerubbabel have laid the foundation of this temple; his hands will also complete it. Then you will know that the Lord Almighty has sent me to you.

¹⁰Who despises the day of small things? Men will rejoice when they see the plumb-line in the hand of Zerubbabel.

(These seven are the eyes of the Lord, which range throughout the earth.)"

Haggai confronts the priests	Haggai 2:10–14
The Lord promises blessing	Haggai 2:15–23
Zechariah's vision of the horses	Zechariah 1:7–17
God's promise to Zerubbabel	Zechariah 4:6–10
Zechariah's vision of the horns	Zechariah 1:18–21
His vision of the measuring line	Zechariah 2:1–13
His vision of the High Priest	Zechariah 3:1–10
His vision of the golden candlestick	Zechariah 4:1–5, 11–14
His vision of the flying scroll	Zechariah 5:1–4
His vision of the woman in the basket	Zechariah 5:5–11

For Thought and Contemplation

Although the phrase, "Thus saith the Lord", is found 1,904 times in the Old Testament, Zechariah uses it, or its equivalent, close on 90 times. How sad that so many modern pulpits lack this kind of authority. Pray today that God will restore the Old Testament note of authority to the present-day Church.

"When Jesus had finished saying these things, the crowds were amazed at his teaching, because he taught as one who had authority, and not as their teachers of the law." (Matt. 7:28–29)

Teaching

Haggai aimed to galvanise the Jews into action and complete rebuilding the temple. Zechariah also reminds the Jews to finish this task and spells out the necessity for God's people to be pure. Zechariah concludes with a vision about the coming Messiah, pointing to Jesus, the coming Messiah: the 'Branch' (3:8), the King Priest (6:13), the humble King, mounted on a donkey (9:9–10), the good shepherd who is sold for thirty pieces of silver (11:4–13) and the one who is pierced (12:10).

A Verse to Remember

"On that day … I will take you, my servant Zerubbabel … and I will make you like my signet ring, for I have chosen you …" (Hag. 2:23).

DAY 259 — The decree discovered

The vision of the four chariots
Zechariah 6:1–8

Symbolic crowning of Joshua
Zechariah 6:9–15

Tattenai and Shethar-Bozenai's question
Ezra 5:3–4

They appeal to Darius
Ezra 5:5–17

Cyrus' decree is discovered
Ezra 6:1–2

Darius adds to it
Ezra 6:6–12

Co-operation of Tattenai and Shethar-Bozenai
Ezra 6:13–14

Insincere fasting condemned
Zechariah 7:1–7

The cause of exile
Zechariah 7:8–14

The Lord's promise
Zechariah 8:1–15

Zechariah 6:9–15

⁹The word of the Lord came to me: ¹⁰"Take [silver and gold] from the exiles Heldai, Tobijah and Jedaiah, who have arrived from Babylon. Go the same day to the house of Josiah son of Zephaniah. ¹¹Take the silver and gold and make a crown, and set it on the head of the high priest, Joshua son of Jehozadak. ¹²Tell him this is what the Lord Almighty says: 'Here is the man whose name is the Branch, and he will branch out from his place and build the temple of the Lord. ¹³It is he who will build the temple of the Lord, and he will be clothed with majesty and will sit and rule on his throne. And he will be a priest on his throne. And there will be harmony between the two.' ¹⁴The crown will be given to Heldai, Tobijah, Jedaiah and Hen son of Zephaniah as a memorial in the temple of the Lord. ¹⁵Those who are far away will come and help to build the temple of the Lord, and you will know that the Lord Almighty has sent me to you. This will happen if you diligently obey the Lord your God."

For Thought and **Contemplation**

An effective father, it has been said, needs two outstanding qualifications: firmness in discipline and a readiness to encourage. Some think God has just one of these characteristics – firmness in discipline – but look again at Zech. 8:15 and remind yourself that God is a Father who not only disciplines, but encourages and cares.

"As a father has compassion on his children, so the Lord has compassion on those who fear him ... from everlasting to everlasting the Lord's love is with those who fear him, and his righteousness with their children's children." (Psa. 103:13 & 17)

The completion of the Temple

DAY 260

Zechariah 9:9-13

⁹Rejoice greatly, O Daughter of Zion!
 Shout, Daughter of Jerusalem!
See, your king comes to you,
 righteous and having salvation,
 gentle and riding on a donkey,
 on a colt, the foal of a donkey.
¹⁰I will take away the chariots from Ephraim
 and the war-horses from Jerusalem,
 and the battle-bow will be broken.
 He will proclaim peace to the nations.
 His rule will extend from sea to sea
 and from the River to the ends of the earth.
¹¹As for you, because of the blood of my covenant with you,
 I will free your prisoners from the waterless pit.
¹²Return to your fortress, O prisoners of hope;
 even now I announce that I will restore twice as much to you.
¹³I will bend Judah as I bend my bow
 and fill it with Ephraim. ...

The Lord promises to restore Israel
Zechariah 8:16–23

Temple completed 516 BC

The Temple is completed
Ezra 6:15

Dedication of the Temple
Ezra 6:16–18

The Passover celebration
Ezra 6:19–22

The Restoration 516–400 BC

In praise of God the Saviour
Psalm 146:1–10

In praise of the Lord
Psalm 111:1–10

The happiness of a good person
Psalm 112:1–10

In praise of the Lord's goodness
Psalm 113:1–9

A man saved from death praises God
Psalm 116:1–19

In praise of the Lord
Psalm 117:1–2

Judgment on neighbouring cities
Zechariah 9:1–8

A divine deliverer
Zechariah 9:9–17

For Thought and **Contemplation**

The Temple project is at last complete – a full twenty-three years after it was begun. God's plans and purposes may be hindered or postponed, but they will ultimately be fulfilled. Has there been a hindering of the divine purpose in your life? Then hold on – the day of its fulfilment will most certainly come.

"Being confident of this, that he who began a good work in you will carry it on to completion until the day of Christ Jesus." (Phil. 1:6)

WEEK 38

Zerubbabel and main party return	Iron Age begins in Britain	Ezra returns	Malachi
500 BC			400 BC
Cyrus	Zechariah Haggai		Nehemiah rebuilds walls of Jerusalem
	2nd Temple built		

DAY 261

Israel's deliverance

The Lord promises deliverance
Zechariah 10:1–12

Destruction to come
Zechariah 11:1–3

The two shepherds
Zechariah 11:4–17

Punishment of Israel's enemies
Zechariah 12:1–9

Israel's repentance and sorrow
Zechariah 12:10–14

Israel's cleansing
Zechariah 13:1–6

The command to kill God's shepherd
Zechariah 13:7–9

Jerusalem and the nations
Zechariah 14:1–15

Israel's restoration
Zechariah 14:16–21

Zechariah 12:10–14

¹⁰"And I will pour out on the house of David and the inhabitants of Jerusalem a spirit of grace and supplication. They will look on me, the one they have pierced, and they will mourn for him as one mourns for an only child, and grieve bitterly for him as one grieves for a firstborn son. ¹¹On that day the weeping in Jerusalem will be great, like the weeping of Hadad Rimmon in the plain of Megiddo. ¹²The land will mourn, each clan by itself, with their wives by themselves: the clan of the house of David and their wives, the clan of the house of Nathan and their wives, ¹³the clan of the house of Levi and their wives, the clan of Shimei and their wives, ¹⁴and all the rest of the clans and their wives.

For Thought and **Contemplation**

Men have predicted that history will reach its climax through a nuclear holocaust. God has determined that it will reach its climax at the return of His Son. Whom do you believe – men or God? Keep Zechariah 14:1–9 before you, and it will hold you fast in the midst of the greatest threat of world destruction.

"For the Lord himself will come down from heaven, with a loud command, with the voice of the archangel and with the trumpet call of God, and the dead in Christ will rise first. After that, we who are still alive and are left will be caught up together with them in the clouds to meet the Lord in the air ..." (1 Thess. 4:16–17)

a bird's eye view of Esther

Place in the Bible	**Main Characters**	**Special Features**
Seventeenth Old Testament book; twelfth book of history.	King Xerxes, Queen Vashti, Esther, Mordecai, Haman.	There is no mention of God anywhere in this book, but from beginning to end God's hand is seen in action.

A beauty contest

DAY **262**

Esther 3:1–6

¹After these events, King Xerxes honoured Haman son of Hammedatha, the Agagite, elevating him and giving him a seat of honour higher than that of all the other nobles. ²All the royal officials at the king's gate knelt down and paid honour to Haman, for the king had commanded this concerning him. But Mordecai would not kneel down or pay him honour.
³Then the royal officials at the king's gate asked Mordecai, "Why do you disobey the king's command?" ⁴Day after day they spoke to him but he refused to comply. Therefore they told Haman about it to see whether Mordecai's behaviour would be tolerated, for he had told them he was a Jew.
⁵When Haman saw that Mordecai would not kneel down or pay him honour, he was enraged. ⁶Yet having learned who Mordecai's people were, he scorned the idea of killing only Mordecai. Instead Haman looked for a way to destroy all Mordecai's people, the Jews, throughout the whole kingdom of Xerxes.

Xerxes' feast
Esther 1:1–8

Vashti's rebellion
Esther 1:9–12

Her dethronement
Esther 1:13–22

New queen sought
Esther 2:1–4

Esther brought to Shushan
Esther 2:5, 7–11

Esther made queen
Esther 2:12–17

Feast in honour of Esther
Esther 2:18–20

Mordecai saves the king's life
Esther 2:21–23

Haman's plot
Esther 3:1–7

Haman gains the king's support
Esther 3:8–11

For Thought and **Contemplation**

Esther won the first-ever "Miss World" beauty contest hands down. Yet her real beauty lay, not in her appearance, but in her character. Men judge the outward appearance, but God judges the heart (1 Sam. 16:7).

"Your beauty should not come from outward adornment ... Instead, it should be that of your inner self, the unfading beauty of a gentle and quiet spirit, which is of great worth in God's sight." (1 Pet. 3:3–4)

Jesus and the Book

Esther knew that she was risking her life. Jesus voluntarily gave up his life to rescue us from the stranglehold of sin, as John chapter 10:15 says: "... I lay down my life for the sheep."

Teaching

This book explains the origin of the Jewish Feast of Purim and how, had it not been for Mordecai's astuteness and Esther's courage, the Jews would have been slaughtered. The Jews believed that God was their deliverer.

A Verse to Remember

"'If you remain silent at this time, relief and deliverance for the Jews will arise from another place, but you and your father's family will perish. And who knows but that you have come to royal position for such a time as this?'" (Esth. 4:14).

Building for God

"So the wall was completed ... with the help of our God." (Neh. 6:15,16)
In December 446 BC, Nehemiah learns from his brother Hanani of the pitiful state of Jerusalem. Broken-hearted, Nehemiah begins a time of confession and intercession to God on His people's behalf (1:6–11).

Nehemiah returns to Judah and despite intimidation his confidence in the Lord never wavers. In 53 days the walls are finished. The returning Jewish exiles make a binding covenant to dedicate themselves and the city to the Lord.

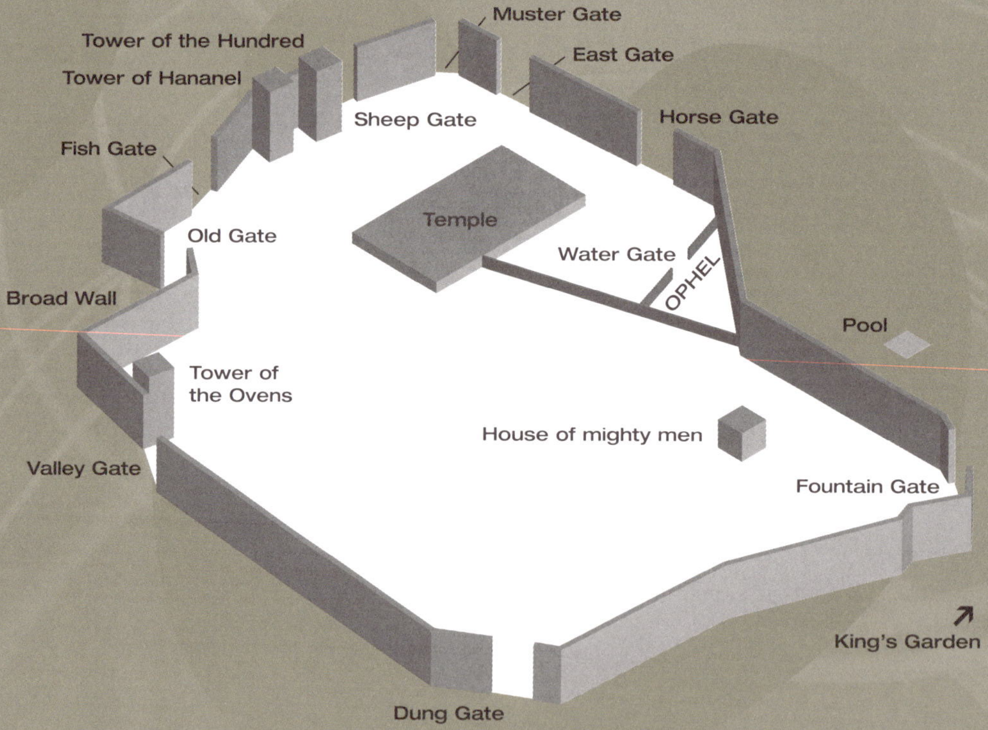

Place names according to RSV, other translations may differ.

The tables are turned

DAY **263**

Esther 4:12–17

¹²When Esther's words were reported to Mordecai, ¹³he sent back this answer: "Do not think that because you are in the king's house you alone of all the Jews will escape. ¹⁴For if you remain silent at this time, relief and deliverance for the Jews will arise from another place, but you and your father's family will perish. And who knows but that you have come to royal position for such a time as this?"

¹⁵Then Esther sent this reply to Mordecai: ¹⁶"Go, gather together all the Jews who are in Susa, and fast for me. Do not eat or drink for three days, night or day. I and my maids will fast as you do. When this is done, I will go to the king, even though it is against the law. And if I perish, I perish."

¹⁷So Mordecai went away and carried out all of Esther's instructions.

The command to annihilate all Jews
Esther 3:12–15

Mordecai enlists Esther's help
Esther 4:1–17

Esther's invitation
Esther 5:1–8

Haman's rage against Mordecai
Esther 5:9–14

The king's sleepless night
Esther 6:1–3

Mordecai honoured
Esther 6:4–14

Haman accused
Esther 7:1–6

Haman hanged
Esther 7:7–10

For Thought and **Contemplation**

Do you believe in prayer? *Really* believe? Esther believed in prayer enough to go to the king at an unappointed time with an unlikely request. Underline Esther 5:1–8 in your Bible as a constant reminder that faith sees the invisible, believes the incredible and receives the impossible.

"Ask and it will be given to you; seek and you will find; knock and the door will be opened to you. For everyone who asks receives; he who seeks finds; and to him who knocks, the door will be opened." (Matt. 7:7–8)

WEEK 38

Zerubbabel and main party return | *Iron Age begins in Britain* | Ezra returns | Malachi
500 BC | | | | 400 BC
Cyrus | Zechariah Haggai | | Nehemiah rebuilds walls of Jerusalem
| 2nd Temple built

DAY 264 — The Jews triumph

The king's edict
Esther 8:1–14

The Jews rejoice
Esther 8:15–17

Their revenge and triumph
Esther 9:1–15

Days of rejoicing
Esther 9:16–19

The Feast of Purim
Esther 9:20–27

Its perpetual celebration
Esther 9:28–32

Mordecai's promotion
Esther 10:1–3

Ezra's commission
Ezra 7:11–20

Esther 10:1–3

¹King Xerxes imposed tribute throughout the empire, to its distant shores. ²And all his acts of power and might, together with a full account of the greatness of Mordecai to which the king had raised him, are they not written in the book of the annals of the kings of Media and Persia? ³Mordecai the Jew was second in rank to King Xerxes, pre-eminent among the Jews, and held in high esteem by his many fellow Jews, because he worked for the good of his people and spoke up for the welfare of all the Jews.

For Thought and **Contemplation**

When you are next tempted to think that God is not working because He does not show Himself to you, read again the story of Esther and realise that He is a God who often works behind the scenes. After all, as this book so wonderfully shows, history is really His-story.

"Though the fig-tree does not bud and there are no grapes on the vines, though the olive crop fails and the fields produce no food, though there are no sheep in the pen and no cattle in the stalls, yet I will rejoice in the Lord, I will be joyful in God my Saviour."
(Habakkuk 3:17–18)

The return to Jerusalem

DAY **265**

Ezra 7:6-10

⁶... this Ezra came up from Babylon. He was a teacher well versed in the Law of Moses, which the Lord, the God of Israel, had given. The king had granted him everything he asked, for the hand of the Lord his God was on him. ⁷Some of the Israelites, including priests, Levites, singers, gate-keepers and temple servants, also came up to Jerusalem in the seventh year of King Artaxerxes.
⁸Ezra arrived in Jerusalem in the fifth month of the seventh year of the king. ⁹He had begun his journey from Babylon on the first day of the first month, and he arrived in Jerusalem on the first day of the fifth month, for the gracious hand of his God was on him. ¹⁰For Ezra had devoted himself to the study and observance of the Law of the Lord, and to teaching its decrees and laws in Israel.

Artaxerxes' decree	Ezra 7:21-26
Ezra's thanksgiving	Ezra 7:27-28
The exiles who returned with Ezra	Ezra 8:1-14
Ezra returns to Jerusalem 458 BC	
The camp site	Ezra 7:9, 8:15
Ezra finds Levites	Ezra 8:16-20
Prayer and fasting	Ezra 8:21-23
The Temple treasures	Ezra 8:24-30
Journey begins	Ezra 8:31
Ezra's arrival at Jerusalem	Ezra 7:6-8, 10, 8:32-36
Ezra's grief	Ezra 9:1-4
His prayer	Ezra 9:5-15

For Thought and **Contemplation**

The secret of Ezra's successful ministry is found in Ezra 7:10. He not only knew what he had to do, but he also did it. As someone has said, "It is of no benefit to know more, unless you first do something with what you know already."

"What good is it, my brothers, if a man claims to have faith but has no deeds? Can such faith save him? ... In the same way, faith by itself, if it is not accompanied by action, is dead." (Jas. 2:14 & 17)

WEEK 38

Zerubbabel and main party return	Iron Age begins in Britain	Ezra returns	Malachi
500 BC			400 BC
Cyrus	Zechariah Haggai		Nehemiah rebuilds walls of Jerusalem
	2nd Temple built		

DAY 266 — Ezra and Nehemiah

Ezra 10:1–8	Ezra plans national gathering
Ezra 10:9–15	He preaches and the people repent
Ezra 10:16–44	Foreign wives divorced
Nehemiah 1:1–4	Nehemiah's grief
Nehemiah 1:5–11	His prayer
	Nehemiah goes to Jerusalem 437 BC
Nehemiah 2:1–6	His request
Nehemiah 5:14	Nehemiah appointed governor
Nehemiah 2:7–9	Letters and escort provided
Nehemiah 2:10	Sanballat and Tobiah's indignation
Nehemiah 2:11–16	Nehemiah's arrival in Jerusalem

Nehemiah 1:5–10

⁵Then I said:
"O Lord, God of heaven, the great and awesome God, who keeps his covenant of love with those who love him and obey his commands, ⁶let your ear be attentive and your eyes open to hear the prayer your servant is praying before you day and night for your servants, the people of Israel. I confess the sins we Israelites, including myself and my father's house, have committed against you. ⁷We have acted very wickedly towards you. We have not obeyed the commands, decrees and laws you gave your servant Moses.

⁸Remember the instruction you gave your servant Moses, saying, 'If you are unfaithful, I will scatter you among the nations, ⁹but if you return to me and obey my commands, then even if your exiled people are at the farthest horizon, I will gather them from there and bring them to the place I have chosen as a dwelling for my Name.' ¹⁰They are your servants and your people, whom you redeemed by your great strength and your mighty hand."

For Thought and **Contemplation**

Although the centre of Israel's prayer life, the Temple, was established, there was still a need to build the walls. Prayer is important, but so is work. As someone once put it: "We must pray as if it all depended on God, and work as though it all depended on us."

"Therefore, my dear friends, as you have always obeyed – not only in my presence, but now much more in my absence – continue to work out your salvation with fear and trembling, for it is God who works in you to will and to act according to his good purpose." (Phil. 2:12–13)

Rebuilding the walls

DAY 267

Nehemiah 4:1-6

¹When Sanballat heard that we were rebuilding the wall, he became angry and was greatly incensed. He ridiculed the Jews, ²and in the presence of his associates and the army of Samaria, he said, "What are those feeble Jews doing? Will they restore their wall? Will they offer sacrifices? Will they finish in a day? Can they bring the stones back to life from those heaps of rubble – burned as they are?"

³Tobiah the Ammonite, who was at his side, said, "What they are building – if even a fox climbed up on it, he would break down their wall of stones!"

⁴Hear us, O our God, for we are despised. Turn their insults back on their own heads. Give them over as plunder in a land of captivity. ⁵Do not cover up their guilt or blot out their sins from your sight, for they have thrown insults in the face of the builders.

⁶So we rebuilt the wall till all of it reached half its height, for the people worked with all their heart.

Nehemiah's encouragement to rebuild	Nehemiah 2:17-18
The contempt of Sanballat and others	Nehemiah 2:19-20
List of builders	Nehemiah 3:1-16
The Levites	Nehemiah 3:17-21
The priests	Nehemiah 3:22-26
Other builders	Nehemiah 3:27-32
Nehemiah overcomes ridicule	Nehemiah 4:1-6
The conspiracy	Nehemiah 4:7-15
Nehemiah's precautions	Nehemiah 4:16-23
The people's complaint	Nehemiah 5:1-5
Nehemiah's rebuke	Nehemiah 5:6-11
The restitution	Nehemiah 5:12-13

For Thought and Contemplation

One of the characteristics of God's people, in the New Testament as well as the Old, is that sometimes, instead of fighting the enemy, they turn to fighting each other. How Satan must enjoy these lapses! Pray that Christians might come to see the stupidity of this.

"How good and pleasant it is when brothers live together in unity! ... It is as if the dew of Hermon were falling on Mount Zion. For there the Lord bestows his blessing, even life for evermore." (Psa. 133: 1 & 3)

WEEK 39

Timeline: Zerubbabel and main party return | Iron Age begins in Britain | Ezra returns | Malachi | 500 BC | 400 BC | Cyrus | Zechariah Haggai 2nd Temple built | Nehemiah rebuilds walls of Jerusalem

DAY 268 — Rebuilding programme completed

Nehemiah's unselfishness
Nehemiah 5:15–19

Plots against Nehemiah
Nehemiah 6:1–14

Rebuilding completed
Nehemiah 6:15–19

Hanani and Hananiah to protect Jerusalem
Nehemiah 7:1–3

The first return
1 Chronicles 9:2–9

The priests
1 Chronicles 9:10–13

The Levites
1 Chronicles 9:14–16

The gatekeepers
1 Chronicles 9:17–27

Other tasks of the Levites
1 Chronicles 9:28–34

The inhabitants of Jerusalem
Nehemiah 11:1–9

Nehemiah 7:1–3

¹After the wall had been rebuilt and I had set the doors in place, the gatekeepers and the singers and the Levites were appointed. ²I put in charge of Jerusalem my brother Hanani, along with Hananiah the commander of the citadel, because he was a man of integrity and feared God more than most men do. ³I said to them, "The gates of Jerusalem are not to be opened until the sun is hot. While the gatekeepers are still on duty, have them shut the doors and bar them. Also appoint residents of Jerusalem as guards, some at their posts and some near their own houses."

For Thought and Contemplation

Ever heard of the "Nehemiah Management Principles"? Then read this book carefully, and you will see how expertly he got God's task done, *through people*. Good supervision, it has been said, is "the art of getting ordinary people to do extraordinary work." Is God saying something to you in all this?

"Just as each of us has one body with many members, and these members do not all have the same function, so in Christ we who are many form one body, and each member belongs to all the others. We have different gifts, according to the grace given us. ..." (Rom. 12:4–6)

WEEK 39

Zerubbabel and main party return | Iron Age begins in Britain | Ezra returns | Malachi
500 BC — 400 BC
Cyrus | Zechariah Haggai 2nd Temple built | Nehemiah rebuilds walls of Jerusalem

Restoration of Israel

Rebuilt walls
Nehemiah Ch. 1–7

- plans received
- building commences
- work is completed

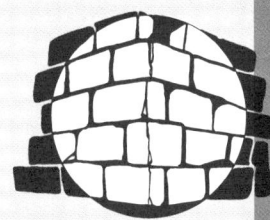

Renewed worship
Neh. Ch. 8–10

- the law is read
- repentance follows
- a celebration of worship

Restored nation
Neh. Ch. 11–13

- people placed in cities
- walls are dedicated
- Temple is cleansed

about 25 years' duration

DAY 269 — The Law is read

The priests
Nehemiah 11:10–14

The Levites
Nehemiah 11:15–18

The gatekeepers
Nehemiah 11:19

Further distribution of the people
Nehemiah 11:20–36

Ezra reads the Law
Nehemiah 7:73, 8:1–12

Feast of Tabernacles
Nehemiah 8:13–18

The people confess their sins
Nehemiah 9:1–4

God's goodness remembered
Nehemiah 9:5–31

Nehemiah 8:1–6

¹... all the people assembled as one man in the square before the Water Gate. They told Ezra the scribe to bring out the Book of the Law of Moses, which the Lord had commanded for Israel. ²So on the first day of the seventh month, Ezra the priest brought the Law before the assembly, which was made up of men and women and all who were able to understand. ³He read it aloud from daybreak till noon as he faced the square before the Water Gate in the presence of the men, women and others who could understand. And all the people listened attentively to the Book of the Law. ⁴Ezra the scribe stood on a high wooden platform built for the occasion. Beside him on his right stood Mattithiah, Shema, Anaiah, Uriah, Hilkiah and Maaseiah; and on his left were Pedaiah, Mishael, Malkijah, Hashum, Hashbaddanah, Zechariah and Meshullam. ⁵Ezra opened the book. All the people could see him because he was standing above them; and as he opened it, the people all stood up. ⁶Ezra praised the Lord, the great God ...

For Thought and **Contemplation**

One of the great principles of Old Testament worship was the way in which they reminded themselves of God's goodness to them in the past. Take a lesson from their example today. Recite at least ten instances of how God has blessed your life in the past year.

"Yet this I call to mind and therefore I have hope: Because of the Lord's great love we are not consumed, for his compassions never fail."
(Lamentations 3:21–22)

---

700 BC | Assyrians besiege Jerusalem | Nahum Zephaniah Josiah Nebuchadnezzar | 600 BC | Daniel taken to Babylon | Jeremiah Habakkuk | Ezekiel | Jerusalem destroyed | FALL OF JUDAH | Exile in Babylon

The covenant

DAY **270**

Nehemiah 9:32–37

³²"Now therefore, O our God, the great, mighty and awesome God, who keeps his covenant of love, do not let all this hardship seem trifling in your eyes – the hardship that has come upon us, upon our kings and leaders, upon our priests and prophets, upon our fathers and all your people, from the days of the kings of Assyria until today. ³³In all that has happened to us, you have been just; you have acted faithfully, while we did wrong. ³⁴Our kings, our leaders, our priests and our fathers did not follow your law; they did not pay attention to your commands or the warnings you gave them. ³⁵Even while they were in their kingdom, enjoying your great goodness to them in the spacious and fertile land you gave them, they did not serve you or turn from their evil ways.
³⁶"But see, we are slaves today, slaves in the land you gave our forefathers so that they could eat its fruit and the other good things it produces. ³⁷Because of our sins, its abundant harvest goes to the kings you have placed over us. ..."

God's goodness and mercy remembered	Nehemiah 9:32–37
Covenant made	Nehemiah 9:38
The people sign the covenant	Nehemiah 10:1–27
The covenant	Nehemiah 10:28–39
The dedication of the wall	Nehemiah 12:27–43
In praise of God the Almighty	Psalm 147:1–20

For Thought and **Contemplation**

In light of what you have read today, this would be an excellent time to renew any promises or vows you have made to the Lord. Are you married? Then spend some quiet moments re-affirming your commitment. Are you single? The commit yourself to serving Him with undivided attention (1 Cor. 7:32–34).

"May the God of peace, who through the blood of the eternal covenant brought back from the dead our Lord Jesus, that great Shepherd of the sheep, equip you with everything good for doing his will, and may he work in us what is pleasing to him, through Jesus Christ, to whom be glory for ever and ever. Amen." (Heb. 13:20–21)

WEEK 39

Zerubbabel and main party return · *Iron Age begins in Britain* · Ezra returns · Malachi
500 BC — 400 BC
Cyrus · Zechariah Haggai 2nd Temple built · Nehemiah rebuilds walls of Jerusalem

DAY 271 — The law of the Lord

A call to praise God
Psalm 148:1–14

Hymns of praise
Psalm 149:1–9, 150:1–6

Tobiah expelled from the Temple
Nehemiah 13:4–9

Temple order restored
Nehemiah 12:44–47

Separation from foreigners
Nehemiah 13:1–3

The law of the Lord
Psalm 119:1–8

Obedience to it
Psalm 119:9–24

Determination to obey
Psalm 119:25–32

A prayer for understanding
Psalm 119:33–40

Trusting God's law
Psalm 119:41–56

Devotion to it
Psalm 119:57–64

The value and justice of it
Psalm 119:65–80

Nehemiah 13:4–9

⁴Before this, Eliashib the priest had been put in charge of the storerooms of the house of our God. He was closely associated with Tobiah, ⁵and he had provided him with a large room formerly used to store the grain offerings and incense and temple articles, and also the tithes of grain, new wine and oil prescribed for the Levites, singers and gatekeepers, as well as the contributions for the priests.

⁶But while all this was going on, I was not in Jerusalem, for in the thirty-second year of Artaxerxes king of Babylon I had returned to the king. Some time later I asked his permission ⁷and came back to Jerusalem. Here I learned about the evil thing Eliashib had done in providing Tobiah a room in the courts of the house of God. ⁸I was greatly displeased and threw all Tobiah's household goods out of the room. ⁹I gave orders to purify the rooms, and then I put back into them the equipment of the house of God, with the grain offerings and the incense.

For Thought and Contemplation

Revival could not come to Israel while Tobiah was living in the Temple. A Tobiah in God's House is like having the devil in the church vestry. Would to God we had men in the Church today who would follow Nehemiah's example, and expel from the midst of God's people all those things which are not of Him.

"Jesus ... overturned the tables of the money changers and the benches of those selling doves. 'It is written,' he said to them, '"My house will be called a house of prayer," but you are making it a "den of robbers".' " (Matt. 21:12–13)

a bird's eye view of Psalms

Place in the Bible

Nineteenth Old Testament book; second book of poetry and wisdom.

Special Features

Israel's hymn book brings together a wide variety of hymns, some praising God, others lamenting national sin, some written for public worship and others for private prayer.

Nehemiah's final reforms

DAY **272**

Nehemiah 13:10–14

¹⁰I also learned that the portions assigned to the Levites had not been given to them, and that all the Levites and singers responsible for the service had gone back to their own fields. ¹¹So I rebuked the officials and asked them, "Why is the house of God neglected?" Then I called them together and stationed them at their posts. ¹²All Judah brought the tithes of grain, new wine and oil into the storerooms. ¹³I put Shelemiah the priest, Zadok the scribe, and a Levite named Pedaiah in charge of the storerooms and made Hanan son of Zaccur, the son of Mattaniah, their assistant, because these men were considered trustworthy. They were made responsible for distributing the supplies to their brothers.
¹⁴Remember me for this, O my God, and do not blot out what I have so faithfully done for the house of my God and its services.

Prayer for deliverance	Psalm 119:81–88
Faith in God's law	Psalm 119:89–96
Love for it	Psalm 119:97–112
Safety in it	Psalm 119:113–128
Desire to obey it	Psalm 119:129–136
Its justice	Psalm 119:137–144
A plea for help	Psalm 119:145–176
True happiness	Psalm 1:1–6
Tithing and worship re-established	Nehemiah 13:10–14
Sabbath keeping violated	Nehemiah 13:15–22

For Thought and **Contemplation**

One of Nehemiah's great reforms was to re-establish the principle of tithing for the support of the priests. The work of God was neglected because the workmen were not properly rewarded. Could this be a reform that is needed in your church? If so, then ask the Lord just what He would have you do about it.

"Each man should give what he has decided in his heart to give, not reluctantly or under compulsion, for God loves a cheerful giver." (2 Cor. 9:7)

Jesus and the Book

Many Psalms which apparently refer to David can be seen to be further fulfilled in Jesus, the Messiah.

Teaching

The Psalms present God as creator, deliverer, protector, forgiver, provider, guide, the One worthy of praise, thanksgiving and worship.

A Verse to Remember

"The Lord is my rock, my fortress and my deliverer; my God is my rock, in whom I take refuge" (Psalm 18:2).

DAY 273 — Malachi's prophecy

Intermarriage rebuked
Nehemiah 13:23–29

Priesthood cleansed
Nehemiah 13:30–31

The Lord's love for Israel
Malachi 1:1–5

The Lord reprimands the priests
Malachi 1:6–14, 2:1–9

The people's unfaithfulness
Malachi 2:10–16

The Lord will judge His people
Malachi 2:17, 3:1–5

The payment of tithes
Malachi 3:6–12

God's promise of mercy
Malachi 3:13–18

Greece the world power 333–63 BC

Coming Day of the Lord
Malachi 4:1–6

Malachi 4:1–6

¹"Surely the day is coming; it will burn like a furnace. All the arrogant and every evildoer will be stubble, and that day that is coming will set them on fire," says the Lord Almighty. "Not a root or a branch will be left to them. ²But for you who revere my name, the sun of righteousness will rise with healing in its wings. And you will go out and leap like calves released from the stall. ³Then you will trample down the wicked; they will be ashes under the soles of your feet on the day when I do these things," says the Lord Almighty.
⁴"Remember the law of my servant Moses, the decrees and laws I gave him at Horeb for all Israel.
⁵"See, I will send you the prophet Elijah before that great and dreadful day of the Lord comes. ⁶He will turn the hearts of the fathers to their children, and the hearts of the children to their fathers; or else I will come and strike the land with a curse."

For Thought and **Contemplation**

The last word of the Old Testament is the "promise of a curse" that would come upon an unfaithful and disobedient people. How different from the last chapters of the New Testament which show all sin removed from the universe and promise eternal joy and everlasting peace.

"Christ redeemed us from the curse of the law by becoming a curse for us, for it is written: 'Cursed is everyone who is hung on a tree.' He redeemed us in order that the blessing given to Abraham might come to the Gentiles through Christ Jesus ..." (Gal. 3:13–14)

Place in the Bible

Thirty-ninth Old Testament book; seventeenth book of prophecy.

Two announcements

DAY **274**

Luke 1:1–4

¹Many have undertaken to draw up an account of the things that have been fulfilled among us, ²just as they were handed down to us by those who from the first were eye-witnesses and servants of the word. ³Therefore, since I myself have carefully investigated everything from the beginning, it seemed good also to me to write an orderly account for you, most excellent Theophilus, ⁴so that you may know the certainty of the things you have been taught.

Prefaces to Synoptic Gospels	Matthew 1:1, Mark 1:1, Luke 1:1–4
Preface to John's Gospel	John 1:1–5
Rome the World Power	63 BC–AD 476
Two genealogies of Jesus Christ	Matthew 1:2–17, Luke 3:23–38
Birth of John the Baptist announced	Luke 1:5–25
Birth of Jesus Christ announced	Luke 1:26–38

For Thought and **Contemplation**

Many Christians skip over the genealogy of Christ because they find it dull and uninteresting. But how wonderfully it underlines the truth that, when Christ came to save, He did not just come *near* to the human race, He came *into* it. The Son of God became the Son of Man, that the sons of men might become the sons of God.

"For to us a child is born, to us a son is given, and the government will be on his shoulders. And he will be called Wonderful Counsellor, Mighty God, Everlasting Father, Prince of Peace." (Isa. 9:6)

Jesus and the Book
Malachi predicts that the prophet Elijah would come before the Messiah, and Jesus identified John the Baptist as this person (Matt. 11:10–11).

Teaching
Hard hearts, abuse of the poor and needy, idolatry and covetousness are the order of the day. God's people need a Deliverer from God's judgment.

A Verse to Remember
"Bring the whole tithe into the storehouse, that there may be food in my house … and see if I will not throw open the floodgates of heaven and pour out so much blessing that you will not have room enough for it" (Mal. 3:10).

Heart to Heart

Section 9

Once again, congratulations. You have now read three-quarters of the Bible and built a solid foundation of truth on which the New Testament can rest. At CWR there are people praying for you to finish the course so even if you are a little behind take comfort from what you have already achieved and press on to reach the goal.

Visit the web site: **www.cover2cover.org**

10

In this section

The birth and childhood of Jesus
John the Baptist's message
Jesus' call of His disciples
His teaching and healing ministry
The triumphal entry into Jerusalem

DAY 275 — The birth of Jesus Christ

Elizabeth's greeting to Mary
Luke 1:39–45

Mary praised God
Luke 1:46–55

The birth of John the Baptist 6 BC

Mary stays with Elizabeth
Luke 1:56

Birth of John the Baptist
Luke 1:57–66

Zechariah's prophecy
Luke 1:67–79

John's early years
Luke 1:80

The announcement to Joseph
Matthew 1:18–24

Birth of Jesus Christ 5 BC

The birth of Jesus
Luke 2:1–7, Matthew 1:25

The angels and the shepherds
Luke 2:8–20

Circumcision of Jesus
Luke 2:21

Presentation in the Temple
Luke 2:22–38

Matthew 1:18–24

[18]This is how the birth of Jesus Christ came about: His mother Mary was pledged to be married to Joseph, but before they came together, she was found to be with child through the Holy Spirit. [19]Because Joseph her husband was a righteous man and did not want to expose her to public disgrace, he had in mind to divorce her quietly. [20]But after he had considered this, an angel of the Lord appeared to him in a dream and said, "Joseph son of David, do not be afraid to take Mary home as your wife, because what is conceived in her is from the Holy Spirit. [21]She will give birth to a son, and you are to give him the name Jesus, because he will save his people from their sins."
[22]All this took place to fulfil what the Lord had said through the prophet: [23]"The virgin will be with child and will give birth to a son, and they will call him Immanuel" – which means, "God with us." [24]When Joseph woke up, he did what the angel of the Lord had commanded him and took Mary home as his wife.

For Thought and Contemplation

How slow and unhurried God must have seemed to those who knew the prophecies concerning Christ's first coming. Yet God is always right on time – never a moment too soon, and never a moment too late. He is a punctual God. Keep this thought in mind the next time you are tempted to think the Almighty's schedules are mistimed.

"But when the time had fully come, God sent his Son, born of a woman, born under law, to redeem those under law, that we might receive the full rights of sons." (Gal. 4:4–5)

a bird's eye view of Luke

Place in the Bible	Written by:	Special Features
Third New Testament book, third Gospel.	Luke.	Dr Luke's observant eye lays special emphasis on certain people and things in his Gospel: prayer, joy, the Holy Spirit, the early life of Jesus, children, women and social outcasts.

Jesus' childhood

DAY **276**

Luke 2:41–49

⁴¹Every year his parents went to Jerusalem for the Feast of the Passover. ⁴²When he was twelve years old, they went up to the Feast, according to the custom. ⁴³After the Feast was over, while his parents were returning home, the boy Jesus stayed behind in Jerusalem, but they were unaware of it. ⁴⁴Thinking he was in their company, they travelled on for a day. Then they began looking for him among their relatives and friends. ⁴⁵When they did not find him, they went back to Jerusalem to look for him. ⁴⁶After three days they found him in the temple courts, sitting among the teachers, listening to them and asking them questions. ⁴⁷Everyone who heard him was amazed at his understanding and his answers. ⁴⁸When his parents saw him, they were astonished. His mother said to him, "Son, why have you treated us like this? Your father and I have been anxiously searching for you." ⁴⁹"Why were you searching for me?" he asked. "Didn't you know I had to be in my Father's house?"

The wise men
Matthew 2:1–12

The flight to Egypt
Matthew 2:13–18

From Egypt to Nazareth
Matthew 2:19–23, Luke 2:39

Jesus' childhood in Nazareth
Luke 2:40

Birth of Paul: AD 10–15 approx.

Jesus in the Temple
Luke 2:41–50

Jesus' early life
Luke 2:51–52

Start of John the Baptist's ministry
Matthew 3:1–6, Mark 1:2–6, Luke 3:1–6, John 1:6–18

For Thought and **Contemplation**

One of the first things children demonstrate when growing up is the truth of the Scripture that says: "Foolishness is bound in the heart of a child" (Prov. 22:15). Foolishness appears in all they say and do. How different with Jesus. His wisdom baffled the sages of His day. And why? Because it was the wisdom of God!

"The Word became flesh and made his dwelling among us. We have seen his glory, the glory of the One and Only, who came from the Father, full of grace and truth." (Jn. 1:14)

Jesus and the Book

Luke presents Jesus Christ as the One who showed compassion to men and women, and who came to seek and to save lost sinners and offer God's priceless gift of salvation.

Teaching

Luke sets down an orderly, meticulous account of the life, death and resurrection of Jesus. His purpose, as stated in 1:3–4, was to strengthen the faith of Gentiles and to show that Jesus Christ is the Saviour of every kind of person in the world.

A Verse to Remember

"'For the Son of Man came to seek and to save what was lost'" (Luke 19:10)

DAY 277 — The temptation of Jesus

John the Baptist's ministry begins AD 25

John the Baptist's message
Matthew 3:7–10, Luke 3:7–14

His introduction of Christ
Matthew 3:11–12, Mark 1:7–8,
Luke 3:15–18, John 1:19–28

The baptism of Jesus
Matthew 3:13–17, Mark 1:9–11,
Luke 3:21–22

John's declaration
John 1:29–34

The temptation in the wilderness
Matthew 4:1–11, Mark 1:12–13, Luke 4:1–13

The first three disciples
John 1:35–42

Philip and Nathanael
John 1:43–51

Luke 4:1–8

¹Jesus, full of the Holy Spirit, returned from the Jordan and was led by the Spirit in the desert, ²where for forty days he was tempted by the devil. He ate nothing during those days, and at the end of them he was hungry. ³The devil said to him, "If you are the Son of God, tell this stone to become bread." ⁴Jesus answered, "It is written: 'Man does not live on bread alone.'" ⁵The devil led him up to a high place and showed him in an instant all the kingdoms of the world. ⁶And he said to him, "I will give you all their authority and splendour, for it has been given to me, and I can give it to anyone I want to. ⁷So if you worship me, it will all be yours." ⁸Jesus answered, "It is written: 'Worship the Lord your God and serve him only.'"

For Thought and **Contemplation**

What a contrast exists between the temptation of the first Adam and that of Christ, who is called in Scripture the last Adam. The first Adam failed while feasting in a garden, but the second Adam triumphed while fasting in a wilderness. And because He triumphed – so can you!

"So it is written: 'The first man Adam became a living being'; the last Adam, a life-giving spirit. The spiritual did not come first, but the natural, and after that the spiritual. The first man was of the dust of the earth, the second man from heaven." (1 Cor. 15:45–47)

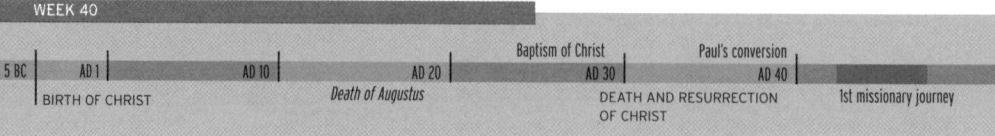

Jesus and John

DAY 278

John 3:25–30

²⁵An argument developed between some of John's disciples and a certain Jew over the matter of ceremonial washing. ²⁶They came to John and said to him, "Rabbi, that man who was with you on the other side of the Jordan – the one you testified about – well, he is baptising, and everyone is going to him."

²⁷To this John replied, "A man can receive only what is given him from heaven. ²⁸You yourselves can testify that I said, 'I am not the Christ but am sent ahead of him.' ²⁹The bride belongs to the bridegroom. The friend who attends the bridegroom waits and listens for him, and is full of joy when he hears the bridegroom's voice. That joy is mine, and it is now complete. ³⁰He must become greater; I must become less."

The wedding in Cana	John 2:1–11
Jesus in Capernaum	John 2:12
Jesus in the Temple	John 2:13–22
Jesus' knowledge of human nature	John 2:23–25
Jesus and Nicodemus	John 3:1–21
Jesus and John	John 3:22–24
John's testimony	John 3:25–36
The imprisonment of John	Luke 3:19–20
Jesus leaves Judea	Matthew 4:12, John 4:1–3
Jesus and the woman at the well	John 4:4–26

For Thought and **Contemplation**

John the Baptist faced a dilemma that, sooner or later, comes to every one of us: who is to be first – me, or Jesus? You know how John decided: it would be Jesus! "He must become greater; I must become less." What decision have you reached about this momentous issue?

"I have been crucified with Christ and I no longer live, but Christ lives in me. The life I live in the body, I live by faith in the Son of God, who loved me and gave himself for me." (Gal. 2:20)

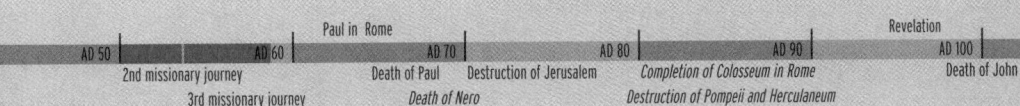

DAY 279

Jesus' early ministry

Jesus in Samaria
John 4:27–42

Jesus preaches the Gospel
Matthew 4:17, Mark 1:14–15,
Luke 4:14–15, John 4:43–45

Jesus heals an official's son
John 4:46–54

Jesus is rejected at Nazareth
Luke 4:16–30

Jesus leaves Nazareth
Matthew 4:13–16

Jesus calls four fishermen
Matthew 4:18–22, Mark 1:16–20,
Luke 5:1–11

Jesus teaches in the synagogue
Mark 1:21–22, Luke 4:31–32

The man with an evil spirit
Mark 1:23–28

Mark 1:21–28

²¹They went to Capernaum, and when the Sabbath came, Jesus went into the synagogue and began to teach. ²²The people were amazed at his teaching, because he taught them as one who had authority, not as the teachers of the law. ²³Just then a man in their synagogue who was possessed by an evil spirit cried out, ²⁴"What do you want with us, Jesus of Nazareth? Have you come to destroy us? I know who you are – the Holy One of God!"
²⁵"Be quiet!" said Jesus sternly. "Come out of him!" ²⁶The evil spirit shook the man violently and came out of him with a shriek.
²⁷The people were all so amazed that they asked each other, "What is this? A new teaching – and with authority! He even gives orders to evil spirits and they obey him." ²⁸News about him spread quickly over the whole region of Galilee.

For Thought and **Contemplation**

Anyone who embarks upon an effective ministry for God will, at some time or other, experience rejection. Jesus did – and so will you. And how you handle that rejection will determine whether your ministry will go backward or forward. Jesus went forward – and in His strength, so can you.

"For we do not have a high priest who is unable to sympathise with our weaknesses, but we have one who has been tempted in every way, just as we are – yet was without sin." (Heb. 4:15)

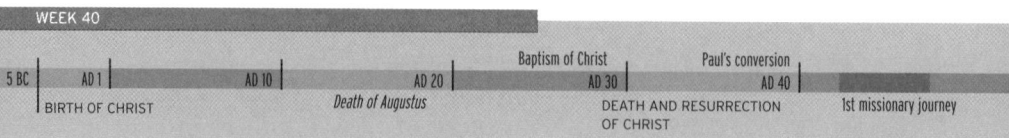

The main highlights of Christ's life

1. **His birth** (Lk. 2:1–7)
2. **The adoration by the shepherds** (Lk. 2:8–20)
3. **The dedication in Jerusalem** (Lk. 2:21–38)
4. **The worship by the wise men** (Matt. 2:1–12)
5. **Flight into Egypt** (Matt. 2:13–18)
6. **Temple visit at age twelve** (Lk. 2:41–50)
7. **His baptism** (Matt. 3:13–17)
8. **His temptation** (Matt. 4:1–11)
9. **Introduction by John the Baptist** (Jn. 1:29)
10. **First Temple cleansing** (Jn. 2:13–25)
11. **Teaching about the new birth** (Jn. 3:1–21)
12. **The choice of the twelve** (Matt. 10:1–4)
13. **Imprisonment and execution of John** (Matt. 14:1–12)
14. **Peter's great confession** (Matt. 16:13–20)
15. **The transfiguration** (Matt. 17:1–13)
16. **His triumphal entry** (Matt. 21:1–11)
17. **Weeping over Jerusalem** (Matt. 23:37–39; Lk. 19:41)
18. **In the upper room** (Jn. 13–14)
19. **In Gethsemane** (Jn. 18:1–11)
20. **His arrest and trials** (Jn. 18:12–19:15)
21. **The crucifixion** (Jn. 19:16–24)
22. **The resurrection** (Matt. 28:1–7)
23. **The ten appearances**
24. **The ascension** (Lk. 24:51)

DAY 280

Jesus heals many

The man with an evil spirit
Luke 4:33–37

Jesus heals many people
Matthew 8:14–17, Mark 1:29–34,
Luke 4:38–41

Jesus in Galilee
Matthew 4:23–25, Mark 1:35–39,
Luke 4:42–44

Jesus heals a leper
Matthew 8:2–4, Mark 1:40–45,
Luke 5:12–16

He heals a paralysed man
Matthew 9:1–8, Mark 2:1–12,
Luke 5:17–26

Luke 5:12–16

¹²While Jesus was in one of the towns, a man came along who was covered with leprosy. When he saw Jesus, he fell with his face to the ground and begged him, "Lord, if you are willing, you can make me clean."
¹³Jesus reached out his hand and touched the man. "I am willing," he said. "Be clean!" And immediately the leprosy left him.
¹⁴Then Jesus ordered him, "Don't tell anyone, but go, show yourself to the priest and offer the sacrifices that Moses commanded for your cleansing, as a testimony to them."
¹⁵Yet the news about him spread all the more, so that crowds of people came to hear him and to be healed of their sicknesses.
¹⁶But Jesus often withdrew to lonely places and prayed.

For Thought and **Contemplation**

Did the healing ministry of Jesus cease when He left this world and returned to heaven? Many think so. What do *you* believe? If you are unsure about this, turn to Hebrews 13:8 and settle the matter once and for all.

"He himself bore our sins in his body on the tree, so that we might die to sins and live for righteousness; by his wounds you have been healed."
(1 Pet. 2:24)

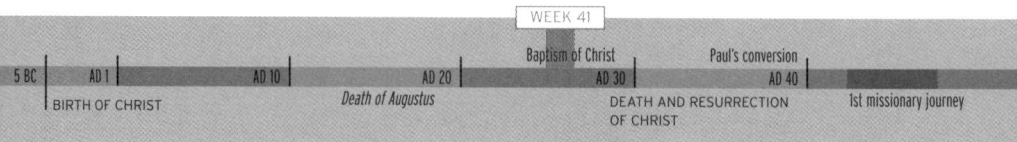

The authority of Jesus

DAY **281**

Mark 2:13–17

¹³Once again Jesus went out beside the lake. A large crowd came to him, and he began to teach them. ¹⁴As he walked along, he saw Levi son of Alphaeus sitting at the tax collector's booth. "Follow me," Jesus told him, and Levi got up and followed him.
¹⁵While Jesus was having dinner at Levi's house, many tax collectors and "sinners" were eating with him and his disciples, for there were many who followed him. ¹⁶When the teachers of the law who were Pharisees saw him eating with the "sinners" and tax collectors, they asked his disciples: "Why does he eat with tax collectors and 'sinners'?"
¹⁷On hearing this, Jesus said to them, "It is not the healthy who need a doctor, but the sick. I have not come to call the righteous, but sinners."

Jesus calls Matthew	Matthew 9:9–13, Mark 2:13–17, Luke 5:27–32
The question about fasting	Matthew 9:14–17, Mark 2:18–22, Luke 5:33–39
The healing at the pool	John 5:1–9
The Jews' displeasure	John 5:10–18
Jesus' response	John 5:19–23
He speaks of His authority	John 5:24–29
His witnesses	John 5:30–47

For Thought and **Contemplation**

Do you know the difference between "power" and "authority"? Imagine a huge transporter coming down the High Street. That's *power*. Then imagine a policeman stepping out, holding up his hand and commanding the huge vehicle to stop. That's *authority*. And Christ gives that same authority to you and me (see Luke 9:1).

"For by him all things were created: things in heaven and on earth, visible and invisible, whether thrones or powers or rulers or authorities; all things were created by him and for him. He is before all things, and in him all things hold together." (Col. 1:16–17)

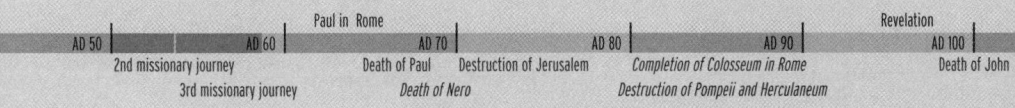

DAY 282 — Jesus chooses the Twelve

The question about the Sabbath
Matthew 12:1–8, Mark 2:23–28, Luke 6:1–5

The man with a withered hand
Matthew 12:9–14, Mark 3:1–6, Luke 6:6–11

Multitudes healed
Matthew 12:15–21, Mark 3:7–12

Jesus chooses the twelve apostles
Mark 3:13–19, Luke 6:12–16

Jesus teaches and heals
Luke 6:17–19

The Sermon on the Mount
Matthew 5:1–20

Luke 6:12–16

[12]One of those days Jesus went out to a mountainside to pray, and spent the night praying to God. [13]When morning came, he called his disciples to him and chose twelve of them, whom he also designated apostles: [14]Simon (whom he named Peter), his brother Andrew, James, John, Philip, Bartholomew, [15]Matthew, Thomas, James son of Alphaeus, Simon who was called the Zealot, [16]Judas son of James, and Judas Iscariot, who became a traitor.

For Thought and **Contemplation**

God calls no one to a special ministry or service for Him without providing the resources by which that ministry can be accomplished. And remember this – no matter the task ahead of you, it is never as great as the power behind you.

"Brothers, think of what you were when you were called. Not many of you were wise by human standards ... But God chose the foolish things of the world to shame the wise; God chose the weak things of the world to shame the strong. He chose the lowly things of this world and the despised things ..." (1 Cor. 1:26–28)

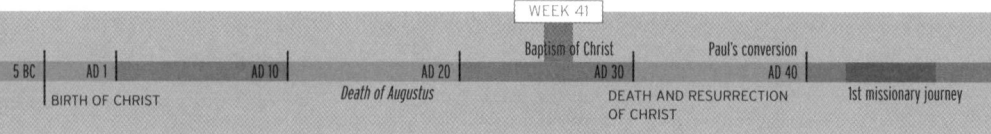

The Sermon on the Mount

DAY 283

Matthew 7:7-12

⁷"Ask and it will be given to you; seek and you will find; knock and the door will be opened to you. ⁸For everyone who asks receives; he who seeks finds; and to him who knocks, the door will be opened.

⁹"Which of you, if his son asks for bread, will give him a stone? ¹⁰Or if he asks for a fish, will give him a snake? ¹¹If you, then, though you are evil, know how to give good gifts to your children, how much more will your Father in heaven give good gifts to those who ask him! ¹²So in everything, do to others what you would have them do to you, for this sums up the Law and the Prophets.

Jesus teaching about anger, adultery and divorce
Matthew 5:21-32

Vows and revenge
Matthew 5:33-42

Love for enemies
Matthew 5:43-48

Teaching about giving
Matthew 6:1-4

Teaching about prayer and fasting
Matthew 6:5-18

Riches in heaven
Matthew 6:19-23

God and possessions
Matthew 6:24-34

Judging others
Matthew 7:1-6

Our heavenly Father
Matthew 7:7-12

Further teaching
Matthew 7:13-23

The wise man and the foolish man
Matthew 7:24-27

Jesus' authority
Matthew 7:28-29

For Thought and **Contemplation**

Some Christians are more concerned about beliefs than behaviour, others about behaviour more than beliefs. The Sermon on the Mount emphasises the necessity of both. Can you spot an area in your life where your doctrine may be right but your actions wrong? Then take whatever steps are necessary to turn it around.

"But the man who looks intently into the perfect law that gives freedom, and continues to do this, not forgetting what he has heard, but doing it – he will be blessed in what he does." (Jas. 1:25)

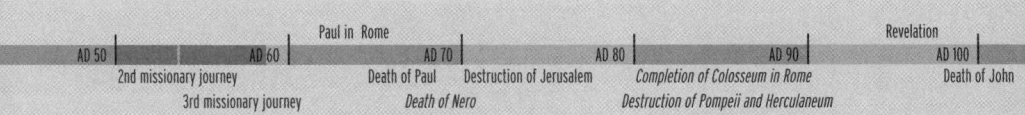

DAY 284

Jesus' teaching

Jesus' teaching about happiness and sorrow
Matthew 8:1, Luke 6:20-26

Treatment of enemies
Luke 6:27-36

Do not judge
Luke 6:37-42

A tree and its fruit
Luke 6:43-45

Wise and foolish builders
Luke 6:46-49

Jesus heals the centurion's servant
Matthew 8:5-13, Luke 7:1-10

He raises a widow's son
Luke 7:11-17

Jesus commends John the Baptist
Luke 7:18-30

Luke 6:46-49

⁴⁶"Why do you call me, 'Lord, Lord,' and do not do what I say? ⁴⁷I will show you what he is like who comes to me and hears my words and puts them into practice. ⁴⁸He is like a man building a house, who dug down deep and laid the foundation on rock. When a flood came, the torrent struck that house but could not shake it, because it was well built. ⁴⁹But the one who hears my words and does not put them into practice is like a man who built a house on the ground without a foundation. The moment the torrent struck that house, it collapsed and its destruction was complete."

For Thought and **Contemplation**

One of the great laws of the personality is that truth does not become part of a person until they begin acting upon it. Progress from merely assenting to Christ's teachings to fully agreeing with them depends on behaving consistently with them. How good are you at not just listening to His words, but acting on them?

"... Jesus said, 'If you hold to my teaching, you are really my disciples. Then you will know the truth, and the truth will set you free.'" (Jn. 8:31-32)

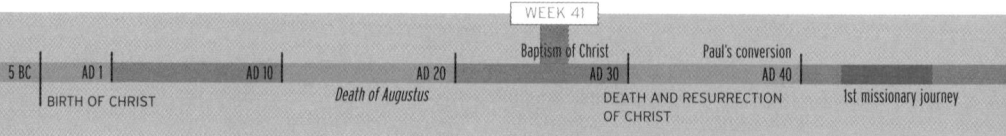

350

Jesus and Beelzebub

DAY **285**

Mark 3:22–27

²²And the teachers of the law who came down from Jerusalem said, "He is possessed by Beelzebub! By the prince of demons he is driving out demons." ²³So Jesus called them and spoke to them in parables: "How can Satan drive out Satan? ²⁴If a kingdom is divided against itself, that kingdom cannot stand. ²⁵If a house is divided against itself, that house cannot stand. ²⁶And if Satan opposes himself and is divided, he cannot stand; his end has come. ²⁷In fact, no-one can enter a strong man's house and carry off his possessions unless he first ties up the strong man. Then he can rob his house.

Jesus condemns wickedness
Matthew 11:16–19, Luke 7:31–35

The unbelieving towns
Matthew 11:20–24

Invitation to rest
Matthew 11:25–30

Jesus at Simon's home
Luke 7:36–50

The women who accompanied Jesus
Luke 8:1–3

Jesus accused of madness
Mark 3:20–21

Jesus and Beelzebub
Matthew 12:22–30, Mark 3:22–27

The unpardonable sin
Matthew 12:31–37, Mark 3:28–30

The folly of seeking a sign
Matthew 12:38–45

For Thought and **Contemplation**

Just as between Christ and Satan there was no collision or compromise, so it must also be with every one of Christ's followers. If you are for God, then you must be *against* the devil. Check up to see if there are any compromises in your life. And if so, decide right now to do something about them.

"Submit yourselves, then, to God. Resist the devil, and he will flee from you. Come near to God and he will come near to you. ..." (Jas. 4:7–8)

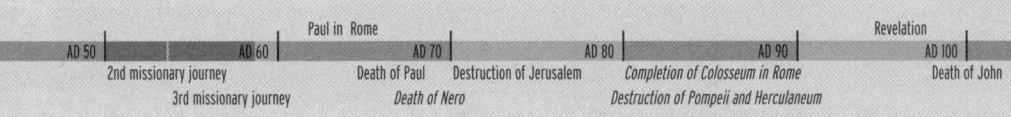

351

DAY 286 — The parables of Jesus

Jesus' mother and brothers
Matthew 12:46–50, Mark 3:31–35, Luke 8:19–21

The parable of the sower
Matthew 13:1–9. Mark 4:1–9, Luke 8:4–8

The purpose of the parables
Matthew 13:10–17, Mark 4:10–12, Luke 8:9–10

The explanation
Matthew 13:18–23, Mark 4:13–20, Luke 8:11–15

A lamp under a bowl
Mark 4:21–25, Luke 8:16–18

The growing seed
Mark 4:26–29

The parable of the weeds
Matthew 13:24–30

Mark 4:26–29

²⁶He also said, "This is what the kingdom of God is like. A man scatters seed on the ground. ²⁷Night and day, whether he sleeps or gets up, the seed sprouts and grows, though he does not know how. ²⁸All by itself the soil produces corn – first the stalk, then the ear, then the full grain in the ear. ²⁹As soon as the grain is ripe, he puts the sickle to it, because the harvest has come."

For Thought and **Contemplation**

In His ministry of teaching, Jesus' goal was never to impress His hearers but to instruct them. How good are you at presenting profound truth with simplicity and directness? Think up a modern parable and then share its truth with someone – today.

"... speaking the truth in love, we will in all things grow up into him who is the Head, that is, Christ." (Eph. 4:15)

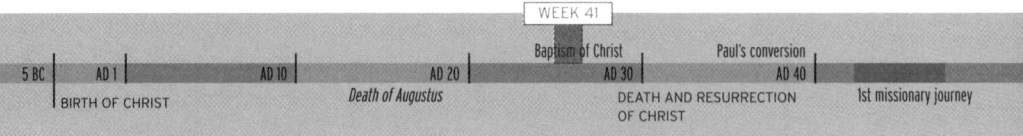

Parables of Jesus

THE PURPOSE of Jesus' parables was to teach in simple, easy-to-understand picture language the message of the kingdom of God. In addition to these, Jesus used epigrams and other memorable sayings, as the Beatitudes and the rest of the Sermon on the Mount show. Jesus used parables so frequently that Mark even says, "[Jesus] did not say anything to them without using a parable" (Mark 4:34).

	Matthew	Mark	Luke
Lamp under a bushel	5:14–15	4:21–22	8:16; 11:33
Houses on rock and on sand	7:24–27		6:47–49
New cloth on an old garment	9:16	2:21	5:36
New wine in old wineskins	9:17	2:23	5:37–38
Sower	13:3–8	4:3–8	8:5–8
The mustard seed	13:31–32	4:30–32	13:18–19
Tares	13:24–30		
Yeast	13:33		13:20–21
Hidden treasure	13:44		
Pearl of great value	13:45–46		
Drag-net	13:47–48		
Lost sheep	18:12–14		15:3–7
Unforgiving servant	18:23–35		
Workers in the vineyard	20:1–16		
Two sons	21:28–31		
Wicked tenants	21:33–41	12:1–9	20:9–16
Invitation to the wedding-feast	22:2–14		
Fig-tree and summer	24:32–33	13:28–29	21:29–32
Ten "bridesmaids"	25:1–13		
Talents/minas	25:14–30		19:12–27
Sheep and goats	25:31–46		
Seedtime to harvest		4:26–29	
Creditor and the debtors			7:41–43
Good Samaritan			10:30–37
Friend in need			11:5–8
Rich fool			12:16–21
Alert servants			12:35–40
Faithful steward			12:42–48
Fig-tree without figs			13:6–9
Wedding-feast			14:7–14
Great banquet			14:16–24
Counting the cost			14:28–33
Lost coin			15:8–10
Prodigal son			15:11–32
Dishonest steward			16:1–8
Rich man and Lazarus			16:19–31
The master and his servant			17:7–10
Persistent widow			18:2–5
Pharisee and the tax collector			18:10–14

DAY 287 — More parables

Parables of the mustard seed and the yeast
Matthew 13:31–33, Mark 4:30–32

Jesus' use of parables
Matthew 13:34–35, Mark 4:33–34

Parable of weeds explained
Matthew 13:36–43

Parable of hidden treasure
Matthew 13:44

Parable of the pearl
Matthew 13:45–46

Parable of the net
Matthew 13:47–50

The householder
Matthew 13:51–53

Jesus calms the storm
Matthew 8:18, 23–27, Mark 4:35–41, Luke 8:22–25

Jesus casts out demons
Matthew 8:28–34, Mark 5:1–20

Matthew 13:36–43

³⁶Then he left the crowd and went into the house. His disciples came to him and said, "Explain to us the parable of the weeds in the field." ³⁷He answered, "The one who sowed the good seed is the Son of Man. ³⁸The field is the world, and the good seed stands for the sons of the kingdom. The weeds are the sons of the evil one, ³⁹and the enemy who sows them is the devil. The harvest is the end of the age, and the harvesters are angels.

⁴⁰"As the weeds are pulled up and burned in the fire, so it will be at the end of the age. ⁴¹The Son of Man will send out his angels, and they will weed out of his kingdom everything that causes sin and all who do evil. ⁴²They will throw them into the fiery furnace, where will be weeping and gnashing of teeth. ⁴³Then the righteous will shine like the sun in the kingdom of their Father. He who has ears, let him hear."

For Thought and **Contemplation**

Someone has said that Christ's parables are not "bedtime stories to put us to sleep, but bugle calls to wake us up". Has something leapt out from these parables and given you a jolt? Good. Now apply its truth to your life without a moment's delay.

"Do not merely listen to the word, and so deceive yourselves. Do what it says. Anyone who listens to the word but does not do what it says is like a man who looks at his face in a mirror and, after looking at himself, goes away and immediately forgets what he looks like." (Jas. 1:22–24)

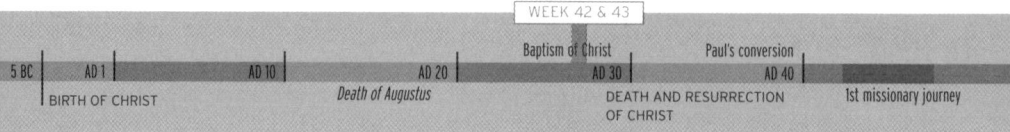

More healings

DAY 288

Matthew 9:27–34

²⁷As Jesus went on from there, two blind men followed him, calling out, "Have mercy on us, Son of David!" ²⁸When he had gone indoors, the blind men came to him, and he asked them, "Do you believe that I am able to do this?"
"Yes, Lord," they replied.
²⁹Then he touched their eyes and said, "According to your faith will it be done to you"; ³⁰and their sight was restored. Jesus warned them sternly, "See that no-one knows about this." ³¹But they went out and spread the news about him all over that region.
³²While they were going out, a man who was demon-possessed and could not talk was brought to Jesus. ³³And when the demon was driven out, the man who had been mute spoke. The crowd was amazed and said, "Nothing like this has ever been seen in Israel."
³⁴But the Pharisees said, "It is by the prince of demons that he drives out demons."

Jesus casts out demons
Luke 8:26–39

The woman who touched Jesus
Matthew 9:18–22, Mark 5:21–34, Luke 8:40–48

Jesus raises Jairus' daughter
Matthew 9:23–26, Mark 5:35–43, Luke 8:49–56

Jesus heals two blind men
Matthew 9:27–31

A dumb man speaks again
Matthew 9:32–34

Jesus rejected again at Nazareth
Matthew 13:54–58, Mark 6:1–6

For Thought and **Contemplation**

The Scripture tells us that "faith comes by hearing, and hearing by the word of God" (Romans 10:17, NKJ). Is there a physical or psychological problem in your life that, despite any help you have received, refuses to budge? Then, with renewed faith, ask Him to make this the day of your deliverance.

"Now faith is being sure of what we hope for and certain of what we do not see." (Heb. 11:1)

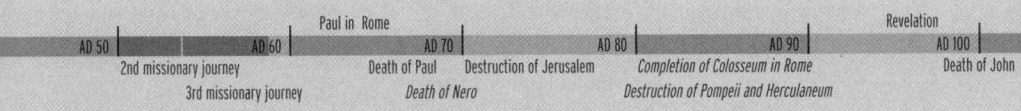

DAY 289 — The mission of the twelve

Jesus sends out the twelve disciples
Matthew 9:35–38, 10:1–4,
Luke 9:1–2

His instructions to them
Matthew 10:5–15, Mark 6:7–11,
Luke 9:3–5

The persecution of the disciples
Matthew 10:16–33

The cost and rewards of discipleship
Matthew 10:34–42, 11:1, Mark 6:12–13,
Luke 9:6

Death of John the Baptist AD 27

Death of John the Baptist
Matthew 14:1–12, Mark 6:14–29,
Luke 9:7–9

Mark 6:7–11

⁷Calling the Twelve to him, he sent them out two by two and gave them authority over evil spirits. ⁸These were his instructions: "Take nothing for the journey except a staff – no bread, no bag, no money in your belts. ⁹Wear sandals but not an extra tunic. ¹⁰Whenever you enter a house, stay there until you leave that town. ¹¹And if any place will not welcome you or listen to you, shake the dust off your feet when you leave, as a testimony against them."

For Thought and **Contemplation**

What a challenge Christ presented to those twelve disciples when He told them to go and do exactly as He had done. But then, as someone has said, "No one has ever tested the resources of God until they come up against that which is humanly impossible."

"I can do everything through him who gives me strength." (Phil. 4:13)

a bird's eye view of Matthew

Place in the Bible	**Written by:**	**Special Features**
First New Testament book; first Gospel.	Matthew.	Five distinct sections record the teaching of Jesus: the Sermon on the Mount (5–7), the Twelve being sent out (10), parables about the Kingdom (13), teaching about discipleship (18), and the coming kingdom (24–25).

The feeding of the five thousand — DAY **290**

Matthew 14:13–19

¹³When Jesus heard what had happened, he withdrew by boat privately to a solitary place. Hearing of this, the crowds followed him on foot from the towns. ¹⁴When Jesus landed and saw a large crowd, he had compassion on them and healed their sick.

¹⁵As evening approached, the disciples came to him and said, "This is a remote place, and it's already getting late. Send the crowds away, so that they can go to the villages and buy themselves some food."

¹⁶Jesus replied, "They do not need to go away. You give them something to eat."

¹⁷"We have here only five loaves of bread and two fish," they answered.

¹⁸"Bring them here to me," he said. ¹⁹And he directed the people to sit down on the grass. Taking the five loaves and the two fish and looking up to heaven, he gave thanks and broke the loaves. Then he gave them to the disciples, and the disciples gave them to the people.

The feeding of the five thousand	Matthew 14:13–21, Mark 6:30–44, Luke 9:10–17, John 6:1–13
Jesus leaves the crowd	Matthew 14:22–23, Mark 6:45–46, John 6:14–15
Jesus walks on the water	Matthew 14:24–33, Mark 6:47–52, John 6:16–21
He heals the sick at Gennesaret	Matthew 14:34–36, Mark 6:53–56

For Thought and **Contemplation**

"A miracle," said C.S. Lewis, "is God taking the ordinary processes of nature and *speeding them up*." Normally, nature takes several seasons to make bread; the wheat, the grain, the flour etc. But what nature takes seasons to do, Christ did in seconds. Carry with you into the day the thrilling fact that God is so much greater than the world He has made.

"Jesus looked at them and said, 'With man this is impossible, but with God all things are possible.'" (Matt. 19:26)

Jesus and the Book

Quoting the Old Testament sixty-five times, Matthew shows how Jesus fulfils the prophecies about the promised Messiah culminating in His death and resurrection from the dead. Out of Matthew's 1,071 verses, 60 per cent are the spoken words of Jesus.

Teaching

Matthew presents Jesus as "King of the Jews" at His birth (Matt. 2:2) and His death (Matt. 27:37). His aim is to show the real nature of His Kingdom, especially in the parables. The Gospel closes with Jesus' command "to make disciples of all nations." (Matt. 28:19)

A Verse to Remember

"You are the Christ, the Son of the living God" (Matt. 16:16).

DAY **291**

The bread of life

The people seek Jesus
John 6:22–24

Jesus teaches about spiritual food
John 6:25–33

Jesus, the bread of life
John 6:34–59

Many disciples desert Jesus
John 6:60–71

The hypocrisy of the scribes and Pharisees
Matthew 15:1–9, Mark 7:1–13

Things that make a person unclean
Matthew 15:10–20, Mark 7:14–23

John 6:34–40

³⁴"Sir," they said, "from now on give us this bread."
³⁵Then Jesus declared, "I am the bread of life. He who comes to me will never go hungry, and he who believes in me will never be thirsty. ³⁶But as I told you, you have seen me and still you do not believe. ³⁷All that the Father gives me will come to me, and whoever comes to me I will never drive away. ³⁸For I have come down from heaven not to do my will but to do the will of him who sent me. ³⁹And this is the will of him who sent me, that I shall lose none of all that he has given me, but raise them up at the last day. ⁴⁰For my Father's will is that everyone who looks to the Son and believes in him shall have eternal life, and I will raise him up at the last day."

For Thought and **Contemplation**

How true it is that, although thousands follow Christ when He gives them what they want, few are prepared to follow Him when He confronts them with what *He* wants. Check up on your own discipleship today. Are you more concerned with what you want, or what *He* wants?

"If you love me, you will obey what I command." (Jn. 14:15)

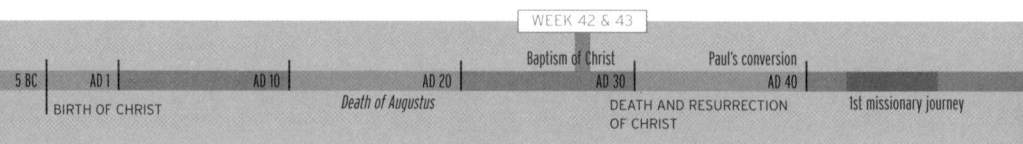

Peter's momentous confession

DAY 292

Matthew 16:13–20

¹³When Jesus came to the region of Caesarea Philippi, he asked his disciples, "Who do people say the Son of Man is?" ¹⁴They replied, "Some say John the Baptist; others say Elijah; and still others, Jeremiah or one of the prophets." ¹⁵"But what about you?" he asked. "Who do you say I am?" ¹⁶Simon Peter answered, "You are the Christ, the Son of the living God." ¹⁷Jesus replied, "Blessed are you, Simon son of Jonah, for this was not revealed to you by man, but by my Father in heaven. ¹⁸And I tell you that you are Peter, and on this rock I will build my church, and the gates of Hades will not overcome it. ¹⁹I will give you the keys of the kingdom of heaven; whatever you bind on earth will be bound in heaven, and whatever you loose on earth will be loosed in heaven." ²⁰Then he warned his disciples not to tell anyone that he was the Christ.

The Syro-Phoenician woman
Matthew 15:21–28, Mark 7:24–30

Jesus heals many
Matthew 15:29–31, Mark 7:31–37

Jesus feeds the four thousand
Matthew 15:32–38, Mark 8:1–9

The demand for a sign
Matthew 15:39, 16:1–4, Mark 8:10–12

The yeast of the Pharisees and Sadducees
Matthew 16:5–12, Mark 8:13–21

Jesus heals a blind man
Mark 8:22–26

Peter's declaration
Matthew 16:13–20

For Thought and **Contemplation**

Do you sometimes find yourself doing what Simon Peter did – one moment listening to the voice of God (Matt. 16:16), the next moment listening to the voice of Satan? (Matt. 16:22) Remember, although you may not be able to avoid hearing Satan's voice, you can most certainly decide to resist him.

"Be self-controlled and alert. Your enemy the devil prowls around like a roaring lion looking for someone to devour. Resist him, standing firm in the faith ..." (1 Pet. 5:8–9)

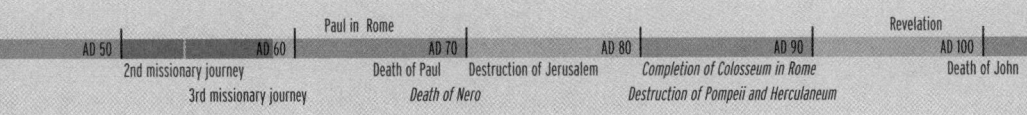

DAY 293

The transfiguration

Peter's declaration
Mark 8:27–30, Luke 9:18–21

Jesus speaks of His suffering and death
Matthew 16:21–23, Mark 8:31–33, Luke 9:22

Jesus speaks about self-denial
Matthew 16:24–28, Mark 8:34–38, 9:1, Luke 9:23–27

The transfiguration
Matthew 17:1–8, Mark 9:2–8, Luke 9:28–36

Question about Elijah
Matthew 17:9–13, Mark 9:9–13

Jesus' ministry of healing and deliverance
Matthew 17:14–21

Luke 9:28–36

[28] About eight days after Jesus said this, he took Peter, John and James with him and went up onto a mountain to pray. [29] As he was praying, the appearance of his face changed, and his clothes became as bright as a flash of lightning. [30] Two men, Moses and Elijah, [31] appeared in glorious splendour, talking with Jesus. They spoke about his departure, which he was about to bring to fulfilment at Jerusalem. [32] Peter and his companions were very sleepy, but when they became fully awake, they saw his glory and the two men standing with him. [33] As the men were leaving Jesus, Peter said to him, "Master, it is good for us to be here. Let us put up three shelters – one for you, one for Moses and one for Elijah." (He did not know what he was saying.) [34] While he was speaking, a cloud appeared and enveloped them, and they were afraid as they entered the cloud. [35] A voice came from the cloud, saying, "This is my Son, whom I have chosen; listen to him." [36] When the voice had spoken, they found that Jesus was alone. ...

For Thought and **Contemplation**

G. Campbell Morgan points out that, according to Luke, Jesus did not go up the mountain to be transfigured – He went up to pray. Prayer was the goal, transfiguration the result. You just cannot predict the outcome of a time of prayer with the Lord. Who knows what will result from your own prayer time today!

"When you pray, go into your room, close the door and pray to your Father, who is unseen. Then your Father, who sees what is done in secret, will reward you." (Matt. 6:6)

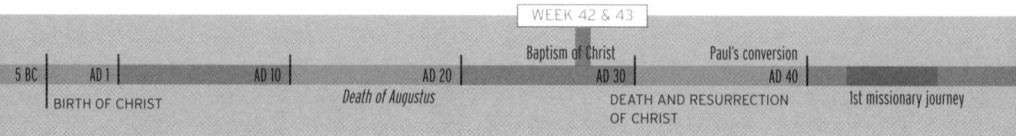

Who's the greatest? — DAY **294**

Mark 9:33–37

³³They came to Capernaum. When he was in the house, he asked them, "What were you arguing about on the road?" ³⁴But they kept quiet because on the way they had argued about who was the greatest.
³⁵Sitting down, Jesus called the Twelve and said, "If anyone wants to be first, he must be the very last, and the servant of all."
³⁶He took a little child and had him stand among them. Taking him in his arms, he said to them, ³⁷"Whoever welcomes one of these little children in my name welcomes me; and whoever welcomes me does not welcome me but the one who sent me."

Jesus' ministry of healing and deliverance
Mark 9:14–29, Luke 9:37–43

Jesus speaks again about His death
Matthew 17:22–23, Mark 9:30–32, Luke 9:44–45

Payment of the Temple tax
Matthew 17:24–27

Who's the greatest?
Matthew 18:1–5, Mark 9:33–37, Luke 9:46–48

Causes of sin
Matthew 18:6–9, Mark 9:42–50

The parable of the lost sheep
Matthew 18:10–14

John is rebuked
Mark 9:38–41, Luke 9:49–50

Teaching on forgiveness and prayer
Matthew 18:15–20

For Thought and **Contemplation**

How do you view spiritual greatness? Being a leader? Lording it over others? That is not greatness; that is smallness. Greatness is the ability to *serve* others, not control them, and that comes only through a right view of God, yourself and others. How much time do you need to spend on improving your "serve"?

"The greatest among you will be your servant. For whoever exalts himself will be humbled, and whoever humbles himself will be exalted." (Matt. 23:11-12)

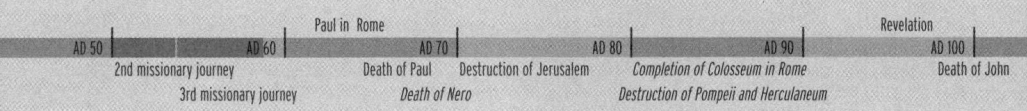

DAY **295** — An unforgiving spirit

The parable of the unforgiving servant
Matthew 18:21–35

Jesus' unbelieving brothers
John 7:1–9

Jesus at the Feast of Tabernacles
John 7:10–13

He teaches in the Temple
John 7:14–31

Guards sent to arrest Him
John 7:32–36

The water of life
John 7:37–39

The dispute
John 7:40–53

The woman caught in adultery
John 8:1–11

The light of the world
John 8:12–20

John 7:37–39

³⁷On the last and greatest day of the Feast, Jesus stood and said in a loud voice, "If anyone is thirsty, let him come to me and drink. ³⁸Whoever believes in me, as the Scripture has said, streams of living water will flow from within him." ³⁹By this he meant the Spirit, whom those who believed in him were later to receive. Up to that time the Spirit had not been given, since Jesus had not yet been glorified.

For Thought and **Contemplation**

One of the most terrible effects of an unforgiving spirit is that it interferes with one's own spiritual assurance. "He who does not offer forgiveness to others," said someone, "destroys the bridge over which God's forgiveness passes to his own heart." Solemn words. Write them on your heart today.

"Be kind and compassionate to one another, forgiving each other, just as in Christ God forgave you." (Eph. 4:32)

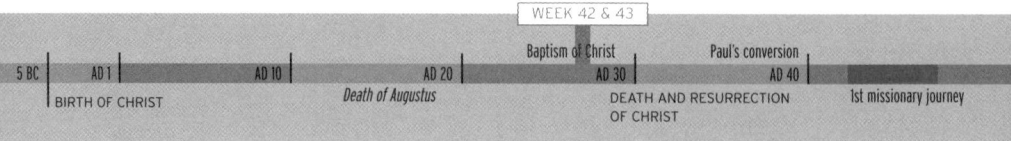

The return of the seventy — DAY **296**

Luke 10:21-24

²¹At that time Jesus, full of joy through the Holy Spirit, said, "I praise you, Father, Lord of heaven and earth, because you have hidden these things from the wise and learned, and revealed them to little children. Yes, Father, for this was your good pleasure.
²²"All things have been committed to me by my Father. No-one knows who the Son is except the Father, and no-one knows who the Father is except the Son and those to whom the Son chooses to reveal him."
²³Then he turned to his disciples and said privately, "Blessed are the eyes that see what you see. ²⁴For I tell you that many prophets and kings wanted to see what you see but did not see it, and to hear what you hear but did not hear it."

Jesus and the Jewish authorities	John 8:21-30
Spiritual freedom	John 8:31-38
Sons of Abraham	John 8:39-41
Children of the devil	John 8:42-47
The claims of Jesus	John 8:48-59
Samaritan opposition	Luke 9:51-56
The cost of following Jesus	Matthew 8:19-22, Luke 9:57-62
Jesus sends out the seventy	Luke 10:1-12
The unbelieving towns	Luke 10:13-16
The return of the seventy	Luke 10:17-20
Jesus' joy	Luke 10:21-24

For Thought and **Contemplation**

What is *your* greatest reason for rejoicing? That your prayers are answered? That devils are subject to you in Jesus' Name? That you are a successful Christian? Our *greatest* reason for rejoicing is the fact that our names are written in heaven (Luke 10:20). Spend as much time as you can today thanking your heavenly Father for this stupendous fact!

"... the rest of my fellow-workers, whose names are in the book of life. Rejoice in the Lord always. I will say it again: Rejoice!" (Phil. 4:3-4)

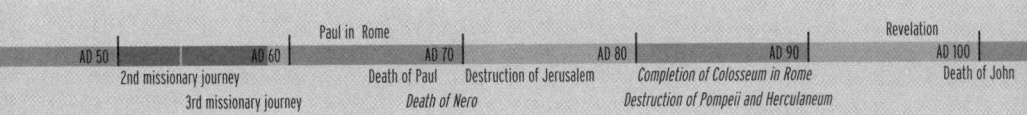

DAY 297 — The Good Shepherd

The parable of the good Samaritan
Luke 10:25–37

Jesus visits Martha and Mary
Luke 10:38–42

The healing of the man born blind
John 9:1–41

The parable of the shepherd
John 10:1–6

Jesus, the Good Shepherd
John 10:7–21

Jesus at the Feast of Dedication
John 10:22–38

Many believe in Him
John 10:39–42

John 10:1–6

¹"I tell you the truth, the man who does not enter the sheep pen by the gate, but climbs in by some other way, is a thief and a robber. ²The man who enters by the gate is the shepherd of his sheep. ³The watchman opens the gate for him, and the sheep listen to his voice. He calls his own sheep by name and leads them out. ⁴When he has brought out all his own, he goes on ahead of them, and his sheep follow him because they know his voice. ⁵But they will never follow a stranger; in fact, they will run away from him because they do not recognise a stranger's voice." ⁶Jesus used this figure of speech, but they did not understand what he was telling them.

For Thought and **Contemplation**

The words, "I am the Good Shepherd", are not a figure of speech; they show that Christ is a loving and concerned protector of His children. Are you overcome with worry and despair? Do you find it difficult to get to sleep at night? Then perhaps, instead of counting sheep, you might try talking to the Shepherd!

"The Lord is my shepherd, I shall not be in want. He makes me lie down in green pastures, he leads me beside quiet waters." (Psa. 23:1–2)

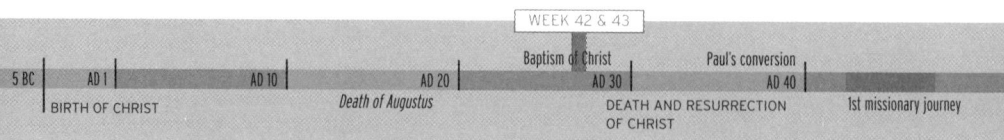

Warnings and encouragements

DAY **298**

Luke 12:4-7

⁴"I tell you, my friends, do not be afraid of those who kill the body and after that can do no more. ⁵But I will show you whom you should fear: Fear him who, after the killing of the body, has power to throw you into hell. Yes, I tell you, fear him. ⁶Are not five sparrows sold for two pennies? Yet not one of them is forgotten by God. ⁷Indeed, the very hairs of your head are all numbered. Don't be afraid; you are worth more than many sparrows."

Jesus' teaching on prayer
Luke 11:1-13

His teaching on Satan's kingdom
Luke 11:14-26

True happiness
Luke 11:27-28

The demand for a miracle
Luke 11:29-32

The light of the body
Luke 11:33-36

Blind guides
Luke 11:37-54

Warning against hypocrisy
Luke 12:1-3

God's care
Luke 12:4-7

Confession or rejection
Luke 12:8-12

The parable of the rich fool
Luke 12:13-21

Trust in God
Luke 12:22-31

Treasure in heaven
Luke 12:32-34

For Thought and **Contemplation**

Recent studies show that millions of people suffer from a low sense of worth. Many feel that they are just names on a computer, or numbers on a card. But in God's sight, every human being is of priceless value. Write out Luke 12:7 on a card and read it at least a dozen times today!

"Your eyes saw my unformed body. All the days ordained for me were written in your book before one of them came to be. How precious to me are your thoughts, O God! How vast is the sum of them!" (Psa. 139:16-17)

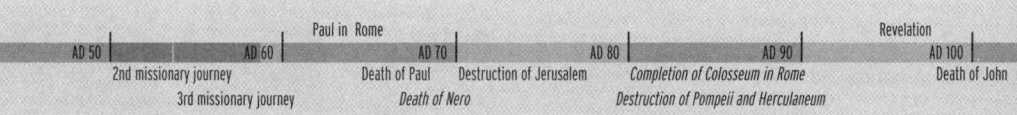

DAY **299**   The kingdom of God

Watchful servants
Luke 12:35–40

Faithful and unfaithful servants
Luke 12:41–48

Jesus, the cause of division
Luke 12:49–53

Interpreting the times
Luke 12:54–59

Repent or perish
Luke 13:1–5

The unfruitful fig tree
Luke 13:6–9

Jesus heals on the Sabbath
Luke 13:10–17

Parables about the kingdom of God
Luke 13:18–21

The narrow door
Luke 13:22–30

Jesus' love for Jerusalem
Luke 13:31–35

Jesus heals a sick man
Luke 14:1–6

Humility and hospitality
Luke 14:7–14

Luke 14:1–6

¹One Sabbath, when Jesus went to eat in the house of a prominent Pharisee, he was being carefully watched. ²There in front of him was a man suffering from dropsy. ³Jesus asked the Pharisees and experts in the law, "Is it lawful to heal on the Sabbath or not?" ⁴But they remained silent. So taking hold of the man, he healed him and sent him away.
⁵Then he asked them, "If one of you has a son or an ox that falls into a well on the Sabbath day, will you not immediately pull him out?" ⁶And they had nothing to say.

For Thought and **Contemplation**

Has it ever occurred to you, as you read the account of Christ's ministry on earth, that He seemed to have little or no concern for His own personal needs? Perhaps it was because, as Hudson Taylor so eloquently said, "God's work done in God's way will never lack God's supply."

"But seek first his kingdom and his righteousness, and all these things will be given to you as well." (Matt. 6:33)

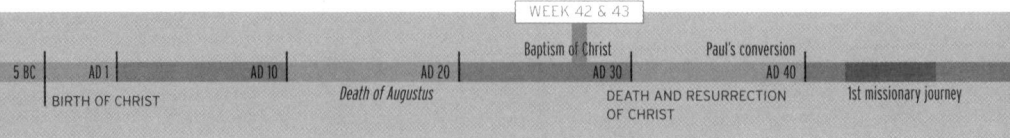

Palestine in the time of Jesus

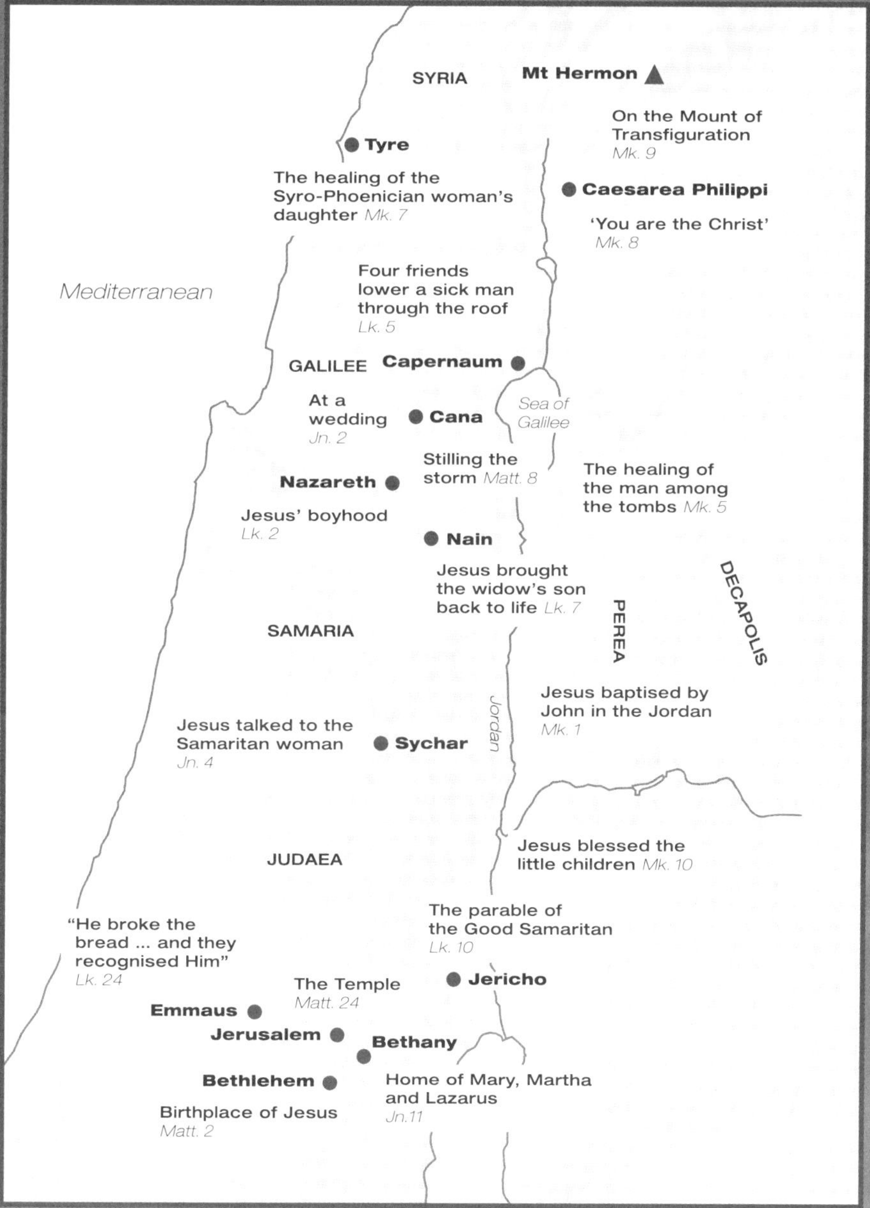

SYRIA

Mt Hermon ▲

Tyre

On the Mount of Transfiguration *Mk. 9*

The healing of the Syro-Phoenician woman's daughter *Mk. 7*

Caesarea Philippi

'You are the Christ' *Mk. 8*

Four friends lower a sick man through the roof *Lk. 5*

Mediterranean

GALILEE   **Capernaum**

At a wedding *Jn. 2*

Cana

Sea of Galilee

Nazareth

Stilling the storm *Matt. 8*

The healing of the man among the tombs *Mk. 5*

Jesus' boyhood *Lk. 2*

Nain

Jesus brought the widow's son back to life *Lk. 7*

PEREA

DECAPOLIS

SAMARIA

Jesus talked to the Samaritan woman *Jn. 4*

Sychar

Jordan

Jesus baptised by John in the Jordan *Mk. 1*

JUDAEA

Jesus blessed the little children *Mk. 10*

"He broke the bread ... and they recognised Him" *Lk. 24*

The parable of the Good Samaritan *Lk. 10*

Emmaus

The Temple *Matt. 24*

Jericho

Jerusalem   **Bethany**

Bethlehem

Home of Mary, Martha and Lazarus *Jn. 11*

Birthplace of Jesus *Matt. 2*

DAY 300 — The challenge of discipleship

The parable of the great banquet
Luke 14:15–24

The cost of discipleship
Luke 14:25–35

The lost sheep
Luke 15:1–7

The lost coin
Luke 15:8–10

The lost son
Luke 15:11–32

The unjust steward
Luke 16:1–13

More teaching
Luke 16:14–18

The rich man and Lazarus
Luke 16:19–31

Luke 14:25–29, 33–35

²⁵Large crowds were travelling with Jesus, and turning to them he said: ²⁶"If anyone comes to me and does not hate his father and mother, his wife and children, his brothers and sisters – yes, even his own life – he cannot be my disciple. ²⁷And anyone who does not carry his cross and follow me cannot be my disciple.

²⁸"Suppose one of you wants to build a tower. Will he not first sit down and estimate the cost to see if he has enough money to complete it? ²⁹For if he lays the foundation and is not able to finish it, everyone who sees it will ridicule him ... ³³In the same way, any of you who does not give up everything he has cannot be my disciple.

³⁴"Salt is good, but if it loses its saltiness, how can it be made salty again? ³⁵It is fit neither for the soil nor for the manure heap; it is thrown out.

"He who has ears to hear, let him hear."

For Thought and **Contemplation**

The Christian Church is desperately in need of a new definition of discipleship. The word has become smudged and discoloured through years of misuse. Read again the meaning of discipleship as presented by Christ in Luke 14:25–35 and ask yourself: Am I truly His disciple?

"... if anyone obeys his word, God's love is truly made complete in him. This is how we know we are in him: Whoever claims to live in him must walk as Jesus did." (1 Jn 2:5–6)

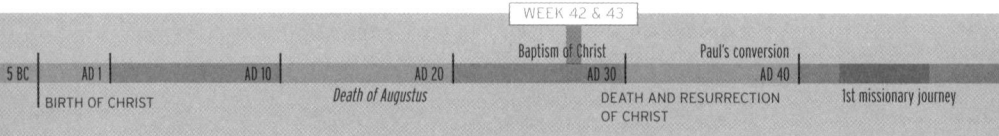

The resurrection and the life

DAY **301**

John 11:17–27

[17]On his arrival, Jesus found that Lazarus had already been in the tomb for four days. [18]Bethany was less than two miles from Jerusalem, [19]and many Jews had come to Martha and Mary to comfort them in the loss of their brother. [20]When Martha heard that Jesus was coming, she went out to meet him, but Mary stayed at home.
[21]"Lord," Martha said to Jesus, "if you had been here, my brother would not have died. [22]But I know that even now God will give you whatever you ask."
[23]Jesus said to her, "Your brother will rise again."
[24]Martha answered, "I know he will rise again in the resurrection at the last day."
[25]Jesus said to her, "I am the resurrection and the life. He who believes in me will live, even though he dies; [26]and whoever lives and believes in me will never die. Do you believe this?"
[27]"Yes, Lord," she told him, "I believe that you are the Christ, the Son of God, who was to come into the world."

The unprofitable servant
Luke 17:1–10

The death of Lazarus
John 11:1–16

Jesus the resurrection and the life
John 11:17–27

Jesus weeps
John 11:28–37

The raising of Lazarus
John 11:38–44

The plot against Jesus
John 11:45–53

Jesus goes to Ephraim
John 11:54

The healing of the ten lepers
Luke 17:11–19

The coming of the kingdom of God
Luke 17:20–37

For Thought and **Contemplation**

Have you ever realised that Jesus did not say, "I am the resurrection and the life" after He rose from the dead, but prior to it? What does this imply? It implies that Jesus was not the Resurrection because He rose from the dead, but He rose from the dead because He was the Resurrection.

"And if the Spirit of him who raised Jesus from the dead is living in you, he who raised Christ from the dead will also give life to your mortal bodies through his Spirit, who lives in you." (Rom. 8:11)

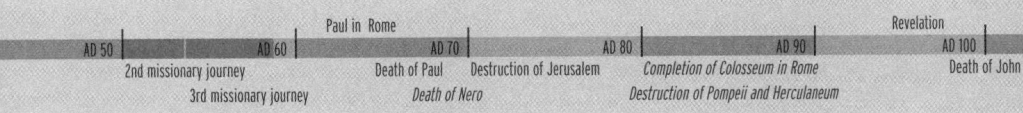

DAY 302

Jesus and divorce

The parable of the persistent widow
Luke 18:1–8

The parable of the Pharisee and the tax collector
Luke 18:9–14

Jesus' teaching about divorce
Matthew 19:1–12, Mark 10:1–12

He blesses little children
Matthew 19:13–15, Mark 10:13–16, Luke 18:15–17

The rich young ruler
Matthew 19:16–30, Mark 10:17–31

Mark 10:2–12
²Some Pharisees came and tested him by asking, "Is it lawful for a man to divorce his wife?"
³"What did Moses command you?" he replied.
⁴They said, "Moses permitted a man to write a certificate of divorce and send her away."
⁵"It was because your hearts were hard that Moses wrote you this law," Jesus replied. ⁶"But at the beginning of creation God 'made them male and female.' ⁷'For this reason a man will leave his father and mother and be united to his wife, ⁸and the two will become one flesh.' So they are no longer two, but one. ⁹Therefore what God has joined together, let man not separate."
¹⁰When they were in the house again, the disciples asked Jesus about this. ¹¹He answered, "Anyone who divorces his wife and marries another woman commits adultery against her. ¹²And if she divorces her husband and marries another man, she commits adultery."

For Thought and **Contemplation**

How do you feel about divorce? God says in the Old Testament that He *hates* it (Mal. 2:16). Britain has a reputation of having one of the highest divorce rates in Europe. Spend a few minutes in prayer today asking God what He would have you do to help stop the break-up of homes and families.

"... God was reconciling the world to himself in Christ, not counting men's sins against them. And he has committed to us the message of reconciliation." (2 Cor. 5:19)

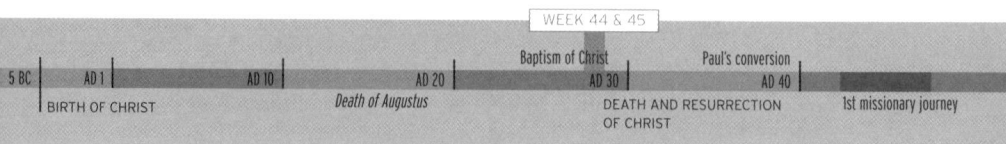

The over-ambitious disciples

DAY 303

Mark 10:35-40, 43-45

35 Then James and John, the sons of Zebedee, came to him. "Teacher," they said, "we want you to do for us whatever we ask."
36 "What do you want me to do for you?" he asked.
37 They replied, "Let one of us sit at your right and the other at your left in your glory."
38 "You don't know what you are asking," Jesus said. "Can you drink the cup I drink or be baptised with the baptism I am baptised with?"
39 "We can," they answered.
Jesus said to them, "You will drink the cup I drink and be baptised with the baptism I am baptised with, 40 but to sit at my right or left is not for me to grant. These places belong to those for whom they have been prepared." ...
43 "Not so with you. Instead, whoever wants to become great among you must be your servant, 44 and whoever wants to be first must be slave of all. 45 For even the Son of Man did not come to be served, but to serve, and to give his life as a ransom for many."

The rich young ruler
Luke 18:18-30

The parable of the workers in the vineyard
Matthew 20:1-16

Jesus speaks of the crucifixion
Matthew 20:17-19, Mark 10:32-34, Luke 18:31-34

The ambition of James and John
Matthew 20:20-28, Mark 10:35-45

The two blind men healed
Matthew 20:29-34

Blind Bartimaeus is healed
Mark 10:46-52, Luke 18:35-43

For Thought and **Contemplation**

How did Jesus deal with problem people in His life, such as His over-ambitious disciples? He turned every problem into a possibility by using it as an opportunity to drive home some new and vital spiritual truth. Put this principle to work in your own life, and it will mean all the difference between success and failure in your relationships.

"A man finds joy in giving an apt reply – and how good is a timely word!" (Prov. 15:23)

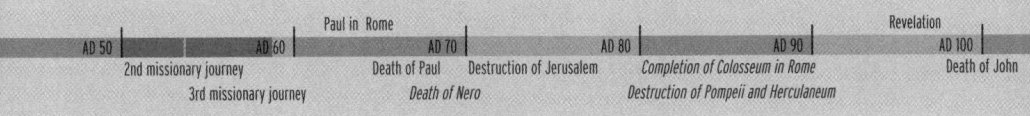

DAY **304**

The triumphal entry

The conversion of Zacchaeus
Luke 19:1–10

The parable of the gold coins
Luke 19:11–27

Jesus arrives at Bethany
John 11:55–57, 12:1

The plot against Lazarus
John 12:9–11

Jesus is anointed at Bethany
John 12:2–8

The triumphant entry into Jerusalem
Matthew 21:1–11, Mark 11:1–11, Luke 19:28–44, John 12:12–19

John 12:12–18

[12] The next day the great crowd that had come for the Feast heard that Jesus was on his way to Jerusalem. [13] They took palm branches and went out to meet him, shouting,
"Hosanna!"
"Blessed is he who comes in the name of the Lord!"
"Blessed is the King of Israel!"
[14] Jesus found a young donkey and sat upon it, as it is written,
[15] "Do not be afraid, O Daughter of Zion;
see, your king is coming,
seated on a donkey's colt."
[16] At first his disciples did not understand all this. Only after Jesus was glorified did they realise that these things had been written about him and that they had done these things to him.
[17] Now the crowd that was with him when he called Lazarus from the tomb and raised him from the dead continued to spread the word. [18] Many people, because they had heard that he had given this miraculous sign, went out to meet him.

For Thought and **Contemplation**

Human nature is such that, on one day, it can receive Christ with palms and rejoicing, and the next day send Him to a cross. Multitudes of people admire Christ, but few become consistent disciples. How about you? Are you just one of Christ's admirers – or a true disciple?

"Dear children, let us not love with words or tongue but with actions and in truth." (1 Jn. 3:18)

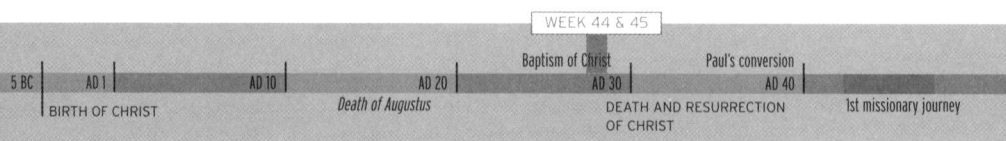

Jesus' authority

DAY 305

Matthew 21:23–27

²³Jesus entered the temple courts, and, while he was teaching, the chief priests and the elders of the people came to him. "By what authority are you doing these things?" they asked. "And who gave you this authority?"

²⁴Jesus replied, "I will also ask you one question. If you answer me, I will tell you by what authority I am doing these things. ²⁵John's baptism – where did it come from? Was it from heaven, or from men?"

They discussed it among themselves and said, "If we say, 'From heaven,' he will ask, 'Then why didn't you believe him?' ²⁶But if we say, 'From men' – we are afraid of the people, for they all hold that John was a prophet."

²⁷So they answered Jesus, "We don't know."

Then he said, "Neither will I tell you by what authority I am doing these things."

Second cleansing of Temple	Matthew 21:12–17, Mark 11:15–19, Luke 19:45–48
Cursing of the fig tree	Matthew 21:18–19, Mark 11:12–14
The fig tree withers	Matthew 21:20–22, Mark 11:20–25
Jesus' authority is challenged	Matthew 21:23–27, Mark 11:27–33, Luke 20:1–8
The parable of the two sons	Matthew 21:28–32
The parable of the wicked tenants	Matthew 21:33–46, Mark 12:1–12, Luke 20:9–19

For Thought and **Contemplation**

The authority of Christ is still questioned today – even by Christians! Someone has said there are usually three reactions given to Christ's words – inattention, irritation or instant obedience. Which of these three reactions is characteristic of your response to Christ's words?

"Whoever has my commands and obeys them, he is the one who loves me. He who loves me will be loved by my Father, and I too will love him and show myself to him." (John 14:21)

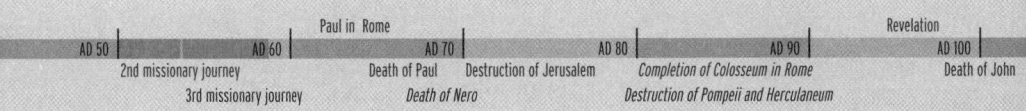

Heart to Heart

Section 10

The wonderful Person of Jesus shines out of the Gospels to heal the sick, comfort the hurt, seek the lost and encourage the faint hearted. You are not just reading about a historical figure but a living Person because Jesus is alive Yesterday, Today and Forever. Praise the name of Jesus.

In this section

Jesus' final week
His trial and crucifixion
The resurrection appearances
The power of Pentecost
Persecution and progress
Paul's founding of new churches

DAY 306 — Jesus silences the opposition

Parable of the wedding feast
Matthew 22:1–14

Jesus is questioned: about paying taxes
Matthew 22:15–22, Mark 12:13–17, Luke 20:20–26

Jesus is questioned: about the resurrection
Matthew 22:23–33, Mark 12:18–27, Luke 20:27–38

Jesus is questioned: about the greatest commandment
Matthew 22:34–40, Mark 12:28–34, Luke 20:39–40

Jesus asks a question
Matthew 22:41–46, Mark 12:35–37, Luke 20:41–44

Mark 12:28–34
[28]One of the teachers of the law came and heard them debating. Noticing that Jesus had given them a good answer, he asked him, "Of all the commandments, which is the most important?" [29]"The most important one," answered Jesus, "is this: 'Hear, O Israel, the Lord our God, the Lord is one. [30]Love the Lord your God with all your heart and with all your soul and with all your mind and with all your strength.' [31]The second is this: 'Love your neighbour as yourself.' There is no commandment greater than these." [32]"Well said, teacher," the man replied. "You are right in saying that God is one and there is no other but him. [33]To love him with all your heart, with all your understanding and with all your strength, and to love your neighbour as yourself is more important than all burnt offerings and sacrifices." [34]When Jesus saw that he had answered wisely, he said to him, "You are not far from the kingdom of God." And from then on no-one dared ask him any more questions.

For Thought and Contemplation

One of the things that contributes to inner conflict in our hearts is the fact that, while we are big enough to ask questions, we are often not big enough to understand the answers. Every question will be answered in eternity. If you can hold on to that in the midst of your perplexity, then you will have discovered one of the greatest secrets of effective Christian living.

"Now we see but a poor reflection as in a mirror; then we shall see face to face. Now I know in part; then I shall know fully, even as I am fully known." (1 Cor. 13:12)

a bird's eye view of Mark

Place in the Bible	Written by:	Special Features
Second New Testament book; second Gospel.	Mark.	Mark may be the shortest Gospel but it is the most action-packed one. It leaves the reader almost breathless, with the word "immediately" coming over forty times, as Mark moves in rapid succession from one event to the next, painting his portrait of Jesus.

Signs of the end

DAY 307

Matthew 24:36-44

³⁶"No-one knows about that day or hour, not even the angels in heaven, nor the Son, but only the Father. ³⁷As it was in the days of Noah, so it will be at the coming of the Son of Man. ³⁸For in the days before the flood, people were eating and drinking, marrying and giving in marriage, up to the day Noah entered the ark; ³⁹and they knew nothing about what would happen until the flood came and took them all away. That is how it will be at the coming of the Son of Man. ⁴⁰Two men will be in the field; one will be taken and the other left. ⁴¹Two women will be grinding with a hand mill; one will be taken and the other left.

⁴²"Therefore keep watch, because you do not know on what day your Lord will come. ⁴³But understand this: If the owner of the house had known at what time of night the thief was coming, he would have kept watch and would not have let his house be broken into. ⁴⁴So you also must be ready, because the Son of Man will come at an hour when you do not expect him."

Jesus denounces the scribes and Pharisees	Matthew 23:1-32, Mark 12:38-40, Luke 20:45-47
Jesus prophesies judgment	Matthew 23:33-36
His lament over Jerusalem	Matthew 23:37-39
The widow's mite	Mark 12:41-44, Luke 21:1-4
The Temple to be destroyed	Matthew 24:1-2
Signs of the end times	Matthew 24:3-31
The parable of the fig tree	Matthew 24:32-35
The coming of the Son of Man	Matthew 24:36-51

For Thought and **Contemplation**

We ought not to forget that the whole point and purpose of prophecy is not only to remind us that Christ is coming, but to remind us that we ought to be *ready* to meet Him. Some Christians regard Christ's second coming as just another doctrinal fact; others regard it as the hope of their existence. What does this truth do for you?

"He who testifies to these things says, 'Yes, I am coming soon.' Amen, Come, Lord Jesus." (Rev. 22:20)

Jesus and the Book

Mark depicts Jesus Christ as both the Son of God ("The beginning of the gospel about Jesus Christ, the Son of God." 1:1), and (in 14 places) the Son of Man who shows his compassion for people (6:34), and can be deeply moved and troubled (14:33).

Teaching

Mark shows Jesus to be the Servant, who gives his life in teaching, healing and caring for others, who is the suffering Servant who dies on the cross, and who calls His followers to be servants in their Master's service.

A Verse to Remember

"The Son of Man did not come to be served, but to serve, and to give his life as a ransom for many'" (Mark 10:45).

DAY **308**

Watch and pray

The destruction of the Temple
Mark 13:1–2, Luke 21:5–6

Events of the end times
Mark 13:3–27, Luke 21:7–28

Parable of the fig tree
Mark 13:28–31, Luke 21:29–33

Warning to be ready
Mark 13:32–37, Luke 21:34–36

Jesus teaches in the Temple
Luke 21:37–38

Parable of the wise and foolish virgins
Matthew 25:1–13

Parable of the talents
Matthew 25:14–30

Luke 21:34–38

³⁴"Be careful, or your hearts will be weighed down with dissipation, drunkenness and the anxieties of life, and that day will close on you unexpectedly like a trap. ³⁵For it will come upon all those who live on the face of the whole earth. ³⁶Be always on the watch, and pray that you may be able to escape all that is about to happen, and that you may be able to stand before the Son of Man."
³⁷Each day Jesus was teaching at the temple, and each evening he went out to spend the night on the hill called the Mount of Olives, ³⁸and all the people came early in the morning to hear him at the temple.

For Thought and **Contemplation**

Ready for a challenge? Then take a pen and a sheet of paper and write down the answers to these two questions. How many talents has God given you? What are you doing with them? In thinking about it, don't forget this point – what you don't *use*, you *lose*.

"... in Christ we who are many form one body, and each member belongs to all the others. We have different gifts, according to the grace given us. ..."
(Rom 12:5–6)

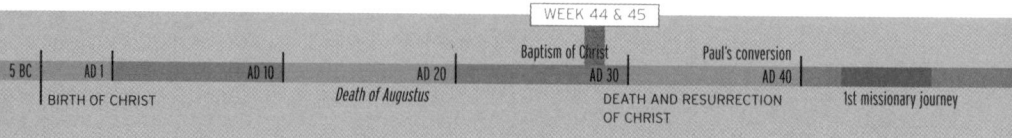

The corn of wheat — DAY **309**

Mark 14:3-9

³While he was in Bethany, reclining at the table in the home of a man known as Simon the Leper, a woman came with an alabaster jar of very expensive perfume, made of pure nard. She broke the jar and poured the perfume on his head.

⁴Some of those present were saying indignantly to one another, "Why this waste of perfume? ⁵It could have been sold for more than a year's wages and the money given to the poor." And they rebuked her harshly.

⁶"Leave her alone," said Jesus. "Why are you bothering her? She has done a beautiful thing to me. ⁷The poor you will always have with you, and you can help them any time you want. But you will not always have me. ⁸She did what she could. She poured perfume on my body beforehand to prepare for my burial. ⁹I tell you the truth, wherever the gospel is preached throughout the world, what she has done will also be told, in memory of her."

The sheep and the goats
Matthew 25:31–46

The plot against Jesus
Matthew 26:1–5, Mark 14:1–2, Luke 22:1–2

Mary anoints Jesus
Matthew 26:6–13, Mark 14:3–9

Judas turns traitor
Matthew 26:14–16, Mark 14:10–11, Luke 22:3–6

Gentiles desire to see Jesus
John 12:20–36

The Jews reject Him
John 12:37–43

Jesus, the Light of the world
John 12:44–50

Preparation for the Passover
Matthew 26:17–19, Mark 14:12–16, Luke 22:7–13

For Thought and **Contemplation**

The last few days of Christ's earthly life occupy more space in the Gospels than any other comparable stage of His ministry. If God regards this period as so significant, should not we? Ask God to help you "enter into His sufferings", as once again you walk the path that leads to Calvary.

"If we endure, we will also reign with him. If we disown him, he will also disown us; if we are faithless, he will remain faithful ..." (2 Tim. 2:12-13)

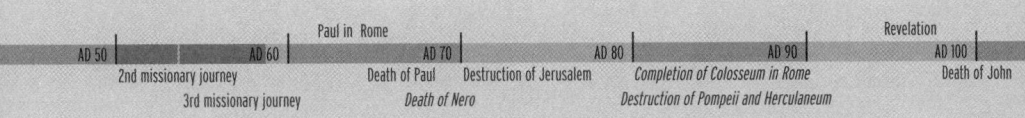

DAY **310** — The Last Supper

Jesus identifies the betrayer
Matthew 26:20–25, Mark 14:17–21, John 13:18–30

Jesus' new commandment
John 13:31–35

He institutes the Lord's Supper
Matthew 26:26–29, Mark 14:22–25, Luke 22:14–23, 1 Corinthians 11:23–26

The disciples' argument
Luke 22:24–30

Jesus washes the disciples' feet
John 13:1–17

He foretells Peter's denial
Matthew 26:31–35, Mark 14:27–31, Luke 22:31–38, John 13:36–38

Luke 22:14-20

¹⁴When the hour came, Jesus and his apostles reclined at the table. ¹⁵And he said to them, "I have eagerly desired to eat this Passover with you before I suffer. ¹⁶For I tell you, I will not eat it again until it finds fulfilment in the kingdom of God."

¹⁷After taking the cup, he gave thanks and said, "Take this and divide it among you. ¹⁸For I tell you I will not drink again of the fruit of the vine until the kingdom of God comes."

¹⁹And he took bread, gave thanks and broke it, and gave it to them, saying, "This is my body given for you; do this in remembrance of me."

²⁰In the same way, after the supper he took the cup, saying, "This cup is the new covenant in my blood, which is poured out for you. ..."

For Thought and **Contemplation**

As you see Christ washing His disciples' feet, or taking the bread into His hands and breaking it – what does it say to you? Is it not saying that the greatest lessons in life are taught, not by words, but by actions? Is your witness for Christ merely by words – or is it also by deeds?

"In the same way, faith by itself, if it is not accompanied by action, is dead." (Jas. 2:17)

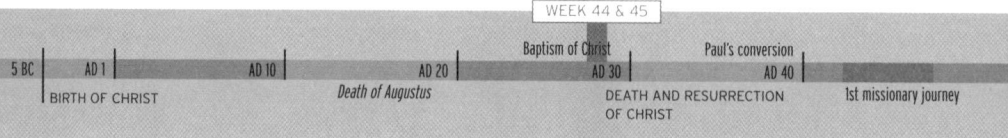

Old Testament
people and places mentioned by Christ

Old Testament reference	Event	New Testament reference
Genesis 1:27; 2:23–24	Creation of Adam and Eve	Mark 10:6–8
Genesis 4:10	Murder of Abel	Luke 11:51
Genesis 6:5–13	Corruption of Noah's day and flood	Luke 17:26,27
Genesis 18:20; 19:24	Corruption of Lot's day and the fire	Luke 17:28,29
Genesis 19:26	Worldliness of Lot's wife	Luke 17:32
Exodus 3:1–6	Moses and the burning bush	Luke 20:37
Exodus 16:15	Moses and the heavenly manna	John 6:31
Numbers 21:8	Moses and the brazen serpent	John 3:14
1 Samuel 21:6	David and the consecrated bread	Matthew 12:3,4
1 Kings 10:1	Solomon and the Queen of Sheba	Matthew 12:42
1 Kings 17:1,9	Elijah, the widow and the famine	Luke 4:25,26
2 Kings 5	Naaman and his leprosy	Luke 4:27
2 Chronicles 24:20,21	The murder of Zechariah	Luke 11:51
Daniel 9:27; 11:31; 12:11	Daniel and the abomination of desolation	Matthew 24:15
Jonah 1:17	Jonah and the fish	Matthew 12:40;16:4
Jonah 3:4–10	The repentance of Nineveh	Luke 11:30; Matthew 12:41

DAY 311 — Jesus comforts His disciples

Jesus, the Way to the Father
John 14:1–14

The promise of the Holy Spirit
John 14:15–31

The true vine
John 15:1–17

Warning about persecution
John 15:18–27, 16:1–4

Jesus teaches about the Comforter
John 16:5–15

He speaks about the Father
John 16:16–28

The disciples' response
John 16:29–30

Jesus promises peace
John 16:31–33

John 16:5–15

⁵"Now I am going to him who sent me, yet none of you asks me, 'Where are you going?' ⁶Because I have said these things, you are filled with grief. ⁷But I tell you the truth: It is for your good that I am going away. Unless I go away, the Counsellor will not come to you; but if I go, I will send him to you. ⁸When he comes, he will convict the world of guilt in regard to sin and righteousness and judgment: ⁹in regard to sin, because men do not believe in me; ¹⁰in regard to righteousness, because I am going to the Father, where you can see me no longer; ¹¹and in regard to judgment, because the prince of this world now stands condemned.

¹²"I have much more to say to you, more than you can now bear. ¹³But when he, the Spirit of truth, comes, he will guide you into all truth. He will not speak on his own; he will speak only what he hears, and he will tell you what is yet to come. ¹⁴He will bring glory to me by taking from what is mine and making it known to you. ¹⁵All that belongs to the Father is mine. ..."

For Thought and Contemplation

Have you ever wondered just how the Holy Spirit goes about comforting us in our trials and difficulties? He follows the model laid down for Him by Christ in John 14. Spend a few moments focusing on how Christ comforted His disciples in this matchless chapter – then compare it with the way the Spirit ministers that selfsame comfort in your heart and life.

"... who comforts us in all our troubles, so that we can comfort those in any trouble with the comfort we ourselves have received from God." (2 Cor. 1:4)

a bird's eye view of John

Place in the Bible	**Written by:**	**Special Features**
Fourth New Testament book; fourth Gospel.	John.	John constantly brings out the meaning of the events in Jesus' life he is describing. John records none of Jesus' parables and carefully chooses from Jesus' numerous miracles seven "signs" which reveal who Jesus Christ really is – the Son of the living God (11:27).

The darkest hour

DAY **312**

John 17:20–26

²⁰"My prayer is not for them alone. I pray also for those who will believe in me through their message, ²¹that all of them may be one, Father, just as you are in me and I am in you. May they also be in us so that the world may believe that you have sent me. ²²I have given them the glory that you gave me, that they may be one as we are one: ²³I in them and you in me. May they be brought to complete unity to let the world know that you sent me and have loved them even as you have loved me.
²⁴"Father, I want those you have given me to be with me where I am, and to see my glory, the glory you have given me because you loved me before the creation of the world.
²⁵"Righteous Father, though the world does not know you, I know you, and they know that you have sent me. ²⁶I have made you known to them, and will continue to make you known in order that the love you have for me may be in them and that I myself may be in them."

Jesus prays for Himself	John 17:1–5
He prays for His disciples	John 17:6–19
He prays for the unity of all Christians	John 17:20–26
In the garden of Gethsemane	Matthew 26:30, 36–46, Mark 14:26, 32–42, Luke 22:39–46, John 18:1
Jesus is betrayed and arrested	Matthew 26:47–55, Mark 14:43–49, Luke 22:47–53, John 18:2–11
The disciples desert Him	Matthew 26:56, Mark 14:50–52

For Thought and **Contemplation**

The great preacher Robert McCheyne once said: "If I could hear Christ praying for me in the next room, I would not fear a million enemies." Listen! He *is* praying for you – *now*. Not in the next room maybe, but before the Throne. Be assured of this – the distance makes no difference!

"Therefore he is able to save completely those who come to God through him, because he always lives to intercede for them." (Heb. 7:25)

Jesus and the Book

John shows that Jesus Christ is God in Jesus' eight "I am" statements.

Teaching

John's aim is in ch. 20:31, "But these are written that you may believe that Jesus is the Christ, the Son of God, and that by believing you may have life in his name." John highlights people's reactions to Jesus Christ – they responded in faith or rejected Him.

A Verse to Remember

"'For God so loved the world that he gave his one and only Son, that whoever believes in him shall not perish but have eternal life'" (John 3:16).

DAY **313**

Trial by the Jews

Jesus before Annas and Caiaphas
John 18:12–14, 19–23

His trial before the Sanhedrin
Matthew 26:57, 59–66, Mark 14:53, 55–64, Luke 22:54, John 18:24

He is mocked and spat on
Matthew 26:67–68, Mark 14:65, Luke 22:63–65

Peter's denial
Matthew 26:58, 69–75, Mark 14:54, 66–72, Luke 22:55–62, John 18:15–18, 25–27

Jesus is condemned
Matthew 27:1–2, Mark 15:1, Luke 22:66–71

Judas' remorse
Matthew 27:3–10, Acts 1:18–19

Matthew 26:59–65

⁵⁹The chief priests and the whole Sanhedrin were looking for false evidence against Jesus so that they could put him to death. ⁶⁰But they did not find any, though many false witnesses came forward.

Finally two came forward ⁶¹and declared, "This fellow said, 'I am able to destroy the temple of God and rebuild it in three days.'"

⁶²Then the high priest stood up and said to Jesus, "Are you not going to answer? What is this testimony that these men are bringing against you?" ⁶³But Jesus remained silent.

The high priest said to him, "I charge you under oath by the living God: Tell us if you are the Christ, the Son of God."

⁶⁴"Yes, it is as you say," Jesus replied. "But I say to all of you: In the future you will see the Son of Man sitting at the right hand of the Mighty One and coming on the clouds of heaven."

⁶⁵Then the high priest tore his clothes and said, "He has spoken blasphemy! Why do we need any more witnesses? Look, now you have heard the blasphemy."

For Thought and **Contemplation**

How amazing that the Son of God, equipped as He was with the power to extricate Himself from difficult situations, chose instead to suffer them. And why? Because as William Penn puts it: "No pain, no palm; no thorns, no throne; no gall, no glory; no cross, no crown."

"... 'If anyone would come after me, he must deny himself and take up his cross and follow me. For whoever wants to save his life will lose it, but whoever loses his life for me will find it.'" (Matt. 16:24–25)

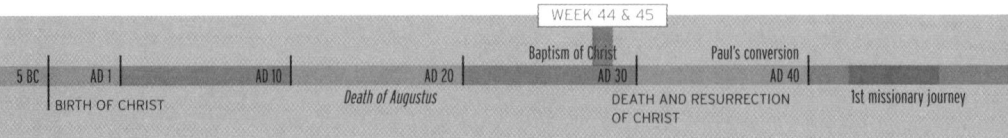

His trial before Pilate

DAY **314**

Matthew 27:11–14

¹¹Meanwhile Jesus stood before the governor, and the governor asked him, "Are you the king of the Jews?"
"Yes, it is as you say," Jesus replied.
¹²When he was accused by the chief priests and the elders, he gave no answer. ¹³Then Pilate asked him, "Don't you hear the testimony they are bringing against you?" ¹⁴But Jesus made no reply, not even to a single charge – to the great amazement of the governor.

Jesus is sent to Pilate
Matthew 27:11–14, Mark 15:2–5,
Luke 23:1–5, John 18:28–38

Herod questions Jesus
Luke 23:6–10

He is sent back to Pilate
Luke 23:11–12

**Barabbas is released,
Jesus is flogged**
Matthew 27:15–26, Mark 15:6–15,
Luke 23:13–25, John 18:39–40, 19:1

Pilate's soldiers mock Jesus
Matthew 27:27–31, Mark 15:16–19,
John 19:2–3

Pilate seeks to release Jesus
John 19:4–12

Pilate's final sentence
John 19:13–16

For Thought and **Contemplation**

The apostle Paul tells us that when Christ stood before Pontius Pilate, He "made the good confession" (1 Tim. 6:13). What does that mean? This: Christ would not allow the actions of Pilate to determine His. He acted, rather than reacted. He *resolved* to remain silent. He *resolved* to go on loving. When we act rather than react to life, then we do as Jesus did – we "make a good confession".

"Whoever acknowledges me before men, I will also acknowledge him before my Father in heaven."
(Matt. 10:32)

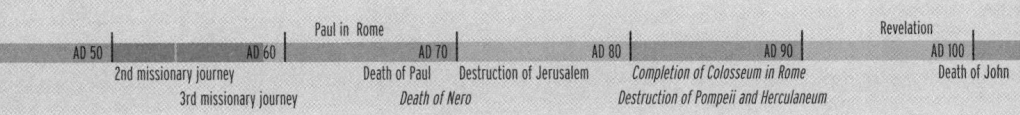

DAY 315 — The Death of Jesus

Jesus' walk to Golgotha
Matthew 27:32–34, Mark 15:20–23,
Luke 23:26–32, John 19:17

Jesus is crucified
Matthew 27:35–44, Mark 15:24–32,
Luke 23:33–43, John 19:18–27

Three hours of darkness
Matthew 27:45–49, Mark 15:33–36,
Luke 23:44–45, John 19:28–29

The death of Jesus AD 29

The death of Jesus
Matthew 27:50, Mark 15:37,
Luke 23:46, John 19:30

His side is pierced
John 19:31–37

Miraculous events at Jesus' death
Matthew 27:51–56, Mark 15:38–41,
Luke 23:47–49

John 19:31–37

³¹Now it was the day of Preparation, and the next day was to be a special Sabbath. Because the Jews did not want the bodies left on the crosses during the Sabbath, they asked Pilate to have the legs broken and the bodies taken down. ³²The soldiers therefore came and broke the legs of the first man who had been crucified with Jesus, and then those of the other. ³³But when they came to Jesus and found that he was already dead, they did not break his legs. ³⁴Instead, one of the soldiers pierced Jesus' side with a spear, bringing a sudden flow of blood and water. ³⁵The man who saw it has given testimony, and his testimony is true. He knows that he tells the truth, and he testifies so that you also may believe. ³⁶These things happened so that the scripture would be fulfilled: "Not one of his bones will be broken," ³⁷and, as another scripture says, "They will look on the one they have pierced."

For Thought and **Contemplation**

No more fitting comment can be found for today's reading than the words which appear on the gravestone of an old Welsh preacher:

*"Had Christ the death of death to death
Not given death by dying,
The gates of life had never been
To mortals open lying."*

"For since death came through a man, the resurrection of the dead comes also through a man. For as in Adam all die, so in Christ all will be made alive." (1 Cor. 15:21–22)

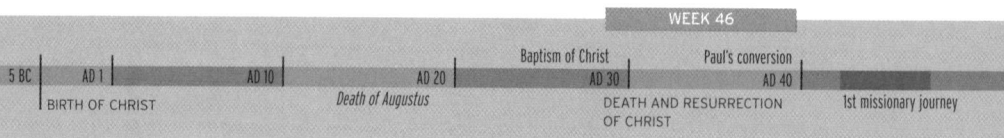

The Resurrection

DAY **316**

John 20:10–17

¹⁰Then the disciples went back to their homes, ¹¹but Mary stood outside the tomb crying. As she wept, she bent over to look into the tomb ¹²and saw two angels in white, seated where Jesus' body had been, one at the head and the other at the foot.
¹³They asked her, "Woman, why are you crying?"
"They have taken my Lord away," she said, "and I don't know where they have put him." ¹⁴At this, she turned round and saw Jesus standing there, but she did not realise that it was Jesus.
¹⁵"Woman," he said, "why are you crying? Who is it you are looking for?"
Thinking he was the gardener, she said, "Sir, if you have carried him away, tell me where you have put him, and I will get him."
¹⁶Jesus said to her, "Mary."
She turned towards him and cried out in Aramaic, "Rabboni!" (which means Teacher).
¹⁷Jesus said, "Do not hold on to me, for I have not yet returned to the Father. Go instead to my brothers and tell them, 'I am returning to my Father ...'"

Jesus' body laid in the tomb
Matthew 27:57–61, Mark 15:42–47, Luke 23:50–56, John 19:38–42

Soldiers put on guard
Matthew 27:62–66

The women visit the tomb
Matthew 28:1–4, Mark 16:1–4, Luke 24:1–2, John 20:1

The angels' message
Matthew 28:5–8, Mark 16:5–8, Luke 24:3–8

Peter and John go to the tomb
Luke 24:9–12, John 20:2–9

Jesus appears to Mary Magdalene
Mark 16:9–11, John 20:10–18

He appears to other women
Matthew 28:9–10

The soldiers are bribed
Matthew 28:11–15

For Thought and **Contemplation**

Perhaps the most important, yet not widely recognised, fact about Joseph's tomb is that it wasn't a tomb at all; it was a room which the everlasting Christ used for a few nights on His way back to glory. As H.R.L. Sheppard put it: "It was inevitable that Christ should die; it was also inevitable He should rise again. *We could expect nothing less of God.*"

"'Where, O death, is your victory? Where, O death, is your sting?'" (1 Cor. 15:55)

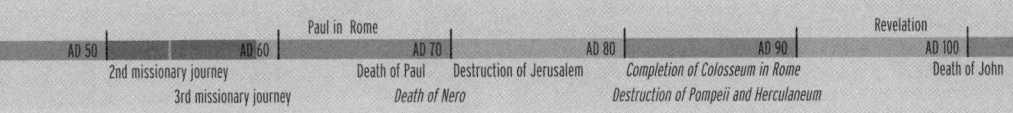

Ten resurrection appearances

First day

1. **To Mary Magdalene in the garden**
   Mk. 16:9; Jn. 20:11–18

2. **To the women returning from the tomb**
   Matt. 28:9–10

3. **To two disciples on the Emmaus Road**
   Lk. 24:13–32; Mk. 16:12–13

4. **To Peter in Jerusalem**
   Lk. 24:34; 1 Cor. 15:5

5. **To ten of His apostles in the upper room**
   Lk. 24:36–43; Jn. 20:19–23

Remaining 40 Days

6. **To the eleven in the upper room**
   Jn. 20:24–29

7. **To seven apostles by the Sea of Galilee**
   John 21:1–24

8. **To the eleven and 500 believers on Mount Tabor**
   Mt. 28:16–20; 1 Cor. 15:6

9. **To the eleven and James, Jesus' half-brother, in Jerusalem**
   Mk. 16:14–18; Lk. 24:44–49; 1 Cor. 15:7

10. **To the eleven on the Mount of Olives**
    Lk. 24:50–53

Jesus appears to many

DAY 317

John 20:24-29

²⁴Now Thomas (called Didymus), one of the Twelve, was not with the disciples when Jesus came. ²⁵So the other disciples told him, "We have seen the Lord!"

But he said to them, "Unless I see the nail marks in his hands and put my finger where the nails were, and put my hand into his side, I will not believe it."

²⁶A week later his disciples were in the house again, and Thomas was with them. Though the doors were locked, Jesus came and stood among them and said, "Peace be with you!" ²⁷Then he said to Thomas, "Put your finger here; see my hands. Reach out your hand and put it into my side. Stop doubting and believe."

²⁸Thomas said to him, "My Lord and my God!"

²⁹Then Jesus told him, "Because you have seen me, you have believed; blessed are those who have not seen and yet have believed."

On the Emmaus Road
Mark 16:12-13, Luke 24:13-32

The disciples report to the eleven
Luke 24:33-35

Jesus appears to the rest of the disciples
1 Corinthians 15:5, Mark 16:14, Luke 24:36-43, John 20:19-25

He appears to Thomas
John 20:26-29

He appears by the Sea of Galilee
John 21:1-14

Jesus reinstates Peter
John 21:15-24

The Great Commission
Matthew 28:16-20, Mark 16:15-18, 1 Corinthians 15:6

Jesus appears to James
1 Corinthians 15:7

For Thought and **Contemplation**

Jesus knew full well the temptation that would come to His disciples to think that they had been mistaken about His resurrection, so He appeared to them over a period of forty days – thus building up the evidence and piling up the proof. How characteristic of Jesus to put the interests of others before His own. Is this one of your characteristics too?

"Each of you should look not only to your own interests, but also to the interests of others. Your attitude should be the same as that of Christ Jesus." (Phil. 2:4-5)

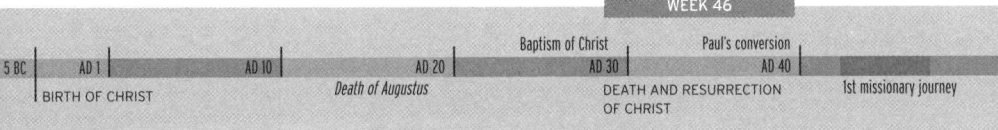

DAY 318 — The Day of Pentecost

The disciples told to wait
Luke 24:44–49, Acts 1:3–8

Jesus' ascension
Mark 16:19–20, Luke 24:50–53, Acts 1:9–12

The purpose of John's Gospel
John 21:25, 20:30–31

Introduction to the Acts
Acts 1:1–2

The disciples in the upper room
Acts 1:13–17, 20–26

The coming of the Holy Spirit
Acts 2:1–13

Peter preaches that Jesus is Christ
Acts 2:14–36

The crowd's response
Acts 2:37–40

Acts 1:3–8

³After his suffering, he showed himself to these men and gave many convincing proofs that he was alive. He appeared to them over a period of forty days and spoke about the kingdom of God. ⁴On one occasion, while he was eating with them, he gave them this command: "Do not leave Jerusalem, but wait for the gift my Father promised, which you have heard me speak about. ⁵For John baptised with water, but in a few days you will be baptised with the Holy Spirit."

⁶So when they met together, they asked him, "Lord, are you at this time going to restore the kingdom to Israel?"

⁷He said to them: "It is not for you to know the times or dates the Father has set by his own authority. ⁸But you will receive power when the Holy Spirit comes on you; and you will be my witnesses in Jerusalem, and in all Judea and Samaria, and to the ends of the earth."

⁹After he said this, he was taken up before their very eyes, and a cloud hid him from their sight.

For Thought and **Contemplation**

Suppose there had been no outpouring of the Spirit on the Day of Pentecost, what kind of Christianity would have faced the world? It would have been the kind found in John 20:19. The Day of Pentecost made a dramatic difference to the disciples – it turned them from men of fear to men of fire. Has it made a similar difference in you? If not, then pray now that God will give you your own *personal* Pentecost.

"Do not get drunk on wine, which leads to debauchery. Instead, be filled with the Spirit." (Eph. 5:18)

a bird's eye view of Acts

Place in the Bible	Written by:	Special Features
Fifth New Testament book; first book of history.	Luke.	The only book to tell in detail what happened between the ascension of Jesus and the spread of the Church.

The power of the early Church

DAY 319

Acts 5:12–16

¹²The apostles performed many miraculous signs and wonders among the people. And all the believers used to meet together in Solomon's Colonnade. ¹³No-one else dared join them, even though they were highly regarded by the people. ¹⁴Nevertheless, more and more men and women believed in the Lord and were added to their number. ¹⁵As a result, people brought the sick into the streets and laid them on beds and mats so that at least Peter's shadow might fall on some of them as he passed by. ¹⁶Crowds gathered also from the towns around Jerusalem, bringing their sick and those tormented by evil spirits, and all of them were healed.

Three thousand added to the Church
Acts 2:41–47

A lame man is healed
Acts 3:1–10

Peter's second sermon
Acts 3:11–26

Peter and John imprisoned
Acts 4:1–4

Their bold testimony
Acts 4:5–14

They refuse to be silenced
Acts 4:15–22

The believers unite in prayer
Acts 4:23–31

The self-sacrifice of the believers
Acts 4:32–37

Death of Ananias and Sapphira
Acts 5:1–11

Many signs and wonders
Acts 5:12–16

For Thought and **Contemplation**

Although the Church of today has grown by leaps and bounds, there are still too many differences between it and the early Church for us to remain comfortable. For example, in Acts, one sermon brought 3,000 converts. Today we have to preach 3,000 sermons to win one convert. What other differences can you think of? Pray that God will help us close this gap.

"Lord, I have heard of your fame;
I stand in awe of your deeds, O Lord.
Renew them in our day, in our time
make them known ..." (Hab. 3:2)

Jesus and the Book

In the sermons and testimonies in Acts the Church is given power by the Holy Spirit to witness boldly to the resurrected Christ and to present Him as the only Saviour. "Salvation is found in no-one else" (4:12).

Teaching

Acts is part two of Luke's Gospel, showing how the message of Jesus spread from Jerusalem through the Roman empire until it arrived in Rome itself. There is a strong emphasis on the activity and transforming power of the Holy Spirit.

A Verse to Remember

"They devoted themselves to the apostles' teaching and to the fellowship, to the breaking of bread and to prayer" (Acts 2:42).

DAY **320**

Stephen, the first martyr

The apostles imprisoned but set free
Acts 5:17–25

They testify to the council
Acts 5:26–33

The advice of Gamaliel
Acts 5:34–39

The apostles are released
Acts 5:40–42

Deacons are appointed
Acts 6:1–7

Stephen is falsely accused
Acts 6:8–15

His defence before the council
Acts 7:1–50

He reproves the Jewish leaders
Acts 7:51–53

Stephen's martyrdom AD 35

Stephen's martyrdom
Acts 7:54–60

Acts 7:54–60

⁵⁴When they heard this, they were furious and gnashed their teeth at him. ⁵⁵But Stephen, full of the Holy Spirit, looked up to heaven and saw the glory of God, and Jesus standing at the right hand of God. ⁵⁶"Look," he said, "I see heaven open and the Son of Man standing at the right hand of God."
⁵⁷At this they covered their ears and, yelling at the top of their voices, they all rushed at him, ⁵⁸dragged him out of the city and began to stone him. Meanwhile, the witnesses laid their clothes at the feet of a young man named Saul.
⁵⁹While they were stoning him, Stephen prayed, "Lord Jesus, receive my spirit." ⁶⁰Then he fell on his knees and cried out, "Lord, do not hold this sin against them." When he had said this, he fell asleep.

For Thought and **Contemplation**

Someone said: "You can't be the salt of the earth without causing someone to smart." Stephen stood up for the truth, and lost his life because of it. How important is truth to you? Maybe it's important enough to live by, but is it important enough to die for?

"... everyone who wants to live a godly life in Christ Jesus will be persecuted." (2 Tim. 3:12)

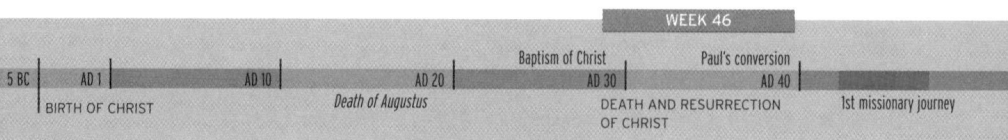

The conversion of Saul

DAY 321

Acts 9:1-9

¹Meanwhile, Saul was still breathing out murderous threats against the Lord's disciples. He went to the high priest ²and asked him for letters to the synagogues in Damascus, so that if he found any there who belonged to the Way, whether men or women, he might take them as prisoners to Jerusalem. ³As he neared Damascus on his journey, suddenly a light from heaven flashed around him. ⁴He fell to the ground and heard a voice say to him, "Saul, Saul, why do you persecute me?" ⁵"Who are you, Lord?" Saul asked.
"I am Jesus, whom you are persecuting," he replied. ⁶"Now get up and go into the city, and you will be told what you must do."
⁷The men travelling with Saul stood there speechless; they heard the sound but did not see anyone. ⁸Saul got up from the ground, but when he opened his eyes he could see nothing. So they led him by the hand into Damascus. ⁹For three days he was blind, and did not eat or drink anything.

Saul persecutes the Church
Acts 8:1-4

Philip's ministry in Samaria
Acts 8:5-13

Simon the sorceror's hypocrisy
Acts 8:14-25

Philip and the Ethiopian eunuch
Acts 8:26-40

Conversion of Saul AD 37

Saul's conversion
Acts 9:1-9

He preaches Christ
Acts 9:10-22

His escape
Acts 9:23-25

His early experiences
Galatians 1:17-19

Barnabas befriends him
Acts 9:26-29

He is sent to Tarsus
Acts 9:30-31

For Thought and **Contemplation**

How were you converted? Was it a dramatic experience like Paul's, or was it simply a quiet conviction that you had passed from death to life? The manner in which we are converted differs, but the results are always the same. Just think – *the spiritual heritage you have in Christ is exactly the same as that of Paul's.*

"... whoever comes to me I will never drive away." (Jn. 6:37)

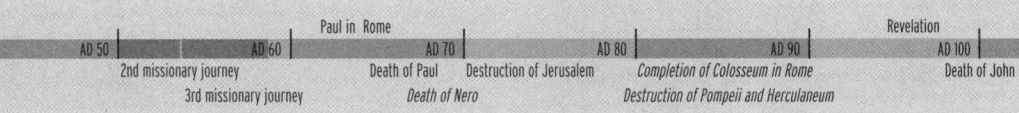

DAY 322

The first Gentile converts

Aeneas is healed
Acts 9:32–35

Dorcas is raised to life
Acts 9:36–43

Cornelius sends for Peter
Acts 10:1–8

Peter's vision
Acts 10:9–18

He goes to Cornelius
Acts 10:19–33

Peter preaches the Gospel
Acts 10:34–43

Gentiles receive the Holy Spirit and are baptised
Acts 10:44–48

The apostles contend with Peter
Acts 11:1–3

Peter's defence
Acts 11:4–18

Acts 10:44–48

⁴⁴While Peter was still speaking these words, the Holy Spirit came on all who heard the message. ⁴⁵The circumcised believers who had come with Peter were astonished that the gift of the Holy Spirit had been poured out even on the Gentiles. ⁴⁶For they heard them speaking in tongues and praising God.

Then Peter said, ⁴⁷"Can anyone keep these people from being baptised with water? They have received the Holy Spirit just as we have." ⁴⁸So he ordered that they be baptised in the name of Jesus Christ. Then they asked Peter to stay with them for a few days.

For Thought and **Contemplation**

What is one of the biggest impediments to the spreading of the gospel? *Bigotry!* Peter resisted the idea that Gentiles should participate in God's salvation until the Lord well and truly re-orientated him. Any bigotry in you? Then take care – God might have to turn you upside down too!

"If you really keep the royal law found in Scripture, 'Love your neighbour as yourself,' you are doing right. But if you show favouritism, you sin and are convicted by the law as law-breakers." (Jas. 2:8–9)

a bird's eye view of **James**

Place in the Bible	**Written by:**
Twentieth New Testament book; fifteenth letter.	James, thought to be the brother of Jesus.

The letter of James

DAY **323**

James 3:13–18

¹³Who is wise and understanding among you? Let him show it by his good life, by deeds done in the humility that comes from wisdom. ¹⁴But if you harbour bitter envy and selfish ambition in your hearts, do not boast about it or deny the truth. ¹⁵Such "wisdom" does not come down from heaven but is earthly, unspiritual, of the devil. ¹⁶For where you have envy and selfish ambition, there you find disorder and every evil practice. ¹⁷But the wisdom that comes from heaven is first of all pure; then peace-loving, considerate, submissive, full of mercy and good fruit, impartial and sincere. ¹⁸Peacemakers who sow in peace raise a harvest of righteousness.

Church established at Antioch	Acts 11:19–24
Paul brought to Antioch	Acts 11:25–26
Gift sent to Jerusalem	Acts 11:27–30
James (John's brother) killed	Acts 12:1–2
James' letter written AD 45	
The letter of James: Temptations try faith	James 1:1–15
God's good gifts	James 1:16–18
Doers of the Word	James 1:19–27
No respect of persons	James 2:1–13
Faith and deeds	James 2:14–26
Use of the tongue	James 3:1–12
True wisdom	James 3:13–18

For Thought and **Contemplation**

Perhaps the greatest lesson that comes out of James' writings is his reminder of the power of the tongue. That "little piece of flesh between the jaws", as Martin Luther called it, takes some taming! In fact the Scripture says that no man can tame it. No *man* perhaps, but with God all things are possible. Have you given God your tongue for taming yet?

"A word aptly spoken is like apples of gold in settings of silver." (Prov. 25:11)

Jesus and the Book

This letter has fifteen mirror images of Jesus' teaching given in the Sermon of the Mount. Matthew 5:10–12, for example, is reflected in James 1:2, "Consider it pure joy, my brothers, whenever you face trials of many kinds ...".

Teaching

James points out that a Christian's belief should be exactly matched by Christian behaviour. James links faith and works together, since works and good deeds done for Christ in His name should always naturally flow out of faith in Christ.

A Verse to Remember

"What good is it, my brothers, if a man claims to have faith but has no deeds? ... faith by itself, if it is not accompanied by action, is dead" (James 2:14, 17).

DAY **324**

Peter's deliverance

Evils that cripple true faith
James 4:1–17

Rich oppressors denounced
James 5:1–6

Exhortation to patience
James 5:7–12

Encouragement to prayer and confessing of faults
James 5:13–20

Peter again imprisoned and freed
Acts 12:3–17

Herod's rage
Acts 12:18–19

Death of Herod
Acts 12:20–23

Paul's first missionary journey AD 45–47

Paul and Barnabas sent out
Acts 12:24–25, 13:1–3

They preach in Cyprus
Acts 13:4–12

John leaves
Acts 13:13

Acts 12:5-10

⁵So Peter was kept in prison, but the church was earnestly praying to God for him. ⁶The night before Herod was to bring him to trial, Peter was sleeping between two soldiers, bound with two chains, and sentries stood guard at the entrance. ⁷Suddenly an angel of the Lord appeared and a light shone in the cell. He struck Peter on the side and woke him up. "Quick, get up!" he said, and the chains fell off Peter's wrists.

⁸Then the angel said to him, "Put on your clothes and sandals." And Peter did so. "Wrap your cloak around you and follow me," the angel told him. ⁹Peter followed him out of the prison, but he had no idea that what the angel was doing was really happening; he thought he was seeing a vision. ¹⁰They passed the first and second guards and came to the iron gate leading to the city. It opened for them by itself, and they went through it. When they had walked the length of one street, suddenly the angel left him.

For Thought and **Contemplation**

What a sad comment it is on human nature, that although the Church prayed for Peter's miraculous deliverance, they seemed unable to believe it when God brought it about. In fact, Peter appeared to have more trouble getting into the prayer meeting than he did in getting out of prison! How ready are you for a miracle?

"Jesus replied, 'What is impossible with men is possible with God.'" (Lk. 18:27)

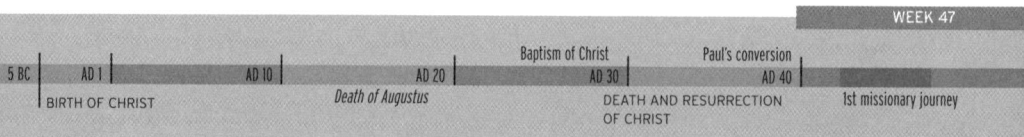

Paul's first missionary journey

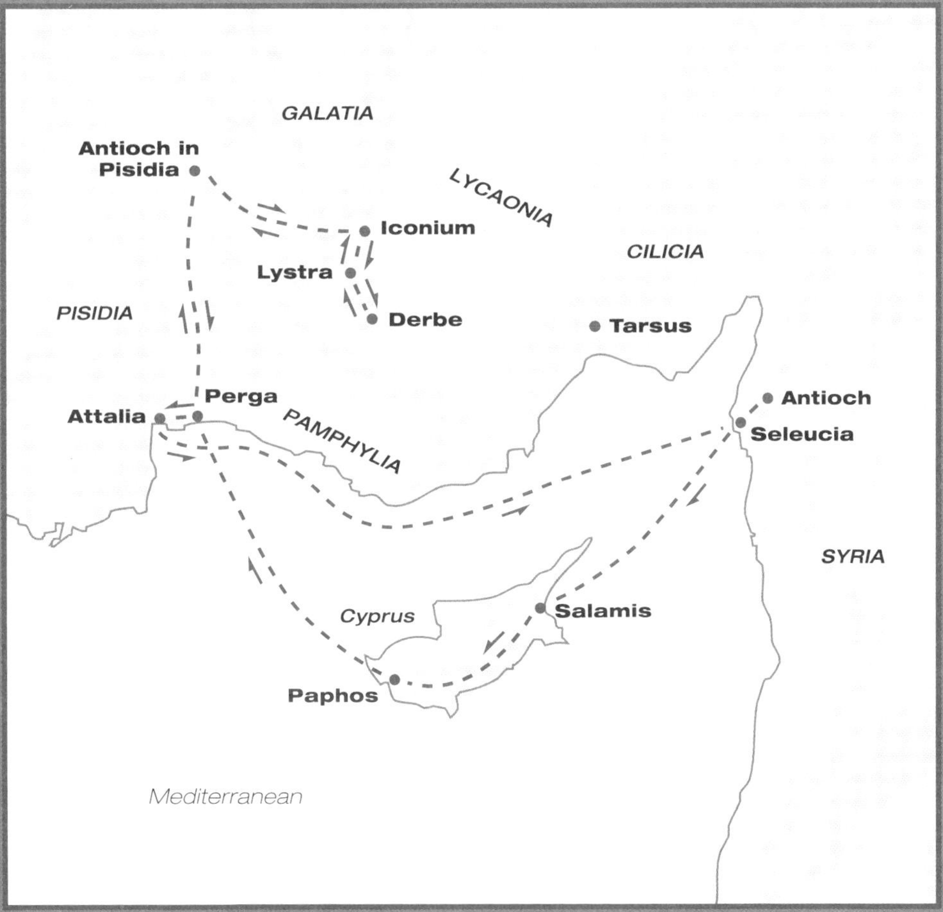

DAY 325 — Paul's first missionary journey

Paul preaches at Antioch (Pisidia)
Acts 13:14–41

The Gentiles receive the message
Acts 13:42–49

The Jews drive out Paul and Barnabas
Acts 13:50–52

They minister in Iconium and Lystra
Acts 14:1–18

Paul is stoned, but revives
Acts 14:19–20

They return to Antioch
Acts 14:21–26

They report back to the church
Acts 14:27–28

The council at Jerusalem
Acts 15:1–12, Galatians 2:7–10

Acts 14:1–7
¹At Iconium Paul and Barnabas went as usual into the Jewish synagogue. There they spoke so effectively that a great number of Jews and Gentiles believed. ²But the Jews who refused to believe stirred up the Gentiles and poisoned their minds against the brothers. ³So Paul and Barnabas spent considerable time there, speaking boldly for the Lord, who confirmed the message of his grace by enabling them to do miraculous signs and wonders. ⁴The people of the city were divided; some sided with the Jews, others with the apostles. ⁵There was a plot afoot among the Gentiles and Jews, together with their leaders, to ill-treat them and stone them. ⁶But they found out about it and fled to the Lycaonian cities of Lystra and Derbe and to the surrounding country, ⁷where they continued to preach the good news.

For Thought and Contemplation

What makes a missionary? Crossing the sea? No – seeing the cross! A missionary (a word, incidentally, you'll not find in the Bible) simply means "someone with a mission". As you study Paul's missionary strategy, spare a moment to consider your own. If you are a Christian, you are "someone with a mission". It may lie across the sea, but, on the other hand, it may lie across the street!

"... Forgetting what is behind and straining towards what is ahead, I press on towards the goal to win the prize for which God has called me heavenwards in Christ Jesus."
(Phil. 3:13–14)

a bird's eye view of **1 & 2 Thessalonians**

Place in the Bible	Written by:	Special Feature
Thirteenth and fourteenth New Testament books; eighth and ninth letters.	Paul.	The second coming of Christ.

Paul's second missionary journey

DAY **326**

Acts 16:27–34

²⁷The jailer woke up, and when he saw the prison doors open, he drew his sword and was about to kill himself because he thought the prisoners had escaped. ²⁸But Paul shouted, "Don't harm yourself! We are all here!"

²⁹The jailer called for lights, rushed in and fell trembling before Paul and Silas. ³⁰He then brought them out and asked, "Sirs, what must I do to be saved?"

³¹They replied, "Believe in the Lord Jesus, and you will be saved – you and your household." ³²Then they spoke the word of the Lord to him and to all the others in his house. ³³At that hour of the night the jailer took them and washed their wounds; then immediately he and all his family were baptised. ³⁴The jailer brought them into his house and set a meal before them; he was filled with joy because he had come to believe in God – he and his whole family.

The decision of the Jerusalem council	Acts 15:13–35
Second missionary journey AD 50–54	
Peter visits Antioch	Galatians 2:11–14
Paul and Barnabas separate	Acts 15:36–41
Paul goes to Macedonia	Acts 16:1–15
He casts out a spirit of divination	Acts 16:16–21
Paul and Silas are imprisoned	Acts 16:22–26
The Philippian jailer	Acts 16:27–34
Paul and Silas freed	Acts 16:35–40
They preach at Thessalonica and Berea	Acts 17:1–13
Paul goes to Athens	Acts 17:14–15

For Thought and **Contemplation**

Paul was not only an effective disciple, but an effective *discipler*. He took Silas and discipled him in the methods of the gospel. Yesterday we asked you to consider your own missionary strategy. Part of that might be to establish some new Christian in the faith. Ask God to show you someone whom you can disciple, then begin to pray for and share with that person as much as and as often as you can.

"Don't let anyone look down on you because you are young, but set an example for the believers in speech, in life, in love, in faith and in purity." (1 Tim. 4:12)

Jesus and the Books

Jesus' return is mentioned over three hundred times in the New Testament, and in 1 Thessalonians 4:17–18 it is meant to encourage Paul's readers.

Teaching

Paul wrote 1 Thessalonians to encourage a group of very new Christians. 2 Thessalonians was written to counter erroneous ideas about the Lord's return and exhorts them to stand firm, reminding them of God's love and faithfulness.

A Verse to Remember

"... warn those who are idle, encourage the timid, help the weak, be patient with everyone" (1 Thess. 5:14).

Paul's second and third missionary journeys

Paul's second journey

Paul's third journey

Paul teaches in Greece

DAY 327

Acts 18:12-17

¹²While Gallio was proconsul of Achaia, the Jews made a united attack on Paul and brought him into court. ¹³"This man," they charged, "is persuading the people to worship God in ways contrary to the law."

¹⁴Just as Paul was about to speak, Gallio said to the Jews, "If you Jews were making a complaint about some misdemeanour or serious crime, it would be reasonable for me to listen to you. ¹⁵But since it involves questions about words and names and your own law – settle the matter yourselves. I will not be a judge of such things." ¹⁶So he had them ejected from the court. ¹⁷Then they all turned on Sosthenes the synagogue ruler and beat him in front of the court. But Gallio showed no concern whatever.

Paul preaches about the true God
Acts 17:16-34

Paul goes to Corinth
Acts 18:1-11

Paul before Gallio
Acts 18:12-17

The first Thessalonian letter:
Their faith, love and patience
1 Thessalonians 1:1-10

Paul's integrity
1 Thessalonians 2:1-12

Their reception of Paul's message
1 Thessalonians 2:13-20

Timothy is sent to encourage them
1 Thessalonians 3:1-8

Paul's prayer
1 Thessalonians 3:9-13

For Thought and **Contemplation**

Someone has described the task of tracing Paul's missionary journeys through the New Testament as "like tracking a bleeding hare across snow". It seemed that wherever he went, he suffered great persecution and, at times, sustained severe bodily harm. What was the secret of his strong spiritual drive? Turn to 2 Corinthians 5:14 and see. Is this your secret too?

"I have fought the good fight, I have finished the race, I have kept the faith." (2 Tim. 4:7)

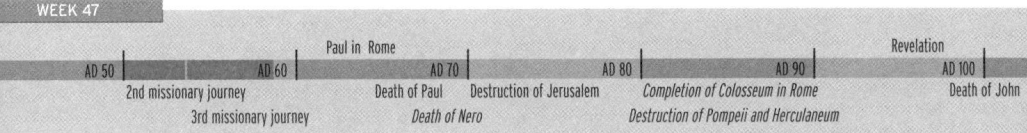

DAY 328 — The Thessalonian letters

Exhortations to love and purity
1 Thessalonians 4:1–12

Comfort concerning those who have died
1 Thessalonians 4:13–18

The Lord's return
1 Thessalonians 5:1–11

Other instructions and conclusion
1 Thessalonians 5:12–28

Second Thessalonian letter: Comfort in persecution
2 Thessalonians 1:1–12

The coming of Christ
2 Thessalonians 2:1–12

Instruction in conduct
2 Thessalonians 2:13–17, 3:1–15

Final prayer
2 Thessalonians 3:16–18

End of Paul's second journey
Acts 18:18–22

1 Thessalonians 4:1–8

¹Finally, brothers, we instructed you how to live in order to please God, as in fact you are living. Now we ask you and urge you in the Lord Jesus to do this more and more. ²For you know what instructions we gave you by the authority of the Lord Jesus.
³It is God's will that you should be sanctified: that you should avoid sexual immorality; ⁴that each of you should learn to control his own body in a way that is holy and honourable, ⁵not in passionate lust like the heathen, who do not know God; ⁶and that in this matter no-one should wrong his brother or take advantage of him. The Lord will punish men for all such sins, as we have already told you and warned you. ⁷For God did not call us to be impure, but to live a holy life. ⁸Therefore, he who rejects this instruction does not reject man but God, who gives you his Holy Spirit.

For Thought and **Contemplation**

Are you aware that the Christians at Thessalonica were comparatively *new* believers? Yet in the short space of these letters, Paul touches on some of the deepest doctrines of the faith. How sad that so many of today's Christians are still "spiritual babes", living on "milk" rather than "meat". Is it time *you* grew up?

"When I was a child, I talked like a child, I thought like a child, I reasoned like a child. When I became a man, I put childish ways behind me."
(1 Cor. 13:11)

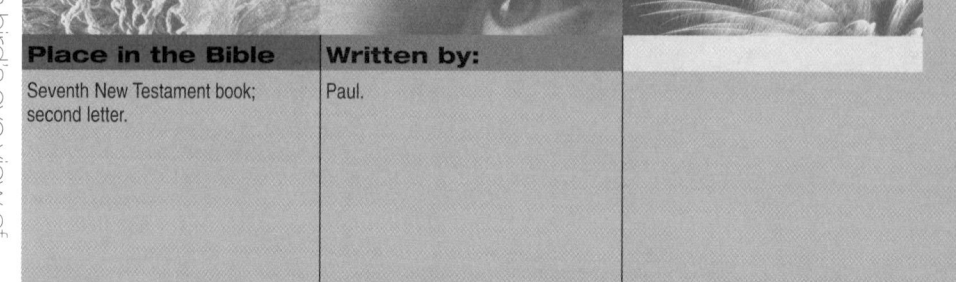

a bird's eye view of **1 Corinthians**

Place in the Bible	Written by:	
Seventh New Testament book; second letter.	Paul.	

Paul's third missionary journey

DAY **329**

Acts 18:23–28

²³After spending some time in Antioch, Paul set out from there and travelled from place to place throughout the region of Galatia and Phrygia, strengthening all the disciples. ²⁴Meanwhile a Jew named Apollos, a native of Alexandria, came to Ephesus. He was a learned man, with a thorough knowledge of the Scriptures. ²⁵He had been instructed in the way of the Lord, and he spoke with great fervour and taught about Jesus accurately, though he knew only the baptism of John. ²⁶He began to speak boldly in the synagogue. When Priscilla and Aquila heard him, they invited him to their home and explained to him the way of God more adequately. ²⁷When Apollos wanted to go to Achaia, the brothers encouraged him and wrote to the disciples there to welcome him. On arriving, he was a great help to those who by grace had believed. ²⁸For he vigorously refuted the Jews in public debate, proving from the Scriptures that Jesus was the Christ.

Third missionary journey AD 54–58
Antioch to Ephesus Acts 18:23–28
Paul teaches at Ephesus Acts 19:1–12
Jewish exorcists disgraced Acts 19:13–20
Demetrius stirs up trouble Acts 19:21–32
The city clerk calms the crowd Acts 19:33–41
First letter to the Corinthians: Paul's greeting 1 Corinthians 1:1–9
Divisions in the church 1 Corinthians 1:10–16
The power of the Gospel 1 Corinthians 1:17–31
God's wisdom revealed by the Spirit 1 Corinthians 2:1–16

For Thought and **Contemplation**

Wherever Paul went, he left behind him a tremendous spiritual impact. You may not be able to make as much impact as Paul, but you ought to be able to make *some* impact. Someone once wrote: "The world doesn't need a definition of religion so much as a demonstration of it." How much impact are you making upon the people you meet day by day?

"My message and my preaching were not with wise and persuasive words, but with a demonstration of the Spirit's power." (1 Cor. 2:4)

Jesus and the Book

Jesus is seen as being relevant to all areas of a Christian's life, for He "has become for us wisdom from God – that is, our righteousness, holiness and redemption" (1 Cor. 1:30).

Teaching

In dealing with the many problems at Corinth, such as division, Christians taking each other to court, abuse of worship services and so on, Paul seeks to bring the Lord Jesus Christ to the centre of their thinking and lives.

A Verse to Remember

"Do you not know that your body is a temple of the Holy Spirit, who is in you, whom you have received from God? You are not your own; you were bought at a price. Therefore honour God with your body" (1 Cor. 6:19–20).

DAY 330 — Straight talking

Christian service evaluated
1 Corinthians 3:1–15

The temple of God
1 Corinthians 3:16–17

All things are ours
1 Corinthians 3:18–23

Paul's apostleship
1 Corinthians 4:1–13

Paul as a father in Christ
1 Corinthians 4:14–21

The Corinthians rebuked concerning incest
1 Corinthians 5:1–8

Discipline of sinning believers
1 Corinthians 5:9–13

Lawsuits rebuked
1 Corinthians 6:1–8

The sacredness of the body
1 Corinthians 6:9–20

1 Corinthians 4:14–21

¹⁴I am not writing this to shame you, but to warn you, as my dear children. ¹⁵Even though you have ten thousand guardians in Christ, you do not have many fathers, for in Christ Jesus I became your father through the gospel. ¹⁶Therefore I urge you to imitate me. ¹⁷For this reason I am sending to you Timothy, my son whom I love, who is faithful in the Lord. He will remind you of my way of life in Christ Jesus, which agrees with what I teach everywhere in every church.

¹⁸Some of you have become arrogant, as if I were not coming to you. ¹⁹But I will come to you very soon, if the Lord is willing, and then I will find out not only how these arrogant people are talking, but what power they have. ²⁰For the kingdom of God is not a matter of talk but of power. ²¹What do you prefer? Shall I come to you with a whip, or in love and with a gentle spirit?

For Thought and **Contemplation**

The ministry of the great apostle Paul was not only winning, but winnowing. He knew no church could grow when its members persisted in their sinful ways – hence his scathing challenges and rebukes. Do any of Paul's words hit home with you? Then do something about it – *now*.

"Therefore, if anyone is in Christ, he is a new creation; the old has gone, the new has come!" (2 Cor. 5:17)

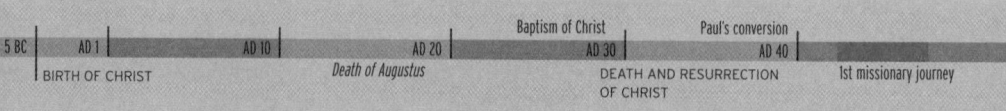

Paul answers questions

DAY **331**

1 Corinthians 9:24–27

²⁴Do you not know that in a race all the runners run, but only one gets the prize? Run in such a way as to get the prize. ²⁵Everyone who competes in the games goes into strict training. They do it to get a crown that will not last; but we do it to get a crown that will last for ever. ²⁶Therefore I do not run like a man running aimlessly; I do not fight like a man beating the air. ²⁷No, I beat my body and make it my slave so that after I have preached to others, I myself will not be disqualified for the prize.

Question about marriage
1 Corinthians 7:1–16

Advice to remain in the same state
1 Corinthians 7:17–31

Advantages of singleness
1 Corinthians 7:32–40

Concerning meat offered to idols
1 Corinthians 8:1–6

Do not cause a brother to sin
1 Corinthians 8:7–13

Paul's rights as an apostle
1 Corinthians 9:1–14

He waives his rights
1 Corinthians 9:15–23

His unfading crown
1 Corinthians 9:24–27

For Thought and **Contemplation**

If you had the privilege of asking Paul a question bearing on some aspect of the Christian life, what would it be? Paul may not be here to answer your enquiry, but keep in mind that every problem relating to Christian life and experience *is answered somewhere in the Word of God.* The better you know your Bible, the more readily you will discover the answers.

"Do your best to present yourself to God as one approved, a workman who does not need to be ashamed and who correctly handles the word of truth."
(2 Tim. 2:15)

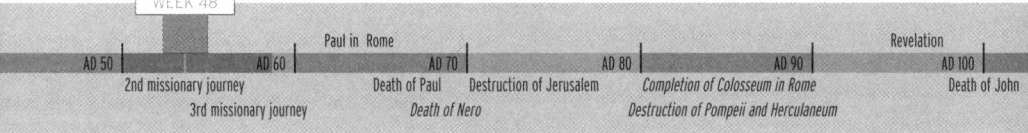

DAY 332 — Paul instructs the church

Jewish heritage reviewed
1 Corinthians 10:1–14

No compromise in relation to the Lord's Supper
1 Corinthians 10:15–22

Doing all to God's glory
1 Corinthians 10:23–33, 11:1

Paul corrects some abuses
1 Corinthians 11:2–16

Right and wrong celebration of the Lord's Supper
1 Corinthians 11:17–22, 27–34

Use of spiritual gifts
1 Corinthians 12:1–11

Comparison with the human body
1 Corinthians 12:12–31

1 Corinthians 11:27–34

[27]Therefore, whoever eats the bread or drinks the cup of the Lord in an unworthy manner will be guilty of sinning against the body and blood of the Lord. [28]A man ought to examine himself before he eats of the bread and drinks of the cup. [29]For anyone who eats and drinks without recognising the body of the Lord eats and drinks judgment on himself. [30]That is why many among you are weak and sick, and a number of you have fallen asleep. [31]But if we judged ourselves, we would not come under judgment. [32]When we are judged by the Lord, we are being disciplined so that we will not be condemned with the world.

[33]So then, my brothers, when you come together to eat, wait for each other. [34]If anyone is hungry, he should eat at home, so that when you meet together it may not result in judgment.

And when I come I will give further directions.

For Thought and **Contemplation**

Although we are indebted to Paul for clear teaching on many issues, one of the greatest debts we owe him is for his instructions on the threefold aspect of Holy Communion. Someone has defined those three aspects in these words – retrospect, introspect, and prospect. Can you discover them?

"... Jesus took bread, gave thanks and broke it, and gave it to his disciples, saying, 'Take and eat; this is my body.' Then he took the cup, gave thanks and offered it to them, saying, 'Drink from it, all of you. This is my blood of the covenant, which is poured out for many ...'" (Matt. 26:26–28)

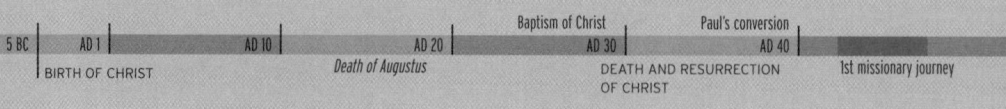

Love – the greatest gift

DAY **333**

1 Corinthians 13:1–7

¹If I speak in the tongues of men and of angels, but have not love, I am only a resounding gong or a clanging cymbal. ²If I have the gift of prophecy and can fathom all mysteries and all knowledge, and if I have a faith that can move mountains, but have not love, I am nothing. ³If I give all I possess to the poor and surrender my body to the flames, but have not love, I gain nothing.

⁴Love is patient, love is kind. It does not envy, it does not boast, it is not proud. ⁵It is not rude, it is not self-seeking, it is not easily angered, it keeps no record of wrongs. ⁶Love does not delight in evil but rejoices with the truth. ⁷It always protects, always trusts, always hopes, always perseveres.

The centrality of love
1 Corinthians 13:1–13

Prophecy to be desired
1 Corinthians 14:1–11

Prophecy builds up the church
1 Corinthians 14:12–25

Orderly worship
1 Corinthians 14:26–40

Paul proves the resurrection
1 Corinthians 15:1–4, 8–28

Objections answered
1 Corinthians 15:29–49

From mortal to immortal
1 Corinthians 15:50–54

The believer's triumph
1 Corinthians 15:55–58

For Thought and **Contemplation**

Most definitions of love focus on exciting or romantic feelings. But although love may *contain* feeling, genuine love is really an action of the will. Charles Finney described it like this: "Love is the bringing about of the highest good in the life of another individual." Examine 1 Corinthians 13 again, and see whether the emphasis is on feelings or the will!

"Whoever does not love does not know God, because God is love." (1 Jn. 4:8)

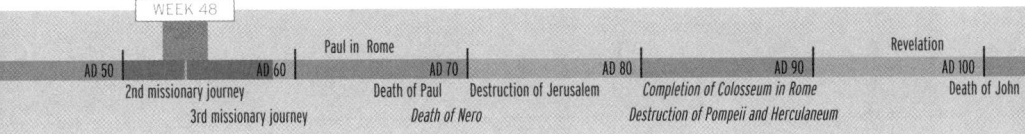

DAY **334** — Paul shares his heart

The collection for the poor
1 Corinthians 16:1–12

Conclusion
1 Corinthians 16:13–24

Paul goes to Macedonia
1 Timothy 1:3, Acts 20:1

Second Corinthian letter: God's comfort in trials
2 Corinthians 1:1–14

Paul's reason for not coming
2 Corinthians 1:15–24

The repentant offender to be restored
2 Corinthians 2:1–11

Paul's triumphant ministry
2 Corinthians 2:12–17

The glorious gospel
2 Corinthians 3:1–18

2 Corinthians 2:12–17

¹²Now when I went to Troas to preach the gospel of Christ and found that the Lord had opened a door for me, ¹³I still had no peace of mind, because I did not find my brother Titus there. So I said good-bye to them and went on to Macedonia.

¹⁴But thanks be to God, who always leads us in triumphal procession in Christ and through us spreads everywhere the fragrance of the knowledge of him. ¹⁵For we are to God the aroma of Christ among those who are being saved and those who are perishing. ¹⁶To the one we are the smell of death; to the other, the fragrance of life. And who is equal to such a task? ¹⁷Unlike so many, we do not peddle the word of God for profit. On the contrary, in Christ we speak before God with sincerity, like men sent from God.

For Thought and **Contemplation**

How do you respond to criticism – with a grudge or with grace? In 2 Corinthians, Paul tells how his character and conduct were under attack. He was charged with fickleness, pride, boasting, weakness, uncouth speech, meanness, dishonesty and unsoundness of mind. How does he respond? Read 2 Corinthians 2:14 once again and you'll see. Is this how you come out when under attack?

"Blessed are you when people insult you, persecute you and falsely say all kinds of evil against you because of me. Rejoice and be glad, because great is your reward in heaven ..." (Matt. 5:11–12)

a bird's eye view of **1 & 2 Timothy & Titus**

Place in the Bible	Written by:	
Fifteenth to seventeenth New Testament books; tenth to twelfth letters.	Paul.	

The Christian as a steward — DAY 335

2 Corinthians 5:16–21

¹⁶So from now on we regard no-one from a worldly point of view. Though we once regarded Christ in this way, we do so no longer. ¹⁷Therefore, if anyone is in Christ, he is a new creation; the old has gone, the new has come! ¹⁸All this is from God, who reconciled us to himself through Christ and gave us the ministry of reconciliation: ¹⁹that God was reconciling the world to himself in Christ, not counting men's sins against them. And he has committed to us the message of reconciliation. ²⁰We are therefore Christ's ambassadors, as though God were making his appeal through us. We implore you on Christ's behalf: Be reconciled to God. ²¹God made him who had no sin to be sin for us, so that in him we might become the righteousness of God.

Paul's sufferings and reward	2 Corinthians 4:1–18
The apostle's hope	2 Corinthians 5:1–10
The new creation	2 Corinthians 5:11–21
The proof of Paul's ministry	2 Corinthians 6:1–10
Separation from unbelievers required	2 Corinthians 6:11–18, 7:1
Paul's heart revealed	2 Corinthians 7:2–16
An example of giving	2 Corinthians 8:1–10
Encouragement to give	2 Corinthians 8:11–15

For Thought and **Contemplation**

Some Christians give like Moses' rock – only when they are struck. Some give like a sponge – only when they are squeezed. But others give like the flowers – because they delight to give. What kind of giver are you?

"Each man should give what he has decided in his heart to give, not reluctantly or under compulsion, for God loves a cheerful giver." (2 Cor. 9:7)

Jesus and the Books

In all three books Jesus is presented as the Saviour of sinners (1 Tim 1:15). Titus sums it up: "our great God and Saviour, Jesus Christ, who gave himself for us to redeem us from all wickedness and to purify for himself a people that are his very own ... (2:13–14).

Teaching

Paul instructs Titus and Timothy concerning the oversight of the churches they are responsible for and the conduct and qualities of those in positions of leadership.

A Verse to Remember

"... he saved us, not because of righteous things we had done, but because of his mercy." (Titus 3:5)

Heart to Heart

Section 11

Did you notice that believers were called "disciples"? They followed the Jesus way of life and allowed the Holy Spirit to discipline them into Christ-like attributes of love and service. They became strong in the faith through the discipline of prayer and studying the Scriptures. You have disciplined yourself this year to read the Bible but remember that true disciples also live out its message.

Visit the web site: **www.cover2cover.org**

12

In this section

The great themes of Paul's letters
Paul's journey to Rome
The letters of Peter and John
Messages to the seven churches
The new heaven and earth

DAY 336

Paul's thorn in the flesh

Paul sends Titus
2 Corinthians 8:16–24, 9:1–5

Results of generosity
2 Corinthians 9:6–15

Paul defends his authority
2 Corinthians 10:1–18

Paul's godly jealousy
2 Corinthians 11:1–15

His boasting
2 Corinthians 11:16–29

He glories in his weaknesses
2 Corinthians 11:30–33

His visions of the Lord
2 Corinthians 12:1–5

The thorn in the flesh
2 Corinthians 12:6–10

2 Corinthians 12:6–10

⁶Even if I should choose to boast, I would not be a fool, because I would be speaking the truth. But I refrain, so no-one will think more of me than is warranted by what I do or say. ⁷To keep me from becoming conceited because of these surpassingly great revelations, there was given me a thorn in my flesh, a messenger of Satan, to torment me. ⁸Three times I pleaded with the Lord to take it away from me. ⁹But he said to me, "My grace is sufficient for you, for my power is made perfect in weakness." Therefore I will boast all the more gladly about my weaknesses, so that Christ's power may rest on me. ¹⁰That is why, for Christ's sake, I delight in weaknesses, in insults, in hardships, in persecutions, in difficulties. For when I am weak, then I am strong.

For Thought and **Contemplation**

A good deal of debate has gone on down the centuries in relation to what exactly Paul's thorn in the flesh was. Some say it was weak eyesight; others that it was recurring malaria, or even a speech impediment. One wag said: "Paul had a thorn in the flesh, and we know little about it. If we had a thorn in the flesh, we would make sure everyone knew *everything* about it." True of you?

"These have come so that your faith – of greater worth than gold, which perishes even though refined by fire – may be proved genuine and may result in praise, glory and honour when Jesus Christ is revealed." (1 Pet. 1:7)

a bird's eye view of **2 Corinthians**

Place in the Bible	**Written by:**
Eighth New Testament book; third letter.	Paul.

Law and grace

DAY **337**

Galatians 2:15–21

¹⁵"We who are Jews by birth and not 'Gentile sinners' ¹⁶know that a man is not justified by observing the law, but by faith in Jesus Christ. So we, too, have put our faith in Christ Jesus that we may be justified by faith in Christ and not by observing the law, because by observing the law no-one will be justified.

¹⁷"If, while we seek to be justified in Christ, it becomes evident that we ourselves are sinners, does that mean that Christ promotes sin? Absolutely not! ¹⁸If I rebuild what I destroyed, I prove that I am a law-breaker. ¹⁹For through the law I died to the law so that I might live for God. ²⁰I have been crucified with Christ and I no longer live, but Christ lives in me. The life I live in the body, I live by faith in the Son of God, who loved me and gave himself for me. ²¹I do not set aside the grace of God, for if righteousness could be gained through the law, Christ died for nothing!"

Paul's effective service
2 Corinthians 12:11–18

His honest dealing
2 Corinthians 12:19–21

Conclusion
2 Corinthians 13:11–14

Paul travels to Corinth
Acts 20:2–3

The Galatian letter:
Paul's gospel from God
Galatians 1:1–16, 20–24

His visit to Jerusalem
Galatians 2:1–6

Justification by faith
Galatians 2:15–21

Bondage under the law
Galatians 3:1–18

The law brings us to Christ
Galatians 3:19–29

For Thought and **Contemplation**

There is a popular idea abroad today that we are only free when we have no restraints placed upon us: no laws, no authority, no responsibility. Galatians shows, as someone put it, that "freedom is not the right to do what we want, but the power to do what we ought".

"... through Christ Jesus the law of the Spirit of life set me free from the law of sin and death." (Rom. 8:2)

Jesus and the Book

In this letter Jesus Christ is presented as the Christian's Lord, "For we do not preach ourselves, but Jesus Christ as Lord, and ourselves as your servants for Jesus' sake" (2 Cor. 4:5).

Teaching

Suffering for the cause of Christ is a recurring theme in this, one of Paul's most autobiographical letters. Set against this is the glory of God which all Christians should reflect increasingly in their lives.

A Verse to Remember

"Therefore, if anyone is in Christ, he is a new creation; the old has gone, the new has come!" (2 Cor. 5:17).

DAY 338 — Paul's three great confessions

Folly of legal observances
Galatians 4:1–20

The bondwoman and the free woman
Galatians 4:21–31

Freedom in Christ
Galatians 5:1–15

The Spirit and the flesh
Galatians 5:16–26

Various exhortations
Galatians 6:1–10

Conclusion
Galatians 6:11–18

Letter to the Romans: Introduction and prayer
Romans 1:1–12

The power of the gospel
Romans 1:13–17

Man's universal sin
Romans 1:18–32

Romans 1:13–17

¹³I do not want you to be unaware, brothers, that I planned many times to come to you (but have been prevented from doing so until now) in order that I might have a harvest among you, just as I have had among the other Gentiles.
¹⁴I am bound both to Greeks and non-Greeks, both to the wise and the foolish. ¹⁵That is why I am so eager to preach the gospel also to you who are at Rome.
¹⁶I am not ashamed of the gospel, because it is the power of God for the salvation of everyone who believes: first for the Jew, then for the Gentile. ¹⁷For in the gospel a righteousness from God is revealed, a righteousness that is by faith from first to last, just as it is written: "The righteous will live by faith."

For Thought and Contemplation

Preachers are often at pains to point out that in Romans 1, Paul shares three great confessions concerning the gospel of Christ: (1) I am a debtor (v.14 AV); (2) I am ready (v.15 AV); (3) I am not ashamed (v.16). Reflect on these three statements for a few minutes and ask yourself: "Is this *my* attitude toward Christ's glorious gospel?"

"I am not ashamed of the gospel, because it is the power of God for the salvation of everyone who believes: first for the Jew, then for the Gentile." (Rom. 1:16)

a bird's eye view of Galatians

Place in the Bible	Written by:
Ninth New Testament book; fourth letter.	Paul.

Justification by faith

DAY **339**

Romans 5:1–5

¹Therefore, since we have been justified through faith, we have peace with God through our Lord Jesus Christ, ²through whom we have gained access by faith into this grace in which we now stand. And we rejoice in the hope of the glory of God. ³Not only so, but we also rejoice in our sufferings, because we know that suffering produces perseverance; ⁴perseverance, character; and character, hope. ⁵And hope does not disappoint us, because God has poured out his love into our hearts by the Holy Spirit, whom he has given us.

All men to be judged by their deeds
Romans 2:1–16

Circumcision alone is insufficient
Romans 2:17–29

The advantages of being a Jew
Romans 3:1–8

All mankind are sinners
Romans 3:9–20

Justification by faith
Romans 3:21–31

Abraham as an illustration
Romans 4:1–25

Results of justification
Romans 5:1–11

Adam and Christ contrasted
Romans 5:12–21

For Thought and **Contemplation**

Justification by faith is one of the greatest truths in the whole of Scripture. It means God accepts us *just-as-if* we had never sinned. Do you understand it? Give yourself this test. List all your Christian activities, then ask yourself: "Am I doing these things in order to be saved, or because I am saved?" If the answer is, "In order to be saved," then you need to think again.

"For all have sinned and fall short of the glory of God, and are justified freely by his grace through the redemption that came by Christ Jesus." (Rom. 3:23–24)

Jesus and the Book

The transforming power of Jesus' cross delivers Christ's followers from the curse of the law: "Christ redeemed us from the curse of the law by becoming a curse for us, for it is written: 'Cursed is everyone who is hung on a tree.'" (Gal. 3:13).

Teaching

Paul expresses his dismay that a group of Christians should revert to their legalistic way of living instead of continuing to live their Christian lives depending solely on Christ. Justification by faith, not by works of the law, is the urgent message of this book.

A Verse to Remember

"I have been crucified with Christ and I no longer live, but Christ lives in me. The life I live in the body, I live by faith in the Son of God, who loved me and gave himself for me" (Gal. 2:20).

DAY **340**

Out of "7" into "8"

Death to sin through baptism into Christ's death
Romans 6:1–14

Servants of righteousness
Romans 6:15–23

Believers united to Christ
Romans 7:1–6

The purpose of the law
Romans 7:7–13

The conflict between the old and new natures
Romans 7:14–25

Freedom from condemnation
Romans 8:1–9

The privileges of the child of God
Romans 8:10–17

Future glory
Romans 8:18–27

More than conquerors
Romans 8:28–39

Romans 8:1–4

¹Therefore, there is now no condemnation for those who are in Christ Jesus, ²because through Christ Jesus the law of the Spirit of life set me free from the law of sin and death. ³For what the law was powerless to do in that it was weakened by the sinful nature, God did by sending his own Son in the likeness of sinful man to be a sin offering. And so he condemned sin in sinful man, ⁴in order that the righteous requirements of the law might be fully met in us, who do not live according to the sinful nature but according to the Spirit.

For Thought and **Contemplation**

Christians sometimes ask each other: Have you stepped our of "7" into "8" yet? They refer, of course, to Romans chapters 7 and 8. In chapter 7, Paul is in deep bondage: in chapter 8, he is gloriously free. What accounts for the difference? *The Holy Spirit*. Has this experience happened to you? If not, ask God to do something for you – today.

"So if the Son sets you free, you will be free indeed." (Jn. 8:36)

a bird's eye view of **Romans**

Place in the Bible	Written by:	
Sixth New Testament book; first letter.	Paul.	

Israel's future restoration

DAY **341**

Romans 10:5–11

⁵Moses describes in this way the righteousness that is by the law: "The man who does these things will live by them." ⁶But the righteousness that is by faith says: "Do not say in your heart, 'Who will ascend into heaven?'" (that is, to bring Christ down) ⁷"or 'Who will descend into the deep?'" (that is, to bring Christ up from the dead). ⁸But what does it say? "The word is near you; it is in your mouth and in your heart," that is, the word of faith we are proclaiming: ⁹That if you confess with your mouth, "Jesus is Lord," and believe in your heart that God raised him from the dead, you will be saved. ¹⁰For it is with your heart that you believe and are justified, and it is with your mouth that you confess and are saved. ¹¹As the Scripture says, "Anyone who trusts in him will never be put to shame."

Paul's concern for the Jews	Romans 9:1–13
God's sovereignty	Romans 9:14–29
Israel's present failure	Romans 9:30–33
Paul's prayer for Israel	Romans 10:1–4
The righteousness of faith	Romans 10:5–11
Jew and Gentile equally in need	Romans 10:12–21
Israel not finally rejected	Romans 11:1–11
They will be grafted back	Romans 11:12–21
Gentiles cautioned against pride	Romans 11:22–32
Praise of God's wisdom and goodness	Romans 11:33–36

For Thought and **Contemplation**

Ready for a searching test? Then here goes. In three chapters you have read today, Paul shows his great knowledge of the Old Testament Scriptures by quoting from ten different books. How many can you identify? 1–4: good! 5–7: very good! 8–10: fantastic!

"For prophecy never had its origin in the will of man, but men spoke from God as they were carried along by the Holy Spirit." (2 Pet. 1:21)

Jesus and the Book

Jesus' death and resurrection are the basis for a Christian's salvation: "all ... are justified freely by his grace through the redemption that came by Christ Jesus. God presented him as a sacrifice of atonement, through faith in his blood" (Rom. 3:23–25).

Teaching

Paul writes that everyone is condemned by God's perfect standard and that the only way a person can ever be accepted by God is through faith in Christ. The result of this new relationship with God is developed in Chapters 6–8 and 12–15.

A Verse to Remember

"I am not ashamed of the gospel, because it is the power of God for the salvation of everyone who believes: first for the Jew, then for the Gentile" (Rom 1:16).

DAY 342 — Practical applications

Call for dedication
Romans 12:1–2

Faithful use of spiritual gifts
Romans 12:3–8

The transformed life
Romans 12:9–21

Obedience to authorities
Romans 13:1–7

Love as the fulfilment of the law
Romans 13:8–14

Warning against judging
Romans 14:1–13

Do not offend a brother
Romans 14:14–23

Maintaining unity
Romans 15:1–14

Paul's future plans
Romans 15:15–29

His request for prayer
Romans 15:30–33

Romans 12:3–8

³For by the grace given me I say to every one of you: Do not think of yourself more highly than you ought, but rather think of yourself with sober judgment, in accordance with the measure of faith God has given you. ⁴Just as each of us has one body with many members, and these members do not all have the same function, ⁵so in Christ we who are many form one body, and each member belongs to all the others. ⁶We have different gifts, according to the grace given us. If a man's gift is prophesying, let him use it in proportion to his faith. ⁷If it is serving, let him serve; if it is teaching, let him teach; ⁸if it is encouraging, let him encourage; if it is contributing to the needs of others, let him give generously; if it is leadership, let him govern diligently; if it is showing mercy, let him do it cheerfully.

For Thought and **Contemplation**

In the first eleven chapters of Romans, Paul has discussed the key doctrines of the Christian faith. Now, however, he moves from doctrine to duty – a necessary consequence. What we believe *must* affect the way we behave. If it doesn't, then it is not "sound doctrine".

"All Scripture is God-breathed and is useful for teaching, rebuking, correcting and training in righteousness, so that the man of God may be thoroughly equipped for every good work."
(2 Tim. 3:16–17)

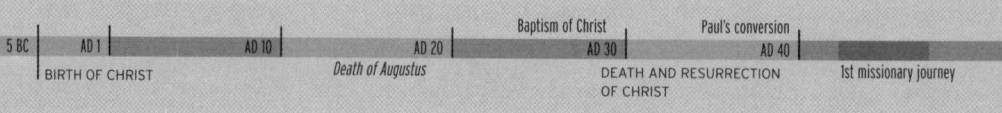

Paul goes to Jerusalem

DAY **343**

Acts 21:13–19

¹³Then Paul answered, "Why are you weeping and breaking my heart? I am ready not only to be bound, but also to die in Jerusalem for the name of the Lord Jesus." ¹⁴When he would not be dissuaded, we gave up and said, "The Lord's will be done."
¹⁵After this, we got ready and went up to Jerusalem. ¹⁶Some of the disciples from Caesarea accompanied us and brought us to the home of Mnason, where we were to stay. He was a man from Cyprus and one of the early disciples.
¹⁷When we arrived at Jerusalem, the brothers received us warmly. ¹⁸The next day Paul and the rest of us went to see James, and all the elders were present. ¹⁹Paul greeted them and reported in detail what God had done among the Gentiles through his ministry.

Personal greetings	Romans 16:1–16
Warning against those who cause divisions	Romans 16:17–20
Further greetings and conclusion	Romans 16:21–27
Paul at Troas	Acts 20:4–12
Paul meets the Ephesian elders	Acts 20:13–17
His farewell address	Acts 20:18–38
From Miletus to Caesarea	Acts 21:1–9
Agabus' prophecy	Acts 21:10–12
Paul goes to Jerusalem AD 58	
Paul travels to Jerusalem	Acts 21:13–19
He takes a vow	Acts 21:20–26

For Thought and **Contemplation**

Did Paul disobey the Holy Spirit in going to Jerusalem? Acts 21:4 certainly seems to suggest so. How careful we must be that our enthusiasm to work for God does not lead us to go ahead of the guidance of God. God's will must take precedence over God's work.

"Instead, you ought to say, 'If it is the Lord's will, we will live and do this or that.'" (Jas. 4:15)

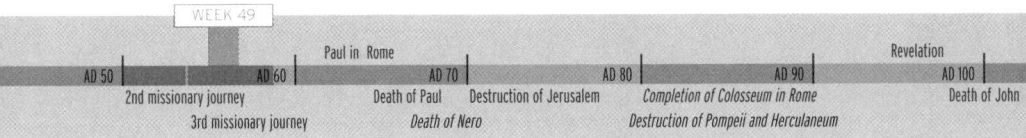

DAY **344** — Paul before the Jews

Paul is seized in the Temple
Acts 21:27–40

His defence before the Jews
Acts 22:1–21

The Jews' rage
Acts 22:22–25

Paul is released
Acts 22:26–30

Paul speaks before the council
Acts 23:1–5

Dissension between the Pharisees and Sadducees
Acts 23:6–10

The Lord's promise
Acts 23:11

The Jews' plot is discovered
Acts 23:12–22

Paul sent to Caesarea
Acts 23:23–35

Acts 23:6–10, 11

⁶Then Paul, knowing that some of them were Sadducees and the others Pharisees, called out in the Sanhedrin, "My brothers, I am a Pharisee, the son of a Pharisee. I stand on trial because of my hope in the resurrection of the dead." ⁷When he said this, a dispute broke out between the Pharisees and the Sadducees, and the assembly was divided. ⁸(The Sadducees say that there is no resurrection, and that there are neither angels nor spirits, but the Pharisees acknowledge them all.) ⁹There was a great uproar, and some of the teachers of the law who were Pharisees stood up and argued vigorously. "We find nothing wrong with this man," they said. "What if a spirit or an angel has spoken to him?" ¹⁰The dispute became so violent that the commander was afraid Paul would be torn to pieces by them. He ordered the troops to go down and take him away from them by force and bring him into the barracks.

For Thought and **Contemplation**

Whether or not we believe Paul was mistaken in going to Jerusalem, it is certain that his arrest there was due to his clear emphasis on the superiority of the Christian faith over every other religion. If you were arrested on that selfsame charge, would there be enough evidence to convict you?

"Jews demand miraculous signs and Greeks look for wisdom, but we preach Christ crucified: a stumbling-block to Jews and foolishness to Gentiles."
(1 Cor. 1:22–23)

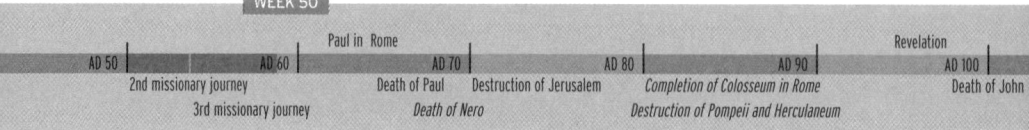

Paul's journey to Rome

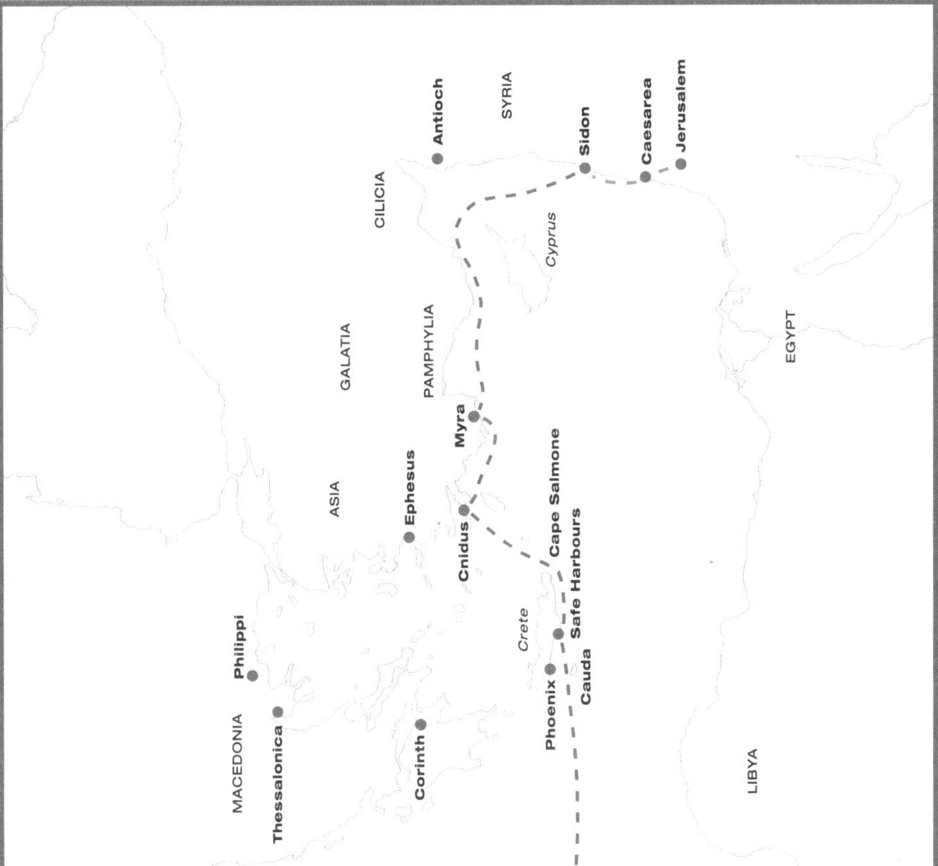

DAY 345 — Paul before the Romans

Tertullus accuses Paul
Acts 24:1–9

Paul's defence before Felix
Acts 24:10–21

Paul kept prisoner at Caesarea
Acts 24:22–27

Paul before Festus
Acts 25:1–9

He appeals to Caesar
Acts 25:10–12

Festus confers with Agrippa
Acts 25:13–27

Paul before Agrippa
Acts 26:1–23

He persuades Festus and Agrippa of his innocence
Acts 26:24–32

Acts 24:22–27

²²Then Felix, who was well acquainted with the Way, adjourned the proceedings. "When Lysias the commander comes," he said, "I will decide your case." ²³He ordered the centurion to keep Paul under guard but to give him some freedom and permit his friends to take care of his needs.

²⁴Several days later Felix came with his wife Drusilla, who was a Jewess. He sent for Paul and listened to him as he spoke about faith in Christ Jesus. ²⁵As Paul discoursed on righteousness, self-control and the judgment to come, Felix was afraid and said, "That's enough for now! You may leave. When I find it convenient, I will send for you." ²⁶At the same time he was hoping that Paul would offer him a bribe, so he sent for him frequently and talked with him. ²⁷When two years had passed, Felix was succeeded by Porcius Festus, but because Felix wanted to grant a favour to the Jews, he left Paul in prison.

For Thought and Contemplation

When faced with a difficult decision, Felix took the path of least resistance. For two years he let Paul's case drag on – all because it was politically inexpedient to release him. Are you facing a difficult decision at the moment? Then here's some good advice – decide *first* to do what God wants, and then all other decisions will fall into line.

"Trust in the Lord with all your heart and lean not on your own understanding; in all your ways acknowledge him, and he will make your paths straight." (Prov. 3:5–6)

---

a bird's eye view of **Philemon**

Place in the Bible	**Written by:**	**Special Feature**
Eighteenth New Testament book; thirteenth letter.	Paul.	The only personal letter of Paul's in the New Testament.

Paul's journey to Rome

DAY **346**

Acts 27:21-26

²¹After the men had gone a long time without food, Paul stood up before them and said: "Men, you should have taken my advice not to sail from Crete; then you would have spared yourselves this damage and loss. ²²But now I urge you to keep up your courage, because not one of you will be lost; only the ship will be destroyed. ²³Last night an angel of the God whose I am and whom I serve stood beside me ²⁴and said, 'Do not be afraid, Paul. You must stand trial before Caesar; and God has graciously given you the lives of all who sail with you.' ²⁵So keep up your courage, men, for I have faith in God that it will happen just as he told me. ²⁶Nevertheless, we must run aground on some island."

Paul sails towards Rome
Acts 27:1-12

They are caught in a storm
Acts 27:13-20

Paul takes command
Acts 27:21-38

They escape safely to land
Acts 27:39-44

The natives receive them kindly
Acts 28:1-10

Journey to Rome AD 60-61

They travel on to Rome
Acts 28:11-16

Letter to Philemon: Greetings
Philemon vv. 1-7

His request on behalf of Onesimus
Philemon vv. 8-22

Conclusion
Philemon vv. 23-25

For Thought and **Contemplation**

Paul's short letter to Philemon is an excellent illustration of what some people call "lathering before you shave". This means emphasising a person's good points before you confront them with their bad points. See how Paul commends before he commands. Now make a decision today that, from now on, you will do the same.

"Be devoted to one another in brotherly love. Honour one another above yourselves." (Rom. 12:10)

Jesus and the Book

The whole letter can be seen as an analogy of the forgiveness a believer discovers in Christ.

Teaching

Paul reminds Philemon of the mercy and grace he has received from Christ and pleads with him to show similar kindness to his runaway slave.

A Verse to Remember

I always thank my God as I remember you in my prayers, because I hear about your faith in the Lord Jesus and your love for all the saints. (Philemon vv. 4-5).

DAY 347 — Paul writes to the Colossians

Paul's prayer for the Colossians
Colossians 1:1–14

The pre-eminence of Christ
Colossians 1:15–23

Paul's labour of love
Colossians 1:24–29, 2:1–3

His joy in them
Colossians 2:4–7

Warning against erroneous beliefs
Colossians 2:8–23

The believer's walk
Colossians 3:1–25, 4:1–6

Closing greetings and instructions
Colossians 4:7–18

Colossians 1:15–23

¹⁵He is the image of the invisible God, the firstborn over all creation. ¹⁶For by him all things were created: things in heaven and on earth, visible and invisible, whether thrones or powers or rulers or authorities; all things were created by him and for him. ¹⁷He is before all things, and in him all things hold together. ¹⁸And he is the head of the body, the church; he is the beginning and the firstborn from among the dead, so that in everything he might have the supremacy. ¹⁹For God was pleased to have all his fullness dwell in him, ²⁰and through him to reconcile to himself all things, whether things on earth or things in heaven, by making peace through his blood, shed on the cross. ²¹Once you were alienated from God and were enemies in your minds because of your evil behaviour. ²²But now he has reconciled you by Christ's physical body through death to present you holy in his sight, without blemish and free from accusation – ²³if you continue in your faith, established and firm, not moved from the hope held out in the gospel. ...

For Thought and **Contemplation**

One of the most important phrases in the Bible is the one found in Colossians 1:27: "Christ in you, the hope of glory." One great preacher, while meditating on these words one day, put his conclusions in this way: "Life with Christ is an endless hope; without Him, it is a hopeless end."

"For by him all things were created: things in heaven and on earth, visible and invisible, whether thrones or powers or rulers or authorities; all things were created by him and for him." (Col. 1:16)

a bird's eye view of **Colossians**

Place in the Bible	**Written by:**	
Twelfth New Testament book; seventh letter.	Paul.	

The letter to the Ephesians

DAY **348**

Ephesians 3:14–21

¹⁴For this reason I kneel before the Father, ¹⁵from whom his whole family in heaven and on earth derives its name. ¹⁶I pray that out of his glorious riches he may strengthen you with power through his Spirit in your inner being, ¹⁷so that Christ may dwell in your hearts through faith. And I pray that you, being rooted and established in love, ¹⁸may have power, together with all the saints, to grasp how wide and long and high and deep is the love of Christ, ¹⁹and to know this love that surpasses knowledge – that you may be filled to the measure of all the fulness of God.
²⁰Now to him who is able to do immeasurably more than all we ask or imagine, according to his power that is at work within us, ²¹to him be glory in the church and in Christ Jesus throughout all generations, for ever and ever! Amen.

The believer's position in Christ	Ephesians 1:1–14
Paul's prayer for wisdom and revelation	Ephesians 1:15–23
The riches of God's grace	Ephesians 2:1–10
Jews and Gentiles one in Christ	Ephesians 2:11–22
The mystery of the Church	Ephesians 3:1–13
Paul's second prayer	Ephesians 3:14–21
Ministries in the Church	Ephesians 4:1–16
The walk of the believer	Ephesians 4:17–32

For Thought and **Contemplation**

Are you feeling a little jaded or under the weather today? Then here's a guaranteed cure. Count the blessings and privileges you have in Christ as outlined in Ephesians 1:3–14. We'll be surprised if you don't break out into a paean of praise. In the Greek verse 3 to verse 14 is one long continuous sentence. It's seemingly endless – just like God's blessings!

"Blessed be the Lord, who daily bears us up; God is our salvation."
(Psa. 68:19, RSV)

Jesus and the Book

His is the all sufficient Saviour according to 1:19–20, "For God was pleased to have all his fulness dwell in him, and through him to reconcile to himself all things … by making peace through his blood, shed on the cross."

Teaching

Christ is supreme and provides complete salvation. The desire to hang on to Jewish ideas about food laws, festivals and circumcision, and to worship angels should evaporate at the sight of Christ.

A Verse to Remember

"We proclaim him, admonishing and teaching everyone with all wisdom, so that we may present everyone perfect in Christ" (Col. 1:28).

DAY 349 — The exaltation of Christ

Life in the Spirit
Ephesians 5:1–21

Application to particular relationships
Ephesians 5:22–33, 6:1–9

The armour of God
Ephesians 6:10–18

Conclusion
Ephesians 6:19–24

Letter to the Philippians: Paul's thanksgiving and prayer
Philippians 1:1–11

He encourages them
Philippians 1:12–30

Christ the believer's example
Philippians 2:1–18

Paul's future plans
Philippians 2:19–30

Philippians 1:3–11

³I thank my God every time I remember you. ⁴In all my prayers for all of you, I always pray with joy ⁵because of your partnership in the gospel from the first day until now, ⁶being confident of this, that he who began a good work in you will carry it on to completion until the day of Christ Jesus.

⁷It is right for me to feel this way about all of you, since I have you in my heart; for whether I am in chains or defending and confirming the gospel, all of you share in God's grace with me. ⁸God can testify how I long for all of you with the affection of Christ Jesus.

⁹And this is my prayer: that your love may abound more and more in knowledge and depth of insight, ¹⁰so that you may be able to discern what is best and may be pure and blameless until the day of Christ, ¹¹filled with the fruit of righteousness that comes through Jesus Christ – to the glory and praise of God.

For Thought and **Contemplation**

The letter to the Philippians was written in a prison cell, but no one would ever know it. One preacher says of this letter: "Philippians with one accord, tells of rejoicing in the Lord." Paul had learned to triumph over all his circumstances. Have you?

"I am not saying this because I am in need, for I have learned to be content whatever the circumstances." (Phil. 4:11)

a bird's eye view of **Ephesians**

Place in the Bible	**Written by:**
Tenth New Testament book; fifth letter.	Paul.

Paul in Rome

DAY 350

Philippians 4:1–7

¹Therefore, my brothers, you whom I love and long for, my joy and crown, that is how you should stand firm in the Lord, dear friends!
²I plead with Euodia and I plead with Syntyche to agree with each other in the Lord. ³Yes, and I ask you, loyal yokefellow, help these women who have contended at my side in the cause of the gospel, along with Clement and the rest of my fellow-workers, whose names are in the book of life.
⁴Rejoice in the Lord always. I will say it again: Rejoice! ⁵Let your gentleness be evident to all. The Lord is near. ⁶Do not be anxious about anything, but in everything, by prayer and petition, with thanksgiving, present your requests to God. ⁷And the peace of God, which transcends all understanding, will guard your hearts and your minds in Christ Jesus.

Paul's earnest desire	Philippians 3:1–21
Exhortation to stand firm	Philippians 4:1–9
Paul's contentment	Philippians 4:10–19
Conclusion	Philippians 4:20–23
Paul's conference with the Jews	Acts 28:17–29
Paul stays in Rome	Acts 28:30–31
Paul released from prison AD 64	
First letter to Timothy: Greeting	1 Timothy 1:1–2
The purpose of the law	1 Timothy 1:4–11
Paul's call	1 Timothy 1:12–17
His charge to Timothy	1 Timothy 1:18–20

For Thought and **Contemplation**

One Christian wrote out Philippians 4:8 in big bold letters and hung it by his television set. "Whatsoever things are true ... honest ... just ... pure ... lovely ... of good report ... think on *these* things." He said it cut down his viewing by 50%. Worth emulating?

"Do not conform any longer to the pattern of this world, but be transformed by the renewing of your mind. Then you will be able to test and approve what God's will is – his good, pleasing and perfect will." (Rom. 12:2)

Jesus and the Book

Paul's phrase "in Christ", or its equivalent, appears over thirty times in Ephesians. What Christ's followers are can be seen from what they are "in Christ".

Teaching

Paul wants believers to realise being "in Christ" means redemption, power, grace and heavenly citizenship and encourages them to go to Christ for spiritual strength. Chapters 4–6 develop how this is worked out in our lives.

A Verse to Remember

"... live a life worthy of the calling you have received. Be completely humble and gentle; be patient, bearing with one another in love" (Eph. 4:1–2).

DAY 351

Paul instructs Timothy

Guidance for the church
1 Timothy 2:1–15

Qualifications of elders
and deacons
1 Timothy 3:1–16

Timothy to be an example
1 Timothy 4:1–16

The work of a minister
1 Timothy 5:1–16

Elders to be respected
1 Timothy 5:17–25

Value of godliness
with contentment
1 Timothy 6:1–10

Paul's charge to Timothy
1 Timothy 6:11–19

Conclusion
1 Timothy 6:20–21

1 Timothy 2:1–7

¹I urge, then, first of all, that requests, prayers, intercession and thanksgiving be made for everyone – ²for kings and all those in authority, that we may live peaceful and quiet lives in all godliness and holiness. ³This is good, and pleases God our Saviour, ⁴who wants all men to be saved and to come to a knowledge of the truth. ⁵For there is one God and one mediator between God and men, the man Christ Jesus, ⁶who gave himself as a ransom for all men – the testimony given in its proper time. ⁷And for this purpose I was appointed a herald and an apostle – I am telling the truth, I am not lying – and a teacher of the true faith to the Gentiles.

For Thought and Contemplation

"Good manners" are a missing ingredient, not only in contemporary society, but also in many of today's Christian communities. Do you know how to "behave in the household of God"? (1 Tim. 3:15) Absorb Paul's teaching in this letter, and never again will you be at a loss to know how to behave in the Master's House.

"... everything should be done in a fitting and orderly way." (1 Cor. 14:40)

a bird's eye view of **Philippians**

Place in the Bible	**Written by:**	**Special Features**
Eleventh New Testament book; sixth letter.	Paul.	The characteristic feature of this letter is the great emphasis on joy.

Order in the Church

DAY **352**

Titus 1:1-5

¹Paul, a servant of God and an apostle of Jesus Christ for the faith of God's elect and the knowledge of the truth that leads to godliness – ²a faith and knowledge resting on the hope of eternal life, which God, who does not lie, promised before the beginning of time, ³and at his appointed season he brought his word to light through the preaching entrusted to me by the command of God our Saviour,

⁴To Titus, my true son in our common faith:

Grace and peace from God the Father and Christ Jesus our Saviour.

⁵The reason I left you in Crete was that you might straighten out what was left unfinished and appoint elders in every town, as I directed you. ...

Letter to Titus: Selection of elders	Titus 1:1–16
Pattern for Christian living	Titus 2:1–15, 3:1–7
Importance of good works	Titus 3:8–11
Final directions	Titus 3:12–15
Peter's first letter: The Christian's security	1 Peter 1:1–12
Exhortation to holiness and love	1 Peter 1:13–25
A chosen people	1 Peter 2:1–10
Patience in suffering	1 Peter 2:11–20
Christ's example	1 Peter 2:21–25

For Thought and **Contemplation**

Read carefully Paul's letter to Titus. It contains some timely words of advice for every Christian, irrespective of their age, sex or level of maturity. Have you spotted a deficiency in your own life, or that of your church, while reading these passages today? Then ask God just what you should do to bring things into harmony with His purposes.

"... each one should retain the place in life that the Lord assigned to him and to which God has called him." (1 Cor. 7:17)

Jesus and the Book

Paul explains how Jesus gives His power in chapter 4:13, "I can do everything through him who gives me strength".

Teaching

As well as the theme of joy Paul teaches believers to be Christlike, especially in humility, and so maintain a spirit of unity. Paul tells his readers ten times how they are to "think" or view life: "Your attitude should be the same as that of Christ Jesus" (Phil. 2:5).

A Verse to Remember

"For to me, to live is Christ and to die is gain" (Phil. 1:21).

DAY 353

Christ our example

The life of peace
1 Peter 3:1–13

Keeping a good conscience
1 Peter 3:14–22

The righteous life
1 Peter 4:1–11

Rejoicing in sufferings
1 Peter 4:12–19

Exhortation to be strong
1 Peter 5:1–9

Concluding prayer
1 Peter 5:10–14

Letter to the Hebrews: Christ greater than angels
Hebrews 1:1–14

He took on man's nature
Hebrews 2:1–9

His sufferings and victory
Hebrews 2:10–18

1 Peter 4:12–19

¹²Dear friends, do not be surprised at the painful trial you are suffering, as though something strange were happening to you. ¹³But rejoice that you participate in the sufferings of Christ, so that you may be overjoyed when his glory is revealed. ¹⁴If you are insulted because of the name of Christ, you are blessed, for the Spirit of glory and of God rests on you. ¹⁵If you suffer, it should not be as a murderer or thief or any other kind of criminal, or even as a meddler. ¹⁶However, if you suffer as a Christian, do not be ashamed, but praise God that you bear that name. ¹⁷For it is time for judgment to begin with the family of God; and if it begins with us, what will the outcome be for those who do not obey the gospel of God? ¹⁸And,
"If it is hard for the righteous to be saved,
 what will become of the ungodly and the sinner?"
¹⁹So then, those who suffer according to God's will should commit themselves to their faithful Creator and continue to do good.

For Thought and **Contemplation**

Are you experiencing some pressure and suffering at the moment? Then make sure you are suffering for doing what is *right*, not for what is *wrong*. Remember to imitate Christ who, "when he was reviled, reviled not again" – then you will be sure of an eternal reward.

"But how is it to your credit if you receive a beating for doing wrong and endure it? But if you suffer for doing good and you endure it, this is commendable before God."
(1 Pet. 2:20)

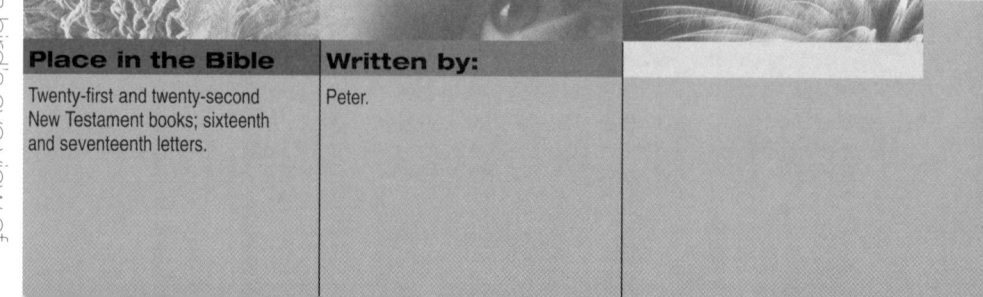

a bird's eye view of **1 & 2 Peter**

Place in the Bible	**Written by:**
Twenty-first and twenty-second New Testament books; sixteenth and seventeenth letters.	Peter.

Christ's pre-eminence

DAY 354

Hebrews 3:1–6

¹Therefore, holy brothers, who share in the heavenly calling, fix your thoughts on Jesus, the apostle and high priest whom we confess. ²He was faithful to the one who appointed him, just as Moses was faithful in all God's house. ³Jesus has been found worthy of greater honour than Moses, just as the builder of a house has greater honour than the house itself. ⁴For every house is built by someone, but God is the builder of everything. ⁵Moses was faithful as a servant in all God's house, testifying to what would be said in the future. ⁶But Christ is faithful as a son over God's house. And we are his house, if we hold on to our courage and the hope of which we boast.

Christ greater than Moses
Hebrews 3:1–6

Warning against unbelief
Hebrews 3:7–13

Necessity for faith
Hebrews 3:14–19

Our Sabbath rest
Hebrews 4:1–13

Christ our High Priest
Hebrews 4:14–16, 5:1–14

Exhortation to go on to maturity
Hebrews 6:1–12

God's unchangeableness
Hebrews 6:13–20

Melchizedek a type of Christ
Hebrews 7:1–28

For Thought and **Contemplation**

The truth of Christ's pre-eminence must be applied, not only to the laws and personalities of the Old Testament, but equally to the many aspects of our own daily lives. Do you, for example, see Christ as superior to your wife, your husband, your bank account, your job and your career? Remember, if you do not crown Him Lord of all, you do not crown Him Lord at all!

"For by him all things were created: things in heaven and on earth, visible and invisible ... all things were created by him and for him. He is before all things, and in him all things hold together." (Col. 1:16–17)

Jesus and the Books

Suffering for Christ and Christ's own suffering are brought together in 1 Peter 4:12–13. Peter recalls Jesus' transfiguration (2 Peter 1:17–18) and writes about his future coming in glory (3:10–13).

Teaching

1 Peter was written to Christians who were suffering for their faith, so Peter writes to bring a message of Christian hope, and to comfort them. 2 Peter counters a different problem – an attack from within – false teachers.

A Verse to Remember

"... no prophecy of Scripture came about by the prophet's own interpretation. For prophecy never had its origin in the will of man, but men spoke from God as they were carried along by the Holy Spirit" (2 Pet. 1:20–21).

DAY 355 — The new covenant

The true High Priest
Hebrews 8:1–5

The new covenant is superior
Hebrews 8:6–13

Description of the tabernacle
Hebrews 9:1–10

Its fulfilment in Christ
Hebrews 9:11–22

Christ's sufficient sacrifice
Hebrews 9:23–28, 10:1–18

True worship
Hebrews 10:19–25

Rejection of Christ fatal
Hebrews 10:26–31

The believer's reward
Hebrews 10:32–39

Examples of faith
Hebrews 11:1–10

Hebrews 8:6–10

⁶But the ministry Jesus has received is as superior to theirs as the covenant of which he is mediator is superior to the old one, and it is founded on better promises. ⁷For if there had been nothing wrong with that first covenant, no place would have been sought for another. ⁸But God found fault with the people and said:

"The time is coming, declares the Lord,
when I will make a new covenant
with the house of Israel
and with the house of Judah.
⁹It will not be like the covenant
I made with their forefathers
when I took them by the hand
to lead them out of Egypt,
because they did not remain
faithful to my covenant,
and I turned away from them,
declares the Lord.
¹⁰This is the covenant I will make
with the house of Israel
after that time, declares the Lord.
I will put my laws in their minds
and write them on their hearts.
I will be their God,
and they will be my people."

For Thought and **Contemplation**

It is important to keep in mind that every Bible doctrine is designed to affect our behaviour. Because Christ is a *better* High Priest ... because He has provided a *better* way ... because He initiates a *better* covenant ... we must respond to that truth with *better* obedience. Make up your mind that, with God's help, you will be a *better* Christian today than you were yesterday.

"For those God foreknew he also predestined to be conformed to the likeness of his Son, that he might be the firstborn among many brothers." (Rom. 8:29)

a bird's eye view of Hebrews

Place in the Bible	**Written by:**
Nineteenth New Testament book; fourteenth letter.	Author unknown.

The superiority of faith

DAY **356**

Hebrews 12:1–6

¹Therefore, since we are surrounded by such a great cloud of witnesses, let us throw off everything that hinders and the sin that so easily entangles, and let us run with perseverance the race marked out for us. ²Let us fix our eyes on Jesus, the author and perfecter of our faith, who for the joy set before him endured the cross, scorning its shame, and sat down at the right hand of the throne of God. ³Consider him who endured such opposition from sinful men, so that you will not grow weary and lose heart.

⁴In your struggle against sin, you have not yet resisted to the point of shedding your blood. ⁵And you have forgotten that word of encouragement that addresses you as sons:
"My son, do not make light of the Lord's discipline,
  and do not lose heart when he rebukes you,
⁶because the Lord disciplines those he loves,
  and he punishes everyone he accepts as a son."

The faith of the patriarchs	Hebrews 11:11–22
Moses and other Old Testament examples	Hebrews 11:23–40
Exhortation to persevere	Hebrews 12:1–13
Following peace and holiness	Hebrews 12:14–17
Superiority of New Testament dispensation	Hebrews 12:18–29
Various exhortations	Hebrews 13:1–19
Conclusion	Hebrews 13:20–25

For Thought and **Contemplation**

What is your favourite definition of faith? A little boy, when asked to define faith, said: "Faith is believing what you know isn't true"! The best definitions, of course, are always Scriptural ones. According to Hebrews, faith is "the evidence of things not seen". "Seeing is believing" is the world's motto. "Not seeing is believing" is the Christian's motto. And why? Because "faith is the evidence of things *not seen*."

"... everyone born of God overcomes the world. This is the victory that has overcome the world, even our faith." (1 Jn. 5:4)

Jesus and the Book
In Hebrews Jesus is portrayed as our Great High Priest.

Teaching
Hebrews focuses on both the humanity and deity of the Lord Jesus Christ. He is presented as our great high priest and sufficient sacrifice to deal with our sin. Readers are exhorted to fix their eyes on Him and press on to maturity.

A Verse to Remember
"Unlike the other high priests, he does not need to offer sacrifices day after day, first for his own sins, and then for the sins of the people. He sacrificed for their sins once for all when he offered himself" (Heb. 7:27).

DAY 357 — Peter's ladder of virtues

Peter's second letter:
Adding to our faith
2 Peter 1:1–11

Peter confirms the truth
of the gospel
2 Peter 1:12–21

Signs of the coming apostasy
2 Peter 2:1–22

Apostasy in the end times
2 Peter 3:1–10

Exhortation to godly living
2 Peter 3:11–18

Letter of Jude:
History of apostasy
Jude vv.1–7

Apostate teachers described
Jude vv.8–19

Encouragement to believers
Jude vv.20–23

Doxology
Jude vv.24–25

2 Peter 1:5–11

⁵For this very reason, make every effort to add to your faith goodness; and to goodness, knowledge; ⁶and to knowledge, self-control; and to self-control, perseverance; and to perseverance, godliness; ⁷and to godliness, brotherly kindness; and to brotherly kindness, love. ⁸For if you possess these qualities in increasing measure, they will keep you from being ineffective and unproductive in your knowledge of our Lord Jesus Christ. ⁹But if anyone does not have them, he is short-sighted and blind, and has forgotten that he has been cleansed from his past sins.
¹⁰Therefore, my brothers, be all the more eager to make your calling and election sure. For if you do these things, you will never fall, ¹¹and you will receive a rich welcome into the eternal kingdom of our Lord and Saviour Jesus Christ.

For Thought and Contemplation

You must have heard at least one sermon on the famous passage found in 2 Peter 1:5–11. Preachers often refer to it as "Peter's ladder of virtues". Go over it again at your leisure some time today, and ask yourself the question: "Which rung am I on?"

"Finally, brothers, whatever is true, whatever is noble, whatever is right, whatever is pure, whatever is lovely, whatever is admirable – if anything is excellent or praiseworthy – think about such things." (Phil. 4:8)

---

a bird's eye view of Jude

Place in the Bible	Written by:	Special Features
Twenty-sixth New Testament book; twenty-first letter.	Jude.	Jude draws illustrations from The book of Enoch (vv. 14–15) and The Assumption of Moses (v.9) which are not in the Bible. Jude does not put them on the same level as Scripture, but realised his readers would be familiar with them.

Second letter to Timothy

DAY 358

2 Timothy 2:1–7

¹You then, my son, be strong in the grace that is in Christ Jesus. ²And the things you have heard me say in the presence of many witnesses entrust to reliable men who will also be qualified to teach others. ³Endure hardship with us like a good soldier of Christ Jesus. ⁴No-one serving as a soldier gets involved in civilian affairs – he wants to please his commanding officer. ⁵Similarly, if anyone competes as an athlete, he does not receive the victor's crown unless he competes according to the rules. ⁶The hardworking farmer should be the first to receive a share of the crops. ⁷Reflect on what I am saying, for the Lord will give you insight into all this.

Paul encourages Timothy	2 Timothy 1:1–18
The good soldier of Christ	2 Timothy 2:1–13
The Lord's faithful servant	2 Timothy 2:14–26
Apostasy in the last days	2 Timothy 3:1–13
The defence of the good soldier	2 Timothy 3:14–17, 4:1–8
Paul deserted by many	2 Timothy 4:9–18
Final greetings	2 Timothy 4:19–22
Martyrdom of Peter and Paul AD 67–68	
First letter of John: Its purpose	1 John 1:1–4
Dealing with sin	1 John 1:5–10

For Thought and **Contemplation**

The second letter to Timothy is really Paul's last will and testament to his spiritual son. What a wealth of wisdom it contains. Pause for a moment, and reflect on what you would write if you had to pass on to a spiritual son or daughter the things you have learned in the Christian life. If you can, write down your conclusions.

"And this is love: that we walk in obedience to his commands. As you have heard from the beginning, his command is that you walk in love." (2 Jn v.6)

Teaching

Ungodly men were threatening to poison the Church with immoral ideals and denial of the gospel. Jude calls his readers to stand firm and persevere in the faith.

A Verse to Remember

"To him who is able to keep you from falling and to present you before his glorious presence without fault and with great joy – to the only God our Saviour be glory, majesty, power and authority, through Jesus Christ ..." (Jude vv. 24–25).

DAY 359 — Love and obedience

Writings of John AD 95–100

Obedience required
1 John 2:1–14

Warning against worldliness and unbelief
1 John 2:15–23

Abiding in Him
1 John 2:24–28

God's love for us
1 John 2:29, 3:1–2

Righteousness and sin
1 John 3:3–10

Love in action
1 John 3:11–24

Overcoming the world
1 John 4:1–6

Love is of God
1 John 4:7–21

Our victory
1 John 5:1–12

Our confidence and security
1 John 5:13–21

1 John 4:7–12

⁷Dear friends, let us love one another, for love comes from God. Everyone who loves has been born of God and knows God. ⁸Whoever does not love does not know God, because God is love. ⁹This is how God showed his love among us: He sent his one and only Son into the world that we might live through him. ¹⁰This is love: not that we loved God, but that he loved us and sent his Son as an atoning sacrifice for our sins. ¹¹Dear friends, since God so loved us, we also ought to love one another. ¹²No-one has ever seen God; but if we love one another, God lives in us and his love is made complete in us.

For Thought and Contemplation

"Love," says Thomas Fuller, a great Christian philosopher, "delights not only to ascend, but also to descend." How true. This is precisely what happened at the first Christmas – Love came *down*. Let that thought simmer in your mind throughout today.

"For God so loved the world that he gave his one and only Son, that whoever believes in him shall not perish but have eternal life." (Jn 3:16)

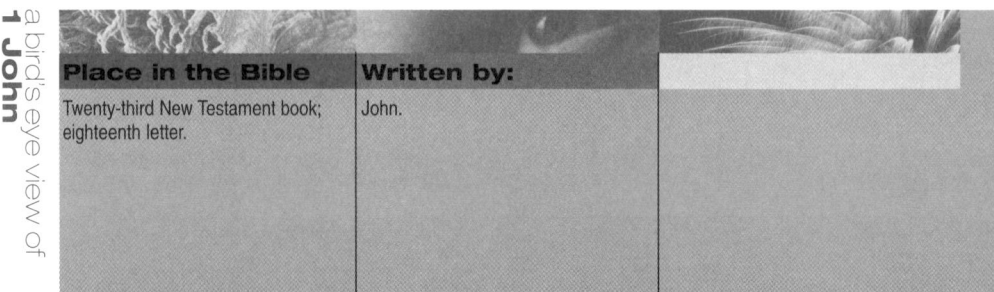

a bird's eye view of **1 John**

Place in the Bible: Twenty-third New Testament book; eighteenth letter.

Written by: John.

Messages to the seven churches

DAY 360

Revelation 2:1–7

¹"To the angel of the church in Ephesus write:
These are the words of him who holds the seven stars in his right hand and walks among the seven golden lampstands: ²I know your deeds, your hard work and your perseverance. I know that you cannot tolerate wicked men, that you have tested those who claim to be apostles but are not, and have found them false. ³You have persevered and have endured hardships for my name, and have not grown weary.
⁴Yet I hold this against you: You have forsaken your first love. ⁵Remember the height from which you have fallen! Repent and do the things you did at first. If you do not repent, I will come to you and remove your lampstand from its place. ⁶But you have this in your favour: You hate the practices of the Nicolaitans, which I also hate.
⁷He who has an ear, let him hear what the Spirit says to the churches. To him who overcomes, I will give the right to eat from the tree of life, which is in the paradise of God.

Second letter of John:
Walking in the truth
2 John vv.1–13

Third letter of John:
Gaius commended
3 John vv.1–8

Concerning Diotrephes
and Demetrius
3 John vv.9–14

The book of Revelation:
Introduction
Revelation 1:1–8

John's vision
Revelation 1:9–20

Message to the church
in Ephesus
Revelation 2:1–7

In Smyrna
Revelation 2:8–11

In Pergamum
Revelation 2:12–17

In Thyatira
Revelation 2:18–29

For Thought and **Contemplation**

What does Christ expect of His Church? The answer lies in His words to the seven churches of Asia. His message to each church is characterised by one important word. *Love*, for example, is the key word for the church at Ephesus. Now find the others.

"... to present her to himself as a radiant church, without stain or wrinkle or any other blemish, but holy and blameless." (Eph. 5:27)

Jesus and the Book

John pictures Jesus as the One who purifies believers from sin: "But if we walk in the light, as he is in the light, we have fellowship with one another, and the blood of Jesus, his Son, purifies us from all sin" (1 John 1:7).

Teaching

John wrote this letter to help Christians know for certain that they were followers of Christ (5:13). Christ's followers have the Holy Spirit resident in them and should be characterised by a special quality of love for fellow Christians.

A Verse to Remember

"This is how we know what love is: Jesus Christ laid down his life for us. And we ought to lay down our lives for our brothers" (1 John 3:16).

DAY **361**

The way to worship

Message to the church in Sardis
Revelation 3:1–6

In Philadelphia
Revelation 3:7–13

In Laodicea
Revelation 3:14–22

The throne of God
Revelation 4:1–11

The sealed book
Revelation 5:1–8

Worship of the Lamb
Revelation 5:9–14

The six seals opened
Revelation 6:1–17

The sealing of the 144,000
Revelation 7:1–8

Revelation 5:9–14
⁹And they sang a new song:
"You are worthy to take the scroll
 and to open its seals,
because you were slain,
 and with your blood you
purchased men for God
 from every tribe and language
and people and nation.
¹⁰You have made them to be a
kingdom and priests to serve our
God,
 and they will reign on the earth."
¹¹Then I looked and heard the
voice of many angels ... ¹²In a loud
voice they sang:
 "Worthy is the Lamb, who was
slain,
 to receive power and wealth and
wisdom and strength
 and honour and glory and praise!"
¹³Then I heard every creature in
heaven and on earth and under
the earth and on the sea, and all
that is in them, singing:
 "To him who sits on the throne
and to the Lamb
 be praise and honour and glory
and power,
 for ever and ever!"
¹⁴The four living creatures said,
"Amen," and the elders fell down
and worshipped.

For Thought and **Contemplation**

"Worship," said A.W. Tozer, "is the missing jewel of the Evangelical Church." It is certainly not the missing jewel in heaven. The 24 elders casting down their crowns is a form of worship. What are you willing to cast down before Him in worship today?

"God is spirit, and his worshippers must worship in spirit and in truth." (Jn 4:24)

a bird's eye view of
2 & 3 John

Place in the Bible	**Written by:**
Twenty-fourth and twenty-fifth New Testament books; nineteenth and twentieth letters.	John.

The seven trumpet judgments

DAY **362**

Revelation 11:15-19

¹⁵The seventh angel sounded his trumpet, and there were loud voices in heaven, which said:
"The kingdom of the world has become the kingdom of our Lord and of his Christ, and he will reign for ever and ever."
¹⁶And the twenty-four elders, who were seated on their thrones before God, fell on their faces and worshipped God, ¹⁷saying:
"We give thanks to you, Lord God Almighty,
 the One who is and who was,
because you have taken your great power
 and have begun to reign.
¹⁸The nations were angry;
 and your wrath has come.
The time has come for judging the dead,
 and for rewarding your servants the prophets
and your saints and those who reverence your name,
 both small and great –
and for destroying those who destroy the earth."
¹⁹Then God's temple in heaven was opened, and within his temple was seen the ark of his covenant.

The multitude in heaven	Revelation 7:9-17
The seventh seal is opened	Revelation 8:1-6
The first four trumpets	Revelation 8:7-13
The fifth and sixth trumpets	Revelation 9:1-21
The angel with the little book	Revelation 10:1-11
The Temple measured	Revelation 11:1-2
The two witnesses	Revelation 11:3-13
The seventh trumpet	Revelation 11:14-19

For Thought and **Contemplation**

If God did not institute a final day of judgment, then the universe would remain unbalanced. Judgment will surely come. If you are a Christian, then rejoice – because for you the judgment has passed. In Christ there is no more condemnation.

"Therefore, there is now no condemnation for those who are in Christ Jesus, because through Christ Jesus the law of the Spirit of life set me free from the law of sin and death." (Rom. 8:1-2)

Jesus and the Book

Deceivers who do not "acknowledge Jesus Christ as coming in the flesh" (v.7) are to be avoided. The key to a relationship with God is continuing in the teaching of Christ (v.9).

Teaching

2 John concentrates on how Christians should not fellowship with false teachers who are enemies of the Christian gospel. 3 John stresses hospitality to true Christians and criticises a church leader for his malicious gossip and hostility to visiting believers.

A Verse to Remember

"Anyone who runs ahead and does not continue in the teaching of Christ does not have God; whoever continues in the teaching has both the Father and the Son" (2 John v. 9).

DAY 363 — The Church and her enemies

The woman, the child and the dragon
Revelation 12:1–8

Satan cast down to the earth
Revelation 12:9–17

The two beasts
Revelation 13:1–15

The mark of the beast
Revelation 13:16–18

The followers of the Lamb
Revelation 14:1–5

The three angels
Revelation 14:6–13

Vision of Christ with a sickle
Revelation 14:14–20

The song of Moses
Revelation 15:1–4

The seven golden vials
Revelation 15:5–8

Revelation 15:1–4

¹I saw in heaven another great and marvellous sign: seven angels with the seven last plagues – last, because with them God's wrath is completed. ²And I saw what looked like a sea of glass mixed with fire and, standing beside the sea, those who had been victorious over the beast and his image and over the number of his name. They held harps given them by God ³and sang the song of Moses the servant of God and the song of the Lamb:

"Great and marvellous are your deeds,
 Lord God Almighty.
Just and true are your ways,
 King of the ages.
⁴Who will not fear you, O Lord,
 and bring glory to your name?
For you alone are holy.
All nations will come
 and worship before you,
for your righteous acts have been revealed."

For Thought and **Contemplation**

There have been many enemies of the Church, but there is a day coming when they will be swept away for ever. Make no mistake about it – truth and righteousness will ultimately triumph.

"Then the end will come, when he hands over the kingdom to God the Father after he has destroyed all dominion, authority and power. For he must reign until he has put all his enemies under his feet."
(1 Cor. 15:24–25)

a bird's eye view of **Revelation**

Place in the Bible	**Written by:**	
Twenty-seventh New Testament book; first book of prophecy.	John.	

The fall of Babylon

DAY 364

Revelation 19:6–10

⁶Then I heard what sounded like a great multitude, like the roar of rushing waters and like loud peals of thunder, shouting:
"Hallelujah!
For our Lord God Almighty reigns.
⁷Let us rejoice and be glad
and give him glory!
For the wedding of the Lamb has come,
and his bride has made herself ready.
⁸Fine linen, bright and clean,
was given her to wear."
(Fine linen stands for the righteous acts of the saints.)
⁹Then the angel said to me, "Write: 'Blessed are those who are invited to the wedding supper of the Lamb!'" And he added, "These are the true words of God."
¹⁰At this I fell at his feet to worship him. But he said to me, "Do not do it! I am a fellow-servant with you and with your brothers who hold to the testimony of Jesus. Worship God! For the testimony of Jesus is the spirit of prophecy."

The seven plagues	Revelation 16:1–21
Vision of the woman sitting on the beast	Revelation 17:1–6
Its interpretation	Revelation 17:7–18
Destruction of Babylon	Revelation 18:1–8
Lament for Babylon	Revelation 18:9–19
The Church to rejoice over her fall	Revelation 18:20–24
Praise given to God	Revelation 19:1–5
The marriage supper of the Lamb	Revelation 19:6–10

For Thought and **Contemplation**

"The Bible", someone said, "is like a tale of two cities – Babylon is one, and Jerusalem the other." Babylon represents sin, Jerusalem represents righteousness. How reassuring to learn that there will be a new Jerusalem, but not a new Babylon. Hallelujah – sin is to be removed – *forever*.

"But you have come to Mount Zion, to the heavenly Jerusalem, the city of the living God. You have come to thousands upon thousands of angels in joyful assembly, to the church of the firstborn, whose names are written in heaven. ..." (Heb. 12:22–23)

Jesus and the Book

This book is a "revelation of Jesus Christ" (Rev. 1:1) and concludes with the words, "'Yes, I am coming soon.' Amen. Come, Lord Jesus. The grace of the Lord Jesus be with God's people. Amen" (Rev. 22:20–21).

Teaching

John relates a series of visions to show that the only One who has authority to judge the world and to reign over it in righteousness is the risen Lord Jesus Christ (Rev. 19:16).

A Verse to Remember

"Now the dwelling of God is with men, and he will live with them. They will be his people, and God himself will be with them and be their God. He will wipe every tear from their eyes. There will be no more death ... or pain, for the old order of things has passed away" (Rev. 21:3–4).

First Adam – Last Adam

First Adam		Last Adam
He brought sin and death into the world	The nature of the act	He brought righteousness and life into the world
In the Garden of Eden	The place of the act	On the cross of Calvary
Disobedience (Gen. 3:6)	The reason for the act	**Obedience** (Lk. 22:42)
Condemnation 1. Immediate judgment upon himself. 2. Imputed judgment upon his posterity. 3. Eternal judgment upon all.	The results from the act	**Justification** 1. Immediate justification 2. Imputed righteousness. 3. Eternal life.
The law served to demonstrate the seriousness of his act	Relationship of the act to law and grace	Grace served to demonstrate the "much more" of his act (Rom. 5:9, 10, 15, 17, 20)
It abounded	The scope of the act	It abounded much more

Satan's destruction

DAY **365**

Revelation 20:7–10

⁷When the thousand years are over, Satan will be released from his prison ⁸and will go out to deceive the nations in the four corners of the earth – Gog and Magog – to gather them for battle. In number they are like the sand on the seashore. ⁹They marched across the breadth of the earth and surrounded the camp of God's people, the city he loves. But fire came down from heaven and devoured them. ¹⁰And the devil, who deceived them, was thrown into the lake of burning sulphur, where the beast and the false prophet had been thrown. They will be tormented day and night for ever and ever.

Christ destroys the beast and his armies
Revelation 19:11–21

The millennium
Revelation 20:1–6

The final battle
Revelation 20:7–10

The great white throne
Revelation 20:11–15

For Thought and **Contemplation**

This earth has witnessed many fierce and bloody battles. But there is a time fixed when the last battle will be fought and never again will the universe resound to the sound of conflict. The devil too, who has always been the instigator of conflict and contention, will be no more. How consoling it is to know that that day will come and Satan will be gone. Hallelujah!

"He who does what is sinful is of the devil, because the devil has been sinning from the beginning. The reason the Son of God appeared was to destroy the devil's work." (1 Jn 3:8)

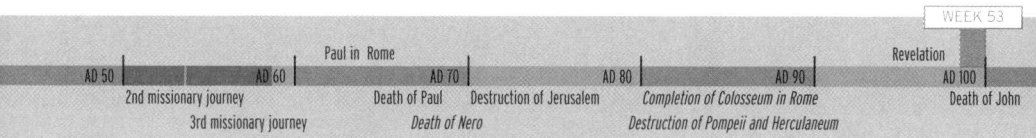

Messages
to the seven churches

+ Pergamum – **TRUTH**

+ Thyatira – **HOLINESS**

+ Sardis – **LIFE**

Smyrna – **SUFFERING** +

+ Philadelphia – **SERVICE**

Ephesus – **LOVE** +

+ Laodicea – **ZEALOUSNESS**

The new heaven and new earth

DAY **366**

Revelation 22:1–5

¹Then the angel showed me the river of the water of life, as clear as crystal, flowing from the throne of God and of the Lamb ²down the middle of the great street of the city. On each side of the river stood the tree of life, bearing twelve crops of fruit, yielding its fruit every month. And the leaves of the tree are for the healing of the nations. ³No longer will there be any curse. The throne of God and of the Lamb will be in the city, and his servants will serve him. ⁴They will see his face, and his name will be on their foreheads. ⁵There will be no more night. They will not need the light of a lamp or the light of the sun, for the Lord God will give them light. And they will reign for ever and ever.

The new heaven and new earth
Revelation 21:1–8

The new Jerusalem
Revelation 21:9–27

The river of life
Revelation 22:1–5

Free invitation to all
Revelation 22:6–19

Final promise and blessing
Revelation 22:20–21

For Thought and **Contemplation**

The Bible ends with the glorious hope of Christ's coming. Notice how the affirmation, "Yes, I am coming soon," is followed by a swift and immediate response – "Amen. Come, Lord Jesus." How swift and immediate is your response to the thought of Christ's coming?

"... 'Amen! Praise and glory and wisdom and thanks and honour and power and strength be to our God for ever and ever. Amen!'" (Rev. 7:12)

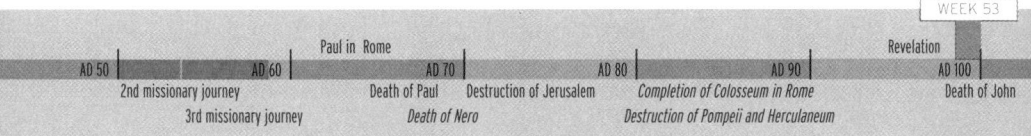

Heart to Heart

Section 12

WELL DONE! You have finished the course and read through the whole Bible. Give yourself a pat on the back. God always gives His Word to accomplish something so take a little time now to reflect on what God has accomplished in you through the reading of His Word. It might be appropriate to share your thoughts and favourite passages with a friend. Remember that expression deepens impression so ask God for opportunities to express and share the truths that He has sown in your heart during this past year.

Visit the web site: **www.cover2cover.org**

Continue to meet God in His Word every day ...

Every Day Light

We've selected six of the best loved editions of *Every Day with Jesus*, arranged them in undated order for a year of daily reading, and given them a touch of luxury to create three very special gift items – for yourself or others.

- Padded front cover
- Gilt-edged pages
- Gold foil lettering on a cloth spine
- Satin ribbon bookmark

Every Day Light
– Light for the Path

The words of Selwyn Hughes and the pictures of Larry Dyke, one of the USA's most well-known artists, are brought together in this third one year devotional in the *Every Day Light* collection to form a very attractive and spiritually powerful publication.

Every Day Light – Light for the Path features a complete commentary by Selwyn Hughes and additional further study sections on six topics:

- The Uniqueness of our Faith
- The Search for Meaning
- The Twenty-third Psalm
- The Spirit-filled Life
- Strong at the Broken Places
- Going Deeper with God

(same text as *Every Day with Jesus – Light for the Path – One Year Devotional Vol. 3*)

Padded Hardback: 400 pages; 135 x 205 mm

Other volumes in the series, featuring paintings by Thomas Kinkade

Every Day Light
– Daily Inspirations

- The Vision of God
- From Confusion to Confidence
- The Beatitudes
- The Power of a New Perspective
- The Corn of Wheat Afraid to Die
- Heaven-sent Revival

(same text as *Every Day with Jesus – A Fresh Vision of God – One Year Devotional Vol. 1*)

Every Day Light
– Water for the Soul

- Staying Spiritually Fresh
- When Sovereignty Surprises
- Rebuilding Broken Walls
- The Character of God
- The Fruit of the Spirit
- The Seven Pillars of Wisdom

(same text as *Every Day with Jesus – Water for the Soul – One Year Devotional Vol. 2*)

Silver medallist ECPA Book Awards 1999

Available from your usual CWR supplier or National Distributor (listed on page 4)

Everyone needs Encouragement

Your Personal Encourager
By Selwyn Hughes

A cutting remark ... plans that fail ... fears and doubts ... a sudden crisis. Who do you turn to for help? This book will show you how to encourage yourself in God. Dealing with issues such as fear, doubts, loneliness, temptation, and bereavement, it covers 40 of life's commonest problems.

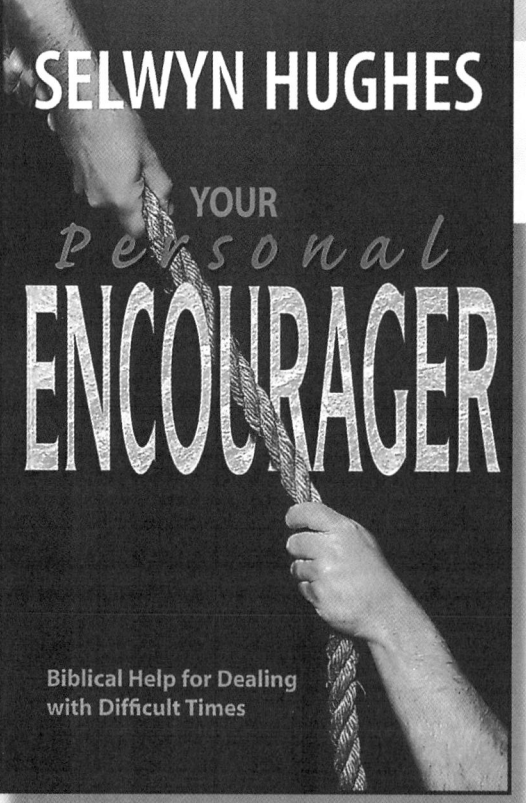

"... a goldmine of helpful advice and Scriptural thinking."
Evangelism Today

Paperback
96 pages,
185 x 123mm

Available from your usual CWR supplier or National Distributor (listed on page 4)